Dictionary of
Information and
Library Management

Specialist dictionaries

Dictionary of Accounting	0 7475 6991 6
Dictionary of Aviation	0 7475 7219 4
Dictionary of Banking and Finance	0 7136 7739 2
Dictionary of Business	0 7475 6980 0
Dictionary of Computing	0 7475 6622 4
Dictionary of Economics	0 7475 6632 1
Dictionary of Environment and Ecology	0 7475 7201 1
Dictionary of Human Resources and Personnel Management	0 7475 6623 2
Dictionary of ICT	0 7475 6990 8
Dictionary of Law	0 7475 6636 4
Dictionary of Leisure, Travel and Tourism	0 7475 7222 4
Dictionary of Marketing	0 7475 6621 6
Dictionary of Media Studies	0 7136 7593 4
Dictionary of Medical Terms	0 7136 7603 5
Dictionary of Nursing	0 7475 6634 8
Dictionary of Politics and Government	0 7475 7220 8
Dictionary of Publishing and Printing	0 7136 7589 6
Dictionary of Science and Technology	0 7475 6620 8

Easier English™ titles

Easier English Basic Dictionary	0 7475 6644 5
Easier English Basic Synonyms	0 7475 6979 7
Easier English Dictionary: Handy Pocket Edition	0 7475 6625 9
Easier English Intermediate Dictionary	0 7475 6989 4
Easier English Student Dictionary	0 7475 6624 0
English Thesaurus for Students	1 9016 5931 3

Check Your English Vocabulary workbooks

Academic English	0 7475 6691 7
Business	0 7475 6626 7
Computing	1 9016 5928 3
Human Resources	0 7475 6997 5
Law	0 7136 7592 6
Leisure, Travel and Tourism	0 7475 6996 7
FCE +	0 7475 6981 9
IELTS	0 7136 7604 3
PET	0 7475 6627 5
TOEFL®	0 7475 6984 3
TOEIC	0 7136 7508 X

Visit our website for full details of all our books: **www.acblack.com**

Dictionary of
Information and
Library Management

second edition

A & C Black • London

www.acblack.com

First published in Great Britain in 1997
This second edition published 2006

A & C Black Publishers Ltd
38 Soho Square, London W1D 3HB

© Janet Stevenson & P. H. Collin 1997
© A & C Black Publishers Ltd 2006

A CIP record for this book is available from the British Library

ISBN-10: 0 7136 7591 8
ISBN-13: 978 0 7136 7591 7

1 3 5 7 9 8 6 4 2

Text Production and Proofreading
Heather Bateman, Helen Liebeck, Katy McAdam

A & C Black uses paper produced with elemental chlorine-free pulp,
harvested from managed sustainable forests.

Text typeset by A & C Black
Printed in Italy by Legoprint

Preface

This dictionary provides a basic vocabulary of terms used in the information and records management industries. It is ideal for all students of librarianship, information science and related subjects, as well as those working for the first time in library, archiving, knowledge management, databasing and research jobs.

Each headword is explained in clear, straightforward English and quotations from specialist publications show how the words are used in context. There are also supplements including a list of major library classification systems, copyright and data protection law, details of book awards and prizes and a list of helpful resources on the Web.

Many thanks to Diana Dixon for her invaluable help and advice during the production of this book.

Pronunciation Guide

The following symbols have been used to show the pronunciation of the main words in the dictionary.

Stress is indicated by a main stress mark (') and a secondary stress mark (,). Note that these are only guides, as the stress of the word changes according to its position in the sentence.

Vowels		*Consonants*	
æ	back	b	buck
ɑː	harm	d	dead
ɒ	stop	ð	other
aɪ	type	dʒ	jump
aʊ	how	f	fare
aɪə	hire	g	gold
aʊə	hour	h	head
ɔː	course	j	yellow
ɔɪ	annoy	k	cab
e	head	l	leave
eə	fair	m	mix
eɪ	make	n	nil
eʊ	go	ŋ	sing
ɜː	word	p	print
iː	keep	r	rest
i	happy	s	save
ə	about	ʃ	shop
ɪ	fit	t	take
ɪə	near	tʃ	change
u	annual	θ	theft
uː	pool	v	value
ʊ	book	w	work
ʊə	tour	x	loch
ʌ	shut	ʒ	measure
		z	zone

A

A3 *adjective* European standard size paper, twice the size of A4: 297 x 420mm

A4 *adjective* European standard size paper, 210 x 297mm

A5 *adjective* European standard size paper, half the size of A4: 148 x 210mm

AACR 2 Rev *noun* Anglo-American cataloguing rules, revised second version

A&I *abbreviation* abstracting and indexing

ABA *abbreviation* American Booksellers' Association

abbreviate /ə'briːvieɪt/ *verb* to make shorter by leaving out some letters or by using only the first few letters of each word

abbreviated entry /ə,briːvieɪtɪd 'entri/ *noun* a shortened form of a bibliographic entry usually giving author, title and date only

abbreviated text /ə,biːvieɪtɪd 'tekst/ *noun* text which is shorter than the original

abbreviation /ə,briːvi'eɪʃ(ə)n/ *noun* a short form of a word

ability /ə'bɪlɪti/ *noun* a quality or skill which makes it possible to do something

-ability /əbɪlɪti/ *suffix* added to adjectives ending in *-able* to form nouns referring to a quality or state, e.g. readability

able /'eɪb(ə)l/ *adjective* quick to learn in an educational environment

abridge /ə'brɪdʒ/ *verb* to make something shorter

abridged document /ə,brɪdʒd 'dɒkjuːmənt/ *noun* a written document which has been made shorter while keeping the main points

abridged edition /ə'brɪdʒd ɪ,dɪʃ(ə)n/ *noun* a shortened text but keeping the main points or story

abridgement /ə'brɪdʒmənt/ *noun* a shortened version of a book

abstract *noun* /'æbstrækt/ a summary of the contents of a document ■ *verb* /æb'strækt/ to summarise the main points of a document

abstracting and indexing /,æbstræktɪŋ ənd 'ɪndeksɪŋ/ *noun* the making of summaries and indexes for articles and books. Abbr **A&I**

abstracting journal /əb'stræktɪŋ ,dʒɜːnəl/ *noun* a journal containing summaries of documents or articles in a given field

ac *abbreviation* **1.** in Internet addresses, the top-level domain for academic organisations **2.** in Internet addresses, the top-level domain for Ascension Island

academic /,ækə'demɪk/ *adjective* relating to studying ■ *noun* a person who teaches or does research usually in higher education

academic library /,ækədemɪk 'laɪbrəri/ *noun* a library which serves an academic community such as a university or college

academic session /,ækədemɪk 'seʃ(ə)n/ *noun* a school or university year, or one complete part of a year, e.g. a term or semester

academy /ə'kædəmi/ *noun* **1.** an educational institution devoted to a particular subject **2.** a secondary school which has been set up in cooperation with private organisations such as businesses or voluntary groups

accent /'æksənt/ *noun* a mark put above or below a letter in writing or printing to show how it should be pronounced

access /'ækses/ *noun* the opportunity or right to use something ○ *They were given access to all relevant information.* ■ *verb* to obtain, examine or be able to reach something ○ *You can access this information in a library or on a computer.*

access code /'ækses kəʊd/ *noun* a code used for information retrieval to show where something can be found

access course /'ækses kɔːs/ *noun* a course of study designed for people without formal educational qualifications, so that they can gain entry to higher education

accessibility /ək,sesɪ'bɪlɪti/ *noun* the quality of being able to be found and used

accessible /ək'sesɪb(ə)l/ *adjective* easy to find and use

accession /ək'seʃ(ə)n/ *noun* a new addition to a library or collection

accession list /ək'seʃ(ə)n lɪst/ *noun* a list of new purchases or additions to a library

accession number /ək'seʃ(ə)n ,nʌmbə/ *noun* a consecutive number used to identify new additions to a library or collection in an inventory system

accession register /ək'seʃ(ə)n ,redʒɪstə/ *noun* a physical record of new purchases or additions to a library or collection

access name /'ækses neɪm/ *noun* a unique name that identifies an object in a database

access number /'ækses ,nʌmbə/ *noun* the telephone number used to link to an Internet service provider or other network provider using a dial-up connection

access point /'ækses pɔɪnt/ *noun* a transceiver in a wireless local area network that connects a wired local area network to wireless devices or that connects wireless devices to each other

access time /'ækses taɪm/ *noun* the time taken to get into a computer program

accompany /ə'kʌmp(ə)ni/ *verb* to play a musical instrument to provide a second part for a piece of music

account /ə'kaʊnt/ *verb* □ **to take account of something, to take something into account** to consider something when you are thinking about a situation

accountant /ə'kaʊntənt/ *noun* a person whose job is to keep the financial accounts for a business

accounting /ə'kaʊntɪŋ/ *noun* the process of keeping financial records for a company or organisation

accounting period /ə'kaʊntɪŋ ,pɪəriəd/ *noun* a period of time at the end of which a company's accounts are closed for checking

accounting year /ə'kaʊntɪŋ ,jɪə/ *noun* any period of twelve months which an organisation uses to control its money ○ *Many universities have an accounting year from August to August.*

accounts /ə'kaʊnts/ *plural noun* detailed records of money received and spent by a business or person

accreditation /ə,kredɪ'teɪʃ(ə)n/ *noun* the granting of official approval to a person or organisation, or the condition of having received this approval

'...the exams, certificates and other pieces of paper that go with CILIP education and accreditation really benefit info pros; raising their profile, and that of the whole profession.' [*Information World Review*]

accumulate /ə'kjuːmjʊleɪt/ *verb* to collect things over a period of time ○ *We have accumulated a large collection of reference materials.*

accumulation /ə,kjuːmjʊ'leɪʃ(ə)n/ *noun* the act of collecting items gained over a period of time

accurate /'ækjʊrət/ *adjective* capable of providing information in accordance with an accepted standard

acetate /'æsɪteɪt/ *noun* transparent plastic used for writing or drawing on, for use with an overhead projector

achievement /ə'tʃiːvmənt/ *noun* something which somebody has succeeded in doing, often after considerable effort

acid-free paper /ˌæsɪd friː 'peɪpə/ *noun* paper which has had certain acid chemicals removed, so that it will not become yellow and brittle with age

acidic paper /əˌsɪdɪk 'peɪpə/ *noun* paper which is made from naturally acidic wood pulp or chemicals used in the manufacturing process, which deteriorates quickly

acid process /'æsɪd ˌprəʊses/ *noun* the process of making chemical paper pulp using acid

acknowledge /ək'nɒlɪdʒ/ *verb* to inform the sender that a message or object has been received

acknowledgement /ək'nɒlɪdʒmənt/ *noun* a piece of text printed at the beginning of a written document thanking people who have helped in its production (NOTE: **Acknowledgement** is usually used in the plural.)

COMMENT: The acknowledgements may also include references to institutions which have given permission to quote copyright material or to use copyright photographs. The acknowledgements are usually placed after the verso of the title page and before the preface; if short, they can be listed at the end of the preface itself.

acoustic hood /əˌkuːstɪk 'hʊd/ *noun* a soundproof covering placed over such things as public telephones or computer printers, to cut out noise

acquiescence /ˌækwi'es(ə)ns/ *noun* agreement with what somebody wants to do

acquire /ə'kwaɪə/ *verb* **1.** to obtain or buy something ○ *to acquire the paperback rights to a new novel* **2.** to gain a skill

acquisition /ˌækwɪ'zɪʃ(ə)n/ *noun* **1.** an object or item which is obtained, purchased or received as a donation to a library **2.** learning or obtaining a skill ○ *The acquisition of a new language is a long process.*

acquisition policy /ˌækwɪ'zɪʃ(ə)n ˌpɒlisi/ *noun* a plan for what types of stock will be bought by a library

'The British Library is to stop collecting every book, magazine and journal printed in Britain because it has nowhere to store them... The government's decision to review the library's acquisition policy follows news that shelves at its new £450m St Pancras site will be full before the building opens.' [*Sunday Times*]

acquisition register /ˌækwɪ'zɪʃ(ə)n ˌredʒɪstə/ *noun* a list of all books and materials obtained by a library

Acrobat /'ækrəʊbæt/ a trademark for a file format developed by Adobe Systems, which describes a graphics, text and indexing system that allows the same screen image or page layout file to be displayed on different hardware

acronym /'ækrənɪm/ *noun* a word made from the initial letters of other words, e.g. DIANE Direct Information Access Network Europe

action shot /'ækʃən ʃɒt/ *noun* a still photograph showing an action taking place

activate /'æktɪveɪt/ *verb* to cause something to start working

active /'æktɪv/ *adjective* busy, being used, working

active database /ˌæktɪv 'deɪtəbeɪs/ *noun* a database file currently being accessed by a database management program

active vocabulary /ˌæktɪv vəʊ'kæbjʊləri/ *noun* the range of words that somebody normally uses in speech or writing, as opposed to words he or she understands when used by others

activity /æk'tɪvɪti/ *noun* a job or task you spend time doing

activity log /æk'tɪvɪti lɒg/ *noun* a written account of things that are done in a given period of time ○ *She kept an activity log of her daily tasks for one week.*

Act of Parliament /ˌækt əv 'pɑːləmənt/ *noun* in the UK, a decision which has been approved by Parliament and so becomes law (NOTE: The US equivalent is **Act of Congress**.)

acute accent /əˌkjuːt 'æksənt/ *noun* a mark usually over the letter e (é) to show how it should be pronounced

ad¹ /æd/ *noun* same as **advertisement**

ad² *abbreviation* in Internet addresses, the top-level domain for Andorra

adapt /ə'dæpt/ *verb* to change a person or thing in order to make it suitable for a specific purpose ○ *Has the play been adapted for the cinema?* ○ *She adapted the story for TV.*

adaptation /ˌædæp'teɪʃ(ə)n/ *noun* a film or play based on a story or novel

adapter /ə'dæptə/ *noun* somebody who adapts a literary work to another format, e.g. a novel to a play

added entry /ˌædɪd 'entri/ *noun* a secondary entry in an index or catalogue

addendum /ə'dendəm/ *noun* an additional section at the end of a document giving extra information (NOTE: The plural is **addenda**.)

addition /ə'dɪʃ(ə)n/ *noun* something extra to what is already there □ **in addition to something** added ○ *There is a lending charge in addition to the reservation fee.*

address /ə'dres/ *noun* **1.** details of where somebody lives or where their business premises are **2.** a label, number or name which locates where information is stored ■ *verb* to deal with something ○ *He addressed the problem.*

addressee /ˌædre'siː/ *noun* the person to whom a letter, package or communication is addressed

address harvester /ə'dres ˌhɑːvɪstə/ *noun* a computer program that collects email addresses from the Internet

adequate /'ædɪkwət/ *adjective* large or good enough for the purpose

adherent /əd'hɪərənt/ *noun* somebody who holds a particular belief or view or supports a particular group

adhesive /əd'hiːsɪv/ *noun* a substance used to make things stick together

adhesive binding /əd,hiːsɪv 'baɪndɪŋ/ *noun* a type of binding where the folds of the signatures are trimmed, and not sewn, the cover being glued to the cut pages. Also called **perfect binding**

ad hoc /ˌæd 'hɒk/ *adjective* unplanned or only organised to meet a particular short-term unexpected situation

adjacent /ə'dʒeɪs(ə)nt/ *adjective* next to or near to something

adjustable shelving /ə ˌdʒʌstəb(ə)l 'ʃelvɪŋ/ *noun* library shelves which can be raised or lowered to meet the requirements of different-sized books

administer /əd'mɪnɪstə/ *verb* to be responsible for managing a company, institution or country

administration /əd,mɪnɪ 'streɪʃ(ə)n/ *noun* **1.** a group of people who are responsible for the management of a company, institution or country **2.** the range of activities connected with management

Adobe /ə'dəʊbi/ a trade name for a leading producer of graphics and desktop publishing software

adopt /ə'dɒpt/ *verb* to accept ideas, plans or attitudes and be willing to carry them out

ADS *abbreviation* advertisement delivery system

adult education /ˌædʌlt ˌedjʊ 'keɪʃ(ə)n/ *noun* courses designed especially for adults outside the formal system of schooling

adult literacy /ˌædʌlt 'lɪt(ə)rəsi/ *noun* the level of reading and writing ability in the adult population of a community

adult literacy programme /ˌædʌlt 'lɪt(ə)rəsi ˌprəʊgræm/ *noun* a programme to teach adults to read and write

advance /əd'vɑːns/ *adjective* happening or arriving before the expected time

advance copy /əd'vɑːns ˌkɒpi/ *noun* a copy of a book sent to people such as reviewers and the author before the official publication date

advanced /əd'vɑːnst/ *adjective* **1.** modern and developed from earlier versions **2.** at a high level of study or achievement ○ *courses for both beginners and advanced students*

advance information sheet /əd ˌvɑːns ˌɪnfə'meɪʃ(ə)n ˌʃiːt/ *noun* full form of **AI**

advance order /əd,vɑːns ˈɔːdə/ *noun* an order for goods or services to be supplied at a later date

advertisement /ədˈvɜːtɪsmənt/ *noun* a notice which shows that something is for sale or that a service is offered or that someone wants something or that a job is vacant, etc. ○ *to put an advertisement in the paper* ○ *to answer an advertisement in the paper*

advertisement delivery system /əd,vɜːtɪsmənt dɪˈlɪv(ə)ri ,sɪstəm/ *noun* a digital file format used in the transmission of mono and colour images. Abbr **ADS**

advertisement file /ədˈvɜːtɪsmənt faɪl/ *noun* a file of advertisements arranged by the name of the product or firm

advertisement page /əd ˈvɜːtɪsmənt peɪdʒ/ *noun* a page facing the title page of a book, which may have a list of other works in the same series or by the same author

advertising /ˈædvətaɪzɪŋ/ *noun* the act of telling people about products or events in order to make them want to buy them or take part

advocacy /ˈædvəkəsi/ *noun* active verbal support for and promotion of a cause

aerial /ˈeəriəl/ *noun* a device which enables a radio or television to receive signals

aero in Internet addresses, the generic top-level domain for the aviation industry

af *abbreviation* in Internet addresses, the top-level domain for Afghanistan

affiliate /əˈfɪlieɪt/ *verb* to form a close official link with an organisation

affirmative /əˈfɜːmətɪv/ *adjective* meaning 'yes' or agreement or approval

afford /əˈfɔːd/ *verb* **1.** to be able to allow something to happen ○ *We cannot afford another argument.* **2.** to have enough money to pay for something

AFNOR /ˈæfnɔː/ *abbreviation* Association Française de Normalisation

A format paperback /,eɪ ,fɔːmæt ˈpeɪpəbæk/ *noun* a paperback with the format 178 x 111mm

After Dark /,ɑːftə ˈdɑːk/ *noun* a non-prime time database service of BRS allowing access to the database at cheaper rates at night

afterword /ˈɑːftəwɜːd/ *noun* a short piece of text placed at the end of a book sometimes used for a note about the author, especially if the author has died since the first printing of the book

ag *abbreviation* in Internet addresses, the top-level domain for Antigua and Barbuda

agate line /ˈægət laɪn/ *noun US* a measure of page space, e.g. in classified advertising, one column wide and 1.8 mm deep

agenda /əˈdʒendə/ *noun* a list of items to be discussed at a meeting

agent /ˈeɪdʒənt/ *noun* somebody who arranges work or business for other people for a fee

age of information /,eɪdʒ əv ,ɪnfə ˈmeɪʃ(ə)n/ *noun* a description of the period in history during the second half of the twentieth century when computers made information easily accessible to large numbers of people

aggregation services /,ægrɪ ˈgeɪʃ(ə)n ,sɜːvɪsɪz/ *plural noun* services which allow information from different places (in digital form) to be available in one single place

'Google was today accused of stifling the media industry's profits by with its news aggregation service. A panel of media executives speaking at the Online Publishers Association conference said that the search engine was infringing on their audience and revenues by aggregating headlines and stories into its Google News service.' [*The Guardian*]

agreement /əˈgriːmənt/ *noun* a formal document stating what two or more people have decided together

Agricultural System for Storing and Subsequently Selecting Information *noun* a software package of particular use to employees in agricultural information. Abbr **ASSASSIN**

ai *abbreviation* in Internet addresses, the top-level domain for Anguilla

AI[1] *noun* a document which is put together by a publishing company to provide marketing information about a book before publication. Full form **advance information sheet**

AI[2] *abbreviation* artificial intelligence

aim /eɪm/ *noun* what an action or plan is intended to achieve

aim for /'eɪm fɔː/ *verb* to plan or hope to achieve something

airmail /'eəmeɪl/ *noun* a system of transporting letters and packages by air

airmail envelope /'eəmeɪl ˌenvələʊp/ *noun* a lightweight envelope usually of blue paper with a red, white and blue striped edging, used for sending letters by air to foreign countries

airport fiction /'eəpɔːt ˌfɪkʃ(ə)n/ *noun* a type of fiction which sells well at airports, generally because it is not serious and is therefore easy to read on a plane journey

al *abbreviation* in Internet addresses, the top-level domain for Albania

ALA *abbreviation* **1.** Associate of the Library Association **2.** American Library Association

album /'ælbəm/ *noun* a collection in book form of short literary or musical pieces or pictures

algorithm /'ælgərɪð(ə)m/ *noun* a logical sequence of steps for solving a problem, often written out as a flow chart, that can be translated into a computer program

alias /'eɪliəs/ *noun* **1.** a name used instead of a real name. ◊ **allonym, pseudonym 2.** a copy of a computer application

align /ə'laɪn/ *verb* to place two objects side by side in a line

alignment /ə'laɪnmənt/ *noun* the ordering of lines of type relative to a margin or line

allocate /'æləkeɪt/ *verb* to give a particular amount of money, goods or tasks to somebody for a particular purpose

allocation /ˌælə'keɪʃ(ə)n/ *noun* the specified amount of something allowed for a particular purpose ○ *All the staff*

had an allocation of time for extra study.

allocation of funds /ˌæləkeɪʃ(ə)n əv 'fʌndz/ *noun* how much money is given to each person or department for a specific purpose

allonym /'ælənɪm/ *noun* a false name often used by authors. ◊ **alias, pseudonym**

all over style /ˌɔːl 'əʊvə ˌstaɪl/ *noun* a style of cover decoration which uses the whole cover instead of just the front

allow /ə'laʊ/ *verb* to give permission

allowance /ə'laʊəns/ *noun* the amount of something given for a specific purpose ○ *They were given an allowance of money to buy children's books.*

all published /ˌɔːl 'pʌblɪʃt/ *noun* a catalogue entry to show that a series or periodical run has not been completed

all rights reserved /ˌɔːl ˌraɪts rɪ'zɜːvd/ *phrase* printed on books and documents to show that they are subject to copyright

allusion book /ə'luːʒ(ə)n ˌbʊk/ *noun* a collection of allusions or references to a writer from other works

almanac /'ɔːlmənæk/ *noun* a book of information, often in tables, about events on particular days of the year such as tides, new moons, times of sunset and festivals

alphabet /'ælfəbet/ *noun* a set of letters or symbols in a fixed order used for writing the words of a language

alphabetical /ˌælfə'betɪk(ə)l/ *adjective* in the same order as the letters of the alphabet

alphabetical index /ˌælfəbetɪk(ə)l 'ɪndeks/ *noun* an index where the items are listed in the order of the letters of the alphabet

alphabetically /ˌælfə'betɪkli/ *adverb* in alphabetical order ○ *The files are arranged alphabetically under the customer's name.*

alphabetical order /ˌælfəbetɪk(ə)l 'ɔːdə/ *noun* arrangement according to the usual order of letters in an alphabet ○ *The authors' names are given in alphabetical order.*

alphabetise /ˈælfəbetaɪz/, **alphabetize** *verb* to sort into alphabetical order

alphanumeric /ˌælfənjʊˈmerɪk/, **alphanumerical** *adjective* using a combination of symbols made up of Roman letters and Arabic numerals including punctuation marks

alphanumeric **data** /ˌælfənjʊmerɪk ˈdeɪtə/ *noun* data shown by the letters of the alphabet and the Arabic numerals

alphanumeric **indexing** /ˌælfənjʊmerɪk ˈɪndeksɪŋ/ *noun* a system which uses both numbers and letters

alpha pulp /ˈælfə pʌlp/ *noun* wood pulp with almost all the cellulose removed

alphasort /ˌælfəˈsɔːt/ *verb* to sort data into alphabetical order

alt *noun* a type of newsgroup on the Internet that contains discussions about alternative subjects

alternate *adjective* /ɔːlˈtɜːnət/ occurring regularly at one time and then missing a time but occurring again the next time ○ *The library van comes on alternate Tuesdays.* ■ *verb* /ˈɔːltəneɪt/ to cause things to happen alternately

alternative /ɔːlˈtɜːnətɪv/ *noun* something that you can do instead of another

alternative **curriculum** /ɔːl ˌtɜːnətɪv kəˈrɪkjʊləm/ *noun* in England and Wales, any available course of study that is not included in the National Curriculum

alternative **title** /ɔːlˌtɜːnətɪv ˈtaɪt(ə)l/ *noun* other title information, also used to describe a subtitle

alumni list /əˈlʌmnaɪ lɪst/ *noun* a list of past members of an educational institution

always-on /ˌɔːlweɪz ˈɒn/ *adjective* relating to a home or business with several computers and mobile phones, in which Internet access is not restricted to specific times

am *abbreviation* in Internet addresses, the top-level domain for Armenia

ambient /ˈæmbiənt/ *adjective* normal background conditions ○ *ambient temperature*

ambiguity /ˌæmbɪˈɡjuːɪti/ *noun* confusion arising from double meanings to words or writing

ambiguous /æmˈbɪɡjuəs/ *adjective* having a double meaning, possible to interpret in more than one way

amend /əˈmend/ *verb* to change something written or said

amendment /əˈmendmənt/ *noun* something that is added to a written or verbal statement in order to change it

amendment record /əˌmendmənt ˈrekɔːd/ *noun* a record containing new information used to update a master record or file

amenities /əˈmiːnɪtiz/ *plural noun* facilities provided for people's convenience or enjoyment

American Booksellers' Association /əˌmerɪkən ˈbʊkseləz əˌsəʊsieɪʃ(ə)n/ *noun* an organisation representing American booksellers, which sponsors an annual convention at which publishing companies have stands showing their new titles. Abbr **ABA** (NOTE: The bookfair sponsored by the ABA, and formerly also called 'the ABA' has changed its name to BookExpo America.)

American Library Association /əˌmerɪkən ˈlaɪbrəri əˌsəʊsieɪʃ(ə)n/ *noun* the oldest and largest library association in the world for the support of qualified librarians and information workers. Abbr **ALA**

American National Standards Institute /əˌmerɪkən ˌnæʃ(ə)nəl ˈstændədz ˌɪnstɪtjuːt/ *noun* an organisation issuing guidelines for production and distribution of goods and services in the USA. Abbr **ANSI**

American Publishers Association /əˌmerɪkən ˈpʌblɪʃəz əˌsəʊsieɪʃ(ə)n/ *noun* an organisation which represents American publishers. Abbr **APA**

American Sign Language /əˌmerɪkən ˈsaɪn ˌlæŋɡwɪdʒ/ *noun* a system of communication used by people with impaired hearing that uses motions or gestures of the hands. Abbr **ASL**

American Society for Information Science /ə,merɪkən sə,saɪəti fər ,ɪnfə'meɪʃ(ə)n ,saɪəns/ *noun* a professional support group for information employees in the USA. Abbr **ASIS**

American Standard Code for Information Interchange /ə ,merɪkən ,stændəd kəʊd fər ,ɪnfəmeɪʃ(ə)n 'ɪntətʃeɪndʒ/ *noun* a computer code which represents alphanumeric characters as binary code. Abbr **ASCII**

ampersand /'æmpəsænd/ *noun* a symbol (&) meaning 'and'

amplifier /'æmplɪfaɪə/ *noun* an electronic device for making signals sound louder

an /ən, æn/ *abbreviation* in Internet addresses, the top-level domain for Netherlands Antilles

analects /'ænəlekts/ *plural noun* a collection of miscellaneous writings

analogue /'ænəlɒg/ *adjective* relating to data in physical rather than numerical form

analogy /ə'nælədʒi/ *noun* a way of describing similarities between two different things

analyse /'ænəlaɪz/ *verb* to examine a situation in detail in order to understand it better

analysis /ə'næləsɪs/ *noun* the process of examining something in detail

analyst /'ænəlɪst/ *noun* a person who analyses data

analytical entry /ænə,lɪtɪk(ə)l 'entri/ *noun* a catalogue entry for a part of a book or periodical which refers to the work containing it

ancestral file /æn,sestrəl 'faɪl/ *noun* a system of backing up computer files, from son to father to grandfather file, where the son is the current working file

anchor /'æŋkə/ *verb* to hold firmly to a solid base

ancillary /æn'sɪləri/ *adjective* supporting the main structure

ancillary worker /æn'sɪləri ,wɜːkə/ *noun* a person in an organisation whose work supports the main aims of the organisation

anecdotal /,ænɪk'dəʊt(ə)l/ *adjective* consisting of or based on second-hand

accounts rather than first-hand knowledge or scientific investigation

animate /'ænɪmeɪt/ *verb* to draw pictures for films which make cartoon characters appear to move

animation /,ænɪ'meɪʃ(ə)n/ *noun* the technique of drawing or photographing successive pictures to create the idea of movement

animator /'ænɪmeɪtə/ *noun* a person who draws or photographs the pictures that make up cartoons

ann. *abbreviation* annals

annal /'æn(ə)l/ *noun* a periodical that records events and reports in a field of research

annals /'æn(ə)lz/ *plural noun* history in general, as it is recorded in books and other documents

annexe *noun* /'æneks/ **1.** an appendix, epilogue or other additional material attached to a larger document **2.** *US* a supplement to a specialised book ■ *verb* /ə'neks/ to attach something such as a document

annotate /'ænəteɪt/ *verb* to add notes to something written in order to explain it more fully

annotated bibliography /,ænəteɪtɪd ,bɪbli'ɒgrəfi/ *noun* a bibliography with notes

annotated catalogue /,ænəteɪtɪd 'kætəlɒg/ *noun* an alphabetical list of items with additional notes of explanation

annotated text /,ænəteɪtɪd 'tekst/ *noun* text with notes written by an editor

annotation /,ænə'teɪʃ(ə)n/ *noun* a note written to explain items in a text

annual /'ænjuəl/ *adjective* **1.** happening once a year **2.** coming out once a year ■ *noun* a book that is published and updated once a year

annually /'ænjuəli/ *adverb* each year ○ *Our prices are raised annually on March 1st.*

annual publication /,ænjuəl ,pʌbli'keɪʃ(ə)n/ *noun* a book, journal or document that is published once a year

annual review /,ænjuəl rɪ'vjuː/ *noun* an inspection that takes place once a year

anon /ə'nɒn/ *abbreviation* anonymous

anonym /'ænənɪm/ *noun* a publication whose author is unnamed or unknown

anonymiser /ə'nɒnɪmaɪzə/, **anonymizer** *noun* a website through which a person browsing can visit the World Wide Web without leaving any trace of their identity

anonymous /ə'nɒnɪməs/ *adjective* of unknown name or authorship

anonymous FTP /ə,nɒnɪməs ef tiː 'piː/ *noun* a type of Internet file transfer in which no password is needed, used by some organisations to make their file archives publicly accessible

ANSI /'ænsi/ *abbreviation* American National Standards Institute

answerphone /'ɑːnsəfəʊn/, **answer machine** *noun* a cassette recorder attached to a telephone which relays a pre-recorded message to callers and records messages

anthologise /æn'θɒlədʒaɪz/, **anthologize** *verb* **1.** to gather works from different writers, musicians or artists into a collection **2.** to compile or publish an anthology

anthology /æn'θɒlədʒi/ *noun* a book that consists of essays, stories or poems by different writers

anticipate /æn'tɪsɪpeɪt/ *verb* to realise in advance that something is going to happen and to prepare for it

Antiope /æn'taɪəpi/ *noun* a French videotext system also known as Teletel

antiquarian /,ænti'kweəriən/ *adjective* relating to or dealing with antiques or antiquities, especially rare and old books. Abbr **antiq.**

antiquary /æn'tɪkwəri/ *noun* a collector, scholar or seller of antiques or antiquities

anti-setoff paper /,ænti 'setɒf ,peɪpə/ *noun* thin transparent paper put between the pages of an expensive illustrated book

antonym /'æntənɪm/ *noun* a word which has the opposite meaning to another word

anycast /'enikɑːst/ *noun* an act of sending data across a computer network from a single user to the nearest receiver

ao *abbreviation* in Internet addresses, the top-level domain for Angola

AP *abbreviation* PUBL Associated Press

a.p. *abbreviation* PUBL author's proof

APA *abbreviation* American Publishers Association

Apocrypha /ə'pɒkrɪfə/ *plural noun* books of the Bible that are included in the Vulgate and Septuagint versions of the Christian Bible, but not in the Protestant Bible or the Hebrew canon

apocryphal /ə'pɒkrəf(ə)l/ *adjective* of unknown authorship, possibly false or exaggerated

'The cardinal's main objection to the book is that it presents itself as a historical document. Acknowledging that the book is a brilliantly marketed page-turner, he accused Brown of relying on apocryphal texts that had been removed from the biblical canon because they were imaginative.' [*Irish Independent*]

apostil /ə'pɒstɪl/ *noun* a margin note or annotation

apostrophe /ə'pɒstrəfi/ *noun* a punctuation mark which indicates either contraction or possession

app. *abbreviation* PUBL appendix

appeal /ə'piːl/ *noun* **1.** the attractiveness of something which makes it popular ○ *The illustrations have a lot to do with the book's continuing appeal.* **2.** a request for something to be reconsidered

append /ə'pend/ *verb* to add extra information to something, especially to a document

appendix /ə'pendɪks/ *noun* a section at the end of a document giving extra information (NOTE: The plural is **appendices** /ə'pendɪsiːz/ .)

COMMENT: Appendices are always printed at the back of a book, always starting on a right-hand page. They must be laid out in a way which shows clearly that they are not part of the main text.

Apple Mac /'æp(ə)l mæk/, **Apple Macintosh computer** a trade name for a range of personal computers developed by Apple Inc. that has a graphical user interface and uses the 68000 family of processors.

applicant /ˈæplɪkənt/ *noun* a person who formally asks to be considered for a job

application /ˌæplɪˈkeɪʃ(ə)n/ *noun* **1.** a written request for something ○ *job application* **2.** the use of a rule or piece of equipment in a particular situation ○ *Computer applications are electronic packages which allow particular tasks to be performed.*

application form /ˌæplɪˈkeɪʃ(ə)n ˌfɔːm/ *noun* a standardised form to be filled in when applying for something

apply for /əˈplaɪ ˈfɔː/ *verb* to make a formal, usually written, request for something

appoint /əˈpɔɪnt/ *verb* to choose somebody to do a job

appreciate /əˈpriːʃieɪt/ *verb* **1.** to understand and know what a situation involves **2.** to like something because you recognise its good qualities **3.** to increase in value

appropriate /əˈprəʊpriət/ *adjective* suitable or acceptable for a particular situation

approve /əˈpruːv/ *verb* to agree to ○ *to approve the terms of a contract* □ **to approve of** to think something is good ○ *They approved of the new signs for the library.*

approximate /əˈprɒksɪmət/ *adjective* not exact, almost correct

aq *abbreviation* in Internet addresses, the top-level domain for Antarctica

AR *abbreviation* aspect ratio

Arabic /ˈærəbɪk/ *adjective* coming from Arabia or from the Arabs

Arabic numerals /ˌærəbɪk ˈnjuːmərəl/, **Arabic numbers** /ˌærəbɪk ˈnʌmbəz/, **Arabic figures** /ˌærəbɪk ˈfɪgəz/ *plural noun* normal numbers (such as 1, 2, 3, etc.) as opposed to Roman numerals (I, II, III, IV, etc.) ○ *the page numbers are written in Arabic figures*

arcane /ɑːˈkeɪn/ *adjective* requiring secret knowledge to be understood

archetype /ˈɑːkɪtaɪp/ *noun* a document or book that illustrates the styles of a particular time and subject

ARCHIE /ˈɑːtʃi/ *noun* retrieval software which gives access to Internet databases

architecture /ˈɑːkɪtektʃə/ *noun* the planning and design of buildings or systems

archival management /ˈɑːkaɪvəl ˌmænɪdʒmənt/ *noun* control of archives

archive /ˈɑːkaɪv/ *noun* **1.** a public record, document or photograph of historical interest kept in an official repository **2.** a collection of documents and records relating to the history of an organisation ■ *verb* to put data in storage

archive file /ˈɑːkaɪv faɪl/ *noun* a file containing data which is out of date, but which is kept for future reference

archive library /ˈɑːkaɪv ˌlaɪbrəri/ *noun* a library which stores and makes accessible historical materials

'The relevant portions of the digital content identified by the editor will be retrieved from the data archive library, automatically transcoded or reformatted as necessary and delivered directly into the nonlinear editing system. The labour efficiencies gained and vast creativity benefits of a digital archive management system are obvious.' [*Broadcast Engineering*]

archivist /ˈɑːkɪvɪst/ *noun* a person who organises archives

area /ˈeəriə/ *noun* a space in a building such as a library, designated for a particular purpose, e.g. reference area

argument /ˈɑːgjʊmənt/ *noun* **1.** a disagreement between two or more people **2.** a set of reasons used to try to convince people

arrange /əˈreɪndʒ/ *verb* to put things into a correct or desired order

arrangement /əˈreɪndʒmənt/ *noun* something that has been planned, agreed or put into order

array /əˈreɪ/ *noun* a set of numbers or symbols, e.g. experimental data, usually arranged in a specific order

art book /ˈɑːt bʊk/ *noun* a book with illustrations, dealing with a painter, sculptor, style of design or other art topic

article /ˈɑːtɪk(ə)l/ *noun* **1.** a piece of writing in a newspaper or magazine **2.** a message sent to an electronic newsgroup

articulated indexing /ɑːˌtɪkjʊleɪtɪd ˈɪndeksɪŋ/ *noun* a method of producing computer-generated subject indexes

articulation of information /ɑːˌtɪkjʊleɪʃ(ə)n əv ˌɪnfəˈmeɪʃ(ə)n/ *noun* the way in which information is presented so that the user can easily access and understand it

artificial indexing language /ˌɑːtɪfɪʃ(ə)l ˈɪndeksɪŋ ˌlæŋgwɪdʒ/ *noun* signs and symbols used as a controlled language in inverted order for subject indexing

artificial intelligence /ˌɑːtɪfɪʃ(ə)l ɪnˈtelɪdʒəns/ *noun* the design and development of computers which attempt to imitate some human characteristics. Abbr **AI**

artificial language /ˌɑːtɪfɪʃ(ə)l ˈlæŋgwɪdʒ/ *noun* a man-made language for use in communicating with computers

artistic map /ɑːˌtɪstɪk ˈmæp/ *noun* a map made by an artist rather than a map maker

artwork /ˈɑːtwɜːk/ *noun* drawings, photographs and text prepared for inclusion in a book or advertisement. Abbr **a/w**

as *abbreviation* in Internet addresses, the top-level domain for American Samoa

ascender /əˈsendə/ *noun* **1.** the part of a lower case letter such as h, d or b that projects above the body of the letter **2.** a lower case letter with an ascender

ascending order /əˌsendɪŋ ˈɔːdə/ *noun* a method of organising things so that each item is bigger than the one before it or comes later in the system ○ *The list was arranged in ascending order from A to Z.*

ASCII /ˈæskiː/ *abbreviation* American Standard Code for Information Interchange

ASCII character /ˈæski ˌkærɪktə/ *noun* a character which is in the ASCII list of codes

ASCII file /ˈæski faɪl/ *noun* a stored file containing only ASCII coded character data ○ *Make an ASCII file of the document for clients who use different word-processing software.*

ASI *abbreviation* Australian Society of Indexers

ASIS *abbreviation* American Society for Information Science

ASL *abbreviation* American Sign Language

ASLIB /ˈæzlɪb/ *abbreviation* Association of Information Management

aspect ratio /ˈæspekt ˌreɪʃiəʊ/ *noun* the ratio of the width to the height of an illustration, used especially in computer graphics. Abbr **AR**

ASSASSIN /əˈsæsɪn/ *abbreviation* Agricultural System for Storing and Subsequently Selecting Information

assemble /əˈsemb(ə)l/ *verb* **1.** to bring the parts of a collection together **2.** to fit the parts of something together to make it whole

assembly language /əˈsembli ˌlæŋgwɪdʒ/ *noun* a low-level computer programming language

assertion /əˈsɜːʃ(ə)n/ *noun* a firm statement of belief

assess /əˈses/ *verb* to judge the importance or value of something

'Measurement is perhaps the least developed aspect of KM because of the inherent difficulty of measuring something that can not bet seen or touched. However, if the discipline of KM is to survive and make a long-lasting contribution, it will need to achieve greater levels of standardization and better metrics to assess its effectiveness.' [*Journal of American Academy of Business*]

assessed work /əˌsest ˈwɜːk/ *noun* assignments that have been judged as part of a course of training

assign /əˈsaɪn/ *verb* to allocate a task to a person or send somebody to work in a particular place

assignment /ə'saɪnmənt/ *noun* a task often given as part of a programme of study

assimilate /ə'sɪmɪleɪt/ *verb* to learn and make use of something

assimilation /ə,sɪmɪ'leɪʃ(ə)n/ *noun* the absorption of ideas or people ○ *The assimilation of immigrants by the host culture is a long process.*

assist /ə'sɪst/ *verb* to help somebody, e.g. by giving them information

assistant /ə'sɪst(ə)nt/ *noun* somebody who is employed to help another in their work

assistant librarian /ə,sɪst(ə)nt laɪ'breəriən/ *noun* somebody who is qualified as a librarian and usually works with a more senior person

associate *noun* /ə'səʊsiət/ somebody you work with ■ *verb* /ə'səʊsieɪt/ to connect something with another having a similar background

association /ə,səʊsi'eɪʃ(ə)n/ *noun* **1.** a group of people or of companies with the same interest ○ *a book trade association* ○ *a printers' association* **2.** a relationship between two or more topics or concepts

association copy /ə,səʊsi'eɪʃ(ə)n ,kɒpi/ *noun* a copy of a book which has a connection with the author, e.g. a copy given by the author to a friend or the author's own copy with his or her notes in it

Association Française de Normalisation /æ,sɒsiæsiɒn frɒn,ses də ,nɔːmæli'zæsiɒn/ *noun* a French official body responsible for issuing standards. Abbr **AFNOR**

Association of Information Management /ə,səʊsieɪʃ(ə)n əv ,ɪnfə'meɪʃ(ə)n ,mænɪdʒmənt/ *noun* a body which gives advice and guidelines on the management of information within companies, and publishes ASLIB Information, ASLIB Proceedings and Journal of Documentation. Abbr **ASLIB**

assume /ə'sjuːm/ *verb* to accept the truth of something or to take something on ○ *He assumed responsibility for the information service.*

asterisk /'æstərɪsk/ *noun* a symbol in the form of a star used to mark things to be noted: * ■ *verb* to mark something with an asterisk or a star-shaped symbol, especially to draw attention to it

asterism /'æstɜːrɪz(ə)m/ *noun* a triangle formed of three asterisks which calls the reader's attention to a following passage

asymmetrical digital subscriber line /,æsɪmetrɪk(ə)l ,dɪdʒɪt(ə)l səb'skraɪbə ,laɪn/ *noun* a high-speed telephone line that can transmit voice and video data over copper wires. Abbr **ADSL**

asynchronous transfer mode /eɪ,sɪŋkrənəs 'trænsfɜː ,məʊd/ *noun* a method for transferring data very quickly using broadband. Abbr **ATM**

asyndetic /,æsɪn'detɪk/ *adjective* without cross-references

at *abbreviation* in Internet addresses, the top-level domain for Austria

athenaeum /,æθə'neɪəm/ *noun* an institution where reading materials are made available to the public, e.g. a library

atlas /'ætləs/ *noun* a book of maps

ATM *abbreviation* asynchronous transfer mode

attach /ə'tætʃ/ *verb* to fasten on ○ *She asked them to attach the documents for her information.* □ **to be attached to** to be working with a company or person for a short time

attachment /ə'tætʃmənt/ *noun* a computer file that is transferred together with an electronic mail message

attend /ə'tend/ *verb* to go to ○ *to attend a meeting* □ **to attend to** to deal with something

attendance /ə'tendəns/ *noun* the number of people at a meeting

attendant /ə'tendənt/ *noun* somebody employed to serve or help members of the public in a public institution or place

attention span /ə'tenʃən spæn/ *noun* the length of time that a person is able to give undivided attention to something

attribute /ə'trɪbjuːt/ *verb* to say that somebody did something ○ *to attribute a piece of writing to a particular person*

attributed author /ə,trɪbjuːtɪd 'ɔːθə/ *noun* the name of a possible author when there is doubt about authenticity

au *abbreviation* in Internet addresses, the top-level domain for Australia

audience /'ɔːdiəns/ *noun* a group of people gathered together to watch or listen to something

audio /'ɔːdiəʊ/ *adjective* relating to material which can be heard

audio book /'ɔːdiəʊ bʊk/ *noun* a book in spoken form recorded on a cassette or CD

audio conference /'ɔːdiəʊ ,kɒnf(ə)rəns/ *noun* a meeting that is held with the use of several linked telephones to connect the people who want to talk together

audio media /'ɔːdiəʊ ,miːdiə/ *noun* communication tools which use sound only, such as radio

audio tape /'ɔːdiəʊ teɪp/ *noun* a tape which is used to record and play back sounds for listening to

audiovisual /,ɔːdiəʊ 'vɪʒʊəl/ *adjective* **1.** relating to sound and vision, especially when combined, e.g. in a presentation using both film and sound recordings ○ *audiovisual media* **2.** relating to hearing and seeing ○ *an audiovisual experience* Abbr **AV**

audiovisual aid /,ɔːdiəʊvɪʒuəl 'eɪd/ *noun* a teaching or lecture aid that combines sound and vision, e.g. in the form of video equipment, software programs or slides accompanied by sound recordings

audiovisual materials /,ɔːdiəʊvɪʒuəl mə'tɪəriəlz/ *plural noun* materials that can be listened to and looked at, such as CDs or slides with recorded speech

audit /'ɔːdɪt/ *verb* to examine something officially to make sure it is correct

Audit Commission /,ɔːdɪt kə'mɪʃ(ə)n/ *noun* a government body which ensures that financial affairs are conducted according to approved standards, and examines the accounts of government departments and local government organisations

audit trail /'ɔːdɪt treɪl/ *noun* **1.** a record of all interactions with a system, kept to assess the level of use **2.** a record showing what operations a computer or computer user has performed in a specific period of time

aural /'ɔːrəl/ *adjective* relating to hearing

aural materials /,ɔːrəl mə'tɪəriəlz/ *plural noun* materials that can be listened to, such as CDs

aural test /'ɔːrəl test/ *noun* a test of an individual's ability to listen and understand

Australian Society of Indexers /ɒ,streɪliən sə,saɪəti əv 'ɪndeksəz/ *noun* a professional support group for professional indexers in Australasia. Abbr **ASI**

authentic /ɔː'θentɪk/ *adjective* known to be real and not a copy

authentication /ɔː,θentɪ'keɪʃ(ə)n/ *noun* a security measure using data encryption that identifies the user and verifies that the message was not tampered with

authenticity /,ɔːθen'tɪsɪti/ *noun* the quality of being authentic

author /'ɔːθə/ *noun* somebody who writes books or articles ■ *verb* **1.** to be the author of something ○ *The book is authored by a college professor.* **2.** to create a multimedia presentation or application by combining text, video, sound and images using a programming language or special multimedia authoring system

author catalogue /'ɔːθə ,kætəlɒg/, **author index** /'ɔːθər ,ɪndeks/ *noun* a catalogue which is organised according to an alphabetical list of writers' surnames

author entry /'ɔːθər ,entri/ *noun* a catalogue entry under the name of the person or organisation responsible for writing or compiling a work

authoring /'ɔːθərɪŋ/ *noun* the act of creating a multimedia application by combining sound, video and images, usually using a script or authoring software

authoring software /ˌɔːθərɪŋ ˈsɒftweə/ *noun* software that allows users to add their own text and to link text, pictures and sound within a given framework

authorise /ˈɔːθəraɪz/, **authorize** *verb* to give official permission for something to be done

Authorised Version /ˈɔːθəraɪzd ˌvɜːʒ(ə)n/ *noun* an English translation of the Bible made in England in 1611 AD. Also called **King James Bible**

authoritative /ɔːˈθɒrɪtətɪv/ *adjective* reliable or official

authority /ɔːˈθɒrɪti/ *noun* an expert in the field

authority control /ɔːˈθɒrɪti kənˌtrəʊl/ *noun* a list of headings used in a retrieval system

'In addition, the ability to reassign records from one authority control heading to another [in the Open Q electronic library system] will aid in correcting the inconsistent author headings.' [*Computers in Libraries*]

authority file /ɔːˈθɒrɪti faɪl/ *noun* a list of authoritative forms to be used in bibliographic records

author's alterations /ˌɔːθəz ˌɔːltəˈreɪʃ(ə)nz/ *plural noun* same as **author's corrections**. Abbr **AA**

author's corrections *plural noun* a change to proofs which is made by an author, and which is charged to the author if too many are made. Also called **author's alterations**. Abbr **AC**

autobiography /ˌɔːtəʊbaɪˈɒɡrəfi/ *noun* an account of a person's life written by that person

auto-encode /ˈɔːtəʊ ɪnˌkəʊd/ *verb* to select keywords automatically by computer

autograph /ˈɔːtəɡrɑːf/ *noun* the signature of somebody famous ■ *verb* to sign a copy of the book ○ *He gave an autographed copy of his novel to the library.*

auto-indexing /ˈɔːtəʊ ˌɪndeksɪŋ/ *noun* the process of automatic indexing using a computer program

automate /ˈɔːtəmeɪt/ *verb* to use machines to do work previously done by people

automatic /ˌɔːtəˈmætɪk/ *adjective* able to operate by itself without constant user input

automatic data processing /ˌɔːtəmætɪk ˈdeɪtə ˌprəʊsesɪŋ/ *noun* data processing done by a computer

automatic indexing /ˌɔːtəmætɪk ˈɪndeksɪŋ/ *noun* using a computer to compile an index to a document by selecting specific words or items in the text

automation /ˌɔːtəˈmeɪʃ(ə)n/ *noun* the use of machines to do work with very little supervision

autonomy /ɔːˈtɒnəmi/ *noun* the opportunity to make one's own decisions without being told what to do by somebody else

auxiliary /ɔːɡˈzɪliəri/ *adjective* used to describe a person or a machine which helps a more important worker

auxiliary language /ɔːɡˌzɪliəri ˈlæŋɡwɪdʒ/ *noun* a language that is used by speakers of other languages in order to communicate

auxiliary number /ɔːɡˌzɪliəri ˈnʌmbə/ *noun* an additional number placed after the class number to allow materials to be further grouped into subgroups

AV *abbreviation* MEDIA audiovisual

availability /əˌveɪləˈbɪlɪti/ *noun* being able to be obtained, used or seen ○ *The new books were given limited availability of one week per person, so that more people could read them.*

available /əˈveɪləb(ə)l/ *adjective* ready to be used ○ *available time or information*

a/w *abbreviation* artwork

award /əˈwɔːd/ *noun* **1.** a prize given for doing something well **2.** a sum of money given for a specific purpose ○ *an award to help you to study* ■ *verb* to give a prize or financial grant

awarding body /əˌwɔːdɪŋ ˈbɒdi/ *noun* an organisation which gives a prize or scholarship

awareness /əˈweənəs/ *noun* knowing about things

axis /ˈæksɪs/ *noun* a fixed line against which other positions can be measured, e.g. the vertical and horizontal axes on a graph (NOTE: The plural is **axes**.)

az *abbreviation* in Internet addresses, the top-level domain for Azerbaijan

B

bachelor's degree /'bætʃələz dɪ ˌgriː/ *noun* a degree awarded on the successful completion of an undergraduate course at a college or university and, at some universities, on completion of a usually short postgraduate course

back /bæk/ *noun* the part of a book where the pages are glued or stitched to the binding ■ *adjective* published or issued at an earlier date

back board /'bæk bɔːd/ *noun* the board which forms the back of a book

backbone /'bækbəʊn/ *noun US* the spine of a book

back catalogue /ˌbæk 'kæt(ə)lɒg/ *noun* the complete collection of recordings, films or books made by an artist or a company to date

back copy /'bæk ˌkɒpi/ *noun* a copy of an old issue of a newspaper or magazine

back cover /ˌbæk 'kʌvə/ *noun* the cover at the back of a book or magazine, which can have publicity matter or details of the author

backdate /bæk'deɪt/ *verb* to make effective from an earlier date than the current one

backdated /bæk'deɪtɪd/ *adjective* with the date written earlier than the current day's date

back flap /ˌbæk 'flæp/, **back jacket flap** /ˌbæk 'dʒækɪt ˌflæp/ *noun* a flap on a book jacket which is folded inside the back cover

background /'bækgraʊnd/ *noun* **1.** the context of a situation, which helps to explain it **2.** scenery behind the main people and objects in a picture or photograph

background colour /ˌbækgraʊnd 'kʌlə/ *noun* the colour of a computer screen display, with characters and graphics displayed in a different foreground colour

background printing /ˌbækgraʊnd 'prɪntɪŋ/ *noun* printing from a computer while it is processing another task

background processing /ˌbækgraʊnd 'prəʊsesɪŋ/ *noun* execution of computer tasks that continues while the user is working with another application. Once started, background tasks such as printing or copying data take place without user input.

backing /'bækɪŋ/ *noun* money or support given to a person or an organisation for a particular project

back issue /'bæk ˌɪʃuː/ *noun US* same as **back number**

back lining /ˌbæk 'laɪnɪŋ/ *noun* a piece of thin cloth or paper glued to the sewn spine of a book before the cover is attached

backlist /'bæklɪst/ *noun* the range of books already published by a publisher that are still in print

backlog /'bæklɒg/ *noun* work waiting to be done and causing delays

back matter /'bæk ˌmætə/ *noun* the parts of a book that appear after the main text, e.g. the index or an appendix

back number /'bæk ˌnʌmbə/ *noun* an edition of a magazine, newspaper or other document which is not the most recent edition

back order /'bæk ˌɔːdə/ *noun* an uncompleted order which is held back for delivery when stock becomes available

backslash /ˈbækslæʃ/ *noun* a punctuation mark ○ *These words are between backslashes.*\

back title /ˈbæk ˌtaɪt(ə)l/ *noun* the title on the spine or back of a book

back up /ˌbæk ˈʌp/ *verb* to make a copy of computer data to keep in case anything goes wrong with the original

backup /ˈbækʌp/ *adjective* assistance ○ *We offer an after sales backup service.* ■ *noun* a duplicate copy of a file on a computer

backup procedure /ˈbækʌp prə ˌsiːdʒə/ *noun* a method of making backup copies of files

backwards compatible /ˌbækwədz kəmˈpætəb(ə)l/ *adjective* relating to a computer hardware or software product that is compatible with its predecessors to the extent that it can use interfaces and data from earlier versions

bail /beɪl/ *noun* a hinged bar on a typewriter or printer that holds the paper steady

.BAK, .bak *suffix* an extension to a filename, indicating a backup version of a file

balance /ˈbæləns/ *verb* a financial term meaning to keep expenditure equal to income ■ *noun* **1.** the positioning of text and graphics on a page in an attractive way **2.** □ **in the balance** not yet decided □ **on balance** phrase used to show that you are giving a considered opinion

bandwidth /ˈbændwɪdθ/ *noun* the capacity, often measured in bits per second, of a communication channel, e.g. a connection to the Internet

bang /bæŋ/ *noun US* in typesetting, the character !

bank /bæŋk/ *noun* somewhere to store things ready for use ■ *verb* □ **to bank on** to rely on something happening

bankrupt /ˈbæŋkrʌpt/ *adjective* not having enough money to pay one's debts

bank sort code /ˌbæŋk ˈsɔːt ˌkəʊd/ *noun* a set of numbers printed on cheques which identifies a particular bank

banned /bænd/ *adjective* prohibited from use by authorities

banner /ˈbænə/ *noun* a heading or title across the width of a page

banner headline /ˌbænə ˈhedlaɪn/ *noun* an extra large newspaper headline

BAPLA /ˈbæplə/ *abbreviation* British Association of Picture Libraries and Agencies

bar /bɑː/ *noun* a thick band of colour ■ *verb* to prevent somebody from doing something or going somewhere

bar chart /ˈbɑː tʃɑːt/ *noun* a graph in which the data is represented by horizontal or vertical bars

barcode /ˈbɑːkəʊd/ *noun* a line of printed stripes of different thickness representing a numeric code which can be read electronically

COMMENT: Barcodes are found on most goods and their packages. The width and position of the stripes is sensed by a light pen or optical wand and provides information about the goods, such as price, stock quantity, etc. The main type of bar code used in Europe is the European Article Number (EAN) or the Universal Product Code (UPC). Barcodes are used on the backs of books, giving their ISBN number, and so helping the computerised stock control in bookshops.

barcode reader /ˈbɑːkəʊd ˌriːdə/, **barcode scanner** /ˈbɑːkəʊd ˌskænə/ *noun* an electronic device used to read barcodes

base /beɪs/ *verb* □ **to base on** to develop an idea from the foundations of a previous idea

baseline /ˈbeɪslaɪn/ *noun* the data used as a reference with which to compare future observations or results

BASIC /ˈbeɪsɪk/ *noun* a computer programming language. Full form **Beginner's All-Purpose Symbolic Instruction Code**

Basic Curriculum /ˌbeɪsɪk kə ˈrɪkjələm/ *noun* in schools in England and Wales, the National Curriculum plus religious education

basic stock /ˌbeɪsɪk ˈstɒk/ *noun* standard titles which are considered necessary to form the core of an authoritative book stock. Also called **core stock**

basis /'beɪsɪs/ *noun* the foundation or reason for something

bastard size /'bɑːstəd saɪz/ *noun* an odd non-standard size of paper

.BAT, .bat *suffix* an extension to a filename, showing that the file is a batch file

batch /bætʃ/ *noun* a group of things which are made or dealt with all at one time

batch control /'bætʃ kən,trəʊl/ *noun* a system for organising groups of products

batch file /'bætʃ faɪl/ *noun* a combination of computer files which are treated as one unit

batch number /'bætʃ ,nʌmbə/ *noun* a number used to identify a particular group

batch processing /'bætʃ ,prəʊsesɪŋ/ *noun* a mode of computer operation in which programs are executed without the user being able to influence processing while it is in progress

'First things first, however. Repcol needs to upgrade its in-house collections system, and build a live link between collections and financials. Repcol runs the collections system on an Informix database, but uses a separate Oracle financials system running on Linux, batch processing transactions.' [*The Australian*]

batch system /'bætʃ ,sɪstəm/ *noun* a way of dealing with tasks in groups

batter /'bætə/ *noun* a defective impression produced by a faulty printing plate

battery /'bæt(ə)ri/ *noun* a large number of things or people

bay /beɪ/ *noun* a space or area used for a particular purpose ○ *a book bay in a library*

bb *abbreviation* in Internet addresses, the top-level domain for Barbados

BBC *abbreviation* British Broadcasting Corporation

BBIP *abbreviation* British Books in Print

bcc *abbreviation* blind carbon copy

.bck *suffix* an extension to a filename, showing that the file is a backup file

bd *abbreviation* **1.** in Internet addresses, the top-level domain for Bangladesh **2.** PUBL bound

bds *abbreviation* PUBL bound in boards

be *abbreviation* in Internet addresses, the top-level domain for Belgium

Beginner's All-Purpose Symbolic Instruction Code *noun* full form of **BASIC**

BEI *abbreviation* British Education Index

benchmark /'bentʃmɑːk/ *noun* something of accepted quality which is used to provide a standard for comparison

beneficial /,benɪ'fɪʃ(ə)l/ *adjective* providing advantage or benefit

Berne Convention /'bɜːn kən ,venʃ(ə)n/ *noun* the international agreement on copyright, signed in Berne in 1886. ◊ **convention**

COMMENT: Under the Berne Convention , any book which is copyrighted in a country which has signed the convention is automatically copyrighted in the other countries. Some countries (notably the USA) did not sign the Convention, and the UCC (Universal Copyright Convention) was signed in Geneva in 1952, under the auspices of the United Nations, to try to bring together all countries under a uniform copyright agreement.

bestseller /best'selə/ *noun* **1.** a popular book of which a very large number of copies are sold **2.** an author who writes bestsellers

bestselling /best'selɪŋ/ *adjective* **1.** far more popular and successful than other products on sale at the same time **2.** making products that are commercially very successful ○ *a bestselling author*

bf *abbreviation* PRINTING boldface

B format paperback /,biː ,fɔːmæt 'peɪpəbæk/ *noun* a paperback with the format 198 x 129mm

bg *abbreviation* in Internet addresses, the top-level domain for Bulgaria

bh *abbreviation* in Internet addresses, the top-level domain for Bahrain

BHI *abbreviation* British Humanities Index

bi *abbreviation* in Internet addresses, the top-level domain for Burundi

biannually /baɪˈænjuəli/ *adverb* issued every two years

bias /ˈbaɪəs/ *noun* an unfair judgement influenced by opinions rather than facts

biased /ˈbaɪəst/ *adjective* holding views based on opinions rather than facts

bias phrase /ˈbaɪəs freɪz/ *noun* in classification, the name of a specific group for whom a work is intended

biblio /ˈbɪbliəʊ/ *noun* bibliographic details printed on the back of the title page

bibliographic /ˌbɪbliəˈɡræfɪk/ *adjective* relating to bibliographies

bibliographical information /ˌbɪbliəɡræfɪk(ə)l ˌɪnfəˈmeɪʃ(ə)n/ *noun* information about a book such as the name of the author, number of pages and ISBN, which is used for library cataloguing

bibliographic control /ˌbɪbliəɡræfɪk kənˈtrəʊl/ *noun* the creation and management of bibliographic records and the system which enables users to access them

'This practical volume addresses the ways a library can manage electronic collections. The goal is to provide an overview of management concerns and issues regarding bibliographic control in an online environment and to suggest tools that are available.' [*Booklist*]

bibliographic database /ˌbɪbliəɡræfɪk ˈdeɪtəbeɪs/ *noun* a database containing bibliographic information, designed to locate specific items

bibliographic details /ˌbɪbliəɡræfɪk ˈdiːteɪlz/ *plural noun* information about a publication, often printed on the back of the title page, which enables it to be identified, e.g. date of publication and ISBN

bibliographic entry /ˌbɪbliəɡræfɪk ˈentri/ *noun* details of written material, set out in a list for reference

bibliography /ˌbɪbliˈɒɡrəfi/ *noun* **1.** a list of books and other written materials on one particular subject **2.** a list of

books or articles referred to in another book or article

bibliomania /ˌbɪbliəʊˈmeɪniə/ *noun* an obsession with collecting books

bibliophile /ˈbɪbliəfaɪl/ *noun* a person who loves books, especially somebody who collects old, rare or beautiful books ○ *The book has been published as a limited edition for bibliophiles.*

bifurcate classification /baɪ ˌfɜːkeɪt ˌklæsɪfɪˈkeɪʃ(ə)n/ *noun* a system of classification based on branching positive and negative pairs

bilingual /baɪˈlɪŋɡwəl/ *adjective* in two languages ○ *a bilingual dictionary* ◊ **monolingual, multilingual**

bilingual text /baɪˌlɪŋɡwəl ˈtekst/ *noun* text which is given in two languages, usually with the texts on facing pages

billion /ˈbɪljən/ *noun* **1.** in the UK, a million million **2.** in the US, a thousand million

bimonthly /baɪˈmʌnθli/ *adjective* issued or published every two months

binary /ˈbaɪnəri/ *adjective* relating to a numerical system using only the digits 0 and 1, used especially in computing

binary file /ˈbaɪnəri faɪl/ *noun* a computer file that contains data in a raw or nontext state made up of characters that only a computer can read. Executable programs are stored and transmitted in binary files, as are most numerical data files.

binary search /ˈbaɪnəri sɜːtʃ/ *noun* a system of searching by repeatedly rejecting one of a pair until the required item is found

binary system /ˈbaɪnəri ˌsɪstəm/ *noun* a number system based on two digits only, usually 1 and 0

bind /baɪnd/ *verb* to join the pages of a book together and enclose them in a cover (NOTE: **binding – bound**)

binder /ˈbaɪndə/ *noun* a person or company that specialises in binding books

bindery /ˈbaɪndəri/ *noun* a factory where books are bound

binding /ˈbaɪndɪŋ/ *noun* **1.** the cover of a book **2.** the act of putting a cover on a book ■ *adjective* demanding an obligation ○ *The contract was binding in law.*

binding record /'baɪndɪŋ ˌrekɔːd/ *noun* a record of all books sent to the binder

bio /'baɪəʊ/ *noun* a biographical work

biodata /'baɪəʊdeɪtə/ *noun* information relating to a particular person and his or her financial, professional or educational history, stored in a database and used, e.g. in banking, job recruiting and marketing

biographee /ˌbaɪɒɡrəˈfiː/ *noun* somebody whose life is described in a biography

biographical   details /ˌbaɪəɡræfɪk(ə)l ˈdiːteɪlz/ *plural noun* information about the main events in somebody's life

biography /baɪˈɒɡrəfi/ *noun* an account of somebody's life and work written by another person

bioinformatics /ˌbaɪəʊˌɪnfə ˈmætɪks/ *noun* the use of computers to extract and analyse biological data, especially in studying DNA

BIS *abbreviation* Business Information Service

bit /bɪt/ *noun* a binary digit, 0 or 1

bit map /'bɪtmæp/, **bitmp** *noun* a file format for storing images in which data in the file represents the value of each pixel

bitmapped font /ˌbɪtmæpt 'fɒnt/ *noun* a screen or printer font with characters formed as a pattern of pixels or dots

bitmapped graphics /ˌbɪtmæpt ˈɡræfɪks/ *plural noun* images whose individual pixels can be controlled by changing the value of the stored bits

BITNET /'bɪtnet/ *noun* a network used to connect mostly academic sites and computers and allows transfer of electronic mail and listserver application

biweekly /baɪˈwiːkli/ *noun* a publication that appears every two weeks

biz *abbreviation* in Internet addresses, the generic top-level domain for businesses

BL *abbreviation* British Library

black box /ˌblæk 'bɒks/ *noun* a device used for converting protocols from one computer system to another, such as for converting data from a micro to a phototypesetter

black list /'blæk lɪst/ *noun* a list of companies, countries or people who are banned from trading or using goods or services ■ *verb* to make a list of untrustworthy people or organisations

black market /ˌblæk 'mɑːkɪt/ *noun* illegal trading

blackout /'blækaʊt/ *noun* the withholding of news or information about a subject, especially by official sources

BLAISE /bleɪz/ *abbreviation* British Library Automated Information Service

BLAISE Records /'bleɪz ˌrekɔːdz/ *plural noun* online machine-readable records from the MARC database for use on automated catalogues

blank /blæŋk/ *noun* an empty space in a form ■ *adjective* empty or with nothing on it ○ *a blank tape* ○ *a blank piece of paper*

blank cheque /ˌblæŋk 'tʃek/ *noun* 1. a bank cheque with the amount of money to be filled in by the recipient 2. the authority to do whatever you consider to be right

blanket agreement /ˌblæŋkɪt ə ˈɡriːmənt/ *noun* agreement which covers many items

blanket order /'blæŋkɪt ˌɔːdə/ *noun* an order with several different items

blast freeze /'blɑːst friːz/ *verb* to reduce the temperature to below freezing using very cold air, sometimes used as a method for conserving wet paper

BLDSC *abbreviation* British Library Document Supply Centre

bleed /bliːd/ *noun* 1. page design where the illustrations run off the edge of the trimmed page ○ *The double-page spreads are all bleeds.* 2. overtrimmed margins when binding, cutting off the edge of the type ■ *verb* to print something, or be printed, so that part of it is cut off by the edge of the page

blind /blaɪnd/ *adjective* done without preparation or the relevant information

blind carbon copy /ˌblaɪnd ˌkɑːbən ˈkɒpi/ *noun* a feature of many electronic mail programs that allows a user to send one message to several users at a time (a carbon copy) but does not display this list to the recipients. Abbr **bcc**

blind reference /ˌblaɪnd ˈref(ə)rəns/ *noun* a reference in a catalogue or index to a heading which has no entry

block capital /ˌblɒk ˈkæpɪt(ə)l/ *noun* an upper case letter, e.g. A, B, C, as opposed to lower case a, b, c

block letter /ˌblɒk ˈletə/ *noun* a compressed sans serif typeface or individual letter

block letter style /ˌblɒk ˈletə ˌstaɪl/ *noun* a style of writing using only capital letters

block markers /ˈblɒk ˌmɑːkəz/ *plural noun* two markers inserted at the start and finish of a section of data to indicate a special block which can then be moved or deleted or copied as a single unit

blog /blɒg/ *noun* ONLINE same as **weblog** ■ *verb* to create or run a weblog

'Employees are no different to customers. They are besieged by information from an increasing number of sources. It places a greater imperative on management to engage with staff first. In a world of blogs and RSS feeds, communications heads increasingly need to make instant decisions based on the speed at which news travels.' [*PR Week*]

blogger /ˈblɒgə/ *noun* a person who creates or runs a weblog

blogosphere /ˈblɒgəˌsfɪə/ *noun* the World Wide Web environment in which bloggers communicate with each other

blogware /ˈblɒgweə/ *noun* computer software tools for creating a weblog

blow up /ˌbləʊ ˈʌp/ *verb* to enlarge a photograph

blowup /ˈbləʊˌʌp/ *noun* a photograph or illustration greatly enlarged for exhibition purposes

BLR&DD *abbreviation* British Library Research & Development Department

blue-pencil /ˌbluː ˈpensɪl/ *verb* to edit a piece of writing by marking it, in order to shorten, censor or delete it

blueprint /ˈbluːprɪnt/ *noun* **1.** a photographic copy of construction plans usually printed in white on blue paper **2.** a detailed plan of something

blurb /blɜːb/ *noun* a short piece of writing that praises and promotes something, especially a paragraph on the cover of a book

blurred /blɜːd/ *adjective* unclear because there is no distinct outline

BMJ *abbreviation* British Medical Journal

.bmp *suffix* a file extension for a bit map file

bn *abbreviation* in Internet addresses, the top-level domain for Brunei

BNB *abbreviation* British National Bibliography

bo *abbreviation* in Internet addresses, the top-level domain for Bolivia

board /bɔːd/ *noun* **1.** thick sturdy material used to form the foundation of book covers, made from pressed fibres and usually covered with cloth or other material **2.** one piece of this material, cut to size **3.** the controlling group of people in a company or organisation also known as the board of directors □ **across the board** decision or action which affects everyone in a particular group

board meeting /ˈbɔːd ˌmiːtɪŋ/ *noun* a meeting of the directors to discuss company business

board room /ˈbɔːd ruːm/ *noun* a room where board meetings are held

Bodleian /ˈbɒdliən/ *noun* the main library of Oxford University, one of England's copyright deposit libraries

body /ˈbɒdi/ *noun* **1.** an official group of people **2.** the main part of the text in a document

boil down /ˌbɔɪl ˈdaʊn/ *verb* to condense or summarise something such as information or text

boilerplate /ˈbɔɪləpleɪt/ *noun* US fixed or formulaic language such as that used in legal forms and documents, e.g. powers of attorney and authors' contracts

bold /bəʊld/ *adjective* having darker, thicker lines than standard type, fonts or lettering ∎ *noun* type, fonts or lettering with darker, thicker lines than is standard, used for emphasis ∎ *verb* to set, print, or display text in bold type

boldface /'bəʊldfeɪs/ *adjective, noun, verb* PRINTING same as **bold**. Abbr **bf**

bold type /'bəʊld taɪp/, **bold face** /'bəʊld feɪs/ *noun* same as **bold**

book /bʊk/ *noun* a collection of pages containing text and sometimes pictures, bound together inside a cover

Book Aid International /,bʊk eɪd ,ɪntə'næʃ(ə)nəl/ *noun* a service which collects unwanted books from individuals and institutions and sends them abroad to help fight illiteracy, and also encourages local publishing

book bay /'bʊk beɪ/ *noun* an area in a library surrounded by bookshelves

bookbinder /'bʊk,baɪndə/ *noun* somebody who binds books, especially as a profession

bookbinding /'bʊk,baɪndɪŋ/ *noun* the art of binding books

book bus /'bʊk bʌs/ *noun* a bus converted to act as a mobile library usually in residential areas

bookcase /'bʊkkeɪs/ *noun* a piece of furniture with shelves for books

book cloth /'bʊk klɒθ/ *noun* a covering material for cased books, especially library editions

book club /'bʊk klʌb/ *noun* a system of buying and selling books by post, usually on specialist subjects

book club edition /'bʊk klʌb ɪ,dɪʃ(ə)n/ *noun* an edition of a book specially printed and bound for a book club for sale to its members

book cover /'bʊk ,kʌvə/ *noun* a paper cover which is put on a book to protect it or to make it attractive. Also called **book jacket**, **book wrapper**

book design /'bʊk dɪ,zaɪn/ *noun* the design of a book, both the typography and the page layout

book designer /'bʊk dɪ,zaɪnə/ *noun* a person who designs books

book distribution /'bʊk ,dɪstrɪbjuːʃ(ə)n/ *noun* a system of delivering books to institutions or people

book donation /'bʊk dəʊ,neɪʃ(ə)n/ *noun* a book given to an organisation as a gift

bookend /'bʊkend/ *noun* one of a pair of supports used to keep a row of books upright

BookExpo America /,bʊkekspəʊ ə'merɪkə/ *noun* a book fair held in Chicago in May/June, formerly called the 'ABA'

book export /'bʊk ,ekspɔːt/ *noun* a book produced in one country and sold in another

book fair /'bʊk feə/ *noun* a trade exhibition with the object of publicising, selling and exchanging books

COMMENT: The major international fairs are held all year round. The most important are the London Book Fair (April); the Bologna Book Fair (April/May); the Paris Salon du Livre (May); the BookExpo America (May/June); the Moscow Book Fair (September); the Frankfurt Book Fair (October). There are many other book fairs in various countries; and many specialised fairs as well. Book fairs have existed as meetings for trade since books were invented: the Frankfurt Book Fair existed even in the later Middle Ages. Originally they were places where merchants could buy and sell manuscripts; they have always had an international element, and even the earliest book fairs were patronised by dealers from various countries in Europe. Book fairs can now be divided into two main categories: (a) rights fairs (like the Frankfurt Book Fair, or the London Book Fair), where publishers sell rights in books to publishers from other countries, and also meet agents and representatives; and (b) selling fairs (such as the Geneva Book Fair) where books can be sold to the visitors from the stands

booking /'bʊkɪŋ/ *noun* an arrangement to reserve something ○ *The bookings were low for the theatre performance.*

book jacket /'bʊk ,dʒækɪt/ *noun* same as **book cover**

bookkeeping /'bʊkkiːpɪŋ/ *noun* the activity of keeping records of the income and expenditure of an organisation or company

book learning /'bʊk ˌlɜːnɪŋ/ *noun* knowledge obtained from books instead of from experience

booklet /'bʊklət/ *noun* a small book with a paper cover, often used for information

book list /'bʊk lɪst/ *noun* a list of books on a specific subject or by a particular author

booklore /'bʊklɔː/ *noun* information about books, especially their authors and the circumstances of their publication

booklouse /'bʊklaʊs/ *noun* a small wingless insect that destroys books by feeding on the paste used in the binding (NOTE: The plural is **booklice**.)

bookmaker /'bʊkmeɪkə/ *noun* a book designer, printer or binder

bookmark /'bʊkmɑːk/ *noun* **1.** a narrow strip of material or paper used to mark the place in a book where the reader has stopped reading temporarily **2.** a code used by a multimedia title or web browser that allows the user to go back to the same point again in the future

book market /'bʊk ˌmɑːkɪt/ *noun* the number of potential buyers for books

bookmobile /'bʊkməˌbiːl/ *noun US* a large motor vehicle equipped as a small lending library, used for taking books to people, especially in rural areas

book paper /'bʊk ˌpeɪpə/ *noun* special paper used for printing books

book plate /'bʊk pleɪt/ *noun* a decorated piece of paper stuck in the front of the book with the name of the owner written or printed on it

book review /'bʊk rɪˌvjuː/ *noun* critical comments on a book, especially when it is first published

bookseller /'bʊkselə/ *noun* a person or company that sells books

bookshelf /'bʊkʃelf/ *noun* a horizontal piece of wood or metal used to store books (NOTE: The plural is **bookshelves**.)

bookshop /'bʊkʃɒp/ *noun* a shop which specialises in selling books

Books in Print /ˌbʊkz ɪn 'prɪnt/ *noun* ♦ **British Books in Print**

bookstall /'bʊkstɔːl/, **bookstand** /'bʊkstænd/ *noun* a table in a market or fair where books are sold

bookstore /'bʊkstɔː/ *noun* **1.** a space in a library devoted to storage of books and documents not frequently used **2.** *US* same as **bookshop**

book token /'bʊk ˌtəʊkən/ *noun* a card bought to give as a gift which can only be used to buy books

book trade /'bʊk treɪd/ *noun* the business of buying and selling books

Book Trust /'bʊk trʌst/ *noun* an independent body, formerly known as the National Book League, which promotes books and reading and also offers an information service

bookwork /'bʊkwɜːk/ *noun* the keeping of financial records

bookworm /'bʊkwɜːm/ *noun* a person who is very fond of reading

'Cardiff is a city of bookworms, compared to its European counterparts. Each resident takes out an average of seven books a year [from the library] – above the European average – but not a patch on Ljubljana in Slovenia, where the figure is 21 books a year.' [*South Wales Echo*]

book wrapper /'bʊk ˌræpə/ *noun* same as **book cover**

Boolean /'buːliən/ *adjective* using a system of symbolic logic that uses combinations of logical operators such as 'AND', 'OR' and 'NOT' to determine relationships between entities. Boolean operations are extensively used in writing computer programs and in computer searches using keywords.

Boolean logic /ˌbuːliən 'lɒdʒɪk/ *noun* rules set down to simplify logical functions in searching

Boolean operator /ˌbuːliən 'ɒpəreɪtə/ *noun* a connecting word or symbol that allows a computer user to include or exclude items in a text search, e.g. 'and', 'or' and 'not'

boost /buːst/ *verb* to increase something ○ *to boost the market for books*

bootleg /'buːtleg/ *adjective* something which is imported or sold illegally

boot up /ˌbuːt 'ʌp/ *verb* to load the operating system or programs automatically into a computer

border /'bɔːdə/ *noun* a strip, line or band around the edge of something

borderline /'bɔːdəlaɪn/ *adjective* only just acceptable ○ *He was a borderline case in the examination, but they allowed him to pass.*

borrow /'bɒrəʊ/ *verb* to take away temporarily with the intention of returning it

borrower card /'bɒrəʊə kɑːd/, **borrower ticket** /'bɒrəʊə ˌtɪkɪt/ *noun* a card issued to a member of a library so that items borrowed can be recorded in his or her name

borrowings /'bɒrəʊɪŋz/ *plural noun* books borrowed from a library

borrowing system /'bɒrəʊɪŋ ˌsɪstəm/ *noun* a system for organising items which are taken away temporarily and need to be returned

bot /bɒt/ *noun* a computer program performing routine or time-consuming tasks such as searching websites automatically or semi-independently

bottom line /ˌbɒtəm 'laɪn/ *noun* the most important consideration in a discussion

bottom price /'bɒtəm praɪs/ *noun* the lowest possible price

bounce /baʊns/ *noun* electronic mail that is returned to the sender because the address is incorrect or the user is not known at the mail server ■ *verb* (*of an e-mail message*) to fail to be delivered ○ *If you send e-mail to an incorrect address it bounces back to your mailbox.*

bound /baʊnd/ *adjective* used to describe a book or other written document that has a permanent, usually hard, cover

bound journal /ˌbaʊnd 'dʒɜːnəl/ *noun* a set of regular journal issues collected in date order and put inside a stiff cover

bounds /baʊndz/ *plural noun* the limits of what can be done

bowdlerise /'baʊdləraɪz/, **bowdlerize** *verb* to change a text by omitting anything which may be thought to be offensive, so called after Thomas Bowdler who in 1818 'cleaned up' an edition of Shakespeare's plays

box /bɒks/ *verb* to pack into boxes for transport or sale

box number /'bɒks ˌnʌmbə/ *noun* a number used as an address, often in reply to an advertisement in a newspaper or magazine

BPM *abbreviation* business process management

br *abbreviation* in Internet addresses, the top-level domain for Brazil

brace /breɪs/ *noun* either of a pair of symbols, { }, used singly in printing or writing to group items together in a table or list or as a pair in mathematical formulae. Also called **curly bracket**

bracket /'brækɪt/ *noun* **1.** a punctuation mark put on either side of a word or phrase to show that it contains additional information ○ *(These words are inside brackets.)* **2.** a piece of metal or wood fastened to a wall to support something

bracket together /ˌbrækɪt tə'geðə/ *verb* **1.** to put two or more things together because they are thought to be similar **2.** to print brackets round several items to show that they are treated in the same way and separated from the rest of the text

Braille /breɪl/ *noun* a system of printing that enables blind people to read by feeling with their fingers letters which are printed as groups of raised dots

Brailler /'breɪlə/ *noun* a machine similar to a typewriter that prints Braille

brainstorm /'breɪnstɔːm/ *verb* to gather together the random thoughts on a given subject of all the people at a meeting or seminar

branch /brɑːntʃ/ *noun* a local subsection of a business or organisation

branching classification /'brɑːntʃɪŋ ˌklæsɪfɪkeɪʃ(ə)n/ *noun* a system of classification with two or more main divisions which can be further subdivided as often as necessary

branch library /ˈbrɑːntʃ ˌlaɪbrəri/ *noun* a library which serves a specific area and is accountable to a main library

branch manager /ˌbrɑːntʃ ˈmænɪdʒə/ *noun* a person who runs a local branch

brand name /ˈbrænd neɪm/ *noun* a version of a product recognised by a name or design

breach /briːtʃ/ *verb* to break an agreement or contract

breach of contract /ˌbriːtʃ əv ˈkɒntrækt/ *noun* failure to carry out the terms of an agreement

break down /ˌbreɪk ˈdaʊn/ *verb* to separate something into smaller parts so that it is easier to deal with

breakdown /ˈbreɪkdaʊn/ *noun* a summary, explanation or analysis of data items collected

break even /ˌbreɪk ˈiːv(ə)n/ *verb* to make enough money to cover one's expenses but making neither a profit nor a loss

break into /ˌbreɪk ˈɪntʊ/ *verb* to use a computer system without permission

bridge /brɪdʒ/ *verb* to overcome differences between people □ **to bridge an information gap** to provide relevant information

brief /briːf/ *noun* a set of instructions needed to perform a task, often used for legal instructions

briefing /ˈbriːfɪŋ/ *noun* a meeting at which people are given instructions and information

British Association of Picture Libraries and Agencies *noun* a support group providing information guidelines and standards for special picture libraries. Abbr **BAPLA**

British Books in Print /ˌbrɪtɪʃ bʊks ɪn ˈprɪnt/ *noun* a publication containing bibliographical details of all published books in the UK. Abbr **BBIP**

British Broadcasting Corporation /ˌbrɪtɪʃ ˈbrɔːdkɑːstɪŋ ˌkɔːpəreɪʃ(ə)n/ *noun* the controlling body for most radio and some television in Britain. Abbr **BBC**

British Council /ˌbrɪtɪʃ ˈkaʊns(ə)l/ *noun* a government-funded body to promote the United Kingdom abroad by means of information offices, cultural relations, educational aid schemes and agencies for low-priced book schemes

British Education Index /ˌbrɪtɪʃ ˌedjʊˈkeɪʃ(ə)n ˌɪndeks/ *noun* an index to articles about education from over 250 periodicals with online access through DIALOG. Abbr **BEI**

British Humanities Index /ˌbrɪtɪʃ hjuːˈmænɪtɪz ˌɪndeks/ *noun* a quarterly index to articles in periodicals about the humanities published by the Library Association. Abbr **BHI**

British Library /ˌbrɪtɪʃ ˈlaɪbrəri/ *noun* the national library of the UK which contains a copy of every publication in Britain through the copyright deposit system. Abbr **BL**

British Library Automated Information Service /ˌbrɪtɪʃ ˌlaɪbrəri ˌɔːtəmeɪtɪd ˌɪnfəˈmeɪʃ(ə)n ˌsɜːvɪs/ *noun* an online information retrieval system provided by the British Library, now divided into BLAISE-LINE standard bibliographic database and BLAISE-LINK online database host. Abbr **BLAISE**

British Library Document Supply Centre /ˌbrɪtɪʃ ˌlaɪbrəri ˌdɒkjʊmənt səˈplaɪ ˌsentə/ *noun* a closed collection kept for use by interlibrary loan. Abbr **BLDSC**

British Library Research & Development Department /ˌbrɪtɪʃ ˌlaɪbrəri rɪˌsɜːtʃ ən dɪ ˈveləpmənt dɪˌpɑːtmənt/ *noun* part of the British Library devoted to research into all aspects of library and information work. Abbr **BLR&DD**

British National Bibliography /ˌbrɪtɪʃ ˌnæʃ(ə)nəl ˌbɪbliˈɒɡrəfi/ *noun* an organisation which issues a weekly list in printed form and on CD-ROM of all the books published in Great Britain and produces monthly and annual cumulative indexes. Abbr **BNB**

British Society of Indexers /ˌbrɪtɪʃ səˌsaɪəti əv ˈɪndeksəz/ *noun* a support association for professional indexers. Abbr **BSI**

British Standards Institution /ˌbrɪtɪʃ ˈstændədz ˌɪnstɪtjuːʃ(ə)n/ *noun* the approved British body for the preparation and publication of national standards for the production of goods and services. Abbr **BSI**

British Talking Book Service for the Blind *noun* an organisation which arranges for written materials to be recorded on to audio tape so that blind people can listen to them

broad /brɔːd/ *adjective* comprehensive in content, knowledge, experience, ability or application

broadband /'brɔːdbænd/ *noun* a connection to the Internet that allows it to remain connected while still using phone and fax facilities on the same line, since many signals can be transmitted simultaneously ■ *adjective* able to transfer large amounts of data at high speed

broadcast /'brɔːdkɑːst/ *noun* a programme made for transmission on radio or television ■ *verb* **1.** to send out words, music or signals by radio waves **2.** to make widely known

broadsheet /'brɔːdʃiːt/ *noun* anything printed on large sheets of paper, but especially one of the more serious newspapers

broad term /'brɔːd tɜːm/ *noun* an indexing term heading a string of narrower terms

brochure /'brəʊʃə/ *noun* a magazine or booklet with pictures giving information about a product or service

broken order /ˌbrəʊkən 'ɔːdə/ *noun* a system which is not in the expected or normal order, used deliberately in unusual circumstances to facilitate use

broker /'brəʊkə/ *noun* a person who does the business of buying and selling for somebody else

brokerage /'brəʊkərɪdʒ/ *noun* the business of buying and selling goods and services for other people

Brown issuing system /'braʊn ˌɪʃuɪŋ ˌsɪstəm/ *noun* a system of recording loans from a library which uses individual book cards, which are kept in members' small cardboard tickets until the book is returned

browse /braʊz/ *verb* **1.** to look through a book, magazine, database or shop in a casual way without definite intentions **2.** to view data in a database or online system

browser /'braʊzə/ *noun* a software program that is used to navigate through WWW pages stored on the Internet. ◊ **web browser**

browsing /'braʊzɪŋ/ *noun* the act of a user moving through text or a multimedia application in no particular order

BRS *noun* an online database host

brush up /ˌbrʌʃ 'ʌp/ *verb* to refresh or renew knowledge of or skill in something

bs *abbreviation* in Internet addresses, the top-level domain for Bahamas

BSI *abbreviation* **1.** British Society of Indexers **2.** British Standards Institution

bt *abbreviation* in Internet addresses, the top-level domain for Bhutan

BTEC /'biːtek/ *noun* a work-related technical qualification, usually at school-leaving level

BUBL /'bʌb(ə)l/ *noun* an electronic discussion list subscribed to by librarians worldwide. Full form **Bulletin Boards for Libraries**

'BUBL is an excellent resource in that it combines classification of resources in a familiar way with hyperlink availability…In our search example, Scientology information is found under "Other Religions" and we have a good online reference to likely impartial information.' [*Law Now*]

Buchmesse /'bʊxmesə/ *noun* a German book fair, such as the Frankfurt Book Fair

buckram /'bʌkrəm/ *noun* a coarse cotton or linen fabric that has been stiffened with starch, gum or latex, used in bookbinding

budget /'bʌdʒɪt/ *noun* a financial plan showing how much money is available and how it is proposed to spend it ■ *verb* to allow pre-determined amounts of money for specific purposes

buffer /'bʌfə/ *noun* a temporary storage area for data being transmitted between two devices that function at different speeds. A buffer enables a faster device such as a computer to complete sending the data and begin another task without waiting for a slower device such as a printer.

bug /bʌg/ *noun* **1.** a problem or mistake in a computer program **2.** a tracking or surveillance device

built-in /ˌbɪlt ˈɪn/ *adjective* included as part of the original structure or plan

built-in obsolescence /ˈbɪlt ɪn ɒbsəˌles(ə)ns/ *noun* deliberate features of the design which will cause a piece of equipment to become out of date and need to be replaced

bulk /bʌlk/ *noun* a large quantity □ **the bulk of something** most of it □ **to buy in bulk** to buy large quantities

bulk purchase /ˌbʌlk ˈpɜːtʃɪs/ *noun* the act of buying a large quantity of something to obtain a cheaper price

bulk storage /ˌbʌlk ˈstɔːrɪdʒ/ *noun* the act of storing large amounts of information on a database

bullet /ˈbʊlɪt/ *noun* a large printed dot used to highlight items in a printed list

bulletin /ˈbʊlɪtɪn/ *noun* a short report on the latest situation

bulletin board /ˈbʊlɪtɪn bɔːd/ *noun* an electronic discussion network and information database

bullet point /ˈbʊlɪt pɔɪnt/ *noun* PRINTING same as **bullet**

bumf /bʌmf/ *noun* unwanted or uninteresting printed material, especially official forms and documents

bundled service /ˌbʌnd(ə)ld ˈsɜːvɪs/ *noun* a collection of several different services sold as a package

bureau /ˈbjʊərəʊ/ *noun* an office organisation or government department that collects and distributes information

burn /bɜːn/ *verb* to copy data on to a CD-ROM or DVD-ROM. It can then be used to transport the content or to create multiple copies.

burnishing /ˈbɜːnɪʃɪŋ/ *noun* the process of polishing the gold or silver leaf on edges of books to give it a brighter appearance

burst /bɜːst/ *noun* an amount of data sent or received in one operation

bus /bʌs/ *noun* **1.** a communication link consisting of a set of leads or wires which connects different parts of a computer hardware system, and over which data is transmitted and received by various circuits in the system **2.** a central source of information which supplies several devices

business /ˈbɪznɪs/ *noun* an organisation that produces and sells goods or provides a service

business card /ˈbɪznɪs kɑːd/ *noun* a small card giving the name and business details of a person

business computer /ˈbɪznɪs kəmˌpjuːtə/ *noun* a powerful small computer which is programmed for special business uses

Business Information Service /ˌbɪznɪs ˌɪnfəˈmeɪʃ(ə)n ˌsɜːvɪs/ *noun* a service to promote awareness of the British Libraries' holdings on business information, based at the Science Reference and Information Service. Abbr **BIS**

business letter /ˈbɪznɪs ˌletə/ *noun* a letter which is sent from one company to another about business matters

businesslike /ˈbɪznɪslaɪk/ *adjective* working in an efficient and timesaving way

business plan /ˈbɪznɪs plæn/ *noun* a proposal for a new business, presented to a bank or other institution when asking for a loan

business process management /ˈbɪznɪs ˌprəʊses ˌmænɪdʒmənt/ *noun* the theory of how to best organise processes in business for maximum efficiency. Abbr **BPM**

business relationship /ˈbɪznɪs rɪˌleɪʃ(ə)nʃɪp/ *noun* the way people in business work together

business school /ˈbɪznɪs skuːl/ *noun* a college where people are taught how to manage a business or other organisation

business system /ˈbɪznɪs ˌsɪstəm/ *noun* a way of organising business following a fixed set of rules

BUSLIB /ˈbɪzlɪb/ *noun* an electronic bulletin board for business libraries

button /ˈbʌt(ə)n/ *noun* a picture on a computer screen which can be used with a mouse to perform specific functions

buy into /ˌbaɪ ˈɪntʊ/ *verb* to buy part of a business or organisation in order to gain some control

buy out /ˌbaɪ 'aʊt/ *verb* to buy somebody's share of a business that you previously owned together

buzzer /'bʌzə/ *noun* an electronic device making a loud hum, often used as an alarm

by *abbreviation* in Internet addresses, the top-level domain for Belarus

byline /'baɪlaɪn/ *noun* a line giving the name of the author of a newspaper or magazine article

by-product /'baɪ ˌprɒdʌkt/ *noun* **1.** something that is an unexpected or unplanned outcome of a situation **2.** something that is produced during the manufacture of something else

byte /baɪt/ *noun* a measurement used to express data or memory capacity of a computer

bz *abbreviation* in Internet addresses, the top-level domain for Belize

C

© *symbol* a symbol denoting copyright, placed by law before the name of the owner of the copyright and the year of first publication

COMMENT: The symbol adopted by the Universal Copyright Convention in Geneva in 1952. Publications bearing the symbol are automatically covered by the convention. The copyright line in a book should give the © followed by the name of the copyright holder and the date.

c *abbreviation* **1.** PUBL chapter **2.** HIST circa

ca *abbreviation* in Internet addresses, the top-level domain for Canada

ca. *abbreviation* circa

cabinet /'kæbɪnət/ *noun* a piece of furniture with doors and drawers used for storing things. ◊ **filing cabinet**

cable /'keɪb(ə)l/ *noun* a flexible wire link for electrical equipment

cable television /ˌkeɪb(ə)l ˌtelɪ'vɪʒ(ə)n/, **cable TV** /ˌkeɪb(ə)l ˌtiː'viː/ *noun* a system whereby signals are relayed to viewers' homes by fibre optic cables often underground

cache /kæʃ/ *noun* an area of high-speed computer memory used for temporary storage of frequently used data ■ *verb* to store data in a cache

cache memory /'kæʃ ˌmem(ə)ri/ *noun* a section of high-speed memory which stores data that the computer can access quickly

CAD /kæd/ *abbreviation* computer-aided design

CAL *abbreviation* computer-aided learning

calculated /'kælkjʊleɪtɪd/ *adjective* planned to have a particular effect

calculator /'kælkjʊleɪtə/ *noun* an electronic device for working out the answers to numerical problems

calendar /'kælɪndə/ *noun* a printed table or chart which shows the days, weeks and months of the year

calendar month /'kælɪndə mʌnθ/ *noun* a period of time, usually 30 or 31 days, measured according to an established western calendar rather than natural changes of the moon

calendar year /ˌkælɪndə 'jɪə/ *noun* a period of time, usually 12 months, measured according to an established western calendar rather than natural changes of the moon

calfskin /'kɑːfskɪn/, **calf** /kɑːf/ *noun* a soft type of leather used in bookbinding

calligraphy /kə'lɪgrəfi/ *noun* the artistic use of handwriting

call mark /'kɔːl mɑːk/ *noun* LIBRARIES same as **shelf mark**

call number /'kɔːl ˌnʌmbə/ *noun* a number used to identify and locate a book. ◊ **spine number**

call slip /'kɔːl slɪp/ *noun* a form for requesting a library book that is not kept on the shelves used by the public

call up /ˌkɔːl 'ʌp/ *verb* to instruct a computer to find and display a particular piece of information

camcorder /'kæmkɔːdə/ *noun* a small video recorder which can be held in the hand

camera-ready /'kæm(ə)rə ˌredi/ *adjective* relating to material in its final publishable format, ready to be photographed or electronically scanned for the purpose of preparing printing plates

camera-ready copy /ˌkæm(ə)rə ˌredi 'kɒpi/, **camera-ready paste-up** /ˌkæm(ə)rə ˌredi 'peɪst ˌʌp/ *noun* a typescript which is ready to be photographed as part of book production. Abbr **CRC, CRPU**

campus /'kæmpəs/ *noun* an area of land containing the main buildings of a college or university

cancel /'kæns(ə)l/ *verb* to cause something such as a cheque or reservation to be no longer valid

cancelbot /'kæns(ə)lbɒt/ *noun* a computer program that cancels unwanted articles sent to an Internet newsgroup by a particular user

cancellation /ˌkænsə'leɪʃ(ə)n/ *noun* an instruction to say that something is no longer needed

cancel out /ˌkæns(ə)l 'aʊt/ *verb* to combine two things having opposite effects so as to produce no effect

candidate /'kændɪdeɪt/ *noun* **1.** a person who is being considered for a job, or who is standing for election **2.** someone who is taking an examination **3.** a person or company that is considered suitable for a particular purpose ○ *Small libraries are likely candidates for closure.*

capability /ˌkeɪpə'bɪlɪti/ *noun* ability to do something ○ *the capability to understand computers*

capable /'keɪpəb(ə)l/ *adjective* able to do things well

capacity /kə'pæsɪti/ *noun* **1.** the amount that something can hold **2.** (*in industry*) the amount that can be produced or work that can be done

capacity planning /kə'pæsɪti ˌplænɪŋ/ *noun* planning work so that the best use is made of the abilities and equipment available

capital /'kæpɪt(ə)l/ *noun* money that is used to set up a business or invested to make more money

capital expenditure /ˌkæpɪt(ə)l ɪk 'spendɪtʃə/ *noun* money spent on equipment or buildings

capital letter /ˌkæpɪt(ə)l 'letə/ *noun* the upper case form of a letter used at the beginning of sentences and names,

e.g. A, B, C as opposed to a, b, c. Abbr **cap**

caption /'kæpʃən/ *noun* a note or heading to a picture or illustration

capture /'kæptʃə/ *verb* to obtain control over something ○ *to capture the market*

carbon copy /ˌkɑːbən 'kɒpi/ *noun* full form of **cc**

card /kɑːd/ *noun* a piece of thick, stiff paper

card catalogue /'kɑːd ˌkætəlɒg/ *noun* a list of contents written on index cards and arranged according to a system which aids retrieval

card file /'kɑːd faɪl/ *noun* COMM, LIBRARIES same as **card index**

card index /'kɑːd ˌɪndeks/ *noun* a series of cards, usually standard size 12.5 x 7.5 cm, used to record holdings and kept in specially designed drawers or boxes

card-index /'kɑːd ˌɪndeks/ *verb* to put information onto a card index

card-index file /'kɑːd ˌɪndeks faɪl/ *noun* information kept on filing cards

career ladder /kə'rɪə ˌlædə/ *noun* the steps by which a person gains promotion in their chosen career

'The need for role models is paramount in a male-dominated industry and, with so few women on the upper rungs of the IT career ladder, a significant change is needed in the way companies recruit and promote their senior IT staff to make a real difference.' [*Evening Standard*]

career stage /kə'rɪə steɪdʒ/ *noun* the level of progress made in promotion

caret mark /'kærət mɑːk/, **caret sign** /'kærət saɪn/ *noun* a proofreading symbol to indicate that something should be inserted into the text

Carnegie library /kɑːˌniːgi 'laɪbrəri/ *noun* a public library system that was developed nationally from money donated by Andrew Carnegie (1835–1919), a Scottish-born American who gave money to public education and libraries

carrel /'kærel/, **carrell** *noun* an enclosed area for private study within a larger space like a classroom or a library

carriage return/line feed /ˌkærɪdʒ rɪˌtɜːn ˈlaɪn ˌfiːd/ *noun* a key that moves the cursor or print head to the beginning of the next line and moves the paper or text up by one line. Abbr **CR/LF**

carry /ˈkæri/ *verb* **1.** to transport something from one place to another **2.** to contain or broadcast ○ *The newspaper carried a full report on the event.*

carry on /ˌkæri ˈɒn/ *verb* to continue to do something

carry out /ˌkæri ˈaʊt/ *verb* to perform a task

carry over /ˌkæri ˈəʊvə/ *verb* (*in accounts*) to take a total from the bottom of one page to the top of the next

carry through /ˌkæri ˈθruː/ *verb* to continue an action until it is finished

cartel /kɑːˈtel/ *noun* a group of similar companies which agree to control prices to prevent competition

cartographer /kɑːˈtɒgrəfə/ *noun* a person who draws maps

cartographic /ˌkɑːtəˈgræfɪk/ *adjective* relating to maps ○ *The library had a large cartographic collection.*

cartography /kɑːˈtɒgrəfi/ *noun* the art of drawing maps

cartoon /kɑːˈtuːn/ *noun* **1.** the first draft of a drawing done on paper which can be transferred to larger paintings **2.** a comic or satirical drawing **3.** an animated film made by photographing a series of drawings

cartridge /ˈkɑːtrɪdʒ/ *noun* a removable device made of a closed box containing a disk, tape, program or data

cartridge paper /ˈkɑːtrɪdʒ ˌpeɪpə/ *noun* strong, thick, usually white paper used for drawing

COMMENT: Cartridge paper is so called because it was originally used for making cartridges for bullets. It is made from chemical pulp, sized, and is very white.

case /keɪs/ *noun* a stiff cardboard cover glued onto a book formed of two pieces of cardboard and the spine ○ *The library edition has a case and jacket.* ■ *verb* to bind a book in a stiff cardboard cover

case binding /ˈkeɪs ˌbaɪndɪŋ/ *noun* **1.** a stiff cardboard cover ○ *The trade edition has a case binding.* **2.** the action of binding a book in a hard cardboard cover

casebound /ˈkeɪsbaʊnd/, **cased** /keɪst/ *adjective* enclosed in a hard cover ○ *The book was available in both casebound and paperback versions.*

cased book /ˌkeɪst ˈbʊk/ *noun* a book which is bound in a hard cover

casein glue /ˈkeɪsiɪn gluː/ *noun* a glue used in bookbinding and in making coated papers, which is almost acid-free

cash book /ˈkæʃ bʊk/ *noun* a book in which a record is kept of income and expenditure

cash flow /ˈkæʃ fləʊ/ *noun* movement of money in and out of a business

cash in /ˌkæʃ ˈɪn/ *verb* to exchange something for what it is worth in cash

cash in on /ˌkæʃ ˈɪn ˌɒn/ *verb* to use a situation to gain advantage for oneself

cash on delivery /ˌkæʃ ɒn dɪ ˈlɪv(ə)ri/ *noun* a phrase meaning that goods must be paid for as soon as they are received. Abbr **C.O.D.**

cash register /ˈkæʃ ˌredʒɪstə/ *noun* a machine which is used to record sales and to add up the amount of money to be paid

cash value /ˈkæʃ ˌvæljuː/ *noun* the amount of money which anyone will pay for something

cassette /kəˈset/ *noun* a small rectangular plastic container for magnetic tape which can be used for recording and playing back speech or music

casual work /ˈkæʒuəl wɜːk/ *noun* jobs done by people employed for a short time

catalogue /ˈkæt(ə)lɒg/ *noun* **1.** a list of priced and illustrated items for sale, presented in book form or in other formats including CD-ROM or video **2.** a list of the holdings in a library, usually arranged according to subject, title or author ■ *verb* **1.** to classify and list items to form a catalogue **2.** to enter something in a catalogue

catalogue card /ˈkætəlɒg kɑːd/ *noun* a small card used for writing catalogue entries and stored in boxes or drawers in a manual catalogue

cataloguer /ˈkætəlɒgə/ *noun* a person who catalogues books in a library

Cataloguing in Publication /ˌkætəlɒgɪŋ ɪn ˌpʌblɪˈkeɪʃ(ə)n/ *noun* a system whereby new books are catalogued before publication by the British Library or by the Library of Congress based on details about each book supplied by the publisher. Abbr **CIP**

catch letter /ˈkætʃ ˌletə/ *noun* a group of letters, usually three, which appears at the top of the page in reference books such as dictionaries or directories, to indicate the first or last word on that page or column

catchword /ˈkætʃwɜːd/ *noun* **1.** a word printed at the top of a page in a dictionary or other reference book, usually the first or last entry for that page **2.** the first word of a page of printed text repeated at the bottom right-hand corner of the previous page, originally placed there to draw the binder's attention to it

catchword index /ˈkætʃwɜːd ˌɪndeks/ *noun* a system which uses a keyword from a title or text to index an item

categorise /ˈkætɪgəraɪz/, **categorize** *verb* to put into a category

category /ˈkætɪg(ə)ri/ *noun* a division or class in a system used to group items according to their type

cater for /ˈkeɪtə fɔː/ *verb* to provide what people need

cathode ray tube /ˌkæθəʊd ˈreɪ ˌtjuːb/ *noun* an output device used in a VDU or phototypesetter for displaying text or figures or graphics. Abbr **CRT**

COMMENT: A CRT consists of a vacuum tube, one end of which is flat and coated with phosphor; the other end contains an electron beam source. Characters becomes visible when the electron beam makes the phosphor coating glow.

CBT *abbreviation* **1.** computer-based training **2.** computer-based tutorial

cc¹ *noun* **1.** used at the ends of letters, memos and reports to indicate that an identical copy has been sent to the named people **2.** a feature of electronic mail software that allows you to send a copy of a message to another user. ◇

blind carbon copy ▶ full form **carbon copy**

cc² /ˌsiː ˈsiː/ *abbreviation* in Internet addresses, the top-level domain for Cocos Islands

CCTV *abbreviation* closed circuit television

cd *abbreviation* in Internet addresses, the top-level domain for Democratic Republic of the Congo

CD *abbreviation* compact disc

CD burner /ˌsiː ˈdiː ˌbɜːnə/ *noun* COMPUT same as **CD writer**

CD-I /ˌsiː ˈdiː aɪ/ *noun* a compact disc with electronic information that can be changed by the user. Full form **compact disc interactive**

CD-ROM /ˌsiː diː ˈrɒm/ *noun* an electronic method of storing large quantities of information which can be read by laser. Full form **compact disc – read only memory**

CD-ROM drive /ˌsiː diː ˈrɒm ˌdraɪv/ *noun* a disk drive that allows a computer to read data stored on a CD-ROM, in which the player spins the disc and uses a laser beam to read etched patterns on the surface of the CD-ROM that represent data bits

CD-ROM player /ˌsiː diː ˈrɒm ˌpleɪə/ *noun* a disc drive that allows a computer to read data stored on a CD-ROM

CD-RW /ˌsiː diː ɑː ˈdʌb(ə)ljuː/ *noun* a compact disc that can have its contents erased and something else recorded onto it many times. Full form **compact disc rewritable**

CD-WO /ˌsiː ˌdʌb(ə)l juː ˈəʊ/ *noun* CD-ROM disc and drive technology that allows a user to write data to the disc once only and is useful for storing archived documents or for testing a CD-ROM before it is duplicated. Full form **compact disc write once**

CD writer /ˌsiː ˈdiː ˌraɪtə/ *noun* a piece of equipment used to record data permanently onto a compact disc

cease /siːs/ *verb* to finish or stop doing something

ceased publication /ˌsiːst ˌpʌblɪ ˈkeɪʃ(ə)n/ *adjective* no longer published, often used to describe serials

cedilla /sə'dɪlə/ *noun* a small mark (ˌ) used in some languages under a letter to change its pronunciation, e.g. under the letter c in French to soften it

CEEFAX /'siːfæks/ *noun* a videotext system used by the BBC for broadcasting textual information

cell /sel/ *noun* a space for information in a table such as a computer spreadsheet, formed where a row and a column intersect

censor /'sensə/ *noun* a person who decides what may be published, shown or distributed to the general public ■ *verb* to edit published material or films with regard to what is considered decent for selling, showing or distributing to the general public

censorship /'sensəʃɪp/ *noun* prohibition of the production, distribution or sale of items considered to be objectionable on political, religious or moral grounds

census /'sensəs/ *noun* an official survey to count and analyse the population of a country

centimetre /'sentɪmiːtə/ *noun* one hundredth part of a metre. Abbr **cm** (NOTE: The US spelling is **centimeter**.)

centralised /'sentrəlaɪzd/, **centralized** *adjective* placed in the middle, often as the most important or controlling feature

centralised copying /ˌsentrəlaɪzd 'kɒpiɪŋ/ *noun* a service for all users located in a central position

centralised purchasing /ˌsentrəlaɪzd 'pɜːtʃɪsɪŋ/ *noun* the method of buying everything needed for an organisation through a central purchasing office

centralised records storage /ˌsentrəlaɪzd 'rekɔːdz ˌstɔːrɪdʒ/ *noun* a system used by organisations by which records are stored in a central unit but can be accessed by all members of the organisation

central processing unit /ˌsentrəl 'prəʊsesɪŋ ˌjuːnɪt/ *noun* the circuits which form the main part of a computer. Abbr **CPU**

Central Statistical Office /ˌsentrəl stə'tɪstɪk(ə)l ˌɒfɪs/ *noun* a government department which produces national statistical publications in the UK. Abbr **CSO**

ceremony /'serɪməni/ *noun* the established order of formal ritual used to mark special occasions

certificate /sə'tɪfɪkeɪt/ *noun* an official document given to confirm facts ○ *birth certificate* ○ *health certificate* ○ *degree certificate*

cf *abbreviation* in Internet addresses, the top-level domain for Central African Republic

C format paperback /ˌsiː ˌfɔːmæt 'peɪpəbæk/ *noun* a paperback with the format 234 x 156mm

cg *abbreviation* in Internet addresses, the top-level domain for Congo

CGI *abbreviation* COMPUT common gateway interface

ch *abbreviation* in Internet addresses, the top-level domain for Switzerland

chained library /'tʃeɪnd ˌlaɪbrəri/ *noun* in former times, a library in which books were chained to desks or shelves to prevent them being stolen (NOTE:.)

chain indexing /'tʃeɪn ˌɪndeksɪŋ/ *noun* an alphabetical system of indexing using subject headings and hierarchical sub-headings

chain list /'tʃeɪn lɪst/ *noun* a list of data with each piece of information providing an address for the next consecutive item in the list

change agent /'tʃeɪndʒ ˌeɪdʒənt/ *noun* a catalyst which causes something to change

channel /'tʃæn(ə)l/ *noun* **1.** the spoken, written or electronic means by which something is passed on **2.** a major interest area on the Internet that is easily accessible. ◊ **information channel 3.** (*in graphics*) one layer of an image that can be worked on separately or which can be used to create special effects

chanop /'tʃænɒp/ *noun* a channel operator, the person who controls the messages within a channel on the Internet

chapbook /'tʃæpbʊk/ *noun* a small booklet of poems, ballads or stories, originally sold by travelling pedlars

chapel /'tʃæp(ə)l/ *noun* **1.** a branch of a trade union in printing and journalism **2.** a meeting of a printers' or journalists' chapel

chapter /'tʃæptə/ *noun* one of the divisions of a book or document

character /'kærɪktə/ *noun* a single letter, number or symbol that can be displayed on a computer screen or printer and represents one byte of data

character byte /'kærɪktə baɪt/ *noun* a byte of data containing the character code and any error check bits

characteristic /ˌkærɪktə'rɪstɪk/ *noun* a typical feature of a person, place or thing

charge /tʃɑːdʒ/ *verb* to ask people to pay for goods or services ○ *He charges £10 an hour.*

charge out /ˌtʃɑːdʒ 'aʊt/ *verb* to make a record of a loan

charging system /'tʃɑːdʒɪŋ ˌsɪstəm/ *noun* any method of recording loans from a library

chart /tʃɑːt/ *noun* a visual representation of information

charter /'tʃɑːtə/ *noun* an official document giving rights to a person, organisation or community

Chartered Institute of Library and Information Professionals *noun* the leading professional body for librarians and information managers in the UK. Abbr **CILIP**

chartered librarian /ˌtʃɑːtəd laɪ'breəriən/ *noun* a librarian who has successfully undertaken training and completed specific tasks, including a professional development report, according to the criteria set by the Library Association

CHC *abbreviation* cyclohexylamine carbonate

CHC paper /ˌsiː eitʃ 'siː ˌpeɪpə/ *noun* paper impregnated with CHC, used to de-acidify the pages of old books

check /tʃek/ *noun* an inspection of something to make sure it is correct ▪ *verb* to look at something closely to make sure there are no mistakes

check digit /'tʃek ˌdɪdʒɪt/ *noun* a number added to a numeric code to enable a computer program to detect any errors in the code

check in /ˌtʃek 'ɪn/ *verb* to record the receipt of something

check into /ˌtʃek 'ɪntʊ/ *verb* to investigate something in order to get more information about it or to establish its truth or accuracy

checklist /'tʃeklɪst/ *noun* **1.** a list which acts as a reminder of things to be done or accounted for **2.** a list used to identify items from a minimum amount of information

check out /ˌtʃek 'aʊt/ *verb* to record the loan of something

chemically pure paper /ˌkemɪkli ˌpjʊə 'peɪpə/ *noun* paper which is acid-free, used to repair or protect old books or maps

cheque /tʃek/ *noun* a method of paying money from a bank account, by filling in a standard form and without using coins or notes (NOTE: The US spelling is **check**.)

chief /tʃiːf/ *adjective* denoting the most important person or part of something ○ *chief librarian*

chief information officer /ˌtʃiːf ˌɪnfə'meɪʃ(ə)n ˌɒfɪsə/ *noun* somebody who has responsibility for the organisation and control of information flow in a company or organisation. Abbr **CIO**

chief knowledge officer /ˌtʃiːf 'nɒlɪdʒ ˌɒfɪsə/ *noun* a senior official whose job it is to maximise a company's efficiency by providing appropriate information about things such as processes, customer relations and the marketplace. Abbr **CKO**

children's annual /'tʃɪldrənz ˌænjuəl/ *noun* a book published each year usually at Christmas, with stories, games and articles, intended for children and often based on a popular TV series or cartoon character

children's book group /ˌtʃɪldrənz 'bʊk ˌgruːp/ *noun* an unofficial group of people whose aim is to encourage the promotion of books to children

children's librarian /'tʃɪldrənz laɪ ˌbreəriən/ *noun* a librarian who specialises in the provision of library services to children

children's library /'tʃɪldrənz ˌlaɪbrəri/ *noun* a library which specialises in providing books usually written specially for children

chip /tʃɪp/ *noun* a small piece of plastic containing a set of electronic instructions to work computers and other machines

Christmas gift book /ˌkrɪsməs 'ɡɪft ˌbʊk/ *noun* a special book which is given as a present at Christmas

chronological order /ˌkrɒnəlɒdʒɪk(ə)l 'ɔːdə/ *noun* the arrangement of things such as records, files or invoices in order of their dates

'…during a state audit his company's seven party planners spent days combing through customer records when they could have been out selling. One suggestion: Make extra copies of invoices and file them in chronological order. 'The lesson is to be so anally prepared you can say immediately, "I've got it",' Mr. Kelly says.' [*Crain's Chicago Business*]

chronological sequence /ˌkrɒnəlɒdʒɪk(ə)l 'siːkwəns/ *noun* arrangement by the order of the time at which events happened

ci *abbreviation* in Internet addresses, the top-level domain for Côte d'Ivoire

CILIP /'sɪlɪp/ *abbreviation* Chartered Institute of Library and Information Professionals

CIO *abbreviation* chief information officer

CIP *abbreviation* Cataloguing in Publication

cipher /'saɪfə/ *noun* a system of writing secrets in code

cir. *abbreviation* PUBL circulation

circa /'sɜːkə/ *preposition* about or approximately, used to show uncertainty especially about numbers or dates ○ *The book was written circa 1760.* Abbr **ca.**

circular /'sɜːkjʊlə/ *noun* a letter or advertisement sent to a large number of people at the same time

circular letter /ˌsɜːkjʊlə 'letə/ *noun* a letter sent to a large number of people conveying the same information

circulate /'sɜːkjʊleɪt/ *verb* to send information to a group of people ○ *They circulated a new list of prices to all their customers.*

circulating library /'sɜːkjʊleɪtɪŋ ˌlaɪbrəri/ *noun* a library run on a commercial basis, where the members pay to borrow books

circulation /ˌsɜːkjʊ'leɪʃ(ə)n/ *noun* **1.** the number of copies of a newspaper or magazine sold each time it is produced **2.** distribution of written materials such as journals or books to people who may be interested in them □ **out of circulation** not available for issue or reference

circulation desk /ˌsɜːkjʊ'leɪʃ(ə)n desk/ *noun* the area of a library where the staff record the loans and returns of books

circumflex accent /'sɜːkəmfleks ˌæksənt/ *noun* a mark (^) used over a vowel in some languages to show pronunciation

citation /saɪ'teɪʃ(ə)n/ *noun* a formal word for quotation or reference

citation index /saɪ'teɪʃ(ə)n ˌɪndeks/ *noun* a list of articles which quote a specific article

citation order /saɪ'teɪʃ(ə)n ˌɔːdə/ *noun* an order of component parts when constructing a classification string

citation search /saɪ'teɪʃ(ə)n sɜːtʃ/ *noun* a search on a database of books that looks for specified words in the author or title fields

cite /saɪt/ *verb* to quote or mention something especially as proof of a point

ck *abbreviation* in Internet addresses, the top-level domain for Cook Islands

CKO *abbreviation* chief knowledge officer

cl *abbreviation* in Internet addresses, the top-level domain for Chile

claim /kleɪm/ *noun* **1.** a demand for something to which you think you have a right **2.** a statement which may be untrue but cannot be proved to be so

class /klɑːs/ *noun* a division of a classification scheme

class entry /'klɑːs ˌentri/ *noun* an entry in a catalogue under the class rather than the specific subject

classic /'klæsɪk/ *noun* a famous work of literature ○ *'The Lord of the Flies' has become a modern classic.* ○ *They have published a series of nineteenth-century classics.*

classical /'klæsɪk(ə)l/ *adjective* consisting of or involving the study of the ancient Greek and Latin languages and literature

classicism /'klæsɪsɪz(ə)m/ *noun* the study or knowledge of ancient Greece and Rome

classicist /'klæsɪsɪst/ *noun* a scholar of ancient Greek and Latin

classics /'klæsɪks/ *noun* the academic study of the languages, literature and history of ancient Greece and Rome

classification /ˌklæsɪfɪ'keɪʃ(ə)n/ *noun* **1.** a division or category within a system according to their degrees of similarity **2.** the process of putting things into groups according to similarities or relationships

classification number /ˌklæsɪfɪ'keɪʃ(ə)n ˌnʌmbə/, **classification mark** /ˌklæsɪfɪ'keɪʃ(ə)n mɑːk/ *noun* a number given to a classification heading in an information retrieval system

classification schedule /ˌklæsɪfɪ'keɪʃ(ə)n ˌʃedjuːl/ *noun* the complete plan and content of a library's cataloguing system

classification string /ˌklæsɪfɪ'keɪʃ(ə)n strɪŋ/ *noun* a sequence working from broad to narrow terms

classification system /ˌklæsɪfɪ'keɪʃ(ə)n ˌsɪstəm/, **classification scheme** /ˌklæsɪfɪ'keɪʃ(ə)n skiːm/ *noun* a system of organising things by dividing them into groups based on their similarities ○ *In libraries books are often arranged according to the Dewey decimal classification system.*

classified /'klæsɪfaɪd/ *adjective* **1.** listed in a catalogue and given an identification **2.** having access restricted to named individuals or groups ○ *The document was classified so only members of the government could read it.*

classified catalogue /ˌklæsɪfaɪd 'kæt(ə)lɒg/ *noun* a list of contents arranged according to the classification system used to control them

classified index /'klæsɪfaɪd ˌɪndeks/ *noun* a list of holdings organised under general headings rather than in one alphabetical sequence ○ *In a classified index, publishers would appear under the general heading 'Publishers' and not in the usual alphabetical order of their names.*

classify /'klæsɪfaɪ/ *verb* **1.** to place into a sequence according to a classification scheme **2.** to restrict the distribution of a document for reasons of security

class list /'klɑːs lɪst/ *noun* a list of the items in a particular class, especially used in archival management

class number /'klɑːs ˌnʌmbə/, **class mark** *noun* a series of letters and/or numbers on a book or other publication in a library identifying it, the category of its subject matter and usually its shelf location

clear /klɪə/ *verb* to delete data from a computer display or storage device

clearing house /'klɪərɪŋ haʊs/ *noun* **1.** an agency or central office where information from various sources is pooled **2.** a central office where orders from many sources are consolidated

clerical error /ˌklerɪk(ə)l 'erə/ *noun* a mistake made by an office worker

click /klɪk/ *verb* to do the action needed to activate a computer mouse ○ *Click three times to highlight the text.*

client /'klaɪənt/ *noun* **1.** a person using the services of a professional organisation **2.** a computer that is connected to a network or the Internet, or that is using the resources of another computer. ◊ **gopher**

clip art /'klɪp ɑːt/ *noun* pre-packaged artwork, available on software for use in documents produced on a computer

clipboard /'klɪpbɔːd/ *noun* a small board with a clip at the top to hold paper, so that it can be carried around and written on

closed access /ˌkləʊzd 'ækses/ *noun* a system of organising a collection so that items must be fetched for users by the staff

closed circuit television /ˌkləʊzd ˌsɜːkɪt ˈtelɪvɪʒ(ə)n/ *noun* an internal video system often used for security purposes or for relaying conferences. Abbr **CCTV**

closed question /ˌkləʊzd ˈkwestʃ(ə)n/ *noun* a question which can be answered by yes or no

closing time /ˈkləʊzɪŋ taɪm/ *noun* the time that an establishment such as a shop, library or bar closes and people have to leave

closure /ˈkləʊʒə/ *noun* the act of closing something down ○ *They are fighting against library closures.*

cloth /klɒθ/ *noun* material used to cover a hardbound book

clothbound /ˈklɒθbaʊnd/ *adjective* used to describe books which are covered in a specific type of material made originally from natural fibres, now often synthetic

cloze test /ˈkləʊz test/ *noun* a test of comprehension and grammar in which a language student supplies appropriate missing words omitted from a text

cluster /ˈklʌstə/ *noun* a small group of similar things

cluster sample /ˈklʌstə ˌsɑːmp(ə)l/ *noun* a method of sampling in statistical analysis, which compares small groups

cm *abbreviation* **1.** in Internet addresses, the top-level domain for Cameroon **2.** centimetre

CM *abbreviation* corporate memory

CMC *abbreviation* computer-mediated communication

cn *abbreviation* in Internet addresses, the top-level domain for China

co *abbreviation* in Internet addresses, the top-level domain for Colombia

coauthor /kəʊˈɔːθə/ *noun* an author who writes something jointly with one or more other authors

cobweb site /ˈkɒbweb saɪt/ *noun* a website that has not been updated for a long time

C.O.D. *abbreviation* cash on delivery

coda /ˈkəʊdə/ *noun* an additional section at the end of a text such as a literary work or speech that is not neces-sary to its structure but gives additional information

code /kəʊd/ *noun* a group of numbers or letters used to identify something. ◊ **barcode**

codebook /ˈkəʊdbʊk/ *noun* a book containing a key to a code or codes

code index /ˈkəʊd ˌɪndeks/ *noun* a system which directs the user to information by use of a code number

coden /ˈkəʊdən/ *noun* a system of classification which combines numbers and letters

code of practice /ˌkəʊd əv ˈpræktɪs/ *noun* a set of written rules describing how people in a particular job or profession are expected to behave

codex /ˈkəʊdeks/ *noun* a handwritten unbound manuscript, especially of an ancient classic

codicil /ˈkəʊdɪsɪl/ *noun* an appendix or supplement to a text

coedition /ˈkəʊɪˌdɪʃ(ə)n/ *noun* the publication of a book by two publishing companies in different countries, where the first company has originated the work and then sells sheets to the second publisher (or licenses the second publisher to reprint the book locally) ○ *We have sold coeditions of our book on garden flowers to publishers in France and Greece.*

coffee table book /ˈkɒfi ˌteɪb(ə)l bʊk/ *noun* a glossy book with many colour illustrations, designed to be browsed through rather than read in full

cognitive processing /ˌkɒgnɪtɪv ˈprəʊsesɪŋ/ *noun* the way in which a person changes external information into patterns of thought and how these are used to form judgments or choices

cognitive science /ˈkɒgnɪtɪv ˌsaɪəns/ *noun* the scientific study of knowledge and how it is acquired, combining aspects of philosophy, psychology, linguistics, anthropology and artificial intelligence

cognizance /ˈkɒgnɪz(ə)ns/ *noun* knowledge or awareness of something

cognizant /ˈkɒgnɪz(ə)nt/ *adjective* having knowledge of something

coherent /kəʊˈhɪərənt/ *adjective* clear and easy to understand

cohesion /kəʊ'hiːʒ(ə)n/ *noun* the state of all parts of an organisation working together to form a united whole

coin /kɔɪn/ *noun* a small, flat piece of metal made and stamped by a government to be used as money ■ *verb* **1.** to make coins from metal **2.** to invent words or phrases

collaborative learning /kə,læb(ə)rətɪv 'lɜːnɪŋ/ *noun* a way of teaching by sharing responsibility for organising learning with the students

collaborator /kə'læbəreɪtə/ *noun* a person who works with another to produce a literary or artistic work

collate /kə'leɪt/ *verb* **1.** to gather pieces of information together **2.** to organise materials into a specific order and check that they are complete

collation /kə'leɪʃ(ə)n/ *noun* **1.** a detailed comparison between different items or forms of information **2.** the assembling of pieces of paper in the right order, particularly the sections of a book prior to binding **3.** the act of compiling a technical description of a book, including its bibliographical details and information about its physical construction

collected works /kə,letɪd 'wɜːks/ *plural noun* all the writings of one author collected and published in one volume

collection /kə'lekʃən/ *noun* a group of similar or related things such as the stock of a special library

collection development /kə 'lekʃən dɪ,veləpmənt/ *noun* the act of expanding a collection, e.g. by providing electronic access to other collections

'A primary source [on deaf issues] for collection development librarians will be Gallaudet University Press, which offers titles on sign language, deaf special education, and deaf history.' [*Library Journal*]

collective /kə'lektɪv/ *noun* a group such as an audience, class or library

collective cataloguing /kə,lektɪv 'kætəlɒɡɪŋ/ *noun* a system used to collect small items together and catalogue them under a heading or collec-

tive title which is given a class number for retrieval

college /'kɒlɪdʒ/ *noun* **1.** an educational institution for higher education, especially one offering courses in specialised or practical subjects **2.** the building or buildings of a college

colon /'kəʊlɒn/ *noun* a punctuation mark (:) used chiefly to introduce lists ○ *The titles were: Rumplestiltskin, Cinderella and Little Red Riding Hood.*

colon classification /'kəʊlɒn ,klæsɪfɪkeɪʃ(ə)n/ *noun* a system of classifying pieces of stored information by their main field of knowledge and then by a number of other attributes (facets) which describe it

colophon /'kɒləfɒn/ *noun* **1.** the symbol or emblem that is printed on a book and represents a publisher or publisher's imprint **2.** the details of the title, printer, publisher and publication date given at the end of a book. Colophons are commonly found in early printed books and in modern private press editions.

COMMENT: Usually the publisher's colophon will appear on the title page and spine of a book, and on all publicity matter; a printer's colophon is likely to appear on private press books and other art books, and is often printed on the last page of the book.

colour coding /'kʌlə ,kəʊdɪŋ/ *noun* a system of organising items by labelling similar contents with the same colour

colour copying /'kʌlə ,kɒpiɪŋ/ *noun* the production of coloured copies of documents

colour supplement /'kʌlə ,sʌplɪmənt/ *noun* **1.** a colour magazine that comes with a weekend newspaper **2.** a section of coloured illustrations in the centre of a book or magazine, often removable

column /'kɒləm/ *noun* **1.** a vertical section of writing in a book, newspaper or magazine **2.** a regular section or article in a newspaper or magazine by the same writer or on the same subject

columnar working /kə,lʌmnə 'wɜːkɪŋ/ *noun* a method of data presentation in which information is shown in columns

columnist /'kɒləmnɪst/ *noun* a journalist who writes a regular column for a newspaper or magazine

com *abbreviation* in Internet addresses, the top-level domain for commercial organisations

combination lock /ˌkɒmbɪ'neɪʃ(ə)n lɒk/ *noun* a lock which can be opened using a pre-set order of numbers

combination ordering /ˌkɒmbɪ'neɪʃ(ə)n ˌɔːdərɪŋ/ *noun* a system whereby several departments join together to order items

combination storage /ˌkɒmbɪ'neɪʃ(ə)n ˌstɔːrɪdʒ/ *noun* a system whereby several departments use communal storage facilities

come into force /ˌkʌm ˌɪntʊ 'fɔːs/ *verb* (*of a law*) to become active or valid

comic /'kɒmɪks/ *noun* **1.** a magazine for children, telling stories written with captions on strips of pictures **2.** a person who makes others laugh ∎ *adjective* causing laughter

comma /'kɒmə/ *noun* a punctuation mark (,) used to show the natural breaks in written sentences

command paper /kə'mɑːnd ˌpeɪpə/ *noun* a government publication containing the proceedings and proposals of government committees

comment /'kɒment/ *noun* a statement which expresses an opinion

commercial /kə'mɜːʃ(ə)l/ *adjective* relating to buying and selling things ○ *Sample only – of no commercial value.*

commercial gateway package /kəˌmɜːʃ(ə)l 'geɪtweɪ ˌpækɪdʒ/ *noun* an electronic code which can be bought for a subscription and which allows access to online databases

commercial information supplier /kəˌmɜːʃ(ə)l ˌɪnfə'meɪʃ(ə)n səˌplaɪə/ *noun* a business which buys and sells information

commercial records centre /kəˌmɜːʃ(ə)l 'rekɔːdz ˌsentə/ *noun* an organisation which keeps records of a business's financial dealings

commitment /kə'mɪtmənt/ *noun* a task which you undertake to do

common query language /ˌkɒmən 'kwɪəri ˌlæŋgwɪdʒ/ *noun* a formal language used to interrogate a database. Abbr **CQL**

commons /'kɒmənz/ *plural noun* data stored in the memory of one computer that is available to all computers linked to it by a network

communicable /kə'mjuːnɪkəb(ə)l/ *adjective* easily communicated

communicate /kə'mjuːnɪkeɪt/ *verb* to give information

communication /kəˌmjuːnɪ'keɪʃ(ə)n/ *noun* **1.** the exchange of information between people, e.g. by means of speaking, writing or using a common system of signs or behaviour **2.** a spoken or written message **3.** the act of giving information

communication channel /kəˌmjuːnɪ'keɪʃ(ə)n ˌtʃæn(ə)l/ *noun* a method used to communicate with other people, e.g. writing or speech

communications /kəˌmjuːnɪ'keɪʃ(ə)nz/ *plural noun* the systems by which information is transmitted

communications audit /kəˌmjuːnɪ'keɪʃ(ə)nz ˌɔːdɪt/ *noun* a survey of the methods used to send information around an organisation

communication skills /kəˌmjuːnɪ'keɪʃ(ə)n skɪl/ *plural noun* the ability to give information clearly and appropriately to other people

'We take for granted that there are basic literacy and numeracy skills. What we want in addition to that is the ability to get on with people, work as part of the team, problem solve and so on. Communication skills… those are the things that are important to us.' [*The Times*]

communication theory /kəˌmjuːnɪ'keɪʃ(ə)n ˌθɪəri/ *noun* the study of all forms of human communication, including branches of linguistics such as semantics as well as telecommunications and other nonlinguistic forms

communicative /kə'mjuːnɪkətɪv/ *adjective* **1.** relating to communication or to systems for communication **2.** (*in foreign language teaching*) stressing the importance of language as a tool for communicating information and ideas

communiqué /kə'mjuːnɪkeɪ/ *noun* an official announcement, especially to the press or public

community /kə'mjuːnɪti/ *noun* a group of people who live in a particular area

community analysis /kə,mjuːnɪti ə'nælɪsɪs/ *noun* a survey of the different types of people who live in a community

community college /kə'mjuːnɪti ,kɒlɪdʒ/ *noun* (*in the UK*) an educational centre with recreational facilities available to the whole community

community information /kə ,mjuːnɪti ,ɪnfə'meɪʃ(ə)n/ *noun* local information relating to a small geographical area

community profiling /kə,mjuːnɪti 'prəʊfaɪlɪŋ/ *noun* a method of local planning in which the needs and resources of a particular community are assessed

compact disc /,kɒmpækt 'dɪsk/ *noun* a coated plastic disc that can record large amounts of data which can be read by laser. Abbr **CD**

compact disc interactive /,kɒmpækt dɪsk ,ɪntər'æktɪv/ *noun* full form of **CD-I**

compact disc player /,kɒmpækt 'dɪsk ,pleɪə/ *noun* an electronic device which uses lasers to read signals on a disc to produce very high quality reproduction

compact disc – read only memory /,kɒmpækt ,dɪsk ,riːd ,əʊnli 'mem(ə)ri/ *noun* full form of **CD-ROM**

compact disc write once /,kɒmpækt dɪsk ,raɪt 'wʌns/ *noun* full form of **CD-WO**

compact video disc /,kɒmpækt 'vɪdiəʊ ,dɪsk/ *noun* a compact disc that plays both sound and pictures

companion /kəm'pænjən/ *noun* a guide or handbook on a particular subject

company /'kʌmp(ə)ni/ *noun* a business which makes money by making or buying and selling goods, or by providing a service

company file /'kʌmp(ə)ni faɪl/ *noun* a file containing and collating information specific to a company

compatible /kəm'pætɪb(ə)l/ *adjective* working well together

compendious /kəm'pendiəs/ *adjective* containing a wide range of information in a concise form

compendium /kəm'pendiəm/ *noun* a book in which two or more previously published books are brought together

competence /'kɒmpɪt(ə)ns/ *noun* knowledge of a language that enables somebody to speak and understand it

competition /,kɒmpə'tɪʃ(ə)n/ *noun* **1.** a situation where two or more companies with similar products try to persuade people to buy theirs **2.** an informal test of skill or ability ○ *The children's library ran a competition to see who read the most books during the school holiday.*

competitor /kəm'petɪtə/ *noun* **1.** a person who takes part in competitions **2.** a person or company that sells similar types of goods or services which can reduce the market for others

compilation /,kɒmpɪ'leɪʃ(ə)n/ *noun* a work produced by combining material from other books or documents

compile /kəm'paɪl/ *verb* to put together different pieces of information in order to make them into one document

compiler /kəm'paɪlə/ *noun* a person who collects and edits material taken from various sources for publication as a new work

compleat /kəm'pliːt/ *adjective* having or exhibiting full knowledge of a particular field or skill

complementary /,kɒmplɪ'ment(ə)ri/ *adjective* fitting well together to make a harmonious whole

completion date /kəm'pliːʃ(ə)n deɪt/ *noun* the date by which something must be finished

compliance certificate /kəm 'plaɪəns sə,tɪfɪkət/ *noun* an official statement that something has passed all the necessary tests for the regulations

compliance test /kəmˈplaɪəns test/ noun a test to ensure that something conforms to the regulations

complimentary copy /ˌkɒmplɪmentəri ˈkɒpi/ noun a copy of a book given free as a favour, reward or mark of respect

component /kəmˈpəʊnənt/ noun a part of something, used together with other parts to create a whole

compose /kəmˈpəʊz/ verb to create a musical or literary work

composer /kəmˈpəʊzə/ noun a person who composes, especially one who writes music

composer entry /kəmˈpəʊzər ˌentri/ noun an entry usually for a musical composition in a catalogue under the name of the composer

composite subject /ˌkɒmpəzɪt ˈsʌbdʒəkt/ noun a classification subject which consists of more than one element

composition /ˌkɒmpəˈzɪʃ(ə)n/ noun the way that the parts of something are put together

compound /ˈkɒmpaʊnd/ adjective made up of a mixture of several components

compound interest /ˌkɒmpaʊnd ˈɪntrəst/ noun money which is paid as interest both on the original capital and also on the interest earned

compound name /ˈkɒmpaʊnd neɪm/ noun a name which has two or more parts joined by a hyphen, e.g. 'Mrs. Brownley-Smith'.

compound subject heading /ˌkɒmpaʊnd ˈsʌbdʒekt ˌhedɪŋ/ noun a heading which consists of words that are always associated together, e.g. 'Treaty of Rome'

compound term /ˈkɒmpaʊnd tɜːm/ noun a name that consists of two words, as in 'primary schools', and could be indexed with a 'see also' reference, e.g. 'schools, see also primary schools'

comprehensive /ˌkɒmprɪˈhensɪv/ adjective covering all the possible aspects of a subject

compression ratio /kəmˈpreʃ(ə)n ˌreɪʃiəʊ/ noun the ratio of the size of an original, uncompressed file to the final, compressed file that has been more efficiently encoded

comprise /kəmˈpraɪz/ verb to be made up of different parts ○ *Overseas students comprise 10% of the college population.*

Compuserve /ˈkɒmpjʊsɜːv/ a trade name for a very large commercial online information service

computer /kəmˈpjuːtə/ noun an electronic machine that processes data very quickly using a stored program

computer-aided design /kəm ˌpjuːtər ˌeɪdɪd dɪˈzaɪn/ noun the use of a computer and graphics terminal to help a designer in his or her work. Abbr **CAD**

computer-aided learning /kəm ˌpjuːtər ˌeɪdɪd ˈlɜːnɪŋ/ noun a form of self-study which can be done with the aid of specially written computer programs. Abbr **CAL**

computer-assisted composition /kəmˌpjuːtər əˌsɪstɪd ˌkɒmpə ˈzɪʃ(ə)n/ noun composition using digitally recorded text, which generates characters and automatically inserts spaces, as well as hyphenating, justifying and paginating

computer-assisted retrieval system /kəmˌpjuːtər əˌsɪstɪd rɪ ˈtriːv(ə)l ˌsɪstəm/ noun an automated method of finding information

computer-based thesaurus /kəm ˌpjuːtə beɪst θɪˈsɔːrəs/ noun a dictionary installed as a word processing facility which checks the spelling in written text and suggests alternatives for misspelt words

computer-based training /kəm ˌpjuːtə beɪst ˈtreɪnɪŋ/ noun a method of teaching which uses computers as the main teaching tool. Abbr **CBT**

computer-based tutorial /kəm ˌpjuːtə beɪst tjuˈtɔːriəl/ noun a software package which teaches the user how to use a program. Abbr **CBT**

computer bureau /kəmˈpjuːtə ˌbjʊərəʊ/ noun an office which offers to do work on its computers for companies that do not own their own computers

computer conferencing /kəm
ˌpjuːtə ˈkɒnf(ə)rənsɪŋ/ *noun* the use
of a number of computers or terminals
connected together to allow a group of
users to communicate

computer crime /kəmˈpjuːtə
kraɪm/ *noun* illegal activities carried
out on or by means of a computer.
Computer crime includes criminal tres-
pass into another computer system,
theft of computerised data and the use
of an online system to commit or aid in
the commission of fraud.

computer error /kəmˌpjuːtər ˈerə/
noun a mistake made by a computer

computer-generated /kəmˌpjuːtə
ˈdʒenəreɪtɪd/ *adjective* produced using
a computer ○ *The book is illustrated
with computer-generated graphics.*

computer graphics /kəmˌpjuːtə
ˈɡræfɪks/ *plural noun* a visual display
of information on a computer screen or
printout, e.g. graphs and charts

computer hardware /kəmˌpjuːtə
ˈhɑːdweə/ *noun* machines used in data
processing, including the computers,
keyboards, monitors and printers, but
not the programs

computer-human interaction
/kəmˌpjuːtə ˌhjuːmən ˌɪntər
ˈækʃ(ə)n/ *noun* same as **human-
computer interaction**

computer illiteracy /kəmˌpjuːtər ɪ
ˈlɪt(ə)rəsi/ *noun* lack of knowledge
about how to use a computer

computer indexing /kəmˌpjuːtər
ˈɪndeksɪŋ/ *noun* automated methods of
producing indexes

computerised /kəmˈpjuːtəraɪzd/,
computerized *adjective* changed from
a manual system to an automated
system ○ *a computerised invoicing
system* ○ *The book was set using computerised typesetting.*

computer laboratory /kəmˈpjuːtə
ləˌbɒrət(ə)ri/ *noun* a room equipped
with several computers, sometimes
networked together, which can be used
for working in or teaching

computer language /kəmˈpjuːtə
ˈlæŋɡwɪdʒ/ *noun* a language made up
of numbers and characters used to give
instructions to a computer

COMMENT: There are three types of
computer languages: machine code,
assembler and high-level language. The
higher the level the language is, the
easier it is to program and understand,
but the slower it is to execute. Common
high-level languages are BASIC, C,
COBOL, FORTRAN, PASCAL,
PROLOG.

computer listing /kəmˌpjuːtə
ˈlɪstɪŋ/ *noun* a printout of a list of items
taken from data stored in a computer

computer-literate /kəmˌpjuːtə
ˈlɪt(ə)rət/ *adjective* having a good
understanding and experience of
working with computers

**computer-mediated communi-
cation** /kəmˌpjuːtə ˌmiːdieɪtɪd kə
ˌmjuːnɪˈkeɪʃ(ə)n/ *noun* communication networks that are accessed through
a computer, e.g. forums, e-mail and
intranets

computer network /kəmˈpjuːtə
ˌnetwɜːk/ *noun* shared use of a series of
interconnected computers, peripherals
and terminals

computer printout /kəmˌpjuːtə
ˈprɪntaʊt/ *noun* a printed copy of information from a computer

computer program /kəmˈpjuːtə
ˌprəʊɡræm/ *noun* instructions to a
computer, telling it to do a particular
piece of work

computer programmer /kəm
ˌpjuːtə ˈprəʊɡræmə/ *noun* a person
who writes computer programs

computer programming /kəm
ˌpjuːtə ˈprəʊɡræmɪŋ/ *noun* the job of
writing programs for computers

computer-readable /kəmˌpjuːtə
ˈriːdəb(ə)l/ *adjective* relating to data in
a form which can be read by a computer

computer services /kəmˌpjuːtə
ˈsɜːvɪsɪz/ *plural noun* 1. support services for computer users 2. work done on
a computer for clients by experts

computer system /kəmˈpjuːtə
ˌsɪstəm/ *noun* a set of programs and
commands which run a computer

computer-telephone integration
/kəmˌpjuːtə ˌtelɪfəʊn ˌɪntɪˈɡreɪʃ(ə)n/
noun a system that allows normal audio
telephone conversations to be transmitted over a computer data network
and controlled by a computer. Abbr **CTI**

computer terminal /kəm'pjuːtə ˌtɜːmɪn(ə)l/ *noun* a keyboard and screen by which information can be put into a computer or called up from a database ○ *a computer system consisting of a microprocessor and six terminals*

computing /kəm'pjuːtɪŋ/ *noun* the activity of using computers or computer software

computing facilities /kəm'pjuːtɪŋ fəˌsɪlɪtɪz/ *plural noun* computers and the services which help the staff of an organisation to use them

concatenate /kən'kætəneɪt/ *verb* to link two or more information units, e.g. character strings or computer files, so that they form a single unit

concentrate /'kɒnsəntreɪt/ *verb* □ **to concentrate on something** to give something all one's attention

concept /'kɒnsept/ *noun* an idea or principle

concept map /'kɒnsept mæp/ *noun* a way of representing knowledge in the form of a diagram, with links indicating the relationships between concepts

conceptual model /kənˌseptʃuəl 'mɒd(ə)l/ *noun* a description of a database in terms of the data it contains and its relationships

concise /kən'saɪs/ *adjective* using as few words as possible to give the necessary information

concordance /kən'kɔːd(ə)ns/ *noun* an alphabetical index of all the words in a document ○ *a concordance to the Bible* ○ *a Shakespeare concordance*

'Logos Bible Software, for example, licenses 50 Bible translations and 5,000 reference works, such as commentaries and concordances, that the company bundles into quickly searchable electronic libraries.' [*The Boston Globe*]

concurrent /kən'kʌrənt/ *adjective* happening at the same time

condition /kən'dɪʃ(ə)n/ *noun* something that must happen before something else is possible

conference /'kɒnf(ə)rəns/ *noun* a meeting often lasting several days

where people discuss a common subject or shared interest

conferencing /'kɒnf(ə)rənsɪŋ/ *noun* the holding of a conference, meeting or discussion in which the participants are linked by telephone, by telephone and video equipment or by computer

confidential /ˌkɒnfɪ'denʃəl/ *adjective* intended to be kept secret ○ *As this information is confidential you must not give it to anyone else.*

configure /kən'fɪgə/ *verb* to plan computer hardware and software so that they will work together

confirm /kən'fɜːm/ *verb* to state that something is definite or true □ **to confirm in writing** to write a letter to say that an agreement is definite

confiscate /'kɒnfɪskeɪt/ *verb* to remove private property as a punishment ○ *The police are allowed to confiscate pornographic material.*

conform /kən'fɔːm/ *verb* **1.** to behave according to accepted standards **2.** to be in accordance with laws or regulations

congestion /kən'dʒestʃən/ *noun* a state where there is too much data for the capacity of a system

conjecture /kən'dʒektʃə/ *noun* a conclusion, judgment or statement based on incomplete or inconclusive information

connect /kə'nekt/ *verb* to join two things together

connectivity /ˌkɒnek'tɪvɪti/ *noun* the ability to communicate with another system or piece of hardware or software, or with an Internet site

connect time /kə'nekt taɪm/ *noun* the period of time a user is logged on to a remote computer, e.g. when browsing the Internet

consecutive /kən'sekjʊtɪv/ *adjective* happening one after the other without interruption

consequence /'kɒnsɪkwəns/ *noun* the result or effect of something happening

conservation /ˌkɒnsə'veɪʃ(ə)n/ *noun* the process of ensuring the survival of materials, e.g. library books, through repair and controlled storage conditions

conservation unit /ˌkɒnsə
'veɪʃ(ə)n ˌjuːnɪt/, **conservation
department** /ˌkɒnsə'veɪʃ(ə)n dɪ
ˌpɑːtmənt/ *noun* a group of people who
take responsibility for the conservation
of library stock

conservator /kən'sɜːvətər/ *noun* a
person who works to conserve things

consignment /kən'saɪnmənt/ *noun*
the delivery of goods

consist of /kən'sɪst ɒv/ *verb* to be
made up of ○ *The committee consists of
librarians and information scientists.*

consonant /'kɒnsənənt/ *noun* all the
letters of the Roman alphabet except the
five vowels

consortium /kən'sɔːtiəm/ *noun* a
group of companies or organisations
working together for a common purpose

construct *noun* /'kɒnstrʌkt/ a
complex idea, built up from various
elements ■ *verb* /kən'strʌkt/ to build or
create something

consultant /kən'sʌltənt/ *noun* an
expert who gives advice in a professional field

consultation /ˌkɒnsəl'teɪʃ(ə)n/
noun a meeting where expert advice is
sought and given

consultation document /ˌkɒnsəl
'teɪʃ(ə)n ˌdɒkjʊmənt/ *noun* a document with proposals on which people's
opinion is requested

consultative leadership style
/kən'sʌltətɪv ˌliːdəʃɪp ˌstaɪl/ *noun* a
way of leading a group by asking them
for their opinions

consumables /kən'sjuːməb(ə)lz/
plural noun items necessary for work
which get used up and need to be
replaced, e.g. stationery

consumer /kən'sjuːmə/ *noun* a
person who buys goods or uses services

consumer characteristics /kən
ˌsjuːmə ˌkærɪktə'rɪstɪks/ *plural noun*
specific features which distinguish one
consumer group from another

consumer demands /kən,sjuːmə
dɪ'mɑːndz/ *plural noun* what the
consumer is asking for

consumer group /kən'sjuːmə
gruːp/ *noun* people in given age,
income or geographic groups who

would have a particular interest in
specific goods or services

consumer needs /kən,sjuːmə
'niːdz/ *plural noun* services that
consumers think are essential

consumer targeting /kən,sjuːmə
'tɑːgɪtɪŋ/ *noun* the act of aiming the
advertising of goods or services at
specific groups of consumers

consumption /kən'sʌmpʃ(ə)n/
noun the act of buying and using up
goods such as food

cont. *abbreviation* PUBL contents

contact name /'kɒntækt neɪm/
noun the name of the person within a
particular department or service who
may be contacted for information

contemporary /kən'temp(ə)rəri/
adjective happening or existing at the
same time as something else

content /'kɒntent/ *noun* information
made available by an electronic medium
or product

content management /'kɒntent
ˌmænɪdʒmənt/ *noun* the act of using a
database system which allows large
amounts of content to be entered,
accessed, edited and stored

'While organisations are building
more elaborate content management
systems, they are failing to address the
need to harness and share knowledge
in meaningful ways. The information
[in these] is just the thin end of a large
and largely unmanageable wedge. The
rest of the wedge comprises human
interaction like face-to-face
conversations, online discussion
groups, weblogs, telephone calls,
instant messages, emails and so on.'
[*Information World Review*]

content provider /'kɒntent prə
ˌvaɪdə/ *noun* a website containing
mainly news or information rather than
commercial facilities such as shopping
or banking, or a business supplying the
information for such a website

content-rich /ˌkɒntent 'rɪtʃ/ *adjective* containing a lot of useful information

contents /'kɒntents/ *plural noun* **1.**
the subject matter of a document or
publication **2.** a list at the front of a
publication that gives the title and

number of the first page of each new chapter or part

contents page /'kɒntents peɪdʒ/ *noun* a page at the beginning of a document listing the things in it

content syndication /'kɒntent ˌsɪndɪkeɪʃ(ə)n/ *noun* the act of making content available to be accessed and reproduced by subscribers

context /'kɒntekst/ *noun* a background situation to an event which helps it to be understood □ **out of context** seen as an individual item not related to its background

contingency fund /kən'tɪndʒənsi fʌnd/ *noun* a sum of money put aside in case it is needed for an unexpected event

contingency plan /kən'tɪndʒənsi plæn/ *noun* a decision about what to do in case of a problem with the original plan ○ *There was a contingency plan to move the book store to the first floor in case of flood danger.*

continuation list /kənˌtɪnjʊ'eɪʃ(ə)n ˌlɪst/ *noun* a method of recording books and documents which are issued in parts and for which there are standing orders

continuous assessment /kənˌtɪnjuəs ə'sesmənt/ *noun* a system of assessing the progress of a student by coursework rather than by an examination at the end

contract /kən'trækt/ *noun* a written legal agreement ○ *The contract is binding on both parties.*

contrast /'kɒntrɑːst/ *noun* a big difference between two things which is clear when they are compared

contribute /kən'trɪbjuːt/ *verb* to provide part of a whole ○ *to contribute an article to a magazine* ○ *to contribute money to help pay for something*

contribution /ˌkɒntrɪ'bjuːʃ(ə)n/ *noun* a piece of material that forms part of a publication or broadcast

control /kən'trəʊl/ *noun* the power or authority to make decisions about how something is managed ▪ *verb* to organise something so that it works the way you want it to

control key /kən'trəʊl kiː/ *noun* a key on a computer which works part of a program

controlled language /kənˌtrəʊld 'læŋgwɪdʒ/ *noun* a limited number of words used for compiling indexes or writing instructions or information

controlled term list /kənˌtrəʊld 'tɜːm ˌlɪst/ *noun* a list of terms with fixed meanings to be used in cataloguing. Also called **controlled vocabulary 2**

controlled vocabulary /kənˌtrəʊld vəʊ'kæbjʊləri/ *noun* **1.** a limited number of words used to make understanding easier for non-native speakers of a language **2.** same as **controlled term list**

controversial /ˌkɒntrə'vɜːʃ(ə)l/ *adjective* causing argument and disagreement

convenient /kən'viːniənt/ *adjective* easy to use and saving time or effort

convention /kən'venʃən/ *noun* **1.** a large meeting of an organisation or political group **2.** an international agreement. ◊ **Berne Convention, Universal Copyright Convention**

COMMENT: Both the Berne Convention and the UCC were drawn up to try to protect copyright from pirates; under the Berne convention, published material remains in copyright until 50 years after the death of the author and for 25 years after publication under the UCC. In both cases, a work which is copyrighted in one country is automatically covered by the copyright legislation of all countries signing the convention.

conventional /kən'venʃ(ə)n(ə)l/ *adjective* conforming to what most people consider to be normal

conversion /kən'vɜːʃ(ə)n/ *noun* changing from one computer system to another

convey /kən'veɪ/ *verb* to make information or ideas known and understood

convince /kən'vɪns/ *verb* to persuade other people to do or believe in something

cookery book /'kʊk(ə)ri bʊk/, **cookbook** /'kʊkbʊk/ *noun* a book which gives recipes for preparing food (NOTE: **Cookbook** is always used in the

US, and the term is becoming much more common in GB English.)

cookie /ˈkʊki/ *noun* a computer file containing information about a user that is sent to the central computer with each request. The server uses this information to customise data sent back to the user and to log the user's requests.

coop *abbreviation* in Internet addresses, the generic top-level domain for non-profit-making cooperatives

coordinate *noun* /kəʊˈɔːdɪnət/ /kəʊˈɔːdɪneɪt/ a value from an axis on a graph, used to locate a specific point ■ *verb* /kəʊˈɔːdɪneɪt/ to combine different items so that they work well together ○ *She is trying to co-ordinate the typesetting, printing and binding in various locations.*

coordinator /kəʊˈɔːdɪneɪtə/ *noun* a person who ensures that people and activities work well together

copier /ˈkɒpiə/ *noun* same as **photocopier**

coping pattern /ˈkəʊpɪŋ ˌpæt(ə)n/, **coping strategy** *noun* a method of managing to deal with problems successfully

copy /ˈkɒpi/ *noun* **1.** something that is made to look exactly the same as the original **2.** the text of a manuscript or advertising material ■ *verb* to make something look exactly the same as the original

copy editor /ˈkɒpi ˌedɪtə/ *noun* a person whose job is to check material ready for printing for accuracy and consistency of typeface, punctuation and layout

copy in /ˌkɒpi ˈɪn/ *verb* to send a copy to somebody, especially a copy of a letter or other document

copy protection /ˈkɒpi prəˌtekʃən/ *noun* a means of preventing unauthorised duplication of computer software

copyright /ˈkɒpiraɪt/ *noun* the legal right, which the creator of an original work has, to only allow copying of the work with permission and sometimes on payment of royalties or a copyright fee

COMMENT: Copyright lasts for 50 years after the author's death according to the Berne Convention, and for 25 years according to the Universal Copyright Convention. In the USA, copyright is for 50 years after the death of an author for books published after January 1st, 1978. For books published before that date, the original copyright was for 28 years after the death of the author, and this can be extended for a further 28 year period up to a maximum of 75 years. In 1995, the European Union adopted a copyright term of 70 years after the death of the author. The copyright holder has the right to refuse or to grant permission to copy copyright material, though under the Paris agreement of 1971, the original publishers (representing the author or copyright holder) must, under certain circumstances, grant licences to reprint copyright material. The copyright notice has to include the symbol ©, the name of the copyright holder and the date of the copyright (which is usually the date of first publication). The notice must be printed in the book and usually appears on the reverse of the title page. A copyright notice is also printed on other forms of printed material such as posters. The change of the term of copyright in the European Union has created problems for publishers and copyright holders, in cases where the author died more than fifty years but less than seventy years ago. In effect, such authors have returned to copyright, and royalties, etc., are due to their estates until the seventy year term expires. This applies to well-known authors such as Beatrix Potter and James Joyce, as well as to composers, such as Elgar.

copyright deposit /ˌkɒpiraɪt dɪˈpɒzɪt/ *noun* the deposit of a copy of a published work in a copyright library, usually the main national library, which is part of the formal copyrighting of published material

copyright deposit library /ˌkɒpiraɪt dɪˈpɒzɪt ˌlaɪbrəri/ *noun* a library that receives a free copy of every book published in the British Isles, belonging to a group of six in England, Scotland, Wales and the Republic of Ireland

copyright fee /ˈkɒpiraɪt fiː/ *noun* money paid to the holder of a copyright for permission to use their work

copyright infringement /ˈkɒpiraɪt ɪnˌfrɪndʒmənt/ *noun* the act of illegally copying or using a work that is covered by copyright law. Also called **infringement of copyright**

copyright law /'kɒpiraɪt lɔː/ *noun* a law which protects the rights to copyright

copyright licence /'kɒpiraɪt ˌlaɪs(ə)ns/ *noun* official permission to produce, copy and sell works that are protected by copyright law

copyright notice /'kɒpiraɪt ˌnəʊtɪs/ *noun* a note in a book showing who owns the copyright and the date of ownership, printed on the verso of the title page

copy typist /'kɒpi ˌtaɪpɪst/ *noun* a person who types from handwritten copy, not from dictation

core competency /ˌkɔː 'kɒmpɪtənsi/ *noun* the basic body of knowledge of a particular area or skill

core curriculum /ˌkɔː kə'rɪkjələm/ *noun* courses in a school or college which are compulsory for all students

core stock /ˌkɔː 'stɒk/ *noun* same as **basic stock**

corner /'kɔːnə/ *verb* to gain control of a particular market

corporate /'kɔːp(ə)rət/ *adjective* **1.** owned by one or more large businesses **2.** shared by all the members of an organisation

corporate author /ˌkɔːp(ə)rət 'ɔːθə/ *noun* a society, institution or government body which publishes documents, and whose name is used as the catalogue heading

corporate database /ˌkɔːp(ə)rət 'deɪtəbeɪs/ *noun* a source of electronic information shared by all members of an organisation

corporate headquarters /ˌkɔːp(ə)rət 'hedkwɔːtəz/ *noun* the head office of a corporation or large business

corporate memory /ˌkɔːp(ə)rət 'mem(ə)ri/ *noun* the basic body of knowledge and information needed for an organisation to work effectively. Abbr **CM**

corporate name /ˌkɔːp(ə)rət 'neɪm/ *noun* the name of a large corporation

corporation /ˌkɔːpə'reɪʃ(ə)n/ *noun* a large company or business

corpus of knowledge /ˌkɔːpəs əv 'nɒlɪdʒ/ *noun* a large collection of the major works about a specific field of knowledge

correct /kə'rekt/ *adjective* accurate and without mistakes ■ *verb* to mark mistakes so that they can be put right

correlation /ˌkɒrə'leɪʃ(ə)n/ *noun* close connections which influence each other

correspondence /ˌkɒrɪ'spɒndəns/ *noun* letters sent and received

correspondent /ˌkɒrɪ'spɒndənt/ *noun* **1.** somebody who writes letters **2.** a television or newspaper reporter on a specialist subject or in a particular area

corrigenda slip /ˌkɒrɪ'gendə ˌslɪp/ *noun* a list of corrections of errors in a printed book, printed on a separate slip of paper and inserted in the bound book

corrupt /kə'rʌpt/ *adjective* **1.** acting dishonestly or illegally **2.** containing errors ○ *corrupt computer data*

cost /kɒst/ *noun* the amount of money needed to buy, do or make something

cost-benefit analysis /ˌkɒst 'benɪfɪt əˌnæləsɪs/ *noun* an investigation of the level of benefit gained from something to decide whether it is worth the expenditure

cost-effective /ˌkɒstɪ 'fektɪv/ *adjective* saving money in comparison with the amount of time or money spent

costly /'kɒstli/ *adjective* very expensive in time, effort or money

co.uk *abbreviation* UK commercial organization

counter /'kaʊntə/ same as **circulation desk**

country code /'kʌntri kəʊd/ *noun* the last part of an e-mail address which indicates the country of origin

course /kɔːs/ *noun* **1.** a programme of study or training, especially one that leads to a qualification from an educational institution **2.** one of several distinct units that together form a programme of study leading to a qualification such as a degree

course book /'kɔːs bʊk/ *noun* a book that is used by students and teachers as the basis of a course of study

coursework /ˈkɔːswɜːk/ *noun* assignments that are done as part of a course

cover /ˈkʌvə/ *noun* the outside of a book, usually made of thicker paper or card

coverage /ˈkʌv(ə)rɪdʒ/ *noun* the time or space given to a topic by the media

cover date /ˈkʌvə deɪt/ *noun* the date which appears on the cover of a publication

cover design /ˈkʌvə dɪˌzaɪn/ *noun* a special design for a book or magazine cover

cover designer /ˈkʌvə dɪˌzaɪnə/ *noun* a person who designs the cover of a book or magazine

covering material /ˈkʌvərɪŋ məˌtɪəriəl/ *noun* material used to make the cover for a book

cover price /ˈkʌvə praɪs/ *noun* the retail price of a book

CPU *abbreviation* central processing unit

CQL *abbreviation* common query language

cr *abbreviation* in Internet addresses, the top-level domain for Costa Rica

craft book /ˈkrɑːft bʊk/ *noun* a book dealing with work done by hand such as knitting, sewing or making models

crash /kræʃ/ *verb* **1.** to come to a sudden stop as a result of an accident **2.** (*of computer systems*) to stop working ▪ *noun* the sudden failure of a computer system

crawler /ˈkrɔːlə/ *noun* a computer program that collects online documents and reference links

CRC *abbreviation* camera-ready copy

credit /ˈkredɪt/ *noun* **1.** a system of paying for goods some time after you have bought them □ **in credit** having money in the bank □ **on credit** to buy goods and pay for them later **2.** acknowledgement of something positive ○ *She gave them credit for their good work.* ▪ *verb* to acknowledge something positive

credit card /ˈkredɪt kɑːd/ *noun* a plastic card issued by banks to their customers which allows them to buy goods on credit or to borrow money

credit limit /ˈkredɪt ˌlɪmɪt/ *noun* the amount of money which is the maximum you can borrow at one time

credit line /ˈkredɪt laɪn/ *noun* a printed acknowledgement of the author or source of material that was included in a publication

credit note /ˈkredɪt nəʊt/ *noun* a note issued by a company stating faulty goods may be replaced with goods to the same value

credits /ˈkredɪts/ *plural noun* notes to acknowledge the contributors to a work, e.g. the owner of a copyright or the designer of a book

creditworthy /ˈkredɪtwɜːði/ *adjective* relating to a person or organisation that has a good record of paying their bills

crime fiction /ˈkraɪm ˌfɪkʃ(ə)n/ *noun* a style of fiction about imaginary crimes and detectives

crime list /ˈkraɪm lɪst/ *noun* a series of books on crime or crime fiction

Crime Writers Association /ˈkraɪm ˌraɪtəz əˌsəʊsieɪʃ(ə)n/ *noun* an organisation in the UK which is responsible for the administration of several annual awards for crime writing

critic /ˈkrɪtɪk/ *noun* a person who writes reviews or gives opinions about books, films, music and art

critical /ˈkrɪtɪk(ə)l/ *adjective* **1.** expressing severe opinions about someone or something **2.** very serious or dangerous

critical factor /ˌkrɪtɪk(ə)l ˈfæktə/ *noun* a factor in a situation which must be considered very carefully because it can have serious effects

criticism /ˈkrɪtɪsɪz(ə)m/ *noun* serious judgement or an expression of disapproval of something

CR/LF *abbreviation* carriage return/line feed

CRLIS *abbreviation* Current Research in Library and Information Science

crosscheck /ˈkrɒstʃek/ *verb* to evaluate the results of an investigation by checking it by an alternative method ○ *The sub-editor should crosscheck the page references against the index.*

'Duplicate versions get into [the] system… Tracking all invoices, performing cross-checks, and singling out those most likely to represent double payments requires constant human surveillance.' [*Information Week*]

cross-index /'krɒs ˌɪndeks/ *verb* **1.** to give a particular item one or more additional entries in an index, under different headings, as cross-references to it **2.** to supply cross-references in something ○ '*Hyde' is cross-indexed to 'Jekyll and Hyde'.*

cross-refer /ˌkrɒs rɪ'fɜː/ *verb* to give a note that tells a reader of a book, index or library catalogue to look in another specified part or on another page of the same work

cross-reference /ˌkrɒs 'ref(ə)rəns/ *noun* a footnote in a document which tells you that there is other relevant information in another part of the document ■ *verb* to make a reference to another part of the book ○ *The various paper sizes are cross-referenced to the appendix.*

cross-searching /'krɒs ˌsɜːtʃɪŋ/ *noun* searching more than one database at the same time using a single search engine or query

cross-section /'krɒs ˌsekʃən/ *noun* a representative sample of a group of people or things

crosstalk /'krɒstɑːk/ *noun* unwanted sounds or other signals picked up by one channel of an electronic communications system from another channel, e.g. between telephones or loudspeakers

crown /kraʊn/ *noun* a size of book based on an old paper size of 15 x 20 inches or 380 x 508mm, so called because the old paper was originally identified by a watermark of a crown

crown octavo /ˌkraʊn ɒk'tɑːvəʊ/ *noun* a size of book, formerly 7 1/2 x 5 inches, now 186 x 123mm

crown quarto /ˌkraʊn 'kwɔːtəʊ/ *noun* a size of book, formerly 10 x 7 1/2 inches, now 246 x 186mm

CRPU *abbreviation* camera-ready paste-up

CRT *abbreviation* cathode ray tube

crucial /'kruːʃ(ə)l/ *adjective* extremely important or essential

cryptanalysis /ˌkrɪptə'næləsɪs/ *noun* the process or science of deciphering coded texts or messages

cryptography /ˌkrɪp'tɒɡrəfi/ *noun* **1.** the study or analysis of codes and coding methods **2.** coded or secret writing

CSO *abbreviation* Central Statistical Office

CTI *abbreviation* computer-telephone integration

cu *abbreviation* in Internet addresses, the top-level domain for Cuba

cultural heritage /ˌkʌltʃər(ə)l 'herɪtɪdʒ/ *noun* the historical artefacts, e.g. art, architecture, texts and other intangibles such as language and folklore, that belong to a culture

'The Community Heritage Grants (CHG) Program aims to preserve and provide access to locally held nationally significant cultural heritage collections… community organisations such as historical societies, museums, public libraries, archives, Indigenous and migrant community groups are eligible to apply.' [*Ayr Advocate*]

culture /'kʌltʃə/ *noun* the ideas, customs and artistic productions of any society

cumulative index /ˌkjuːmjʊlətɪv 'ɪndeks/ *noun* an index that is built up by additions to all the previously published entries at specified times

curator /kjʊ'reɪtə/ *noun* a person responsible for managing a museum or art gallery

curiosa /ˌkjʊəri'əʊsə/ *plural noun* books or other texts dealing with unusual topics, especially erotica

curly bracket /ˌkɜːli 'brækɪt/ *noun* same as **brace**

current /'kʌrənt/ *adjective* happening at the present time

current awareness /ˌkʌrənt ə'weənəs/ *noun* the level to which somebody knows what is the most up-to-date information on specific subjects

current awareness service /ˌkʌrənt ə'weənəs ˌsɜːvɪs/ *noun* an organisation or individual who notifies customers of the most up-to-date information in their field

current journal /ˌkʌrənt ˈdʒɜːnəl/, **current serial** /ˌkʌrənt ˈsɪəriəl/ *noun* the latest edition of a regular publication

Current Research in Library and Information Science /ˌkʌrənt rɪ ˌsɜːtʃ ɪn ˌlaɪbrəri ənd ˌɪnfəˈmeɪʃ(ə)n ˌsaɪəns/ *noun* a quarterly journal with abstracts of current research. Abbr **CRLIS**

curriculum /kəˈrɪkjʊləm/ *noun* all the courses that are taught in a school or college

curriculum vitae /kəˌrɪkjʊləm ˈviːtaɪ/ *noun* a brief summary of somebody's personal details, education and career. Abbr **CV**

cursor /ˈkɜːsə/ *noun* a mark on a computer screen which can be moved around and which indicates where anything that is input will appear

COMMENT: Cursors can take several forms, such as a square of bright light, a bright underline or a flashing light.

custodian /kʌˈstəʊdiən/ *noun* an overseer of the contents of a museum, library or other public institution

customer /ˈkʌstəmə/ *noun* a person who buys a product or uses a service

customer account /ˈkʌstəmər ə ˌkaʊnt/ *noun* a system whereby a customer can buy things and pay for them at set times, e.g. a bill for online searches which is paid monthly

customer details /ˌkʌstəmə ˈdiːteɪlz/ *plural noun* a record of the transactions with any one particular customer

customer file /ˈkʌstəmə faɪl/ *noun* details of a customer kept as a record by a company

customise /ˈkʌstəmaɪz/, **customize** *verb* to adapt something to a particular person's requirements

customised interface /ˌkʌstəmaɪzd ˈɪntəfeɪs/ *noun* a computer system that has been adapted to a particular user's needs

cut /kʌt/ *verb* to delete data on a computer, often in order to insert it somewhere else

cut-and-paste /ˌkʌt ən ˈpeɪst/ *noun* a facility of computers allowing data to be deleted in one place and inserted in another

cut flush /ˌkʌt ˈflʌʃ/ *adjective* used to describe a book which has been trimmed so that the cover does not stick out further than the pages

cutout book /ˈkʌtaʊt bʊk/ *noun* a children's book where the illustrations can be cut out to make models or figures

cutting /ˈkʌtɪŋ/ *noun* an item cut from a newspaper or periodical (NOTE: The US equivalent is **clipping**.)

cv *abbreviation* in Internet addresses, the top-level domain for Cape Verde

CV *abbreviation* curriculum vitae

cx *abbreviation* in Internet addresses, the top-level domain for Christmas Island

cy *abbreviation* in Internet addresses, the top-level domain for Cyprus

cybercrime /ˈsaɪbəkraɪm/ *noun* crime carried out on the Internet, e.g. hacking into protected information

cyberlaw /ˈsaɪbələː/ *noun* the body of laws relating to computers, information systems and networks

cybernetics /ˌsaɪbəˈnetɪks/ *noun* the study of how machines can be made to imitate human actions

cyberphobia /ˌsaɪbəˈfəʊbiə/ *noun* a pathological fear of computers and information technology

cyberspace /ˈsaɪbəspeɪs/ *noun* the notional environment in which electronic information exists or is exchanged ○ *We met by writing to each other on the world wide web in cyberspace.*

cybrary /ˈsaɪbrəri/ *noun* **1.** a guide to the information available on the World Wide Web on a particular topic **2.** an information-gathering service using the Internet

cyclopedia /ˌsaɪkləˈpiːdiə/ *noun* PUBL same as **encyclopedia**

D

dagger /'dægə/ *noun* **1.** a second reference mark for footnotes **2.** a mark signifying 'dead' when placed before an English name ► symbol †

daily /'deɪli/ *adjective* happening every day ■ *noun* a newspaper published every weekday

daisy wheel printer /'deɪzi wiːl ˌprɪntə/ *noun* a device for printing work from a computer, which uses a wheel-shaped printing head with the characters at the ends of spokes

damages /'dæmɪdʒɪz/ *plural noun* money that is paid by court order to somebody to compensate for harm done to them or to their reputation

darkroom /'dɑːkruːm/ *noun* a room protected from daylight and using infrared light only, where films can be developed and printed

dash /dæʃ/ *noun* a punctuation mark (-) that is a short horizontal line used to mark off a section of a sentence

data /'deɪtə bæŋk/ *noun* information usually in the form of facts or statistics which can be analysed ○ *The data is easily available.* (NOTE: **Data** is histori-cally a plural noun but is now usually treated as a singular.)

data acquisition /'deɪtə ˌækwɪzɪʃ(ə)n/, **data collection** /'deɪtə kəˌlekʃən/ *noun* the gathering of data about a particular subject

data administration /'deɪtə ədˌmɪnɪstreɪʃ(ə)n/ *noun* same as **data management**

data administrator /'deɪtə ədˌmɪnɪstreɪtə/ *noun* a control section of a database management system

data analysis /'deɪtə əˌnæləsɪs/ *noun* the act of drawing conclusions from data

data bank /'deɪtə bæŋk/ *noun* a large store of information, especially kept in or available to a computer, sometimes consisting of several databases

database /'deɪtəbeɪs/ *noun* **1.** soft-ware which enables the user to organise data for easy retrieval **2.** a collection of data stored in a computer which can be easily and quickly retrieved

database administrator /ˌdeɪtəbeɪs əd'mɪnɪstreɪtə/ *noun* a person who undertakes responsibility for the control of a database

database language /'deɪtəbeɪs ˌlæŋgwɪdʒ/ *noun* any one of a series of languages, e.g. data description language, that makes up a database management system

database management system /ˌdeɪtəbeɪs 'mænɪdʒmənt ˌsɪstəm/ *noun* a series of computer programs which allows the user to create and maintain databases. Abbr **DBMS**

database mapping /'deɪtəbeɪs ˌmæpɪŋ/ *noun* a description of the way in which the records and fields in a data-base are related

database publishing /'deɪtəbeɪs ˌpʌblɪʃɪŋ/ *noun* publishing information selected from a database, either online where the user pays for it on a per-page inspection basis, or as a CD-ROM

database schema /'deɪtəbeɪs ˌskiːmə/ *noun* a way in which a data-base is organised and structured

database server /ˌ(...ₒₒ)/ *noun* a piece of database management software that runs on a server computer on a network and is used in a client-server system

data capture /'deɪtə ˌkæptʃə/ *noun* the act of collecting data and converting it into a form compatible with computers

data compression /'deɪtə kəmˌpreʃ(ə)n/ *noun* a means of reducing the size of blocks of data by removing spaces, empty sections and unused material

data entry /ˌdeɪtə 'entri/ *noun* a method of putting data into a computer

data file /'deɪtə faɪl/ *noun* a computer file storing data rather than program instructions

data handling /'deɪtə ˌhændlɪŋ/ *noun* same as **data preparation**

data management /'deɪtə ˌmænɪdʒmənt/ *noun* the maintenance and updating of a database. Also called **data administration**

data mining /'deɪtə ˌmaɪnɪŋ/ *noun* the process of locating previously unknown patterns and relationships within data using a database application, e.g. finding customers with common interests in a retail establishment's database

data modelling /'deɪtə ˌmɒd(ə)lɪŋ/ *noun* the act of making a graphic representation of interlinked data, so that an efficient database for it can be designed

data network /'deɪtə ˌnetwɜːk/ *noun* a system which allows transmission of data to a number of linked computers

data preparation /'deɪtə ˌprepəreɪʃ(ə)n/ *noun* the conversion of data into a machine-readable format. Also called **data handling**

data processing /'deɪtə ˌprəʊsesɪŋ/ *noun* the process of selecting and examining data in a computer to produce information in a special form. Abbr **DP**

data protection /'deɪtə prəˌtekʃən/ *noun* the procedure of making sure that data is not copied by an unauthorised user

Data Protection Act /ˌdeɪtə prə'tekʃən ˌækt/ *noun* a piece of legislation passed in 1984 in the UK that requires any owner of a database that contains personal details to register

data retrieval /ˌdeɪtə rɪ'triːv(ə)l/ *noun* the process of searching, selecting and reading data from a stored file

data security /'deɪtə sɪˌkjʊərɪti/ *noun* the protection of electronic data so that it cannot be accessed by unauthorised people

'Chubb offers first-party coverage for internal losses caused by a data security breach. For example, if a retailer suffered a breach of its customers' credit card information, Chubb's policy would cover the costs of notifying customers, regaining stolen credit card information and upgrading its system.' [*Business Insurance*]

data services /'deɪtə ˌsɜːvɪsɪz/ *plural noun* public services such as telephones, which allow data to be transmitted

datasheet /'deɪtəʃiːt/ *noun* a document accessible on the Internet that gives a detailed description of something, especially a product

DATASTAR /'deɪtəstɑː/ *noun* a Swiss-based online database host

data storage /'deɪtə ˌstɔːrɪdʒ/ *noun* the ability to store data in the memory of a computer

data warehouse /'deɪtə ˌweəhaʊs/ *noun* a database used for analysing overall business strategy rather than routine operations

date /deɪt/ *verb* to record on a document the date when it is written or received

date label /'deɪt ˌleɪb(ə)l/ *noun* a label pasted in a library book so that the date for return can be stamped on it

date of publication /ˌdeɪt əv ˌpʌblɪ'keɪʃ(ə)n/ *noun* same as **publication date**

datum /'deɪtəm/ *noun* a piece of information (NOTE: **Datum** is the singular of **data**.)

day release /ˌdeɪ rɪ'liːs/ *noun* a system of training by which employees are allowed a regular day each week to attend college

DBMS *abbreviation* database management system

DCMI *abbreviation* Dublin Core Metadata Initiative

DD *abbreviation* double density

DDC *abbreviation* Dewey decimal classification

DDS *abbreviation* Dewey decimal system

de *abbreviation* in Internet addresses, the top-level domain for Germany

deaccession /ˌdiək'seʃ(ə)n/ *verb* to remove a book or work of art from the collection of a library or museum and sell it

deacidify /ˌdiːə'sɪdɪfaɪ/ *verb* to remove the acid from paper. ◇ **CHC paper**

deadline /'dedlaɪn/ *noun* the stated time or date by which work must be finished

Dead White European Male /ˌded waɪt ˌjʊərəpiːən 'meɪl/ *noun* a conventionally important historical figure, especially one of the writers and thinkers whose works have traditionally formed the basis of academic study in Europe and North America. Abbr **DWEM**

debate /dɪ'beɪt/ *noun* a meeting about a question in which at least two opinions are expressed ∎ *verb* to discuss something, considering arguments for and against it

Debrett /də'bret/ *noun* a publication that lists members of the British aristocracy

decade /'dekeɪd/ *noun* a period of ten years, especially one that begins with a year ending in 0

decay /dɪ'keɪ/ *verb* to become old, rotten, weak or corrupt

decentralise /diː'sentrəlaɪz/, **decentralize** *verb* to move departments away from the main administrative area and give more power to local branches

decimal /'desɪm(ə)l/ *adjective* counting in base ten

decimal classification system /ˌdesɪm(ə)l ˌklæsɪfɪ'keɪʃ(ə)n ˌsɪstəm/ *noun* a system of organising items using a numerical order in base ten

decimal point /ˌdesɪm(ə)l 'pɔɪnt/ *noun* a dot or comma which separates whole numbers from decimal fractions, e.g. in 2.75

COMMENT: The dot should be raised above the line, though it is never printed in this way by computer printers. Note that the decimal point is used in English-speaking countries, and that in most other countries the decimal is indicated by a comma.

decipher /dɪ'saɪfə/ *verb* to work out what something means, even if it is difficult to read or understand

decision support system /dɪ 'sɪʒ(ə)n səˌpɔːt ˌsɪstəm/ *noun* a suite of programs that helps a manager reach decisions using previous decisions, information, and other databases

declarative knowledge /dɪ ˌklærətɪv 'nɒlɪdʒ/ *noun* same as **propositional knowledge**

declarative memory /dɪˌklærətɪv 'mem(ə)ri/ *noun* human memory of learned facts and events. Compare **procedural memory**

declassify /diː'klæsɪfaɪ/ *verb* to state that information or documents no longer have security classification and are not secret

decode /diː'kəʊd/ *verb* to change information which has been written in code into ordinary language

decrease *noun* /'diːkriːs/ a reduction in the size or quantity of something ∎ *verb* /dɪ'kriːs/ to make something smaller

dedicate /'dedɪkeɪt/ *verb* to print a special note in a book offering it to somebody, usually a relative or friend, as a token of affection ○ *He dedicated the book of poetry to his wife and daughters.*

dedicated /'dedɪkeɪtɪd/ *adjective* reserved for a particular use

dedicated channel /ˌdedɪkeɪtɪd 'tʃæn(ə)l/ *noun* a communications channel reserved for a particular use or user

dedicated line /ˌdedɪkeɪtɪd 'laɪn/ *noun* a telephone line assigned to a designated user, usually to provide a permanent connection to the Internet

dedicated word processor
/ˌdedɪkeɪtɪd ˈwɜːd ˌprəʊsesə/ *noun* a
small computer which has been config-
ured to do only word processing

dedication /ˌdedɪˈkeɪʃ(ə)n/ *noun*
words used to offer a book, work or
performance to honour somebody

deduct /dɪˈdʌkt/ *verb* to remove
something from a total

deduction /dɪˈdʌkʃən/ *noun* an
amount removed from a total sum

deep Web /ˌdiːp ˈweb/ *noun* search-
able databases accessible through the
Internet, which must be searched using
CQL queries and not with an ordinary
Web search engine. Also called **hidden
Web**, **invisible Web**. Compare **surface
Web**

de facto /ˌdeɪ ˈfæktəʊ/ *adjective*
accepted as fact by reason of usage ○ *He
was the de facto ruler although he had
no legal right to the position.*

default /dɪˈfɔːlt/ *noun* failure to carry
out a contract ■ *verb* to fail to carry out
the terms of a contract, especially to fail
to pay back a debt ○ *The company is in
default on their repayments.*

default setting /dɪˈfɔːlt ˌsetɪŋ/ *noun*
the setting that a computer or printer
will use if no other instructions are
given

defect /ˈdiːfekt/ *noun* a fault in a
machine

defective /dɪˈfektɪv/ *adjective* not
working properly

define /dɪˈfaɪn/ *verb* to explain the
meaning of something

definition /ˌdefɪˈnɪʃ(ə)n/ *noun* a
statement of meaning, especially in a
dictionary

degree /dɪˈgriː/ *noun* a qualification
awarded by a university or college
following successful completion of a
course of study or period of research, or
a similar qualification granted as an
honour

degree of automation /dɪˌgriː əv
ˌɔːtəˈmeɪʃ(ə)n/ *noun* the level of use of
electronic machines

'In order to optimise our business and
improve our bottom line, we need to
automate the flows of information as
much as possible. Data integration

processes are key to this high degree
of automation, the combined increases
in availability and quality of data they
provide translate into an immediate
increase in operational efficiency.'
[*M2 Presswire*]

de jure /ˌdeɪ ˈdʒʊəri/ *adjective* by
legal right, though not necessarily in
fact

delay /dɪˈleɪ/ *noun* a cause of something happening later than planned ■
verb to cause something to happen later
than planned

delegate *noun* /ˈdelɪgət/ a person
elected to speak for or represent others
■ *verb* /ˈdeləgeɪt/ to give some of one's
responsibility to others for a period of
time

delegation /ˌdelɪˈgeɪʃ(ə)n/ *noun* the
act of delegating

delete /dɪˈliːt/ *verb* to remove information that has been written down or
stored in a computer ■ *noun* an instruction given to a computer to remove a
section of text

delete character /dɪˌliːt ˈkærɪktə/
noun a special code used to indicate
data or text to be removed

delete key /dɪˈliːt kiː/ *noun* a
computer key that moves the cursor to
erase characters, or removes highlighted text

Delphes /delf/ *noun* a French network
of economic and business information
produced by the French Chambers of
Commerce

DELPHI /ˈdelfi/ *noun* a commercial
online information service

de luxe edition /ˌdɪ ˈlʌks ɪˌdɪʃ(ə)n/
noun a special edition of a book, printed
on very good quality paper and with an
expensive binding, selling for a higher
price than a standard edition

demand /dɪˈmɑːnd/ *noun* the number
of people wanting to buy something ○
There is not much demand for this item.
■ *verb* to ask for something in a forceful
way

demand forecasting /dɪˈmɑːnd
ˌfɔːkɑːstɪŋ/ *noun* a prediction of the
number of items which will be sold or
used

demarcation /ˌdiːmɑːˈkeɪʃ(ə)n/ *noun* a boundary or limit separating ideas or groups

demography /dɪˈmɒgrəfi/ *noun* the study of changes in population

Demon Internet Systems /ˌdiːmən ˈɪntənet ˌsɪstəmz/ *noun* a UK provider of gateways to the Internet

demonstrate /ˈdemənstreɪt/ *verb* **1.** to show people how to do something **2.** to make an idea clear to people **3.** to show that you have a skill or quality

demy octavo /ˌdemi ɒkˈtɑːvəʊ/ *noun* a book format, formerly 8 3/4 x 5 inches, now 216 x 138mm

demy quarto /ˌdemi ˈkwɔːtəʊ/ *noun* a book format, formerly 11 1/4 x 8 3/4 inches, now 279 x 219mm

density /ˈdensɪti/ *noun* the level of darkness of an image

COMMENT: Scanner software produces various shades of grey by using different densities or arrangements of black and white dots and/or different sized dots.

deny access /dɪˌnaɪ ˈækses/ *verb* **1.** to refuse permission to enter **2.** to refuse permission to use an information system

departmental information system /ˌdɪpɑːtment(ə)l ˌɪnfəˈmeɪʃ(ə)n ˌsɪstəm/ *noun* a system of organising information specific to one department

dependency level /dɪˈpendənsi ˌlev(ə)l/ *noun* a degree to which somebody is dependent on another person or a system

dependent on /dɪˈpendənt ɒn/ *adjective* needing something in order to survive or function

deploy /dɪˈplɔɪ/ *verb* to place people or resources where they will be most useful

deposit /dɪˈpɒzɪt/ *noun* **1.** an amount of money paid in part payment **2.** an amount of money that a person gives when they borrow something and which is returned to them when the item is returned undamaged **3.** documents placed in a record office for safe keeping **4.** a legal requirement for one copy of any published book to be sent to a national deposit library ■ *verb* to give a copy of a book to a deposit library as

part of the process of publishing the book

deposit library /dɪˈpɒzɪt ˌlaɪbrəri/ *noun* a national library to which a publisher has by law to give a copy of each book published

COMMENT: In the British Isles, the deposit libraries are the British Library, the Bodleian Library at Oxford, Cambridge University Library, the National Library of Scotland and the Library of Trinity College Dublin; the Welsh National Library may also receive copies.

depth indexing /ˈdepθ ˌɪndeksɪŋ/ *noun* the indexing of different subjects within the body of a document

deputation /ˌdepjʊˈteɪʃ(ə)n/ *noun* a group of people who act as representatives of a larger group

descending order /dɪˌsendɪŋ ˈɔːdə/ *noun* a method of organising things so that each item is smaller than the one before it or comes before it in an established order ○ *They were arranged in descending order from Z to A.*

descriptive list /dɪˈskrɪptɪv lɪst/ *noun* a list of holdings with a brief description of their contents to enable users to decide which they want

descriptor /dɪˈskrɪptə/ *noun* a code or symbol given to a document to identify it for the purposes of retrieval

desiderata /dɪˌzɪdəˈrɑːtə/ *plural noun* a list of books and documents required

design /dɪˈzaɪn/ *verb* to plan what something new will be like

desk /desk/ *noun* a writing table in an office or study

desk accessory /ˈdesk əkˌsesəri/ *noun* a device for use on a desk, e.g. a light or a desktop computer

desk diary /ˈdesk ˌdaɪəri/ *noun* a book with blank pages organised by dates, which can be kept on a desk, to record appointments and commitments

desktop /ˈdesktɒp/ *noun* a display on a computer screen comprising background and icons representing equipment, programs and files

desktop computer /ˌdesktɒp kəmˈpjuːtə/ *noun* a computer, usually with a keyboard and monitor, which is small enough to be used on a desk

desktop PC /ˌdesktɒp piː ˈsiː/ *noun* an IBM-compatible computer which can be placed on a user's desk, comprising a system unit with main electronics, disk drive and controllers, and a separate monitor and keyboard

desktop publishing /ˌdesktɒp ˈpʌblɪʃɪŋ/ *noun* the design and layout of text and graphics using a small computer with a specific software application package and a printer. Abbr **DTP**

desktop unit /ˌdesktɒp ˈjuːnɪt/ *noun* a computer or machine that will fit onto a desk

destination /ˌdestɪˈneɪʃ(ə)n/ *noun* **1.** the place where something is sent **2.** the location where data is sent on a network

detail /ˈdiːteɪl/ *noun* a small condition or fact ■ *verb* to list or give full information about things

detailed enquiry /ˌdiːteɪld ɪn ˈkwaɪri/ *noun* an investigation which lists all the small features of an event or situation

developed country /dɪˌveləpt ˈkʌntri/ *noun* a rich industrialised country

developing country /dɪˌveləpɪŋ ˈkʌntri/ *noun* a country where industry is not yet well developed but which is moving towards it

developing market /dɪˌveləpɪŋ ˈmɑːkɪt/ *noun* an area where the sale of goods or services is increasing

development strategy /dɪ ˈveləpmənt ˌstrætədʒi/ *noun* policies and methods for future development

devise /dɪˈvaɪz/ *verb* to design or work out a plan or system

Dewey decimal classification /ˌdjuːi ˈdesɪm(ə)l ˌsɪstəm/, **Dewey decimal system** *noun* a system of classifying library books that divides them into ten main classes, divided in turn into categories with three-digit numbers and subcategories with numbers after a decimal point. Abbr **DDC**, **DDS**

DfES *abbreviation* Department for Education and Skills

diacritical marks, **diacritics**, **diacriticals** *plural noun* marks made above normal letters to show a change of pronunciation or stress

COMMENT: The commonest diacritics are the accents in European languages and the dots indicating vowels in Arabic.

diaeresis, **dieresis** *noun* a printed sign, formed of two dots printed above a vowel (ë)

COMMENT: In English the diaeresis is now uncommon, but was used in words such as 'naïve' and 'coördinate' to show that the two vowels were pronounced separately and not as a diphthong; it is still used in many European languages and indicates a change in pronunciation of a vowel. In German it is called the umlaut.

diagnose /ˈdaɪəgnəʊz/ *verb* to identify what is wrong

diagnosis /ˌdaɪəgˈnəʊsɪs/ *noun* the act of identifying the reason for a fault or problem

diagonal /daɪˈægən(ə)l/ *noun* a slanting line from a top corner to the opposite bottom corner

diagram /ˈdaɪəgræm/ *noun* a chart or graph that illustrates something such as a statistical trend ■ *verb* to make a diagram that represents or illustrates something

dial /ˈdaɪəl/ *verb* to use a series of numbers to make a telephone connection

dialling code /ˈdaɪəlɪŋ kəʊd/ *noun* numbers used in the telephone system to identify towns, countries or individual phone lines and so enable connection by phone or fax

dialling tone /ˈdaɪəlɪŋ təʊn/ *noun* a sound made by a telephone line when it is available for use

DIALOG /ˈdaɪəlɒg/ *noun* an online database host

dialogue /ˈdaɪəlɒg/ *noun* **1.** a written conversation in a book or play **2.** the exchange of ideas or opinions, especially between those with different viewpoints

dialogue box /ˈdaɪəlɒg bɒks/ *noun* a small rectangular window displayed on a computer screen that conveys information to, or requires a response from, the user

dial-up /ˈdaɪəl ʌp/ *adjective* requiring a computer modem and telephone line to establish communication with another computer or a network

DIANE /daɪˈæn/ ♦ **Euronet/Diane**

diary /ˈdaɪəri/ *noun* **1.** a detailed daily record of the events in a person's life written in a book **2.** a small book with dates and blank spaces used to record appointments

dictate /dɪkˈteɪt/ *verb* to speak words for somebody to write down or for a machine to record

dictating machine /dɪkˈteɪtɪŋ mə ˌʃiːn/ *noun* a recording machine which records what someone says so that it can be typed later

dictionary /ˈdɪkʃən(ə)ri/ *noun* a book or compact disc containing the words of a language arranged alphabetically with their meanings

COMMENT: The term 'dictionary' really applies to a book where the words are defined, but not necessarily explained; an 'encyclopaedia' is a book where the words are explained, but not always defined. A 'Dictionary of Gardening' is probably in fact an encyclopaedia, since it may give details of how to grow plants, rather than defining what each plant or process is. This present dictionary has many encyclopaedic sections, such as this one.

dictionary catalogue /ˈdɪkʃən(ə)ri ˌkætəlɒg/ *noun* a catalogue in which all the entries such as author, title and subject are placed in one alphabetical sequence

Dictionary of National Biography /ˌdɪkʃən(ə)ri əv ˌnæʃ(ə)nəl baɪˈɒgrəfi/ *noun* an alphabetical listing of famous people within a country, with brief biographical details. Abbr **DNB**

didactic /daɪˈdæktɪk/ *adjective* relating to speech or writing that is intended to teach, especially on moral issues

didactics /daɪˈdæktɪks/ *noun* the science or profession of teaching

differ /ˈdɪfə/ *verb* to be unlike something else in some way

differential /ˌdɪfəˈrenʃəl/ *noun* the difference between two values in a scale

digest /ˈdaɪdʒest/ *noun* a book which summarises a series of reports, especially one that collects summaries of court decisions and is used as a reference tool by lawyers

digipad /ˈdɪdʒipæd/ *noun* same as **digitising pad**

digit /ˈdɪdʒɪt/ *noun* any of the numbers from 0 to 9

digital /ˈdɪdʒɪt(ə)l/ *adjective* representing physical quantities in numerical form

digital computer /ˌdɪdʒɪt(ə)l kəmˈpjuːtə/ *noun* a computer that calculates on the basis of binary numbers

digital data network /ˌdɪdʒɪt(ə)l ˈdeɪtə ˌnetwɜːk/ *noun* a network designed specifically for the transmission of digital data as distinct from networks such as the telephone system which are analogue

digital divide /ˌdɪdʒɪt(ə)l dɪˈvaɪd/ *noun* the difference in opportunities available to people who have access to modern information technology and those who do not

digital font /ˌdɪdʒɪt(ə)l ˈfɒnt/ *noun* a font that has been digitised so that it can be stored in a computer

digital image processing /ˌdɪdʒɪt(ə)l ˈɪmɪdʒ ˌprəʊsesɪŋ/ *noun* a wide range of techniques used to generate, process and reproduce images by digital computers

digital learning /ˌdɪdʒɪt(ə)l ˈlɜːnɪŋ/ *noun* education using electronic tools, e.g. interactive software

digital library /ˌdɪdʒɪt(ə)l ˈlaɪbrəri/ *noun* a store of digital reference materials, e.g. electronic journals and database-based information

'Researchers can perform their research without regard to physical location, interacting with colleagues, accessing instrumentation, sharing data and computational resources, and accessing information and data in digital libraries and repositories.' [*States News Service*]

digital nervous system /ˌdɪdʒɪt(ə)l ˈnɜːvəs ˌsɪstəm/ *noun* a digital information system that gathers, manages and distributes knowledge in a way that allows an organisation to respond quickly and effectively to events in the outside world

digital object identifier /ˌdɪdʒɪt(ə)l ˌɒbjekt aɪˈdentɪfaɪə/ *noun* an identifying symbol for a web file that redirects users to any new Internet location for that file. Abbr **DOI**

digital preservation /ˌdɪdʒɪt(ə)l ˌpresəˈveɪʃ(ə)n/ *noun* the act of preserving data by putting it into electronic form, which can be copied, stored and distributed easily and without loss of quality

digital proofs /ˌdɪdʒɪt(ə)l ˈpruːfs/ *plural noun* proofs taken from digital files prior to film output at high or low resolution

digital reference services /ˌdɪdʒɪt(ə)l ˈref(ə)rəns ˌsɜːvɪsɪz/ *plural noun* searchable information in electronic form, provided by a library or other service

digital scanning /ˌdɪdʒɪt(ə)l ˈskænɪŋ/ *noun* the reading of an image such as a printed character by a computer, done by building it up as a series of dots in the computer memory

digital video disc /ˌdɪdʒɪt(ə)l ˈvɪdiəʊ ˌdɪsk/ *noun* full form of **DVD**

digitisable /ˈdɪdʒɪtɪzəb(ə)l/ *adjective* able to be converted into digital form for distribution via the Internet or other networks

digitise /ˈdɪdʒɪtaɪz/, **digitize** *verb* to change analogue signals such as pictures or sound into numerical data which can be processed by a computer

digitised letterforms /ˌdɪdʒɪtaɪzd ˈletəfɔːmz/ *plural noun* the shapes of characters which have been scanned and then stored as a series of dots in the computer memory

digitised photograph /ˌdɪdʒɪtaɪzd ˈfəʊtəgrɑːf/ *noun* an image or photograph that has been scanned to produce an analogue signal which is then converted to digital form and stored in a computer or displayed on a screen

digitising pad /ˈdɪdʒɪtaɪzɪŋ pæd/ *noun* a sensitive surface that translates the position of a pen into numerical form, so that drawings can be entered into a computer. Also called **digipad**

digizine /ˈdɪdʒiːn/ *noun* a magazine that is delivered in digital form either on the Internet or on a CD-ROM

dime novel /ˈdaɪm ˌnɒv(ə)l/ *noun* a cheap paperback novel

diploma /dɪˈpləʊmə/ *noun* an official statement that somebody has successfully completed a course or passed an examination

diplomacy /dɪˈpləʊməsi/ *noun* **1.** management of relations between countries **2.** tact in dealings with people ○ *Librarians sometimes need to use diplomacy when dealing with library users.*

direct access /daɪˌrekt ˈækses/ *noun* the ability to use information without the need for an intermediary person

direct connection /daɪˌrekt kəˈnekʃən/ *noun* a fast permanent connection linking a computer or system to a network such as the Internet. It can be used at any time and is much faster than a dial-up connection.

direct entry /daɪˌrekt ˈentri/ *noun* an index entry in which a multi-word subject uses the usual word order instead of an inverted word sequence

direct mail /daɪˌrekt ˈmeɪl/ *noun* a system of selling goods by sending publicity material about them through the post

director /daɪˈrektə/ *noun* **1.** the top person in the management of a group, company or organisation **2.** a person who directs a play or film

directorate /daɪˈrekt(ə)rət/ *noun* the board of directors of a company

directory /daɪˈrekt(ə)ri/ *noun* a book or database which lists the names and details of people or companies in a specific geographical or subject area

disadvantage /ˌdɪsədˈvɑːntɪdʒ/ *noun* a factor in a situation which causes problems

disapplication /ˌdɪsæplɪˈkeɪʃ(ə)n/ *noun* a special exemption from the National Curriculum given to a school

disaster plan /dɪˈzɑːstə plæn/ *noun* a plan for what to do if a disaster occurs

discharge /dɪsˈtʃɑːdʒ/ *verb* to cancel the record of a loan from a library when the book or other item is returned

discipline /'dɪsɪplɪn/ *noun* a field of academic study

discount /'dɪskaʊnt/ *noun* a reduction in the price of something

discovery /dɪ'skʌv(ə)ri/ *noun* the act of finding out something that nobody knew about previously

discretion /dɪ'skreʃ(ə)n/ *noun* the ability to deal with confidential situations or information without causing embarrassment ○ *I leave the matter to your discretion.* □ **at someone's discretion** when something is done because of somebody's decision and not according to a fixed rule

discretionary income /dɪˌskreʃ(ə)n(ə)ri 'ɪnkʌm/ *noun* money which is allocated to a person or a department according to the decisions of people in authority and not according to fixed rules

disinformation /ˌdɪsɪnfə'meɪʃ(ə)n/ *noun* false or deliberately misleading information, often put out as propaganda

disingenuous /ˌdɪsɪn'dʒenjuəs/ *adjective* withholding or not taking account of known information

disk /dɪsk/ *noun* a flat, round plastic device coated with magnetised material which can be used to store information readable by a computer. Also called **disc**

disk drive /'dɪsk draɪv/ *noun* a slot in which to place a floppy disk so that a computer can read the data on it

diskette /dɪ'sket/ *noun* a small portable lightweight disk which can be used in personal computers

Disk Operating System /ˌdɪsk 'ɒpəreɪtɪŋ ˌsɪstəm/ *noun* the section of the operating system in a computer that controls the disk and file management. Abbr **DOS**

disk reader /'dɪsk ˌriːdə/ *noun* a device which will read the contents of a disk into a main computer system

display /dɪ'spleɪ/ *noun* an exhibition for public viewing ■ *verb* to set up or arrange to be viewed

display case /dɪ'spleɪ keɪs/ *noun* a glass box which protects items but allows them to be seen

displayed text /dɪˌspleɪd 'tekst/ *noun* text that is laid out by indenting or being placed in a box, so as to make it different from the rest of the text

display material /dɪ'spleɪ məˌtɪəriəl/ *noun* items that can be used for an exhibition

display space /dɪ'spleɪ speɪs/ *noun* the available memory or amount of screen for showing graphics or text

display stand /dɪ'spleɪ stænd/ *noun* a portable board which can be set on legs and used to display information

display unit /dɪ'spleɪ ˌjuːnɪt/ *noun* a computer terminal or piece of equipment that is capable of showing data or information, usually by means of a CRT

disposal list /dɪs'pəʊzəl lɪst/ *noun* instructions for the disposal of documents by destruction or temporary or permanent preservation

dispose of /dɪs'pəʊz ɒv/ *verb* to throw away or destroy

disseminate /dɪ'semɪneɪt/ *verb* to spread news and information widely

dissemination /dɪˌsemɪ'neɪʃ(ə)n/ *noun* the act of distributing something such as information throughout an area

dissertation /ˌdɪsə'teɪʃ(ə)n/ *noun* a written account of research

distance learning /'dɪstəns ˌlɜːnɪŋ/ *noun* courses which can be studied at home and sent to a tutor by mail or e-mail

distort /dɪ'stɔːt/ *verb* to give a false or dishonest account of something

distributed library /dɪˌstrɪbjʊtɪd 'laɪbrəri/ *noun* **1.** a collection of resources that come from different places but can be accessed from a single point, e.g. in electronic form **2.** resources which are the private collections of people working in a particular field, and which can be shared with others, e.g. by post

'The patent defines a comprehensive software application that provides a secure, high performance distributed library for cataloguing, distributing, tracking, reporting and managing intellectual property.' [*BusinessWire*]

distribution /ˌdɪstrɪˈbjuːʃ(ə)n/ *noun* the delivery of goods or information to people or organisations

distribution channel /ˌdɪstrɪˈbjuːʃ(ə)n ˌtʃæn(ə)l/ *noun* the method by which things are sent to other people, e.g. e-mail, post or retail shops

distribution list /ˌdɪstrɪˈbjuːʃ(ə)n lɪst/ *noun* a list of people to whom copies of a document should be sent

diversity /daɪˈvɜːsɪti/ *noun* the range of variation within a group of people or situations

divinity calf /dɪˈvɪnɪti kɑːf/ *noun* a type of binding used for religious books, made of dark brown calf leather

division /dɪˈvɪʒ(ə)n/ *noun* a department in a large organisation

dj *abbreviation* in Internet addresses, the top-level domain for Djibouti

dk *abbreviation* in Internet addresses, the top-level domain for Denmark

dm *abbreviation* in Internet addresses, the top-level domain for Dominica

DNB *abbreviation* Dictionary of National Biography

DNS *abbreviation* COMPUT domain name service

do *abbreviation* in Internet addresses, the top-level domain for Dominican Republic

Doctor of Philosophy /ˌdɒktə əv fɪˈlɒsəfi/ *noun* the highest level of university degree, awarded to somebody who has successfully completed a lengthy piece of original research. Abbr **PhD**

document /ˈdɒkjʊmənt/ *noun* any form of information in printed or electronic form, e.g. maps, manuscripts or computer software

document address class /ˌdɒkjʊmənt əˈdres ˌklɑːs/ *noun* a number or symbol indicating the location of a document in store

documentalist /ˌdɒkjʊˈmentəlɪst/ *noun* a specialist in documentation

documentary /ˌdɒkjʊˈment(ə)ri/ *noun* a film relating true facts rather than telling a story ■ *adjective* based on written evidence in documents

documentation /ˌdɒkjʊmenˈteɪʃ(ə)n/ *noun* documents provided or collected together as evidence or as reference material

documentation centre /ˌdɒkjʊmenˈteɪʃ(ə)n ˌsentə/ *noun* an information source such as a website which pulls together documents and official publications into a central database which can then be accessed by the public

document control /ˈdɒkjʊmənt kənˌtrəʊl/ *noun* the way in which documents are organised to provide easy retrieval

document delivery /ˈdɒkjʊmənt dɪˌlɪv(ə)ri/ *noun* a service that provides specialised archived documents in electronic form to customers for a fee

document management /ˈdɒkjʊmənt ˌmænɪdʒmənt/ *noun* the storage and retrieval of documents in paper or electronic format

'We have also invested heavily in educating African companies about the benefits of document management systems, and how traditional paper-based processes for dealing with incoming and outgoing business documents no longer make good business sense.' [*M2 Presswire*]

document paper /ˈdɒkjʊmənt ˌpeɪpə/ *noun* special-sized paper used for legal and other documents, which is suitable for writing on

document reader /ˈdɒkjʊmənt ˌriːdə/ *noun* a mechanism for reading text into a computer

document retrieval system /ˌdɒkjʊmənt rɪˈtriːv(ə)l ˌsɪstəm/ *noun* a system which produces a complete copy of a document rather than a citation or reference

document supply centre /ˌdɒkjʊmənt səˈplaɪ ˌsentə/ *noun* a division of a lending library, which supplies copies of documents often through an inter-library loan system

dog-eared /ˈdɒg ɪəd/ *adjective* used to describe a book whose corners are bent and worn

DOI *abbreviation* digital object identifier

do-it-yourself handbook /ˌduː ɪt jəˈself ˌhændbʊk/, **do-it-yourself manual** /ˌduː ɪt jəˈself ˌmænjuəl/

noun a handbook showing how to do repairs or construction work around the house (NOTE: US English is **how-to book**.)

dollar sign /'dɒlə saɪn/ *noun* a printed or written character ($) used in some computer languages to identify a variable as a string type

domain /dəʊ'meɪn/ *noun* the part of an e-mail address after the @ sign

domain name /dəʊ'meɪn neɪm/ *noun* the sequence of words, phrases, abbreviations or characters that serves as the Internet address of a computer or network

domain name service /dəʊ'meɪn neɪm/ *noun* an Internet service which translates domain names into IP addresses. Abbr **DNS**

donation /dəʊ'neɪʃ(ə)n/ *noun* a gift of something, especially for a good cause

DOS /dɒs/ *abbreviation* Disk Operating System

dossier /'dɒsieɪ/ *noun* a collection of documents relating to a person or topic

dot /dɒt/ *noun* a punctuation mark (.) used to separate the various components of an Internet address

dot address /'dɒt ə,dres/ *noun* the common notation for Internet addresses in the form A.B.C.D., each letter representing, in decimal notation, one byte of a four-byte address. Also called **dotted quad**, **dotted decimal notation**, **dotted quad address**

dot matrix printer /,dɒt 'meɪtrɪks ,prɪntə/ *noun* a printer which uses a series of closely spaced dots and prints out line by line

double-check /,dʌb(ə)l 'tʃek/ *verb* to check something a second time to be sure of its accuracy

double dagger /,dʌb(ə)l 'dægə/ *noun* a third reference mark for footnotes

double density /,dʌb(ə)l 'densəti/ *noun* a system to double the storage capacity of a disk drive by doubling the number of bits which can be put on the disk surface. Abbr **DD**

double density disk /,dʌb(ə)l ,densɪti 'dɪsk/ *noun* a disk that can store two bits of data per unit area compared to a standard disk

double elephant /,dʌb(ə)l 'elɪfənt/ *noun* **1.** a large size of drawing paper (40 x 27 inches) **2.** *US* a book size up to 50 inches high

double-page spread /,dʌb(ə)l peɪdʒ 'spred/ *noun* a feature or article that fills two facing pages of a newspaper or magazine

double-sided /,dʌb(ə)l 'saɪdɪd/ *adjective* can be used on both sides

double-sided disk /,dʌb(ə)l ,saɪdɪd 'dɪsk/ *noun* a computer disk which has been sensitised on both sides, and can store twice the amount of data of an ordinary disk

double spread /,dʌb(ə)l 'spred/ *noun* PUBL same as **double-page spread**

doublure /dʌb'ljʊə/ *noun* a lining, especially one made of leather or highly decorated, inside the cover of a book

down /daʊn/ *adjective* used to indicate that a computer is out of action

down cursor key /'daʊn ,kɜːsə ,kiː/ *noun* one of the four direction keys on a computer keyboard

download /,daʊn'ləʊd/ *verb* to move information from one electronic source to another storage device ○ *He downloaded the records from the main database to his own personal database.*

downloadable fonts /,daʊnləʊdəb(ə)l 'fɒnts/ *plural noun* fonts or typefaces stored on a disk, which can be downloaded or sent to a printer and stored in temporary memory or RAM

downtime /'daʊntaɪm/ *noun* the time during which a computer is unusable

DP *abbreviation* data processing

draft /drɑːft/ *noun* **1.** a rough form of something written, drawn or planned ○ *The editor has seen the first draft of her new novel.* **2.** a written order for money to be transferred from one bank to another

draft copy /'drɑːft ,kɒpi/ *noun* the first copy of a book or document which will be changed before it becomes the final version

drawback /'drɔːbæk/ *noun* an aspect of something which is a problem and makes it less acceptable

drawing pin /'drɔːɪŋ pɪn/ *noun* a pin with a flat head used for attaching notices to a board

draw up /ˌdrɔː 'ʌp/ *verb* to prepare and write out a document

dredge up /ˌdredʒ 'ʌp/ *verb* to bring something to light from an obscure source, e.g. to recall something bad that happened long ago or unearth some scandalous information

drill down /ˌdrɪl 'daʊn/ *verb* to access data or information organised in hierarchical form by starting from general information and moving through increasingly detailed data

drilldown /'drɪldaʊn/ *noun* an act of accessing data or information organised in hierarchical form

drilled and strung /ˌdrɪld ən 'strʌŋ/ *adjective* bound by making holes through each leaf or signature, and then attaching them together with a thread

drop-down menu /ˌdrɒp daʊn 'menjuː/ *noun* a vertical list of options that appears on clicking on an item on a computer screen. It remains visible until one of the options has been selected by clicking on it.

DTP *abbreviation* desktop publishing

Dublin Core Metadata Initiative /ˌdʌblɪn kɔː 'metədeɪtə ɪˌnɪʃətɪv/ *noun* an organisation which promotes the standardisation of metadata used in information retrieval. Abbr **DCMI**

due /djuː/ *adjective* **1.** expected to arrive or happen at a particular time □ **due to** because of **2.** referring to the date when books are expected to be returned to a library

due date /'djuː deɪt/ *noun* the date by which something on loan should be returned

dues /djuːz/ *plural noun* **1.** money that is paid regularly to an organisation to which you belong **2.** books for which orders have been taken, but which cannot be supplied until fresh stock arrives. This is because they are either subscription orders recorded for a new title or orders for a backlist title which is being reprinted.

dummy run /'dʌmi rʌn/ *noun* a trial or test procedure to see if something works properly

duodecimo /ˌdjuəʊ'dekɪməʊ/ *noun* PRINTING same as **twelvemo**

duplexing /'djuːpleksɪŋ/ *noun* sending information in two directions simultaneously

duplicate *noun* /'djuːplɪkət/ an extra copy of a book or document already in stock ▪ *verb* /'djuːplɪkeɪt/ to make an exact copy of something

duplicate entry /ˌdjuːplɪkət 'entri/ *noun* an index entry of the same subject matter under two headings

duplicate title /ˌdjuːplɪkət 'taɪt(ə)l/ *noun* a reprint which contains a copy of the original title page as well as its own

duplicating paper /'djuːplɪkeɪtɪŋ ˌpeɪpə/ *noun* special quality paper used for photocopying

dust jacket /'dʌst ˌdʒækɪt/, **dust cover** /'dʌst ˌkʌvə/ *noun* a paper book cover, often illustrated, which protects the hard binding of the book and can be removed

DVD /ˌdiː viː 'diː/ *noun* an optical compact disc that can store a large quantity of video, audio or other information. Full form **digital video disc**

DVD-ROM /ˌdiː viː 'diː ˌrɒm/ *noun* a high-capacity optical disc on which data can be stored but not altered. Full form **digital video disc read only memory**

Dvorak keyboard /'dvɔːræk ˌkiːbɔːd/ *noun* a keyboard with frequently used keys placed near the centre for quicker typing

DWEM *abbreviation* Dead White European Male

dz *abbreviation* in Internet addresses, the top-level domain for Algeria

E

earmark /ˈɪəmɑːk/ *verb* to put on one side for a particular purpose

e-book /ˈiː bʊk/ *noun* a battery-powered portable reading device displaying text on a high-resolution screen. Also called **electronic book**

'Almost every IT expert in the world is agreed that the book faces a revolutionary challenge from e-books and e-paper. Carr says: "In the next five to 10 years, maybe much sooner, we'll see a decent, ultra-lightweight, portable e-paper device that allows book lovers to download titles straight from the internet".' [*The Observer*]

ecclesiastical library /ɪˌkliːzɪ ˈæstɪk(ə)l ˌlaɪbrəi/ *noun* a library made up predominantly of religious writings, especially used as research centre for the study of theology

ECDL *abbreviation* European Computer Driving Licence

ECM *abbreviation* enterprise content management

e-collaboration /ˈiː kə ˌlæbəreɪʃ(ə)n/ *noun* collaboration among people or organisations made possible by means of electronic technologies such as the Internet, video conferencing and wireless devices

economic plan /ˌiːkənɒmɪk ˈplæn/ *noun* a policy for economic development in a country

economies of scale /ɪˌkɒnəmiz əv ˈskeɪl/ *noun* achieving savings by producing very large quantities

e-copy /ˈiː ˌkɒpi/ *noun* an electronic copy of a document, especially an e-mail text that has a primary destination as an electronic message and a secondary destination as a printed copy

ed. *abbreviation* PUBL edition

EDI *abbreviation* electronic data interchange

edifying /ˈedɪfaɪŋ/ *adjective* providing morally useful knowledge or information

edit /ˈedɪt/ *verb* **1.** to change, correct or modify text or films **2.** to prepare a document for publication

edit. *abbreviation* PUBL edition

edited /ˈedɪtɪd/ *adjective* relating to work consisting of one or several separate items prepared for publication by somebody other than the author

editing run /ˈedɪtɪŋ rʌn/ *noun* processing carried out to check that new data meets certain requirements before actually analysing the data and its information content

editing terminal /ˈedɪtɪŋ ˌtɜːmɪn(ə)l/ *noun* a computer terminal on which text is shown which can be edited

edition /ɪˈdɪʃ(ə)n/ *noun* a particular version of a book, magazine, newspaper or TV or radio programme which is printed or broadcast at one time

editio princeps /ɪˌdɪtiəʊ ˈprɪnseps/ *noun* the first printed edition of a piece of writing

editor /ˈedɪtə/ *noun* **1.** a person who changes or corrects text or films **2.** a person in charge of publishing a newspaper or magazine who makes the final decisions about the contents and format

editorial /ˌedɪˈtɔːriəl/ *noun* the main article in a newspaper, written by the editor

editorial board /ˌedɪˌtɔːriəl 'bɔːd/ noun a group of people with the power to make decisions about the contents of documents

EDP abbreviation electronic data processing

edu abbreviation US educational organization

educate /'edjʊkeɪt/ verb to give knowledge to or develop the abilities of somebody by teaching

educated /'edjʊkeɪtɪd/ adjective having the benefit of experience or knowledge

education /ˌedjʊ'keɪʃ(ə)n/ noun **1.** the imparting and acquiring of knowledge through teaching and learning, especially at a school or similar institution **2.** the knowledge or abilities gained through being educated **3.** training and instruction in a particular subject, e.g. health matters **4.** the study of the theories and practices of teaching **5.** the system of educating people in a community or society

educational /ˌedjʊ'keɪʃ(ə)nəl/ adjective **1.** giving knowledge, instruction or information **2.** relating to or concerned with education

educational animation /ˌedjʊkeɪʃ(ə)nəl ˌænɪ'meɪʃ(ə)n/ noun animation that is specifically designed to aid learning

educational discount /ˌedjuː 'keɪʃn(ə)l ˌdɪskaʊnt/ noun the amount of money taken off the price of goods when they are bought for teaching purposes

educational list /ˌedjʊ'keɪʃ(ə)nəl lɪst/ noun a group of books published by one publisher for the educational market

Educational Resources Information Centre /ˌedjʊkeɪʃ(ə)nəl rɪ ˌzɔːsɪz ˌɪnfə'meɪʃ(ə)n ˌsentə/ noun a US research centre which catalogues, abstracts and indexes educational research documents. Abbr **ERIC**

educational software % /ˌedjuː 'keɪʃ(ə)nəl ˌsɒftweə/ noun a set of computer programs designed to meet educational needs

edutainment /ˌedjʊ'teɪnmənt/ noun television programmes, computer software or other media content intended both to entertain and educate users

ee abbreviation in Internet addresses, the top-level domain for Estonia

effective /ɪ'fektɪv/ adjective producing the desired results

efficient /ɪ'fɪʃ(ə)nt/ adjective using the minimum expenditure of effort and money

EFL abbreviation EDUC English as a Foreign Language

EFT abbreviation electronic file transfer

eg abbreviation in Internet addresses, the top-level domain for Egypt

e-GIF /'iː ˌɡɪf/ noun a framework for the technical standards that apply to the exchange of information between the government and companies, or the government and individuals. Full form **Electronic Government Interoperability Framework**

e-government /'iː ˌɡʌv(ə)nmənt/ noun increased efficiency in communication between government and communities, using electronic delivery of information

eh abbreviation in Internet addresses, the top-level domain for Western Sahara

EIC abbreviation European Information Centres

eighteenmo /ˌeɪtiːn'məʊ/ noun same as **octodecimo**

18mo abbreviation eighteenmo

eightvo /'eɪtvəʊ/ noun same as **octavo**

8vo abbreviation octavo

EIS noun easy-to-use software providing information to a manager or executive about his or her company. Full form **executive information system**

e-learning /'iː ˌlɜːnɪŋ/ noun the acquisition of knowledge and skill using electronic technologies such as computer- and Internet-based courseware and local and wide area networks

electoral register /ɪˌlekt(ə)rəl 'redʒɪstə/ noun a list of names of people who are eligible to vote in an election

electrical /ɪˈlektrɪk(ə)l/ *adjective* relating to anything which works by electricity

electrician /ɪˌlekˈtrɪʃ(ə)n/ *noun* a person who installs and repairs electrical equipment

electronic book /ˌelektrɒnɪk ˈbʊk/ *noun* same as **e-book**

electronic conference /ˌelektrɒnɪk ˈkɒnf(ə)rəns/ *noun* a way of discussing a topic with several people simultaneously by using a computer network

electronic data interchange /ˌelektrɒnɪk ˈdeɪtə ˌɪntətʃeɪndʒ/ *noun* a system of sending commercial data over a network or telephone line using an electronic mail system. Abbr **EDI**

electronic data processing /ˌelektrɒnɪk ˈdeɪtə ˌprəʊsesɪŋ/ *noun* computer-based tasks involving the input and manipulation of data, usually using database programs. Abbr **EDP**

electronic funds transfer /ˌelektrɒnɪk ˈfʌndz ˌtrænsfɜː/ *noun* the use of computers to transfer money to and from banks. Abbr **EFT**

Electronic Government Interoperability Framework *noun* full form of **e-GIF**

electronic journal /ˌelektrɒnɪk ˈdʒɜːn(ə)l/ *noun* a journal that is transmitted via a computer network

'Unlike print journals, which libraries own and can keep forever, electronic journals are provided to libraries under a kind of lease. Libraries pay for the privilege of having access to the journals online. But many libraries fear they won't be able to retrieve back issues should this access abruptly end.'

[*The Chronicle of Higher Education*]

electronic journalism /ˌelektrɒnɪk ˈdʒɜːn(ə)lɪz(ə)m/ *noun* news coverage that is transmitted electronically, e.g. by television or over the Internet

electronic library /ˌelektrɒnɪk ˈlaɪbrəri/ *noun* texts and documents that are available through a computer network

electronic magazine /ˌelektrɒnɪk ˌmægəˈziːn/ *noun* a magazine that is distributed online over a computer network rather than being printed on paper

electronic mail /ˌelektrɒnɪk ˈmeɪl/ *noun* same as **e-mail**

electronic mailbox /ˌelektrɒnɪk ˈmeɪlbɒks/ *noun* a system for holding messages until the receiver is ready to use the computer to access them

electronic point of sale /ˌelektrɒnɪk ˌpɔɪnt əv ˈseɪl/ *noun* full form of **EPOS**

electronic publishing /ˌelektrɒnɪk ˈpʌblɪʃɪŋ/ *noun* the process and business of producing books or journals in electronic form, e.g. as e-books or for online access

electronic record /ˌelektrɒnɪk ˈrekɔːd/ *noun* details of an item stored in a computer

electronic records management /ˌelektrɒnɪk ˈrekɔːdz ˌmænɪdʒmənt/ *noun* the process of ensuring that information held in electronic form, such as documents or data, is stored in such a way that it can easily be accessed and cannot accidentally be destroyed. Abbr **ERM**

electronic rights /ˌelektrɒnɪk ˈraɪts/ *plural noun* the right to publish and sell copyright material using electronic devices such as CD-ROM or the Internet

electronic surveillance /ˌelektrɒnɪk səˈveɪləns/ *noun* the gathering of information using electronic devices such as video cameras, especially in crime detection and prevention or in espionage

electronic typewriter /ˌelektrɒnɪk ˈtaɪpraɪtə/ *noun* a typewriter using an electronic keyboard linked, via a buffer, to an electrically driven printing mechanism, also with the facility to send or receive character data from a computer

element /ˈelɪmənt/ *noun* **1.** one of the single parts that make up a whole **2.** the basic and most important part of a subject

elephant /ˈelɪfənt/ *noun* a former book size, 23 x 14 inches. ◊ **double elephant**

elephant folio /ˈelɪfənt ˌfəʊliəʊ/ *noun* a book size from 61 to 63.5 cm/24 to 25 inches in height

élite /eɪˈliːt/ *noun* a group of the most powerful, rich or talented people in a society

élitism /ɪˈliːtɪz(ə)m/ *noun* the belief that a society should be ruled by a group who are considered to be superior to others

ELT *noun* the teaching of English to non-native speakers of English. Full form **English Language Teaching**

e-mail /ˈiː meɪl/ *noun* messages sent on a computer using a modem and telephone lines to other users of a network or bulletin board. Also called **electronic mail**

e-mail address /ˈiː meɪl əˌdres/ *noun* details of how somebody can be contacted through an electronic mailing system

e-mail shorthand /ˈiː meɪl ˌʃɔːthænd/ *noun* the set of acronyms and abbreviations for common phrases originally used in e-mail and subsequently in chat rooms, instant messaging and newsgroup postings

embedded command /ɪmˌbedɪd kəˈmɑːnd/ *noun* a printing command which is keyboarded into text, and which appears on the screen but does not appear in the final printed document

e-media /ˈiː ˌmiːdiə/ *noun* computers, computer networking and multimedia, forming an integrated system. Also called **new media**

emphasis /ˈemfəsɪs/ *noun* extra force given to a word or activity in order to make it seem important

emphasise /ˈemfəsaɪz/, **emphasize** *verb* to show that something is particularly important

empirical research /emˌpɪrɪk(ə)l rɪˈsɜːtʃ/ *noun* research based on experiments

employee /ɪmˈplɔɪiː/ *noun* somebody who is paid by another person for the work they do

employer /ɪmˈplɔɪə/ *noun* somebody who provides work for other people and pays them to do it

employment agency /ɪmˈplɔɪmənt ˌeɪdʒənsi/ *noun* an organisation that earns money by helping other people to find work

employment statistics /ɪmˈplɔɪmənt stəˌtɪstɪks/ *plural noun* facts and figures about the number of people in and out of work in a society, often published as a government document

enable /ɪnˈeɪb(ə)l/ *verb* to make it possible for something to happen

encapsulate /ɪnˈkæpsjʊleɪt/ *verb* to capture the main points of something in a very small space or within a single object or event

encapsulated PostScript /ɪnˌkæpsjʊleɪtɪd ˈpəʊstskrɪpt/ *noun* PostScript commands that describe an image or page contained within a file that can be placed within a graphics or DTP program. Abbr **EPS**

encapsulated PostScript file /ɪnˌkæpsjʊleɪtɪd ˈpəʊstskrɪpt ˌfaɪl/ *noun* a file that contains encapsulated PostScript instructions together with a preview bitmap image. Abbr **EPSF**

enclose /ɪnˈkləʊz/ *verb* to send something in the same envelope

encode /ɪnˈkəʊd/ *verb* to translate plain text into a code (NOTE: The US equivalent is **encrypt**.)

encourage /ɪnˈkʌrɪdʒ/ *verb* to support somebody or something actively

encrypt /ɪnˈkrɪpt/ *verb* to convert plaintext to a secure coded form, using a cipher system ○ *the encrypted text can be sent along ordinary telephone lines*

encryption /ɪnˈkrɪpʃən/ *noun* the conversion of plaintext to a secure coded form by means of a cipher system

'The VPN solution will provide user confidentiality and authenticity through data encryption which allows only authorised users to access corporate networks.' [*DMEurope*]

encyclopedia /ɪnˌsaɪkləˈpiːdiə/, **encyclopaedia** *noun* a book or set of books offering comprehensive information on all or specialised areas of knowledge. Also called **cyclopedia**

encyclopedic /ɪnˌsaɪkləˈpiːdɪk/ *adjective* covering or including a broad range of detailed knowledge such as is found in an encyclopedia

encyclopedism /ɪnˌsaɪkləˈpiːdɪz(ə)m/ *noun* comprehensive learning or knowledge

encyclopedist /ɪnˌsaɪkləˈpiːdɪst/ *noun* a compiler of or contributor to an encyclopedia

ending /ˈendɪŋ/ *noun* the final part of a document

end matter /ˈend ˌmætə/ *noun* PUBL same as **back matter**

endnote /ˈendnəʊt/ *noun* a note of comment or reference placed at the end of a chapter, book or essay

endorse /ɪnˈdɔːs/ *verb* **1.** to sign something on the back **2.** to show approval or support of people or events

endpaper /ˈendpeɪpə/ *noun* a blank piece of thicker paper inserted as part of the binding of a book, one half pasted to the cover and the other half partly pasted to the first or last page

end user /ˌend ˈjuːzə/ *noun* a user of a computer program or any electronic system

energy-saving device /ˌenədʒi ˌseɪvɪŋ dɪˈvaɪs/ *noun* a machine that uses a minimum of power

engaged tone /ɪnˈɡeɪdʒd təʊn/ *noun* a sound made by a telephone when the line is in use

English /ˈɪŋɡlɪʃ/ *noun* the English language, together with literature written in it, as a subject of study

engrave /ɪnˈɡreɪv/ *verb* to cut a design on metal, wood or glass

enhance /ɪnˈhɑːns/ *verb* to make something clearer ○ *to enhance a photograph*

enhancement /ɪnˈhɑːnsmənt/ *noun* an add-on device which improves the performance of a computer and so adds value

enlarge /ɪnˈlɑːdʒ/ *verb* to make something bigger

enlargement /ɪnˈlɑːdʒmənt/ *noun* the process or result of making something bigger

enlighten /ɪnˈlaɪt(ə)n/ *verb* to give clarifying information to somebody

enquiry /ɪnˈkwaɪri/ *noun* a request for information

enquiry desk /ɪnˈkwaɪri desk/ *noun* a desk in a library or information centre where people can ask for information

enquiry service /ɪnˈkwaɪri ˌsɜːvɪs/ *noun* a system for providing answers to enquiries

enquiry work /ɪnˈkwaɪri wɜːk/ *noun* the work of a reference librarian in finding answers to questions

enrich /ɪnˈrɪtʃ/ *verb* to improve by adding something

enrol /ɪnˈrəʊl/ *verb* to sign up to join a group or start a course (NOTE: The US spelling is **enroll**.)

ensure /ɪnˈʃʊə/ *verb* to make certain that something happens

enter /ˈentə/ *verb* **1.** to go into a room or building **2.** to write information in a book or computer **3.** to cause a computer to activate instructions

enterprise content management /ˌentəpraɪz ˈkɒntent ˌmænɪdʒmənt/ *noun* the technologies used to manage, store and deliver content and documents related to organisational processes. Abbr **ECM**

entitle /ɪnˈtaɪt(ə)l/ *verb* to give a title to something such as a book ○ *He is the author of a book entitled 'Decline and Fall'.*

entity /ˈentɪti/ *noun* something which exists in its own right separate from other things

entry /ˈentri/ *noun* a single record in a database, dictionary or catalogue

entry word /ˈentri wɜːd/ *noun* the first word of an entry in a catalogue except the articles 'the', 'a', 'an'

envelope /ˈenvələʊp/ *noun* a paper cover which can be sealed and used to send a letter through the post

envelope window /ˈenvələʊp ˌwɪndəʊ/ *noun* a see-through panel in an envelope which allows the address on the letter to be seen

environmental planning /ɪn ˌvaɪərənment(ə)l ˈplænɪŋ/ *noun* the process of making decisions about the use of the environment to cause the least damage to human and natural inhabitants

ephemera /ɪ'femərə/ *plural noun* items relating to a specific event or topic which are designed to last for a very short time, e.g. theatre programmes, pamphlets or newspaper cuttings

'Libraries have to make room for new books by discarding outdated ephemera, but dumping all older books is a disgrace and a disservice to users. The problem is that deciding what to keep takes more knowledge than many library managers have, so they adopt the motto "when in doubt, chuck it out".' [*Bristol Evening Post*]

epic /'epɪk/ *noun* **1.** a long poem telling stories of brave actions of historic heroes or gods, or the early history of a nation **2.** a long book or film telling an epic type of story

epigraph /'epɪgræf/ *noun* a quotation used at the beginning of a book, as part of the prelims

epithet /'epɪθet/ *noun* a descriptive additional name used to describe particular attributes of a person

epitome /ɪ'pɪtəmi/ *noun* the essential matter of a work contained in an abridged version of a work

EPOS /'iːpɒs/ *noun* a system where sales are charged automatically to a customer's credit card and stock is controlled by the shop's computer. Full form **electronic point of sale**

EPS *abbreviation* encapsulated Post-Script

EPSF *abbreviation* encapsulated Post-Script file

equal /'iːkwəl/ *adjective* same in size, amount or degree

equalise /'iːkwəlaɪz/, **equalize** *verb* to make things equal

equate /ɪ'kweɪt/ *verb* to say that one thing is the same as another

equipment /ɪ'kwɪpmənt/ *noun* machinery and furniture needed to make an office or factory work

equitable /'ekwɪtəb(ə)l/ *adjective* indicating that everyone and everything is treated equally

equivalent /ɪ'kwɪvələnt/ *adjective* having the same value

er *abbreviation* in Internet addresses, the top-level domain for Eritrea

era /'ɪərə/ *noun* a period of time seen as a single unit because it has a common feature ○ *the era of apartheid in South Africa*

erase /ɪ'reɪz/ *verb* **1.** to remove marks from paper **2.** to delete something from a computer

eraser /ɪ'reɪzə/ *noun* a piece of rubber used to remove pencil marks from paper

ergonomics /ˌɜːgə'nɒmɪks/ *noun* the study of people at work with the aim of improving safety and making machines and equipment easier to use

ergonomist /ɜː'gɒnəmɪst/ *noun* a scientist who studies people at work and tries to improve their working conditions

ERIC /'erɪk/ *abbreviation* Educational Resources Information Centre

ERM *abbreviation* electronic records management

erratum slip /e'rɑːtəm slɪp/, **errata slip** /e'rɑːtə slɪp/ *noun* a small piece of paper inserted into a book with corrections to important mistakes which have been noticed since the book was printed (NOTE: The plural of **erratum** is **errata**.)

error detection /'erə dɪˌtekʃ(ə)n/ *noun* the use of special software such as a spellchecker to find mistakes in a document

error rate /'erə reɪt/ *noun* the number of mistakes per page or per thousand entries

erudite /'erʊdaɪt/ *adjective* having or showing great knowledge gained from study and reading

erudition /ˌerʊ'dɪʃ(ə)n/ *noun* knowledge acquired through study and reading

es *abbreviation* in Internet addresses, the top-level domain for Spain

ESA/IRS *abbreviation* European Space Agency Information Relay Service

e-service delivery /'iː ˌsɜːvɪs dɪ ˌlɪv(ə)ri/ *noun* providing services over the Internet, e.g. information delivery, stock check and reservations for a library

'The 'Top of the Web' survey will provide instantaneous feedback to webmasters about the quality of their e-service... At the same time, the questionnaire results will point to those aspects of e-service delivery which can be considered 'best practice', within such areas as filing an on-line tax return, registering a change of address or applying for a copy of one's birth certificate.' [*EUROPEMEDIA*]

ESL *abbreviation* EDUC English as a Second Language

ESOL /'i:sɒl/ *abbreviation* EDUC English for Speakers of Other Languages

ESP *abbreviation* EDUC English for Special Purposes

esparto /ɪs'pɑːtəʊ/ *noun* a type of thick smooth paper made from a South American grass, which is very good for writing or printing, or as the body in coated papers, but is liable to tear and is now not often used

essential /ɪ'senʃəl/ *adjective* absolutely necessary to a person, situation or activity

establish /ɪ'stæblɪʃ/ *verb* **1.** to create something in a permanent way **2.** to prove that something is definitely true

estimate /'estɪmeɪt/ *verb* to calculate an amount or quantity approximately

e-system /'i: ˌsɪstəm/ *noun* an electronic communications or information system

et *abbreviation* in Internet addresses, the top-level domain for Ethiopia

et al. *abbreviation* used to mean 'and the others' (NOTE: From the Latin phrase 'et alia'.)

etc. /ˌ_ˌ_ˌ_/ *abbreviation* used to mean 'and the rest' (NOTE: From the Latin phrase 'et cetera'.)

Ethernet /'i:θənet/ *noun* a standard defining the protocol and signalling method of a local area network

ethnic number /'eθnɪk ˌnʌmbə/ *noun* a number added to a classification symbol to arrange books by language or race

EU *abbreviation* European Union

Euro /'jʊərəʊ/ *noun* the official currency of 12 countries in the European Union

Eurolug /'jʊərəʊlʌg/ *abbreviation* European Online User Group

Euronet/Diane /ˌjʊərəʊnet daɪ'æn/ *noun* telephone networks accessible by a modem and computer covering the countries of the European Union for the transmission of information

European Computer Driving Licence /ˌjʊərəpiːən kəmˌpjuːtə 'draɪvɪŋ ˌlaɪs(ə)ns/ *noun* a standard European qualification in basic computing skills. Abbr **ECDL**

European Information Centres /ˌjʊərəpiːən ˌɪnfə'meɪʃ(ə)n ˌsentəz/ *plural noun* business information centres in all European Union countries sponsored by the EU. Abbr **EIC**

European Institute for Information Management /ˌjʊərəpiːən ˌɪnstɪtjuːt fər ˌɪnfə'meɪʃ(ə)n ˌmænɪdʒmənt/ *noun* a public establishment under the Luxembourg National Ministry of Education which provides postgraduate training for specialists in information management

European Online User Group /ˌjʊərəpiːən ˌɒnlaɪn 'juːzə ˌgruːp/ *noun* an association of European libraries and database users formed to encourage coordination in responses to developments in manufacturing. Abbr **Eurolug**

European Space Agency Information Relay Service *noun* an online database host. Abbr **ESA/IRS**

European Union /ˌjʊərəpiːən 'juːniən/ *noun* the political and economic community of European countries. Abbr **EU**

Eurostat /'jʊərəʊstæt/ *noun* the statistical office of the European Union

evaluate /ɪ'væljueɪt/ *verb* to assess how good something is by looking at the way it works

even number /ˌiːv(ə)n 'nʌmbə/ *noun* a number which can be divided by two to give a whole number

evidence /'evɪd(ə)ns/ *noun* things that you have seen or experienced which make you believe that something is true

evidence gathering /ˈevɪd(ə)ns ˌgæð(ə)rɪŋ/ *noun* software that can gather information about the state of a computer system which has crashed or suffered some incident

evolution /ˌiːvəˈluːʃ(ə)n/ *noun* the process of gradual change and development

examination /ɪgˌzæmɪˈneɪʃ(ə)n/ *noun* a written or spoken test of ability or knowledge

example /ɪgˈzɑːmpəl/ *noun* something that represents or is typical of a particular group

exceed /ɪkˈsiːd/ *verb* to be greater than a limit ○ *He exceeded the speed limit.*

exception /ɪkˈsepʃən/ *noun* things which are different and not included

exception listing /ɪkˈsepʃən ˌlɪstɪŋ/ *noun* the listing of items which are not included in a computer program

exception report /ɪkˈsepʃən rɪˌpɔːt/ *noun* a report which only gives items which do not fit in the general rule or pattern

exception reporting /ɪkˈsepʃən rɪˌpɔːtɪŋ/ *noun* a system of information distribution that passes on only information that is new and out of the ordinary, in order to avoid overloading recipients with information that is out of date or has already been transmitted to them

excerpt /ˈeksɜːpt/ *noun* a section or passage taken from a longer work such as a book, film, musical composition or document

excess /ˈekses/ *adjective* more than is necessary or normal

exclamation mark /ˌekskləˈmeɪʃ(ə)n mɑːk/ *noun* a punctuation mark (!) used to express surprise

exclude /ɪkˈskluːd/ *verb* to leave something or somebody out deliberately

.exe /ˈeksi/ *suffix* a file extension for a program file. Full form **executable**

execute /ˈeksɪkjuːt/ *verb* to carry out a plan or process

executive /ɪgˈzekjʊtɪv/ *noun* somebody who is employed by a company or organisation at a senior level

exemplar /ɪgˈzemplɑː/ *noun* a copy of a book or text, especially one from which further copies have originated

exempt /ɪgˈzempt/ *adjective* to be allowed not to have to perform a duty, service or payment

exercise /ˈeksəsaɪz/ *noun* a short piece of work designed to help you learn something

exhaustive search /ɪgˌzɔːstɪv ˈsɜːtʃ/ *noun* a search through a database or library which covers all known records

exhibit /ɪgˈzɪbɪt/ *noun* an item displayed in a museum, art gallery or court of law ■ *verb* to put something in a public place for people to look at

exhibition /ˌeksɪˈbɪʃ(ə)n/ *noun* a collection of objects displayed in a public place

exhibitor /ɪgˈzɪbɪtə/ *noun* a person whose work is being displayed

ex libris /ˌeks ˈlɪbriːs/ *phrase* used on book plates followed by a name to show who the owner is (NOTE: From a Latin phrase meaning 'from the books of'.)

expenditure /ɪkˈspendɪtʃə/ *noun* the total amount of money spent on something

expense /ɪkˈspens/ *noun* money spent while doing something connected with one's work

expense account /ɪkˈspens əˌkaʊnt/ *noun* an arrangement with a company by which they pay for necessary work expenses

experiment /ɪkˈsperɪmənt/ *noun* a scientific test done to prove or discover something

experimental strategy /ɪkˌsperɪˈment(ə)l ˌstrætədʒi/ *noun* a policy of trying out new ideas and methods to see how they work

expert /ˈekspɜːt/ *noun* somebody with a great deal of knowledge, or skill or experience in a particular subject or activity ■ *adjective* having a great deal of knowledge, skill or experience in a particular subject or activity

expertise /ˌekspəˈtiːz/ *noun* special skills or knowledge in a particular field

expert system /ˈekspɜːt ˌsɪstəm/ *noun* **1.** software which applies the

knowledge of experts in a field to solve problems and partly replicates human decision making **2.** a type of computer program that can analyse a set of problems and recommend a course of action for the user

expert user /ˌeksp3ːt ˈjuːzə/ *noun* somebody who uses a service very efficiently because they have experience

expire /ɪkˈspaɪə/ *verb* to reach the end of the period of time for which something is valid

expiry date /ɪkˈspaɪəri deɪt/ *noun* the date on which something such as a document, membership or piece of software ceases to be valid

explicit knowledge /ɪkˌsplɪsɪt ˈnɒlɪdʒ/ *noun* human knowledge that takes the form of learned facts and which can be documented. Compare **tacit knowledge**

exponent /ɪkˈspəʊnənt/ *noun* somebody who argues in support of an idea

export /ɪkˈspɔːt/ *verb* to convert data from a computer program into a form suitable for a different program or environment

export edition /ˈekspɔːt ɪˌdɪʃ(ə)n/ *noun* a special edition printed for the export market

exporter /ɪkˈspɔːtə/ *noun* a person or company that sells goods and sends them to foreign countries

exposé /ɪkˈspəʊzeɪ/ *noun* a piece of writing that reveals the truth about a situation, often involving something shocking

express /ɪkˈspres/ *verb* to state what you think or feel

expression /ɪkˈspreʃ(ə)n/ *noun* **1.** a word or phrase **2.** a mathematical formula

expurgated edition /ˈekspəgeɪtɪd ɪˌdɪʃ(ə)n/ *noun* an edition of a book that has had parts removed which are judged to be offensive

extend /ɪkˈstend/ *verb* to make something longer

Extensible Markup Language /ɪk ˌstensɪb(ə)l ˈmɑːkʌp ˌlæŋgwɪdʒ/ *noun* COMPUT full form of **XML**

extension card /ɪkˈstenʃən kɑːd/ *noun* a second or subsequent card used in a manual catalogue when the information is too long for one card

extent /ɪkˈstent/ *noun* the number of pages in a book ○ *You need to put the extent and trimmed page size into the catalogue.* ○ *If you don't know the extent of the book yet, how can you order the paper for it?*

external /ɪkˈstɜːn(ə)l/ *adjective* coming from outside

external auditor /ɪkˌstɜːn(ə)l ˈɔːdɪtə/ *noun* a person from outside an organisation who checks its accounts

external consultant /ɪkˌstɜːn(ə)l kənˈsʌltənt/ *noun* an expert in a field who comes in from outside an organisation to give advice

external reader /ɪkˌstɜːn(ə)l ˈriːdə/ *noun* a person who is allowed to use a library which is otherwise limited to specific groups of members

extra- /ekstrə/ *prefix* indicating that something is from outside ○ *extra-mural studies*

extra bound book /ˌekstrə baʊnd ˈbʊk/ *noun* a book that is specially bound and finished by hand

extract /ˈekstrækt/ *noun* a small part of a piece of writing or music which is printed or played separately

COMMENT: Long extracts quoted in a text are often set indented, and in a smaller size than the text matter.

extranet /ˈekstrənet/ *noun* an extension of the intranet of a company or organisation, giving authorised outsiders controlled access to the intranet

extrapolate /ɪkˈstræpəleɪt/ *verb* to use logic applied to known facts to calculate what is likely to happen in the future

eye strain /ˈaɪstreɪn/ *noun* a pain in the eyes caused by looking at something such as small print or a computer screen for too long

'Computer-related injuries have become one of the banes of modern life, according to a recent ICM survey. Problems include repetitive strain injury (RSI), eye strain, and head, back and neck aches… we should all take a short exercise break every hour to reduce muscle tension caused by a rigid posture.' [*The Mail on Sunday*]

e-zine /'iː ziːn/ *noun* a website with contents and layout modelled on a print magazine

F

fable /ˈfeɪb(ə)l/ *noun* a short story which aims to teach a moral lesson

face /feɪs/ *noun* the front cover of a book

facet /ˈfæsɪt/ *noun* (*in classification*) the whole group of divisions when a subject is subdivided

COMMENT: There are five kinds of facet in a class: personality, matter, energy, space and time.

facilitate /fəˈsɪlɪteɪt/ *verb* to make something possible or easier to do, e.g. by providing information

facilitator /fəˈsɪlɪteɪtə/ *noun* somebody who makes it possible for other people to do things

facility /fəˈsɪlɪti/ *noun* a piece of equipment that makes it easy to do something

facing /ˈfeɪsɪŋ/ *adjective* opposite ○ *The picture was on the facing page.*

facing pages /ˌfeɪsɪŋ ˈpeɪdʒɪz/ *plural noun* the two pages that are visible when a book is open

facsimile /fækˈsɪmɪli/ *noun* an exact copy of an original

facsimile edition /fækˈsɪmɪli ɪ ˌdɪʃ(ə)n/ *noun* a book or print that is reprinted in exactly the same style as an earlier edition, often being a photographic reproduction of the original

fact /fækt/ *noun* something that is known or accepted to be true

fact-finding /ˈfækt ˌfaɪndɪŋ/ *adjective* intended to find out information about something ■ *noun* activity that is intended to find out information about something

factor /ˈfæktə/ *noun* one aspect which affects an event, situation or decision

factual /ˈfæktʃuəl/ *adjective* based on fact

faculty /ˈfæk(ə)lti/ *noun* a group of departments in a university or college within the same academic area ○ *The library school is within the faculty of humanities and education studies.*

fail /feɪl/ *verb* to be unsuccessful or not work properly

fail-safe /ˈfeɪl seɪf/ *adjective* designed in such a way that nothing dangerous can happen if any part goes wrong

fair copy /ˌfeə ˈkɒpi/ *noun* the final version of work which has no mistakes

fake /feɪk/ *noun* **1.** something or somebody who is not what they pretend to be **2.** a false, and usually worthless, copy

fallback system /ˈfɔːlbæk ˌsɪstəm/ *noun* a system that can be used if the one in use fails

false /fɔːls/ *adjective* not correct or based on wrong information

false alarm /ˌfɔːls əˈlɑːm/ *noun* a warning of something bad that does not actually happen

false drop /ˌfɔːls ˈdrɒp/ *noun* **1.** a citation that does not relate to the subject being searched **2.** an irrelevant reference in indexing

false friend /ˌfɔːls ˈfrend/ *noun* a word which appears to be similar in meaning to a word in a different language, but actually is not

false positive /ˌfɔːls ˈpɒzɪtɪv/ *noun* an instance of a search program or database mistakenly returning something that is unrelated to the search term

'Echoing remarks he made last year, the geneticist said the criminal DNA database was not sophisticated enough to prevent false positives. "The chances of two unrelated people matching is 1 in 10 trillion – that is not good enough".' [*The Guardian*]

falsify /'fɔːlsɪfaɪ/ *verb* to change information so that it is no longer true or accurate

family /'fæm(ə)li/ *noun* **1.** a group of all the characters belonging to the same typeface, including all the different fonts **2.** a group of related things such as plants, animals or languages, used as the basis of classification

family name /'fæm(ə)li neɪm/ *noun* a surname

fan /fæn/ *noun* a cooling device often built into electric machines so that they do not overheat

fan-fold /'fæn fəʊld/ *adjective* referring to a way of folding paper so that information can be printed on different parts of it as in a pamphlet

FAQ /fæk, ˌef eɪ 'kjuː/ *abbreviation* frequently asked questions

far-sighted /ˌfɑː 'saɪtɪd/ *adjective* good at guessing what will happen in the future

fascicle /'fæskɪk(ə)l/ *noun* a section of a book published in instalments as a volume or pamphlet

fast /fɑːst/ *adverb* fixed or held very firmly

fatal error /ˌfeɪt(ə)l 'erə/ *noun* a mistake that causes a computer program to crash

fault /fɔːlt/ *noun* a weakness or imperfection in something

fault tolerance /'fɔːlt ˌtɒlərəns/ *noun* the ability of a computer or network to preserve the integrity of data during a malfunction

faulty /'fɔːlti/ *adjective* not working properly

fax /fæks/ *noun* an exact copy of a document sent electronically to a distant receiver using the telephone network ■ *verb* to send an exact copy of a document using the telephone network

fax gateway /'fæks ˌgeɪtweɪ/ *noun* a computer or piece of software that allows users to send e-mail or other information as a fax transmission to a remote fax machine

feasibility study /ˌfiːzə'bɪlɪti ˌstʌdi/ *noun* a survey and report about the usefulness and potential of a plan or policy to see if it will work

feasible /'fiːzɪb(ə)l/ *adjective* possible to make or achieve

featherweight antique paper /ˌfeðəweɪt æn'tiːk ˌpeɪpə/ *noun* light, very thick paper, formerly used for children's books (NOTE: The US English is **high-bulk antique**.)

feature /'fiːtʃə/ *noun* **1.** a special characteristic of something **2.** a special article in a newspaper, magazine or broadcast programme

fee /fiː/ *noun* money paid for a service

feed /fiːd/ *verb* to put information into a computer

feedback /'fiːdbæk/ *noun* comments from users or customers about what has been proposed or done

feint /feɪnt/ *noun* very light lines on writing paper

Fellow of the Library Association /ˌfeləʊ əv ðə 'laɪbrəri əˌsəʊsieɪʃ(ə)n/ *noun* the highest qualification awarded by the Library Association. Abbr **FLA**

festschrift /'festʃrɪft/ *noun* a volume of writings by various people collected in honour of somebody such as a writer or scholar

fiche /fiːʃ/ ♦ **microfiche**

fiction /'fɪkʃən/ *noun* stories about imaginary people and events

field /fiːld/ *noun* a section containing individual data in a record, e.g. a person's name or address

field engineer /'fiːld ˌendʒɪnɪə/ *noun* a maintenance worker who travels to companies or individual customers to service their machines

field of study /ˌfiːld əv 'stʌdi/ *noun* an academic area of knowledge being studied in depth

field separator /'fiːld ˌsepəreɪtə/ *noun* a code showing the end of one field and the start of the next

field tested /'fiːld ˌtestɪd/ *adjective* relating to a product or plan that has been tested in a real situation

fieldwork /'fiːldwɜːk/ *noun* the gathering of information about a subject by carrying out a direct investigation rather than reading or talking about it

figure /ˈfɪɡə/ *noun* a printed and numbered line illustration, map or chart in a document

file /faɪl/ *noun* **1.** a cardboard holder for papers which can fit in the drawer of a filing cabinet **2.** a collection of information about a particular person or thing **3.** (*in computing*) a set of stored, related data with its own name □ **on file** kept in a list for reference

file cards /ˈfaɪl kɑːdz/ *plural noun* cards with information written on them which can be stored in a given order to aid retrieval of the information

file copy /ˈfaɪl ˌkɒpi/ *noun* a copy of a document which is kept for reference in an office, or a copy of a published book kept in the library of the publisher

file extension /ˈfaɪl ɪkˌstenʃən/ *noun* a set of characters following the dot after the name of a DOS file, identifying the file type

file header /ˈfaɪl ˌhedə/ *noun* information about a file stored at the beginning of the file

file length /ˈfaɪl leŋθ/ *noun* the number of characters or bytes in a stored file

file maintenance /ˈfaɪl ˌmeɪntənəns/ *noun* the practice of keeping files up to date by changing, adding or deleting entries

'One of the most important CD-Roms to have in such an emergency is Norton SystemWorks 2003. It is a suite of programs that could help revive the computer and even salvage lost or corrupted files. SystemWorks can clean up the machine and make file maintenance a breeze with a simple mouse click.' [*The Daily Telegraph*]

file management /ˈfaɪl ˌmænɪdʒmənt/ *noun* a set of instructions used to create and maintain a file

file manager /ˈfaɪl ˌmænɪdʒə/ *noun* a computer program that arranges and manipulates files and directories

filename /ˈfaɪlneɪm/ *noun* a set of characters, sometimes restricted in number, serving as an identifying title

for a computer file and often including a file extension

file protection /ˈfaɪl prəˌtekʃən/ *noun* software or another device used to prevent any accidental deletion or overwriting of a computer file

file recovery /ˈfaɪl rɪˌkʌvəri/ *noun* software that allows a computer file that has been accidentally deleted or damaged to be recovered

file server /ˈfaɪl ˌsɜːvə/ *noun* **1.** software used to manage and store users' files in a network **2.** the number of independent systems sharing a resource or providing a particular service within a network

file storage /ˈfaɪl ˌstɔːrɪdʒ/ *noun* methods of storing files on a disc or tape

file transfer /ˈfaɪl ˌtrænsfɜː/ *noun* moving a file from one area of computer memory to another

file transfer protocol /ˈfaɪl ˌtrænsfɜː ˌprəʊtəkɒl/ *noun* a TCP/IP standard for transferring files between computers. Abbr **FTP**

filing /ˈfaɪlɪŋ/ *noun* the process of putting things in order according to a set system

filing basket /ˈfaɪlɪŋ ˌbɑːskɪt/, **filing tray** /ˈfaɪlɪŋ treɪ/ *noun* a container kept on a desk for documents which have to be filed

filing cabinet /ˈfaɪlɪŋ ˌkæbɪnət/ *noun* a metal box with several drawers used for storing files

filing clerk /ˈfaɪlɪŋ klɑːk/ *noun* a clerk who files documents

filing code /ˈfaɪlɪŋ kəʊd/, **filing rule** /ˈfaɪlɪŋ ruːl/ *noun* an explicit direction based on a recognised code for filing entries in a catalogue

filing system /ˈfaɪlɪŋ ˌsɪstəm/ *noun* any method of organising documents so that they can be retrieved easily

filing tray /ˈfaɪlɪŋ treɪ/ *noun* a container often kept on a desk for storing documents prior to filing

fillet /ˈfɪlɪt/ *noun* a thin decorative line impressed onto the cover of a book, or the tool used to make it

fill in /ˌfɪl ˈɪn/ *verb* to write in the information required ○ *to fill in a form*

fill out /ˌfɪl 'aʊt/ *verb* to write the required information in the blank spaces on a form ○ *To get customs clearance you must fill out three forms.*

film /fɪlm/ *noun* **1.** a strip of light-sensitive material used in a camera to take photographs **2.** a story or event recorded on film to be shown in the cinema or on television **3.** a very thin layer of powder or grease

film laminate /'fɪlm ˌlæmɪnət/ *noun* very thin plastic film attached to the cover or jacket of a book for protection

film library /'fɪlm ˌlaɪbrəri/ *noun* a collection of films and video recordings, classified for easy retrieval

film strip /'fɪlm strɪp/ *noun* a strip of 16mm or 35mm film bearing up to fifty frames of still photographs with pictures and captions, sometimes with sound track attached

filter /'fɪltə/ *verb* **1.** to select information which is to be passed on **2.** to allow information to come out very gradually

finals /'faɪn(ə)lz/ *plural noun* the last examinations in a university or college course

finance /'faɪnæns/ *noun* money needed to pay for a project ■ *verb* to provide the money for a project

finance department /'faɪnæns dɪ ˌpɑːtmənt/ *noun* the people in an organisation who manage the accounts

financial /faɪ'nænʃəl/ *adjective* relating to or involving money

financial implications /faɪ,nænʃəl ˌɪmplɪ'keɪʃ(ə)nz/ *plural noun* the consequences of a decision in terms of how much it will cost

financial planning /faɪ,nænʃəl 'plænɪŋ/ *noun* the process of working out the most efficient way to use what money is available

financial sector /faɪ,nænʃ(ə)l 'sektə/ *noun* the part of the economy that is involved with money transactions

financial year /faɪ,nænʃəl 'jɪə/ *noun* a period of twelve months which can start at any point within the calendar year, used for managing the budgets of an organisation and assessing profit and loss ○ *The university's financial year*

runs from 31st July to 1st August in the next year.

finding aid /'faɪndɪŋ eɪd/ *noun* a system to aid retrieval such as a classification scheme, catalogue or index

finding list catalogue /,faɪndɪŋ lɪst 'kætəlɒg/ *noun* a catalogue with only brief author entries

findings /'faɪndɪŋz/ *plural noun* information obtained as a result of investigation or research

fine /faɪn/ *noun* an amount of money that has to be paid as a penalty ■ *verb* to make somebody pay money as a punishment ○ *She was fined because the library books were overdue.* ■ *adjective* very thin, soft or small

fine print /'faɪn prɪnt/ *noun* the small print in a contract or agreement, which may refer to unfavourable terms and could be overlooked when signing the contract

fine-tune /,faɪn 'tjuːn/ *verb* to adjust something by very small amounts

finger /'fɪŋgə/ *noun* a software program that will retrieve information about a user based on their e-mail address ■ *verb* to use a finger program to obtain information about somebody

firewall /'faɪəwɔːl/ *noun* a piece of computer software intended to prevent unauthorised access to system software or data

first-class /,fɜːst 'klɑːs/ *adjective* **1.** of the highest or best quality **2.** of the best level of service, e.g. in mail or travel

first edition /,fɜːst ɪ'dɪʃ(ə)n/ *noun* one of the first number of copies printed from the same type at the same time

first impression /,fɜːst ɪm 'preʃ(ə)n/, **first printing** /,fɜːst 'prɪntɪŋ/ *noun* the first printing of a book

first word entry /,fɜːst 'wɜːd ,entri/ *noun* an entry under the first word of the title excluding 'the', 'a', 'an'

fit /fɪt/ *verb* to be the right size or shape ■ *adjective* to be physically capable of doing something

five laws of library science /,faɪv lɔːz əv 'laɪbrəri ,saɪəns/ *plural noun* library laws established by S. R. Ranganathan.

COMMENT: The laws are: 1. Books are for use. 2. Every reader his book. 3. Every book its reader. 4. Save the time of the reader. 5. A library is a growing organism.

fixed back /ˈfɪkst bæk/ *noun* a cover that is glued to the back of the pages of a book

fixed length record /ˌfɪkst leŋθ ˈrekɔːd/ *noun* a computer record which will only accept information in a pre-set number of characters

fj *abbreviation* in Internet addresses, the top-level domain for Fiji

FLA *abbreviation* Fellow of the Library Association

flag /flæg/ *verb* to use a computer code to mark a record as part of a subset ■ *noun* a mark which is attached to information in a computer so that the information can be found easily

flap /flæp/ *noun* either of the two parts of a dust jacket that fold inside a book's cover and are usually printed with information about the book or author

flash drive /ˈflæʃ draɪv/ *noun* a small plastic device functioning as a disk drive, containing memory chips that retain their contents without electrical power and that have a capacity of between 16 megabytes and 2 gigabytes of data

flat back /ˈflæt bæk/ *noun* the spine of a book which is flat and not curved or 'rounded'

flexibility /ˌfleksɪˈbɪlɪti/ *noun* ability to adapt to various situations or conditions

flexible /ˈfleksɪb(ə)l/ *adjective* able to be altered or changed

flexible learning /ˌfleksɪb(ə)l ˈlɜːnɪŋ/ *noun* a system of teaching which provides for people of all ages and educational backgrounds

flexible working hours /ˌfleksɪb(ə)l ˈwɜːkɪŋ ˌaʊəz/ *noun* a system whereby employees can start or stop work at hours to suit themselves as long as they work a certain number of hours in a week

flier /ˈflaɪə/ *noun* a small advertising leaflet designed to encourage customers to ask for more information

flood /flʌd/ *noun* a large number of things or a large amount of information ■ *verb* □ **to flood the market** to make a very large number of a particular item available for sale at one time, usually forcing the price down

floor plan /ˈflɔː plæn/ *noun* a diagram showing the layout of a building

floppy /ˈflɒpi ˈdɪsk/, **floppy disk** /ˌflɒpi ˈdɪsk/ *noun* a small disk for storing computer information ○ *The data is on 3 1/2 inch floppies.*

Florence Agreement /ˈflɒrəns əˌgriːmənt/ *noun* a UNESCO agreement adopted in 1952 which reduces tariffs and trade obstacles to the international export and import of books, documents and other educational scientific and cultural material

floriation /ˌflɒriˈeɪʃ(ə)n/ *noun* tooled decoration on leather binding, in the form of little flowers

flowchart /ˈfləʊtʃɑːt/, **flow diagram** /ˈfləʊ ˌdaɪəgræm/ *noun* a diagram showing the sequence of steps in a process

flush with /ˈflʌʃ wɪθ/ *adjective* level with ○ *The pages were trimmed flush with the covers.*

flyleaf /ˈflaɪliːf/ *noun* an endpaper in a book

flysheet /ˈflaɪʃiːt/ *noun* a two- or four-page tract or circular

fm *abbreviation* in Internet addresses, the top-level domain for Micronesia

FM *abbreviation* frequency modulation

fo *abbreviation* in Internet addresses, the top-level domain for Faroe Islands

focus /ˈfəʊkəs/ *verb* to concentrate one's attention on something

focus group /ˈfəʊkəs gruːp/ *noun* a small group of representative people who are questioned about their opinions as part of political or market research

fold /fəʊld/ *verb* to bend something, e.g. a piece of paper, so that one part covers another

-fold /fəʊld/ *suffix* **1.** combining with numbers to indicate that something has that number of parts ○ *The problem was three-fold.* **2.** indicating that something has been multiplied by that number ○

The number of library users rose tenfold after the advertising campaign.

fold-out /ˈfəʊld aʊt/ *noun* a sheet that is put folded into a magazine or book and can be unfolded to give a much wider page, used especially for plans and maps

foliation /ˌfəʊliˈeɪʃ(ə)n/ *noun* the numbering of consecutive pages in a book or manuscript

folio /ˈfəʊliəʊ/ *noun* **1.** a book made with paper of a large size **2.** a large sheet of paper folded twice across the middle to make four pages of a book **3.** a page number

follow-up /ˈfɒləʊ ʌp/ *noun* a book, film, article or report that continues a story or provides further information

font /fɒnt/ *noun* a set of characters in a typeface of all the same style, i.e. the same size, weight and orientation

COMMENT: Each typeface will be available in many different fonts (Univers, for example, was designed in 21 different fonts) and these will include the different point sizes and weights, such as bold and italic. In metal setting, the font would contain different quantities of each character, according to the frequency of use of the characters. English fonts will contain capitals, small capitals, lower case, punctuation marks, numerals, ligatures and common symbols, making about 150 sorts in all. English fonts contain some accents and special characters, but many accents which are standard in, say German or Spanish fonts, are not included in English. British fonts contain the pound and the dollar signs, but American fonts are likely not to have the pound sign.

font size /fɒnt saɪz/ *noun* the size of the characters in a text

font type /fɒnt taɪp/ *noun* the style of the characters used in printing

foolscap /ˈfuːlskæp/ *noun* a large non-metric size of paper longer than A4, about 34cm x 43cm

COMMENT: Foolscap takes it name from a watermark of a clown's hat used in early papers; foolscap folio is 13 1/2 x 8 1/2 inches; foolscap quarto is 8 1/2 x 6 3/4 inches and foolscap octavo is 6 3/4 x 4 1/4 inches.

foot /fʊt/ *noun* the bottom part of a page ○ *He signed it at the foot of the page.*

footer /ˈfʊtə/ *noun* a repeated message at the bottom of every page in a document

footnote /ˈfʊtnəʊt/ *noun* a note, usually in a smaller type size, at the bottom of a page, which refers to the text above and is for reference only

COMMENT: Footnotes are best printed at the bottom of a page, as the name suggests, if they are essential to the understanding of the text. They can also be printed at the end of a chapter or at the end of a book, especially if they are simply further references or supply bibliographic details. In learned journals it is common for them to be printed at the end of the chapter, which makes the typesetting of the main text much simpler. Reference numbers to footnotes are printed in small superscript numbers after the relevant word in the text, and in books the numbers usually run from the beginning of the text to the end of the book, consecutively. In journals formed of several different articles, each article has its own footnote numbering series.

footprint /ˈfʊtprɪnt/ *noun* **1.** the area covered by a transmitting device such as a satellite or antenna **2.** the area that a computer takes up on a desk

forbid /fəˈbɪd/ *verb* to give instructions that something must not be done

forbidden book /fəˌbɪdən ˈbʊk/ *noun* a book that has been forbidden by a censor

forecast /ˈfɔːkɑːst/ *noun* a prediction or estimate of what is likely to happen in the future

foredge /ˈfɔːredʒ/, **fore-edge** /ˈfɔːr edʒ/ *noun* the front edge of trimmed pages in a bound book, i.e. the opposite edge to the spine

COMMENT: Early bound books were displayed with this edge facing out on the shelf, hence the name; the title was written or printed on this edge of the pages.

foredge margin /ˈfɔːredʒ ˌmɑːdʒɪn/ *noun* the margin along the foredge of a book. Compare **gutter**

foreground /ˈfɔːɡraʊnd/ *noun* the front part of an illustration which seems nearest to the viewer

foreign /ˈfɒrɪn/ *adjective* belonging to or originating from a different country

foreign-language edition /ˌfɒrɪn ˈlæŋgwɪdʒ ɪˌdɪʃ(ə)n/ *noun* an edition of an English-language text in translation

foreign market /ˌfɒrɪn ˈmɑːkɪt/ *noun* other countries where exports are sold

'…we discovered that the German market has different brochure sizes and types to the UK. This caused such consternation when the German site administrators uploaded their own brochures that we had to modify the content management system… Companies like WebtraffIQ, fhios and Bunnyfoot Universality provide products and services that can help design professionals get to grips with foreign markets.' [*Revolution*]

forename /ˈfɔːneɪm/ *noun* a person's first or given name

forename entry /ˈfɔːneɪm ˌentri/ *noun* an entry in a catalogue under the author's first name instead of the surname

foreseeable future /fɔːˈsiːəbl ˈfjuːtʃə/ *noun* the near future which can be reasonably predicted

foreword /ˈfɔːwɜːd/ *noun* a piece of text at the beginning of a book as an introduction, often written by a person other than the author

forgery /ˈfɔːdʒəri/ *noun* **1.** a false copy made with the intention to deceive **2.** the act of making things intended to deceive

form /fɔːm/ *noun* a pre-printed document with spaces where information can be entered

formality /fɔːˈmælɪti/ *noun* something which must be done but which will not change the situation ○ *The decision is just a formality which is not expected to affect the market.*

format /ˈfɔːmæt/ *noun* the size, shape and arrangement of a document ■ *verb* to arrange text on screen as it will appear in printed form on paper

formatted /ˈfɔːmætɪd/ *adjective* **1.** made ready for use by a computer **2.** arranged in a particular format

formatter /ˈfɔːmætə/ *noun* hardware or software that arranges text or data according to certain rules

formatting program /ˈfɔːmætɪŋ ˌprəʊɡræm/ *noun* a program for automatically putting a computer text into a certain page format

form entry /ˈfɔːm ˌentri/ *noun* a catalogue entry under the form in which a book is written ○ *Form entries in the catalogue were poetry, drama, fiction, etc.*

form mode /ˈfɔːm məʊd/ *noun* a display method on a data entry terminal, in which the form is displayed on the screen and the operator enters relevant details

formula /ˈfɔːmjʊlə/ *noun* a set of numbers, letters or symbols which represents a mathematical or scientific rule (NOTE: The plural is **formulae**.)

fortnightly /ˈfɔːtnaɪtli/ *adjective* happening every two weeks

FORTRAN /ˈfɔːtræn/ *noun* a computer programming language for scientific matter. Full form **formula translator**. ◊ assembly language

48mo *abbreviation* forty-eightmo

forty-eightmo /ˌfɔːtiˈeɪtməʊ/ *noun* a book printed with 48 pages from a sheet. Abbr **48mo**

forum /ˈfɔːrəm/ *noun* **1.** a place or meeting at which matters can be discussed **2.** an Internet discussion group for people who share a special interest in something

forward /ˈfɔːwəd/ *adjective* at or moving towards the front of something or the future ■ *verb* to send on a letter which has arrived at an address from which the intended recipient has moved

forwarding address /ˈfɔːwədɪŋ əˌdres/ *noun* an address which you give to somebody when you move so that they can send your mail to you

foundation subject /faʊnˈdeɪʃ(ə)n ˌsʌbjekt/ *noun* any of ten subjects specified in the 1988 National Curriculum that must be studied in schools in England and Wales, three of which have priority as core subjects

4o *abbreviation* quarto

foxed /fɒkst/ *adjective* denoting books or paper stained with yellowish-brown spots from having been kept in damp conditions

foxing /ˈfɒksɪŋ/ *noun* brown spots or stains on paper caused by poor storage, usually found on older documents or books

foxy /ˈfɒksi/ *adjective* PUBL same as **foxed**

foyer /ˈfɔɪeɪ/ *noun* an area just inside the main entrance of a large building where people meet

fr *abbreviation* in Internet addresses, the top-level domain for France

frame of reference /ˌfreɪm əv ˈref(ə)rəns/ *noun* a particular set of ideas or beliefs on which to base one's judgement of other things

framework /ˈfreɪmwɜːk/ *noun* a set of rules or ideas that can be used to decide how to behave ○ *They were able to contain the changes within the framework of the old system.*

Frankfurt Book Fair /ˌfræŋkfɜːt ˈbʊk ˌfeə/ *noun* the most important of the international book fairs, held each year in October as a meeting place for book publishers, printers, literary agents and booksellers

franking machine /ˈfræŋkɪŋ mə ˌʃiːn/ *noun* a machine which prints a sign on letters to show that the postage has been paid

fraud /frɔːd/ *noun* deception or trickery carried out to secure an unfair gain or advantage

free /friː/ *adjective* **1.** available for use **2.** not needing to be paid for

-free /friː/ *suffix* added to adjectives to show that they do not have the thing mentioned ○ *acid-free*

freedom /ˈfriːdəm/ *noun* the state of being free to say or do what you want without restriction

freedom of information /ˌfriːdəm əv ˌɪnfəˈmeɪʃ(ə)n/ *noun* the state of having free access to all published information in any format

Freedom of Information Act /ˌfriːdəm əv ˌɪnfəˈmeɪʃ(ə)n ˌækt/ *noun* a law in the UK which deals with access to information held by public bodies

freedom of speech /ˌfriːdəm əv ˈspiːtʃ/, **freedom of the press** /ˌfriːdəm əv ðə ˈpres/ *noun* the state of being free to write, say or publish what

you want without fear of prosecution as long as you do not break the law

free enterprise /ˌfriː ˈentəpraɪz/ *noun* an economic system where businesses compete for profit without much government control

freehand /ˈfriːhænd/ *adjective* done without the help of instruments

free indexing /ˈfriː ˌɪndeksɪŋ/ *noun* natural language indexing which has no vocabulary controls

freelance /ˈfriːlɑːns/ *adverb* working for anyone who will pay for your skills rather than employed by one company

free market /ˌfriː ˈmɑːkɪt/ *noun* an economic system in which the production and sale of goods is controlled by the buyers and sellers rather than the government

Freenet /ˈfriːnet/ *noun* community-based access to the Internet, usually run by volunteers in the USA

free of charge /ˌfriː əv ˈtʃɑːdʒ/ *adjective* not needing to be paid for

free term list /ˈfriː tɜːm ˌlɪst/ *noun* a list of terms or indicators to which others can be freely added

free text searching /ˌfriː ˈtekst ˌsɜːtʃɪŋ/ *noun* online searching using natural language rather than a controlled vocabulary and any aspect of the record as a search term

free translation /ˌfriː trænsˈleɪʃ(ə)n/ *noun* a rough translation which gives the general meaning without translating the text word for word

freeze /friːz/ *verb* **1.** to stop and display a single frame from a film, TV programme or video tape **2.** to stop funds or credits being paid

frequency /ˈfriːkwənsi/ *noun* **1.** the number of times that something happens in a given period of time **2.** a term used to describe the wavelength of broadcast transmissions

frequency modulation /ˈfriːkwənsi ˌmɒdjuleɪʃ(ə)n/ *noun* a radio broadcasting band which reduces interference. Abbr **FM**

frequently asked questions /ˌfriːkwənt(ə)li ɑːskd ˈkwestʃənz/

plural noun a list of the most common questions on a particular subject, with answers, provided on a website or leaflet. Abbr **FAQ**

frequent user /ˌfriːkwənt ˈjuːzə/ *noun* somebody who makes use of a service very often

front cover /ˌfrʌnt ˈkʌvə/ *noun* the cover on the front of a book or magazine, with the title and usually an attractive, eye-catching design

front end /ˈfrʌnt end/ *noun* the visible part of an application that is seen by a user and is used to view and work with information

front flap /ˌfrʌnt ˈflæp/, **front jacket flap** /ˌfrʌnt ˈdʒækɪt ˌflæp/ *noun* a flap on a book jacket which is tucked into the front cover of a book, usually with a blurb on it

frontispiece /ˈfrʌntɪspiːs/ *noun* a picture at the beginning of a book opposite the title page

front matter /ˈfrʌnt ˌmætə/ *noun* same as **prelims**

front page /ˌfrʌnt ˈpeɪdʒ/ *noun* the first page of a newspaper which contains the most important or interesting news

FTP *abbreviation* file transfer protocol

fugitive material /ˈfjuːdʒɪtɪv mə ˌtɪəriəl/ *noun* ephemera produced for short-term purposes and interest

full binding /ˈfʊl ˌbaɪndɪŋ/, **whole binding** /ˈhəʊl ˌbaɪndɪŋ/ *noun* cased binding, where the case is completely covered with a piece of material such as cloth or leather, as opposed to half binding. Also called **whole binding**

full bound book /ˌfʊl baʊnd ˈbʊk/ *noun* a book with a full binding

full catalogue entry /ˌfʊl ˈkætəlɒg ˌentri/ *noun* full details of a publication

full leather binding /ˌfʊl ˈleðə ˌbaɪndɪŋ/ *noun* a binding on a hardcover book where the whole book is covered with leather

full stop /ˌfʊl ˈstɒp/ *noun* a punctuation mark (.) which indicates the end of a sentence

full text database /ˌfʊl tekst ˈdeɪtəbeɪs/ *noun* a database which allows full text retrieval

'The price [for the resource] ranges from $300 (for the Index only to libraries serving a smaller number of users) to $5000 (for the full-text database to schools, colleges, and public libraries serving a larger number of users).' [*Library Journal*]

full text retrieval /ˌfʊl tekst rɪ ˈtriːv(ə)l/, **full text searching** /ˌfʊl tekst ˈsɜːtʃɪŋ/ *noun* online searching in which every word of the source document can be retrieved

full text search /ˌfʊl tekst ˈsɜːtʃ/ *noun* a search for something carried out through all the text in a file or database rather than limited to an area or block

function /ˈfʌŋkʃən/ *noun* the purpose or role of something

functional /ˈfʌŋkʃən(ə)l/ *adjective* useful or practical rather than attractive

functional illiterate /ˈfʌŋkʃ(ə)nəl ɪ ˌlɪtərət/ *noun* somebody whose reading and writing abilities are inadequately developed to meet everyday needs

functional literacy /ˈfʌŋkʃ(ə)nəl ˌlɪt(ə)rəsi/ *noun* the level of skill in reading and writing that a person needs to cope with everyday adult life

function code /ˈfʌŋkʃən kəʊd/, **function key** /ˈfʌŋkʃən kiː/ *noun* a code or key which makes a part of a computer program work

funding /ˈfʌndɪŋ/ *noun* money provided for a particular purpose

furnish /ˈfɜːnɪʃ/ *verb* to provide or supply something

further education /ˌfɜːðər ˌedjʊ ˈkeɪʃ(ə)n/ *noun* a system of education for people over the official school leaving age

future policy /ˌfjuːtʃə ˈpɒlɪsi/ *noun* plans for the development of an organisation in the near future

fuzzy logic /ˌfʌzi ˈlɒdʒɪk/ *noun* logic that allows for imprecise or ambiguous answers to questions, forming the basis of computer programming designed to mimic human intelligence

fuzzy search /ˈfʌzi sɜːtʃ/ *noun* a computer search that returns not only exact matches to the search request, but also close matches that include possibilities and allow for such things as spelling errors

fx *abbreviation* in Internet addresses, the top-level domain for France, Metropolitan

G

g *abbreviation* gram

ga *abbreviation* in Internet addresses, the top-level domain for Gabon

gain /ɡeɪn/ *noun* an improvement or increase ■ *verb* □ **to gain access to** to get into something such as a record or file

gap /ɡæp/ *noun* a space between two things, ideas or periods of time

garbage /ˈɡɑːbɪdʒ/ *noun* data or information that is no longer required because it is out of date or incorrect

garbage in garbage out /ˌɡɑːbɪdʒ ɪn ˌɡɑːbɪdʒ ˈaʊt/ *phrase* an expression meaning that the accuracy and quality of information that is outputted depends on the quality of the input. Abbr **GIGO**

COMMENT: GIGO is sometimes taken to mean 'garbage in gospel out', meaning that whatever wrong information is put into a computer people will always believe the output is true.

garner /ˈɡɑːnə/ *verb* to collect or accumulate something such as information or facts

gatefold /ˈɡeɪtfəʊld/ *noun* a page in a publication that is larger than the other pages and is folded to fit

gatekeeper /ˈɡeɪtˌkiːpə/ *noun* an online computer host which allows users to access a database

gateway /ˈɡeɪtweɪ/ *noun* a software translation device which allows users working in one network to access another

'In addition, the company is offering the IP Drum Mobile Skype Cables, which connect a Nokia or Sony Ericsson mobile phone to a computer, creating a gateway from Skype to the mobile network. Incoming Skype calls are then forwarded through the mobile phone connected to the computer to the mobile phone the user is carrying.' [*Internet Business News*]

gateway page /ˈɡeɪtweɪ peɪdʒ/ *noun* the initial webpage that a visitor to a website sees and that contains key words and phrases that enable a search engine to find it

gather /ˈɡæðə/ *verb* to compile something such as information or ideas from various sources

gazette /ɡəˈzet/ *noun* a record of public events, journal or other official information document published periodically

gazetteer /ˌɡæzəˈtɪə/ *noun* an index of geographical place names

gd *abbreviation* in Internet addresses, the top-level domain for Grenada

ge *abbreviation* in Internet addresses, the top-level domain for Georgia

gender-free language /ˌdʒendə friː ˈlæŋɡwɪdʒ/ *noun* language that is deliberately used to avoid reference to either men or women, as when the leader of a committee is described as a chairperson instead of the chairman

genealogical tree /ˌdʒiːnɪəlɒdʒɪk(ə)l ˈtriː/ *noun* a tree-structured diagram showing the relationships of the members of a family from the past to the present

genealogy /ˌdʒiːniˈælədʒi/ *noun* the study of the history of the members of a family

general /ˈdʒen(ə)rəl/ *adjective* for all or most people, cases or things

general books /ˈdʒen(ə)rəl bʊks/ *plural noun* books which may interest the adult public, usually not including children's books, fiction or specialised books

generalia class /ˌdʒenəˈreɪliəˌklɑːs/ *noun* a classification for books on a variety of subjects, e.g. encyclopedias

general index /ˈdʒen(ə)rəl ˌɪndeks/ *noun* an index which covers all items in a book

generalisation /ˌdʒen(ə)rəlaɪˈzeɪʃ(ə)n/, **generalization** *noun* a statement that is mostly true but not based on specific facts

general knowledge /ˌdʒen(ə)rəl ˈnɒlɪdʒ/ *noun* knowledge of a broad range of facts or subjects

general packet radio service /ˌdʒen(ə)rəl ˌpækɪt ˈreɪdiəʊ ˌsɜːvɪs/ *noun* full form of **GPRS**

general public /ˌdʒen(ə)rəl ˈpʌblɪk/ *noun* ordinary people

general purpose /ˌdʒen(ə)rəl ˈpɜːpəs/ *adjective* something that can be used for a variety of uses

general reference /ˌdʒen(ə)rəl ˈref(ə)rəns/ *noun* a reference in a catalogue directing users to a number of more specific entries

generate /ˈdʒenəreɪt/ *verb* to cause something to start and develop

generation /ˌdʒenəˈreɪʃ(ə)n/ *noun* **1.** a stage of development in the design and manufacture of machines ○ *fifth generation computers* **2.** the period of time in which people can grow up and have children, usually 25 to 30 years

generic relationship /dʒəˌnerɪk rɪˈleɪʃ(ə)nʃɪp/ *noun* a link in a classification scheme ○ *There is a generic relationship between the genus and species.*

generic searching /dʒəˌnerɪk ˈsɜːtʃɪŋ/ *noun* a type of online searching using a memory to store broader and related headings to the subject being searched

generic top-level domain /dʒəˌnerɪk tɒp ˌlev(ə)l dəˈmeɪn/ *noun* full form of **gTLD**

Geneva Convention /dʒɪˌniːvə kənˈvenʃ(ə)n/ *noun* ♦ **Universal Copyright Convention**

genre /ˈʒɒnrə/ *noun* a category or style of writing, art or music ○ *Science fiction is his favourite genre.*

genuine /ˈdʒenjuɪn/ *adjective* exactly what it is said to be

geographic filing /ˌdʒiəgræfɪk ˈfaɪlɪŋ/ *noun* a system of filing items according to their place of origin

geographic location /ˌdʒiəgræfɪk ləʊˈkeɪʃ(ə)n/ *noun* the place, building, unit or site where an item is stored

get back /ˌget ˈbæk/ *verb* to have something returned to you

get down /ˌget ˈdaʊn/ *verb* **1.** to write down what somebody says **2.** to fetch something from a high place ○ *get down a book from a high shelf*

get into /ˌget ˈɪntuː/ *verb* to become involved with an activity

gf *abbreviation* in Internet addresses, the top-level domain for French Guiana

gg *abbreviation* in Internet addresses, the top-level domain for Guernsey

gh *abbreviation* in Internet addresses, the top-level domain for Ghana

ghost /gəʊst/ *noun* LITERAT same as **ghostwriter** ■ *verb* to be the ghostwriter of a work

ghostwriter /ˈgəʊstˌraɪtə/ *noun* somebody who writes something for or with somebody else, the other person receiving sole credit as the author

gi *abbreviation* in Internet addresses, the top-level domain for Gibraltar

GIF /gɪf/ a trade name for a graphics file format for a file containing a bitmapped image. Full form **Graphics Interchange Format**

.gif *suffix* a file extension for a GIF file. Full form **Graphics Interchange Format**

GIF file /ˌdʒiː aɪ ˈef faɪl/ *noun* a graphics file format for a file containing a bitmapped image

gift /gɪft/ *noun* something given as a present

gigabyte /ˈgɪgəbaɪt/ *noun* 1,000,000,000 bytes

GIGO /ˈgaɪgəʊ/ *abbreviation* garbage in garbage out

gilt /gɪlt/ *noun* a shiny material, usually gold, used as a thin covering to other material

gilt edge /ˈgɪlt edʒ/ *noun* a gold edge to a page of a book, so that when the book is closed it looks like a gold block

gilt-edged /ˈgɪlt edʒd/ *adjective* denoting a book with a gilt edge to the pages

give /gɪv/ *verb* to impart or convey something such as information or advice to somebody

given name /ˈgɪv(ə)n neɪm/ *noun* a person's first name, used by their family and friends

glazed morocco /ˌgleɪzd mə ˈrɒkəʊ/ *noun* polished goatskin leather, used as a binding material

global /ˈgləʊb(ə)l/ *adjective* covering everything

Global Books in Print /ˌgləʊb(ə)l bʊks ɪn ˈprɪnt/ *noun* a worldwide listing on CD-ROM of all books in print

global replace /ˌgləʊb(ə)l rɪˈpleɪs/ *noun* a word-processing function meaning to replace a particular word, group of words, letter or symbol by a different word or words

global search /ˌgləʊb(ə)l ˈsɜːtʃ/ *noun* a computing function which looks through a whole document or database for a particular word or symbol

global search and replace /ˌgləʊb(ə)l ˌsɜːtʃ ən rɪˈpleɪs/ *noun* a search and replace function which is applied to a whole computer file

global village /ˌgləʊb(ə)l ˈvɪlɪdʒ/ *noun* the whole world considered as a single community served by electronic media and information technology

'Given the open architecture of the world wide web, anyone operating a website has access to a worldwide audience – the internet has fuelled globalisation and the 'global village' has become reality.' [*M2 presswire*]

gloss /glɒs/ *noun* a short definition, explanation or translation of a word or phrase that may be unfamiliar to the reader, often located in a margin or collected in an appendix or glossary

glossary /ˈglɒsəri/ *noun* 1. an alphabetical list of the specialist words used in a document, with definitions 2. a list of specialised terms with explanations or translations ○ *glossary of chess terms* ○ *an English-Chinese business glossary*

gloss over /ˌglɒs ˈəʊvə/ *verb* to intentionally leave out negative information, or treat something superficially, in order to make it appear more attractive or acceptable

glossy /ˈglɒsi/ *adjective* smooth and shiny

gm *abbreviation* 1. in Internet addresses, the top-level domain for Gambia 2. gram

gn *abbreviation* in Internet addresses, the top-level domain for Guinea

gnostic /ˈnɒstɪk/ *adjective* relating to knowledge, especially knowledge of spiritual truths

GNVQ /ˌdʒiː en viː ˈkjuː/ *noun* in the United Kingdom, a qualification designed to provide vocationally orientated skills and knowledge for progression from school to employment or university. Full form **General National Vocational Qualification**

goal /gəʊl/ *noun* 1. what somebody is trying to achieve 2. the final state reached when a task is finished

goal-setting /ˈgəʊl ˌsetɪŋ/ *noun* a policy discussion which agrees what a group, company or organisation hopes to achieve

goatskin /ˈgəʊtskɪn/ *noun* leather from the skin of a goat, called morocco when used for binding

go by /ˌgəʊ ˈbaɪ/ *verb* to treat advice or information as reliable or true

go list /ˈgəʊ lɪst/ *noun* a list of terms or characters to be included in a printout. Compare **stop list**

gone to press /ˌgɒn tə ˈpres/ *adjective* used to indicate that text has gone for printing and it is too late to make corrections

Google /ˈguːg(ə)l/ a trade name for a popular search engine

go on /ˌgəʊ ˈɒn/ *verb* to use something as reliable information

gopher /ˈgəʊfə/ *noun* a servicing device within the Internet which allows access by allowing links between systems

gossip /ˈgɒsɪp/ *noun* a conversation or report about other people's behaviour, which is often exaggerated and not always completely true

gov *abbreviation* in Internet addresses, the generic top-level domain for government organisation

government library /ˌgʌvənmənt ˈlaɪbrərɪz/ *noun* a library that exists for each of the major departments of the government, e.g. Dept of Employment library

government publication /ˌgʌvənmənt ˌpʌblɪˈkeɪʃ(ə)n/ *noun* a publication with information which is written and published by government departments, often of a statistical nature

gp *abbreviation* in Internet addresses, the top-level domain for Guadeloupe

GPRS /ˌdʒiː piː ɑːr ˈes/ *noun* a system that provides immediate and continuous access to the Internet from wireless devices such as mobile phones. Full form **general packet radio service**

gq *abbreviation* in Internet addresses, the top-level domain for Equatorial Guinea

gr *abbreviation* in Internet addresses, the top-level domain for Greece

grade /greɪd/ *noun* a mark given to a piece of coursework or an examination which indicates the level of success attained ■ *verb* to judge or measure the quality of something

graduate /ˈgrædʒuət/ *noun* a person who has successfully completed a first degree course at a university

graduate trainee /ˌgrædʒuət treɪ ˈniː/ *noun* a person who has graduated in one subject and is receiving further training in a specialist skill

gram /græm/ *noun* a measurement of weight which is used to indicate the quality of paper ○ *80g paper is standard copier quality*. Abbr **g**

grammar check /ˈgræmə tʃek/ *noun* a software facility which enables the user to check the grammatical accuracy of work done on a word processor

grammatical error /grəˌmætɪk(ə)l ˈerə/ *noun* word usage which breaks the rules of a language

graph /grɑːf/ *noun* a mathematical diagram which visually shows the relationship between two or more sets of variables

graphic /ˈgræfɪk/ *adjective* concerned with drawing

graphic display /ˌgræfɪk dɪsˈpleɪ/ *noun* a computer screen that is able to present graphical information

graphic display resolution /ˈgræfɪk dɪˌspleɪ ˌrezəluːʃ(ə)n/ *noun* the number of pixels that a computer is able to display on the screen

graphic novel /ˌgræfɪk ˈnɒv(ə)l/ *noun* a fictional story for adults published in the form of a comic strip

graphics /ˈgræfɪks/ *plural noun* pictures or lines drawn to represent information

graphics file /ˈgræfɪks faɪl/ *noun* a binary file which contains data describing an image ○ *There are many standards for graphics files including TIFF, IMG and EPS.*

graphics file format /ˈgræfɪks faɪl ˌfɔːmæt/ *noun* a method by which data describing an image is stored

Graphics Interchange Format /ˈgræfɪks ˌɪntətʃeɪndʒ ˌfɔːmæt/ *noun* full form of **GIF**

graphics pad /ˈgræfɪks pæd/, **graphics tablet** /ˈgræfɪks ˌtæblət/ *noun* a flat device that allows a user to input graphical information into a computer by drawing on its surface

graph paper /ˈgrɑːf ˌpeɪpə/ *noun* paper which is printed with measured squares so that it can be used for drawing graphs

grave accent /ˌgrɑːv ˈæksənt/ *noun* a mark placed over a vowel (e.g. è)†to show how it should be pronounced

COMMENT: Grave accents are used in French (è, à, ù) to indicate a pronunciation change or a spelling change. They are used in other languages to show stress.

gremlin /ˈgremlɪn/ *noun* a tiny mischievous spirit said to be the cause of an unexplained problem or fault, especially in a machine or system

grey literature /ˈgreɪ ˌlɪt(ə)rətʃə/ *noun* **1.** in-house publications, e.g. parish magazines or technical reports **2.**

articles and information published, especially on the Internet, without a commercial purpose or the mediation of a commercial publisher

grey scale /ˈgreɪ skeɪl/ *noun* shades which are produced from displaying what should be colour information on a monochrome monitor

grid /grɪd/ *noun* a system of numbered squares allowing points to be easily plotted or located

COMMENT: Grids are used by designers and pasteup artists for laying out magazines and books, where the page size, type area and general layout remain the same for each page. The designer will prepare a master grid, showing the basic proportions of the page, with its trim size, type area, headlines, folio positions, margins, etc., and this is used when pasting up each page.

grid reference /ˈgrɪd ˌref(ə)rəns/ *noun* a set of numbers from the X and Y axes giving the location of a point on a map

gross /grəʊs/ *noun* the total amount before any deductions have been made

gross income /ˌgrəʊs ˈɪnkʌm/ *noun* the total amount of money earned before any deductions e.g. for tax

gross weight /ˌgrəʊs ˈweɪt/ *noun* the total weight of something including all packaging

ground rent /ˈgraʊnd rent/ *noun* rent paid by a tenant of a building to the owner of the land on which it is built

grounds /graʊndz/ *plural noun* a reason or justification for something

group /gruːp/ *noun* a collection of people or things that are in the same place at the same time or have something in common

group consensus /ˌgruːp kənˈsensəs/ *noun* the combined feelings of a group of people about a decision. Also called **groupthink**

group manager /ˌgruːp ˈmænɪdʒə/ *noun* a person who has responsibility for the organisation of a group of people

groupthink /ˈgruːpθɪŋk/ *noun* same as **group consensus**

groupware /ˈgruːpweə/ *noun* software designed to be shared collaboratively by a number of users on a computer network

growing demand /ˌgrəʊɪŋ dɪˈmɑːnd/ *noun* an increasing number of people who want to use a product or service

growth /grəʊθ/ *noun* an increase in the size, wealth or importance of something

Grub Street /ˈgrʌb striːt/ *noun* the name of a street in London which was inhabited mainly by writers, now the general name for low-paid journalism

gs *abbreviation* in Internet addresses, the top-level domain for South Georgia

gsm, g/m² *noun* a way of showing the weight of paper used in printing. Full form **grams per square metre**

gt *abbreviation* in Internet addresses, the top-level domain for Guatemala

gTLD *noun* the portion of an Internet address that identifies it as belonging to a specific generic domain class, e.g. com, edu or gov. Full form **generic top-level domain**

gu *abbreviation* in Internet addresses, the top-level domain for Guam

guarantee /ˌgærənˈtiː/ *noun* a written promise that any faults in a purchase which show within a given period of time will be repaired free of charge

guess /ges/ *noun* an attempt to answer a question when you do not have the information needed

guesstimate /ˈgestɪmət/ *noun* an approximate calculation based entirely on guesswork

guest book /ˈgest bʊk/ *noun* a book in which people write their names and addresses when they stay at a hotel or guest house

guide /gaɪd/ *noun* **1.** a book of instructions **2.** a person who shows people the way

guidebook /ˈgaɪdbʊk/ *noun* a book containing information for tourists about a country, place or institution

guide letters /ˈgaɪd ˌletəz/ *plural noun* large letter signs to indicate the location of items in a library

guidelines /ˈgaɪdlaɪnz/ *plural noun* a written code of practice about how to do things in a particular field of work

guides /gaɪdz/ *noun* a system of signs to help people to find their way around a building

guiding /ˈgaɪdɪŋ/ *noun* same as **guides**

guild /gɪld/ *noun* an association of people with similar interests or skills who join together to support each other

guillotine /ˈgɪlətiːn/ *noun* a device used for cutting and trimming paper

Gutenberg Bible /ˈgʊtənbɜːg ˌbaɪb(ə)l/ *noun* the first large book to be printed in Europe from movable type, in around 1455

gutter /ˈgʌtə/ *noun* the inside margin between two pages of type

gutter press /ˈgʌtə pres/ *noun* a name for the tabloid newspapers which print large amounts of gossip rather than factual news. ◊ **yellow press**

gw *abbreviation* in Internet addresses, the top-level domain for Guinea-Bissau

gy *abbreviation* in Internet addresses, the top-level domain for Guyana

H

hack /hæk/ *verb* to gain access illegally to a computer system or program ■ *noun* a writer who produces poor quality material only for money

hacker /'hækə/ *noun* somebody who gains access to other people's computer files without their permission

half binding /'hɑːf ˌbaɪndɪŋ/ *noun* bookbinding in which the back and sometimes the corners of a book are bound in one material and the sides in another

half bound book /'hɑːf baʊnd ˌbʊk/ *noun* a book with a style of binding which was common from the beginning of the 19th century, where binding leathers or vellum were used on the spine and corners and the rest of the boards were covered with marbled paper or plain paper and cloth

half leather binding /ˌhɑːf ˌleðə 'baɪndɪŋ/ *noun* a binding on a hardcover book, where the spine and corners are covered with leather and the rest is left in ordinary cloth or paper

half title /'hɑːf ˌtaɪt(ə)l/ *noun* the first page of a book with only the title and not the details of the publisher or author

halftone /'hɑːftəʊn/, **half-tone** *noun* **1.** continuous shading of a printed area **2.** a shade of grey appearing to be half way between white and black **3.** an illustration made using the halftone process ○ *a book with 25 halftone illustrations* ○ *The book is illustrated with twenty halftones.* ○ *We need a full page halftone facing the beginning of the chapter.*

COMMENT: Halftones are made by breaking up a continuous tone pattern into a series of dots of varying sizes. When printed, the dots appear to merge into a continuous tone, though if you look at them closely the dots are visible. The dots are created by scanning or by photographing the original through a screen, which is a mesh of criss-cross lines or a series of dots.

halftone screen /'hɑːftəʊn skriːn/ *noun* a screen with cross lines or a grid of dots used for preparing a halftone illustration

half-yearly /ˌhɑːf 'jɪəli/ *adjective* **1.** happening every six months ○ *a half-yearly magazine* **2.** referring to a period of six months ○ *half-yearly royalty statement* ■ *adverb* every six months ○ *we pay some royalties half-yearly*

halt /hɔːlt/ *verb* to stop completely, although usually temporarily

handbook /'hændbʊk/ *noun* a book of advice and instructions

hand-held /'hænd held/ *adjective* small and light enough to be used while held in the hand ○ *hand-held video camera*

handle /'hænd(ə)l/ *noun* **1.** a computer user's nickname or screen name **2.** (*in a graphics or DTP program*) a small square that is displayed on the edge of a frame, object or image ■ *verb* to deal with or accept responsibility for a situation or people

handout /'hændaʊt/ *noun* a printed paper which supports a talk or lecture with summaries or other information

handover period /'hændəʊvə ˌpɪəriəd/ *noun* a period of time when the outgoing holder of a job works with the new person to make sure they have all the necessary knowledge of the work

'Advocates of outsourcing argue that it allows companies to focus on their core business, improve employee services and cut costs. Initially, costs rose in the deal because the two were running parallel services during the handover period.' [*Financial Times*]

handshake /'hændʃeɪk/, **handshaking** /'hændʃeɪkɪŋ/ *noun* a term in computing which indicates that two machines are compatible and can transfer information to each other

hands-on experience /ˌhændz ɒn ɪk'spɪəriəns/ *noun* the ability to actually use machines or equipment rather than just learning about them

hands-on training /ˌhændz ɒn 'treɪnɪŋ/ *noun* a method of teaching using practical experience rather than just theory

handwriting /'hændraɪtɪŋ/ *noun* a system of putting words on paper using a pen or pencil ○ *Everyone has their own distinctive style of handwriting.*

handwritten /ˌhænd'rɪt(ə)n/ *adjective* written with a pen or pencil rather than printed by a machine

hang up /ˌhæŋ 'ʌp/ *verb* to end a phone call by putting the receiver down

Hansard /'hænsɑːd/ *noun* a written account of the proceedings of the UK Parliament

hardback /'hɑːdbæk/ *noun* a copy of a book with a board cover. Compare **paperback**

hardbound /'hɑːdbaʊnd/ *adjective* bound as a book in a stiff cover

hard copy /ˌhɑːd 'kɒpi/ *noun* a printed version of a document held on a computer

hardcover /'hɑːdkʌvə/ *noun* PUBL same as **hardback**

hard disk /ˌhɑːd 'dɪsk/ *noun* a rigid magnetic disk usually built into a computer, which can store much more data than a floppy disk

hardware /'hɑːdweə/ *noun* the machinery of a computer, rather than the programs written for it

hardware costs /'hɑːdweə kɒsts/ *plural noun* the capital costs of buying computer equipment and other machinery

hardware resources /'hɑːdweə rɪˌzɔːsɪz/ *plural noun* the amount of computer equipment and machinery available for use

Harvard system /'hɑːvəd ˌsɪstəm/ *noun* a bibliographic reference system, used in academic publishing, in which the author and date are given in the text and the full reference is supplied in a general list of references

hash /hæʃ/, **hashmark** /'hæʃmɑːk/ *noun* **1.** a symbol (#) used to indicate the word 'number' in addresses ○ *RD#3 (Rural District Number 3)* **2.** a symbol used on telephones for a variety of functions

head /hed/ *noun* the top or most important part or person □ **per head** referring to the cost or amount for each person

head crash /'hed kræʃ/ *noun* failure in a disk drive, where the read/write head touches the surface of the disk, causing damage and data loss

headed stationery /ˌhedɪd 'steɪʃ(ə)n(ə)ri/ *noun* notepaper which has the name and address of the person or organisation it belongs to printed at the top of each sheet

header /'hedə/ *noun* **1.** (*in a document*) a piece of text that appears at the very top of each page, containing e.g. the chapter name and the page number. ◊ **footer 2.** the beginning of an e-mail message with full information about the recipient's address, sender's name and address and any delivery options

header block /'hedə blɒk/ *noun* a block of data at the beginning of a file, which contains the file characteristics

heading /'hedɪŋ/ *noun* a word, phrase, title or name at the beginning of a page, section or catalogue entry

head librarian /ˌhed laɪ'breəriən/ *noun* a qualified librarian who is in charge of a library or district

headline /'hedlaɪn/ *noun* **1.** the title at the top of a page or article in a newspaper story **2.** a spoken list of items to be covered in a radio or TV news bulletin

head of department /ˌhed əv dɪ'pɑːtmənt/ *noun* a person who is responsible for a group of people working in the same department

head office /ˌhed 'ɒfɪs/ *noun* the main office of a company or organisation which has branch offices in other places

headphones /'hedfəʊnz/ *plural noun* a pair of small speakers worn over the ears to listen to speech or music

headquarters /hed'kwɔːtəz/ *plural noun* the main administrative office of an organisation

headword /'hedwɜːd/ *noun* the main entry word in a dictionary

help line /'help laɪn/ *noun* a telephone number dedicated to a specific topic which people can ring for advice and help

help menu /'help ˌmenjuː/ *noun* a list of options available which instruct people how to use a computer program

help screen /'help skriːn/ *noun* a screen containing writing which explains how to use a computer program

Heritage Lottery Fund /ˌherɪtɪdʒ 'lɒtəri ˌfʌnd/ *noun* a public body which distributes money raised by the National Lottery in the UK to heritage organisations, including libraries and archiving services. Abbr **HLF**

Her Majesty's Inspectorate /ˌhɜː ˌmædʒəstiːz ɪn'spekt(ə)rət/, **Her Majesty's Inspector** *noun* a British government department or official responsible for inspecting teaching in schools. Abbr **HMI**

Her Majesty's Stationery Office /ˌhɜː ˌmædʒəstɪz 'steɪʃ(ə)n(ə)ri ˌɒfɪs/ *noun* the publications office of the British government. Abbr **HMSO**

heuristic /hjʊə'rɪstɪk/ *adjective* solving problems by using reasoning and experience rather than standard formulae

heuristic searching /hjʊə'rɪstɪk ˌsɜːtʃɪŋ/ *noun* a method of searching which modifies the search according to each piece of information as it is found

'The GA is one of the emerging heuristic searching techniques that is suitable for solving complex combinatorial problems (Reeves,

1993). The GA was invented and developed to mimic some of the processes observed in natural selection, initially by Holland and his associates at the University of Michigan in the 1960s.' [*Integrated Manufacturing Systems*]

hidden agenda /ˌhɪd(ə)n ə'dʒendə/ *noun* the unspoken intentions behind a decision or action

hidden Web /'hɪd(ə)n web/ *noun* same as **deep Web**

hide /haɪd/ *noun* leather made from the skin of animals older than a calf, used for binding large-format books

hierarchical /ˌhaɪə'rɑːkɪk(ə)l/ *adjective* relating to data arranged in a tree structure with defined layers

hierarchical classification /ˌhaɪərɑːkɪk(ə)l ˌklæsɪfɪ'keɪʃ(ə)n/ *noun* a system of classifying items with the broadest terms at the top and working down to more specific narrow terms

hierarchical database /ˌhaɪərɑːkɪk(ə)l 'deɪtəbeɪs/ *noun* the organisation of information in a database so that records can be related to each other within a defined structure

hierarchical search /ˌhaɪərɑːkɪk(ə)l 'sɜːtʃ/ *noun* a search in a catalogue using an upwards chain of entries from most to least specific

hierarchy /'haɪərɑːki/ *noun* a system of ranking things or people according to their importance

hi fi /'haɪ 'faɪ/ *abbreviation* high fidelity ■ *noun* a set of stereo equipment with speakers and amplifiers used for playing records, tapes and CDs

high density disk /ˌhaɪ ˌdensɪti 'dɪsk/ *noun* a computer floppy disk capable of storing a quantity of data

higher education /ˌhaɪər edjʊ 'keɪʃ(ə)n/ *noun* education that takes place at universities or colleges usually after the age of 18, leading towards an academic qualification

higher learning /ˌhaɪə 'lɜːnɪŋ/ *noun* education or study at university level

Higher National Certificate /ˌhaɪə ˌnæʃ(ə)nəl sə'tɪfɪkət/ *noun* awarded at

British colleges in technical subjects. Abbr **HNC**

Higher National Diploma /ˌhaɪə ˌnæʃ(ə)nəl dɪˈpləʊmə/ *noun* an advanced qualification in technical subjects. Abbr **HND**

high flier /ˌhaɪ ˈflaɪə/ *noun* a person who is very capable, ambitious and likely to reach the top ranks of their career

high-level language /ˌhaɪ ˌlev(ə)l ˈlæŋgwɪdʒ/ *noun* a computer programming language that is easy to use and uses natural language

high-level talks /ˌhaɪ ˌlev(ə)l ˈtɔːks/ *plural noun* discussions involving senior people in politics or business

highlight /ˈhaɪlaɪt/ *verb* to colour or mark text on a document or computer screen to make it stand out from the rest

high-resolution /ˌhaɪ ˌrezə ˈluːʃ(ə)n/ *adjective* relating to the ability to display or detect a very large number of pixels per unit area. Abbr **hi-res**

COMMENT: Currently, high-resolution graphics displays can show images at a resolution of 1024x1024 pixels, high-resolution printers can print at 600 or 800 dots per inch and a high-resolution scanner can scan at a resolution of 800 or 1200 dots per inch.

high-specification /ˌhaɪ ˌspesɪfɪ ˈkeɪʃ(ə)n/ *adjective* having a high level of accuracy or quality

high-speed /ˈhaɪ spiːd/ *adjective* operating at faster than usual speed

high-tech /ˌhaɪ ˈtek/ *adjective* using advanced technology

hi-res /ˌhaɪ ˈreɪz/ *abbreviation* high-resolution

histogram /ˈhɪstəgræm/ *noun* a graph on which the data is represented by vertical or horizontal bars

historical background /hɪs ˌtɒrɪk(ə)l ˈbækgraʊnd/ *noun* the reasons why something has developed over a period of time to its present form

historical value /hɪsˌtɒrɪk(ə)l ˈvæljuː/ *noun* something that helps in the understanding of past events

hit /hɪt/ *noun* a successful match when searching a database

hit list /ˈhɪt lɪst/ *noun* a list of people or organisations that are most likely to do something or have something done to them ○ *The local council had hit lists of branch libraries which were either likely to support their projects or which they were going to close.*

hit rate /ˈhɪt reɪt/ *noun* the number of relevant titles found during a database search

hk *abbreviation* in Internet addresses, the top-level domain for Hong Kong

HLF *abbreviation* Heritage Lottery Fund

hm *abbreviation* in Internet addresses, the top-level domain for Heard and McDonald Islands

HMI *abbreviation* **1.** human machine interface **2.** Her Majesty's Inspectorate

HMSO *abbreviation* Her Majesty's Stationery Office

hn *abbreviation* in Internet addresses, the top-level domain for Honduras

HNC *abbreviation* Higher National Certificate

HND *abbreviation* Higher National Diploma

holding area /ˈhəʊldɪŋ ˌeəriə/ *noun* a space allocated to the temporary storage of semi-current materials

holding file /ˈhəʊldɪŋ faɪl/ *noun* a computer file in which work waits until it can be processed

holdings /ˈhəʊldɪŋz/ *plural noun* the stock of books and other items kept by a library

holiday period /ˈhɒlɪdeɪ ˌpɪəriəd/ *noun* the time of year during which most people take their annual holidays

hologram /ˈhɒləgræm/ *noun* a three-dimensional photographic image created by laser beams

holograph /ˈhɒləgrɑːf/ *noun* a book or document written in the author's own handwriting

home computer /ˌhəʊm kəm ˈpjuːtə/ *noun* a stand-alone personal computer used at home

homepage /ˈhəʊmpeɪdʒ/ *noun* **1.** the opening page of an Internet website **2.** somebody's personal website on the Internet, often containing personal data, photographs or contact information

homograph /ˈhɒməʊɡrɑːf/ *noun* a word having the same spelling but different meaning from another, as with 'spell' meaning 'witchcraft' and 'spell' meaning 'to write words correctly'

COMMENT: Homographs are to be avoided where possible as headings when indexing.

homonym /ˈhɒmənɪm/ *noun* a word with the same sound and perhaps the same spelling another but with a different meaning, as with 'counter' meaning 'library issue desk' and 'counter' meaning 'machine for counting'

homophone /ˈhɒməfəʊn/ *noun* a word with the same sound but different spelling and meaning from another, such as 'threw' meaning 'past tense of throw' and 'through', which is a preposition

honorarium /ˌɒnəˈreəriəm/ *noun* a payment made for professional services which are usually provided without charge

honorary /ˈɒnərəri/ *adjective* **1.** relating to a position or role that is held as an honour, without payment **2.** relating to a title or qualification that is given as a reward, not because it has been worked for in the usual way

horizontal format /ˌhɒrɪzɒnt(ə)l ˈfɔːmæt/ *noun US* a book format where the spine and foredge are shorter than the top and bottom edges (NOTE: The UK term is **landscape format**.)

hospital library /ˈhɒspɪtl ˈlaɪbri/ ♦ **library**

host /həʊst/ *noun* the main computer in a system which allows access to online databases ■ *verb* to provide storage space on a server computer where a user can store files or data, often used to store the files required for a website

host computer /ˌhəʊst kəmˈpjuːtə/ *noun* the controlling computer in a multi-user system

host service /ˈhəʊst ˌsɜːvɪs/ *noun* a company that provides connections to the Internet and storage space on its computers which can store the files for a user's website

hotline /ˈhɒtlaɪn/ *noun* a direct telephone line giving direct access, used e.g. for quick ordering, for complaints or between heads of governments

hot link /ˌhɒt ˈlɪŋk/ *noun* a command within a hypertext program that links a hotspot or hotword on one page with a second destination page which is displayed if the user selects the hotspot

hotspot /ˈhɒtspɒt/ *noun* a special area on an image or display that does something when the cursor is moved on to it ○ *The image of the trumpet is a hotspot and will play a sound when you move the pointer over it.*

hotword /ˈhɒtwɜːd/ *noun* a word within displayed text that does something when the cursor is moved on to it or it is selected

hourly /ˈaʊəli/ *adjective* happening every hour

house journal /ˈhaʊs ˌdʒɜːn(ə)l/ *noun* an internal magazine giving information and news to the employees of a company or organisation. Also called **house magazine**

'…the new premises are said to be 'a sixth of the cost' and have better facilities for training and meetings… the organisation will offer a full package of membership benefits as before – including Aslib journals from Emerald, a range of training courses, and the monthly Managing Information house journal.' [*Information World Review*]

housekeeping /ˈhaʊskiːpɪŋ/ *noun* the work necessary to maintain any system of filing whether manual or computerised

house magazine /ˈhaʊs mægə ˌziːn/ *noun* same as **house journal**

house organ /ˈhaʊs ˌɔːɡən/ *noun* a magazine published by a business or other organisation for its employees or customers, containing information about the company, its products and its employees

house style /ˌhaʊs ˈstaɪl/ *noun* a style of writing and presentation that is specific to a particular group, company or organisation

COMMENT: The aim of a house style is to give consistency to all the products of a publishing house, thus making them more recognisable to the reading public. In the case of magazines, contributors will be sent a style sheet which shows how they should lay out their contributions. A house style will cover many aspects of layout, such as headlines, position of folios, typefaces and sizes; it will also cover details of spelling and punctuation: the form for writing dates (1st January 1999 or January 1st, 1999 or 1st Jan. 1999 or 01.01.99, etc.); the use of full stops after abbreviations (Mr or Mr., P.O.Box or PO Box, etc.). Most publishing companies have their own style sheets which are given to editors and form part of the training programme for new editorial and production staff. Many printers as well as publishers have their own house style and many follow the style of one of the University Presses (Oxford and Cambridge).

hr *abbreviation* in Internet addresses, the top-level domain for Croatia

ht *abbreviation* in Internet addresses, the top-level domain for Haiti

HTML /ˌeɪtʃ tiː em 'el/ *noun* a series of special codes which define the typeface and style that should be used when displaying the text and also allow hypertext links to other parts of the document or to other documents. Full form **HyperText Markup Language.** ◊ **Internet**, **SGML**, **XML**

.html *suffix* a file extension for an HTML file. Full form **HyperText Markup Language**

HTTP /ˌeɪtʃ tiː tiː 'piː/ *noun* a series of commands used by a browser to ask an Internet web server for information about a webpage. Full form **hypertext transfer protocol**

hu *abbreviation* in Internet addresses, the top-level domain for Hungary

human /'hjuːmən/ *adjective* concerning people rather than animals

human capital /ˌhjuːmən 'kæpɪt(ə)l/ *noun* the knowledge and skills that employees have, which are considered a resource of the company

human-computer interaction /ˌhjuːmən kəmˌpjuːtə ˌɪntər'ækʃən/ *noun* the field of study relating to the interface between computers and users

human factors /ˌhjuːmən 'fæktəz/ *plural noun* the needs of human beings

which must be considered when planning automation of an office

humanities /hjuː'mænɪtiz/ *plural noun* subjects of study concerned with human ideas and behaviour, e.g. literature and philosophy

Humanities Online Bulletin Board /hjuːˌmænɪtiz ˌɒnlaɪn 'bʊlətɪn ˌbɔːd/ *noun* an online current awareness service for the humanities. Abbr **HUMBUL**

human machine interface /ˌhjuːmən mə'ʃiːn ˌɪntəfeɪs/ *noun* the way that a computer screen appears to the user. Abbr **HMI**

human resources /ˌhjuːmən rɪ'sɔːsɪz/ *plural noun* the staff of an organisation or company, which can provide skills to do specific jobs

HUMBUL /'hʌmbʌl/ *abbreviation* Humanities Online Bulletin Board

hybrid /'haɪbrɪd/ *noun* a mixture of different things

hymn book /'hɪm bʊk/ *noun* a book containing the words, and sometimes the music, of church songs

hyperlink /'haɪpəlɪŋk/ *noun* a word, symbol, image or other element in a hypertext document that links to another element in the same document or in another hypertext document

hypermedia /'haɪpəmiːdiə/ *noun* a hypertext system that supports the linking of graphics, audio and video elements, and text

hypertext /'haɪpətekst/ *noun* **1.** a multimedia system of organising information in which certain words in a document link to other documents and display the text when the word is selected **2.** a way of linking one word or image on an Internet page to another page in which clicking on certain words or images moves the user directly to the relevant new page

HyperText Markup Language /'haɪpətekst ˌmaːkʌp ˌlæŋwɪdʒ/ *noun* full form of **HTML**

hypertext transfer protocol /ˌhaɪpətekst 'trænsfɜː ˌprəʊtəkɒl/ *noun* full form of **HTTP**

hyphen /ˈhaɪf(ə)n/ *noun* a punctuation mark (-) used to join two words together, as in 'two-sided'

hyphenated /ˈhaɪfəneɪtɪd/ *adjective* formed of two words joined by a hyphen

hyphen stringing /ˈhaɪfən ˌstrɪŋɪŋ/ *noun* the process of using hyphens to combine terms

hypothesis /haɪˈpɒθəsɪs/ *noun* a theory which has not yet been tested to prove its truth (NOTE: The plural is **hypotheses**.)

hypothetical /ˌhaɪpəˈθetɪk(ə)l/ *adjective* based on suggestions rather than proved or tested

I

IA *abbreviation* information architecture

IAA *abbreviation* International Aerospace Abstracts

IAP *abbreviation* ONLINE Internet access provider

IBA *abbreviation* Independent Broadcasting Association

IBIS Information Services Ltd /ˈaɪbɪs/ *noun* a company providing a subject-coded file of information about libraries and staff in academic libraries worldwide

IBM-compatible /ˌaɪ biː em kəm ˈpætɪb(ə)l/ *adjective* referring to a computer which is able to run standard IBM software

ICIC *abbreviation* International Copyright Information Centre

icon /ˈaɪkɒn/ *noun* 1. a picture or symbol that is universally recognised to be representative of something 2. a graphic symbol used in computing to represent different functions of a program

iconography /ˌaɪkəˈnɒgrəfi/ *noun* the set of symbols or images used in a particular field of activity such as music or cinema and recognised by people as having a particular meaning

-ics *suffix* forming nouns referring to a science, art or branch of knowledge

id *abbreviation* ONLINE in Internet addresses, the top-level domain for Indonesia

ID /ˌaɪ ˈdiː/ *noun* proof of identity

IDD *abbreviation* international direct dialling

identical /aɪˈdentɪk(ə)l/ *adjective* exactly the same

identification /aɪˌdentɪfɪˈkeɪʃ(ə)n/ *noun* any means used to establish who somebody is, e.g. a document, mark, number or password

identifier /aɪˈdentɪfaɪə/ *noun* 1. the grammatical term for the definite and indefinite articles in English 2. any tag, flag or mark put on a computer file to differentiate it from others

identify /aɪˈdentɪfaɪ/ *verb* to recognise or indicate what something is

identity number /aɪˈdentɪti ˌnʌmbə/ *noun* a unique number which can be used as a password for accessing a computer system

idiom /ˈɪdiəm/ *noun* an expression which has a different meaning from the separate meanings of the words and is peculiar to a language so that it cannot be literally translated

idle /ˈaɪd(ə)l/ *adjective* waiting to be used

ie *abbreviation* in Internet addresses, the top-level domain for Ireland

IEEE *abbreviation* Institute of Electrical and Electronics Engineers

IFLA *abbreviation* International Federation of Library Associations and Institutions

IG *abbreviation* information governance

ignorance /ˈɪgnərəns/ *noun* a lack of knowledge about something

ignorant /ˈɪgnərənt/ *adjective* 1. lacking knowledge or education in general or in a specific subject 2. caused by a lack of knowledge, understanding or experience

IIS *abbreviation* Institute of Information Scientists

IKBS *abbreviation* INFO SCI intelligent knowledge-based system

il *abbreviation* in Internet addresses, the top-level domain for Israel

ILL *abbreviation* inter-library loan

illegal /ɪˈliːg(ə)l/ *adjective* not allowed by law

illegible /ɪˈledʒɪb(ə)l/ *adjective* so badly written that it cannot be read

illiteracy /ɪˈlɪt(ə)rəsi/ *noun* the inability to read or write

illiterate /ɪˈlɪt(ə)rət/ *adjective* unable to read or write

illuminate /ɪˈluːmɪneɪt/ *verb* **1.** to illustrate a medieval manuscript **2.** to shine light on something **3.** to make things clear by explaining them

illuminated /ɪˈluːmɪneɪtɪd/ *adjective* **1.** denoting a manuscript that is decorated with gold paint and colours **2.** filled with light

illumination /ɪˌluːmɪˈneɪʃ(ə)n/ *noun* the painting of initial letters in manuscripts with gold, silver and colours

illustrate /ˈɪləstreɪt/ *verb* **1.** to draw pictures or diagrams to put into written text **2.** to make a point clear by using examples or stories

illustrated /ˈɪləstreɪtɪd/ *adjective* of a text, with pictures and diagrams included ○ *The book is illustrated with twenty-five full-colour plates.*

illustration /ˌɪləˈstreɪʃ(ə)n/ *noun* a picture, chart or diagram which helps to explain the words of a book or talk

illustrator /ˈɪləstreɪtə/ *noun* a person who does the drawings or pictures for a book

im *abbreviation* in Internet addresses, the top-level domain for Isle of Man

image /ˈɪmɪdʒ/ *noun* **1.** a picture or reflection of somebody or something **2.** in computing, an exact replica of an area of memory

image enhancer /ˈɪmɪdʒ enˌhɑːnsə/ *noun* an electronic device that makes the picture clearer

image processing /ˈɪmɪdʒ ˌprəʊsesɪŋ/ *noun* the analysis of information contained in an image, usually by electronic means or using a computer which provides the analysis or recognition of objects in the image

image processor /ˈɪmɪdʒ ˌprəʊsesə/ *noun* an electronic device that analyses the information in an image to enable recognition

image scanner /ˈɪmɪdʒ ˌskænə/ *noun* an electronic device that converts pictures or drawings into machine-readable form

imaging /ˈɪmɪdʒɪŋ/ *noun* a technique for creating pictures on a computer screen

imp. *abbreviation* PUBL imprimatur

impact /ˈɪmpækt/ *noun* a strong effect or influence on something

impart /ɪmˈpɑːt/ *verb* to communicate information or knowledge

implement /ˈɪmplɪˌment/ *verb* to put a plan into action

'The enterprise edition of the Blackboard Learning System seamlessly integrates with many other technology tools used by academic institutions… According to Barbara Newland, "Moving to the enterprise edition will enable the university to implement its e-learning strategy which aims to enhance the student experience".' [*M2 Presswire*]

implementation /ˌɪmplɪmənˈteɪʃ(ə)n/ *noun* **1.** the carrying out of plans or systems **2.** the latest version, particularly of software

implication /ˌɪmplɪˈkeɪʃ(ə)n/ *noun* something suggested by a situation, words or events

imply /ɪmˈplaɪ/ *verb* to suggest that something is true without actually saying so

import *noun* /ˈɪmpɔːt/ the importance of something because of the way it is likely to affect outcomes ○ *They discussed matters of great import.* ■ *verb* /ɪmˈpɔːt/ **1.** to buy goods or services in one country and bring them to one's own for sale ○ *We use paper imported from Scandinavia.* **2.** to bring something in from outside a system ○ *You can import images from the CAD package into the DTP program.* **3.** to convert a file stored in one format to the default format used by a program ○ *Select import if you want to open a TIFF graphics file.*

impression /ɪmˈpreʃ(ə)n/ *noun* the number of copies of a book or document printed on the same print run ○ *The book is in its third impression.*

imprimatur /ˌɪmprɪˈmeɪtə/ *noun* **1.** authority to do, say or print something **2.** an authorisation allowing a book or other work to be published, now usually confined to works sanctioned by the Roman Catholic Church

imprint /ˈɪmprɪnt/ *noun* **1.** the publisher's or printer's name which appears on the title page of a book or document or in the bibliographical details **2.** a mark made by firmly pressing something onto a surface

COMMENT: Catalogues, advertisements and fliers do not need to have an imprint, but almost all other printed matter (books, newspapers, and even political leaflets) must carry two imprints: that of the publisher and of the printer. In a book, the imprints will normally appear on the reverse of the title page as part of the bibliographic information; in some countries it is usual to have the printer's imprint at the end of the book. In a magazine, imprints may be listed along with other details of the editors and other staff members.

improvise /ˈɪmprəvaɪz/ *verb* **1.** to make something from whatever materials are available rather than using the proper ones **2.** to carry out an activity using one's initiative rather than planning it carefully in advance

impulse /ˈɪmpʌls/ *noun* **1.** a short electrical signal **2.** a sudden desire to do something without thinking about it or planning it first

IMS *abbreviation* INFO SCI information management system

in /ɪn/ *preposition* used to introduce adjectival and adverbial phrases □ **in alphabetical order** organised according to the same order as the letters in the alphabet □ **in ascending order** organised with the smallest item first and working up to the biggest □ **in charge of** in control and able to make decisions □ **in descending order** organised so that the biggest item is first and working down to the smallest □ **in detail** paying attention to all the aspects of something however small ○ *to describe something in detail* □ **in fact** used to emphasise the reality of a situation or to introduce more precise information ○ *In fact this is what really happened.* □ **in house** produced internally by a company or organisation and relating to internal matters ○ *an in-house magazine* □ **in order of importance** organised with the most important item first □ **in place** in the right position □ **in practice** what is done rather than what is talked about or theorised ○ *It was supposed to happen but in practice it had to be cancelled.* □ **in sequence** organised to occur one after another according to a pre-determined order □ **in stages** done in small parts ○ *She learned computing in stages.* □ **in stock** available for immediate purchase or loan □ **in subject order** arranged under headings which relate alphabetically to the subject of the document □ **in terms of** to talk about something specifying which particular aspects you are considering ○ *We discussed what was needed in terms of equipment.* □ **in the case of** in the particular situation under discussion ○ *Difficult decisions must be made in the case of closure of district libraries.* □ **in the long run** eventually ○ *In the long run automation of the library benefited everybody.* □ **in the long term** over a long period of time ○ *In the long term automation will be seen to be good for the library.* □ **in theory** what is supposed to happen but probably will not ○ *In theory the librarians will be given time off for study, but more likely they will not be able to go.* □ **in working order** functioning efficiently ○ *All the computers are in good working order now.* □ **in writing** written down, not spoken ○ *Make sure that you get the contract in writing.* ■ *adverb* done internally by a company ○ *The work is being done in-house.*

in- /ɪn/ *prefix* added to some words to create the opposite meaning, e.g. 'correct' – 'incorrect'

inaccessible /ˌɪnəkˈsesɪb(ə)l/ *adjective* impossible or very difficult to reach

inaccurate /ɪnˈækjʊrət/ *adjective* not correct

inbuilt /'ɪnbɪlt/ *adjective* included as an integral part of a system

inbuilt facility /ˌɪnbɪlt fə'sɪlɪti/ *noun* a feature that is included in the original design

incentive /ɪn'sentɪv/ *noun* anything which encourages extra effort

incentive payment /ɪn'sentɪv ˌpeɪmənt/ *noun* extra money that is paid to encourage somebody to work harder

incidental /ˌɪnsɪ'dent(ə)l/ *adjective* something happening or existing in connection with something else more important ○ *The librarians were allowed to claim for the incidental expenses when they went to the conference.*

incidental music /ˌɪnsɪ'dent(ə)l ˌmjuːzɪk/ *noun* music written to provide the background to a play or film

include /ɪn'kluːd/ *verb* to make one thing part of another

inclusive /ɪn'kluːsɪv/ *adjective* counted in with other aspects ○ *Prices are inclusive of VAT.*

income-generating /'ɪŋkʌm ˌdʒenəreɪtɪŋ/ *adjective* producing money from activities

incoming /'ɪnkʌmɪŋ/ *adjective* coming in from outside ○ *incoming messages on the computer*

incompatible /ˌɪnkəm'pætɪb(ə)l/ *adjective* unable to exist or be used together

incorporate /ɪn'kɔːpəreɪt/ *verb* to include one thing as part of another

increase /ɪn'kriːs/ *verb* to make something larger in amount

incunable /ɪn'kjuːnəb(ə)l/ *noun* PRINTING same as **incunabulum**

incunabulum /ˌɪnkju'næbjʊləm/ *noun* a book printed from movable type before 1501 (NOTE: The plural is **incunabula**.)

incur /ɪn'kɜː/ *verb* to cause something to happen

indent /ɪn'dent/ *verb* to leave a space at the beginning of a passage of writing

indentation /ˌɪnden'teɪʃ(ə)n/ *noun* a space of a set size left at the beginning of a line of text

independent /ˌɪndɪ'pendənt/ *adjective* not connected to, influenced by or needing other people or machines to be able to exist or work

Independent Broadcasting Association /ˌɪndɪpendənt 'brɔːdkɑːstɪŋ əˌsəʊsieɪʃ(ə)n/ *noun* an organisation which controls all broadcasting companies in the UK except the BBC. Abbr **IBA**

index /'ɪndeks/ *noun* **1.** an alphabetical list of items contained in a book, document or computer memory **2.** a system by which the changes in the value of something can be compared or measured ○ *International financial indexes compare the value of shares.* **3.** a finding guide to information on a specific topic ■ *verb* to compile an alphabetical list of contents

index card /'ɪndeks kɑːd/ *noun* a small card containing information and usually arranged alphabetically in a card index box

index entry /'ɪndeks ˌentri/ *noun* an item with bibliographic details written in an index or catalogue

indexer /'ɪndeksə/ *noun* a person who compiles indexes for books

indexing /'ɪndeksɪŋ/ *noun* the use of alphabetical methods to organise information

COMMENT: An index is usually set in smaller type than the text and in two or more columns to the page. Normally an index will begin on a right-hand page, and will be folioed consecutively from the text pages. Bold and italic can be used to highlight important or less important items in an index (as, for example, the page references to illustrations). It is always useful to have a note at the beginning of an index to explain how it has been compiled and the meaning of the various typefaces or symbols used. Indexing was formerly done manually, with the indexer going through the text and making filing cards for the items; there are now computer indexing programs, in which the words in the text are flagged and the computer then automatically lists them in alphabetical order, together with the numbers of the pages on which the words fall.

indexing at source /ˌɪndeksɪŋ æt 'sɔːs/ *noun* publication of index data at the same time as a periodical article

indexing chain /'ɪndeksɪŋ tʃeɪn/ *noun* a chain of classification numbers produced using hierarchical steps from a subject heading

indexing keyword /ˌɪndeksɪŋ 'kiːwɜːd/ *noun* a heading word used to indicate the contents of a document and used in online searching

indexing language /'ɪndeksɪŋ ˌlæŋgwɪdʒ/ *noun* language used in building library or book indexes

index language /'ɪndeks ˌlæŋgwɪdʒ/ *noun* controlled vocabulary used to compile a subject index

index-linked /ˌɪndeks 'lɪŋkt/ *adjective* linked to inflation and so changing each time inflation or the cost of living rises or falls

Index Translationum /ˌɪndeks trænsˌlɑːtiˈəʊnem/ *noun* a list of all translations published in the world, published each year by UNESCO

india paper /'ɪndiə ˌpeɪpə/ *noun* extremely thin good-quality opaque paper, about 30gsm, which is nevertheless quite strong, used for printing books with a large number of pages such as bibles which would be very thick if ordinary paper were used

indicate /'ɪndɪkeɪt/ *verb* to show something

indicator /'ɪndɪkeɪtə/ *noun* **1.** something that shows whether a thing exists **2.** the state of a process, as in closed access libraries showing the number of books 'in' and 'out'

indirect /ˌɪndaɪ'rekt/ *adjective* not done by the shortest or most obvious method

individual /ˌɪndɪ'vɪdʒuəl/ *adjective* relating to one single person or thing rather than to a group

individual password /ˌɪndɪvɪdjuəl 'pɑːswɜːd/ *noun* a personal code allowing access to a computer system

induce /ɪn'djuːs/ *verb* to persuade, influence or cause a situation to happen

induction course /ɪn'dʌkʃən kɔːs/ *noun* a course for new entrants to a company, organisation or institution which gives basic information to help them settle in

industrial archaeology /ɪn ˌdʌstriəl ˌɑːkiˈɒlədʒi/ *noun* the study of buildings related to the industrial revolutions in the developed world

inexpensive /ˌɪnɪk'spensɪv/ *adjective* not costing much money

inexperienced /ˌɪnɪk'spɪəriənst/ *adjective* having little or no experience in a particular activity

infect /ɪn'fekt/ *verb* to copy to a computer system a computer virus that is capable of damaging the system's programs or data

inference /'ɪnf(ə)rəns/ *noun* the act of deducing information from given data

inference control /'ɪnf(ə)rəns kən ˌtrəʊl/ *noun* a way of determining which information can be released on a computer without disclosing personal information about an individual

influence /'ɪnfluəns/ *noun* the power to affect people's actions ■ *verb* to cause something or somebody to change

info *abbreviation* in Internet addresses, the generic top-level domain for general use

informatics /ˌɪnfɔː'mætɪks/ *noun* a collective term for the technologies concerned with the computerised collection, processing and transmission of information

information /ˌɪnfə'meɪʃ(ə)n/ *noun* knowledge given to somebody in a form they can understand

information accessibility /ˌɪnfəmeɪʃ(ə)n æk,sesə'bɪlɪti/ *noun* an indication of how easily information is available to users

information accuracy /ˌɪnfəmeɪʃ(ə)n 'ækjʊrəsi/ *noun* an indication of how correct a piece of information is

information age /ˌɪnfə'meɪʃ(ə)n ˌeɪdʒ/ *noun* a period characterised by widespread electronic access to information through the use of computer technology

information analyst /ˌɪnfə 'meɪʃ(ə)n ˌænəlɪst/ *noun* a person who studies information and draws conclusions

information appliance /ˌɪnfə
ˈmeɪʃ(ə)n əˌplaɪəns/ *noun* a small
portable digital information-processing
machine compatible with an electronic
network

information architecture /ˌɪnfə
ˈmeɪʃ(ə)n ˌɑːkɪtektʃə/ *noun* the design
of something such as a website or database so that the information is presented
in the most efficient and accessible
manner. Abbr **IA**

information brokerage /ˌɪnfə
ˈmeɪʃ(ə)n ˌbrəʊkərɪdʒ/ *noun* the business of buying and selling information
for other people

information bureau /ˌɪnfə
ˈmeɪʃ(ə)n ˌbjʊərəʊ/ *noun* an office that
gives information

information centre /ˌɪnfəˈmeɪʃ(ə)n
ˌsentə/ *noun* an office where people can
make enquiries

information channel /ˌɪnfə
ˈmeɪʃ(ə)n ˌtʃæn(ə)l/ *noun* the means
by which information is distributed

information commons /ˌɪnfə
ˈmeɪʃ(ə)n ˌkɒmənz/ *noun* a community in which information belonging to
members is freely distributed among
everybody

information completeness
/ˌɪnfəmeɪʃ(ə)n kəmˈpliːtnəs/ *noun* an
indication of whether the information
covers all the aspects required

information definition /ˌɪnfə
ˈmeɪʃ(ə)n ˌdefɪnɪʃ(ə)n/ *noun* a technique for deciding exactly what the
enquirer needs to know

information design /ˌɪnfə
ˈmeɪʃ(ə)n dɪˌzaɪn/ *noun* the shaping
and presentation of information in a
way that best serves the needs of users

information desk /ˌɪnfəˈmeɪʃ(ə)n
desk/ *noun* a place in a library or information centre where questions will be
answered

information engineer /ˌɪnfə
ˈmeɪʃ(ə)n ˌendʒɪnɪə/ *noun* a computer
expert who works with information
systems

information explosion /ˌɪnfə
ˈmeɪʃ(ə)n eksˌpləʊʒ(ə)n/ *noun* a situation in which there is a lot of information available because of technology

information flow /ˌɪnfəˈmeɪʃ(ə)n
ˌfləʊ/ *noun* the distribution of information within an organisation

information governance /ˌɪnfə
ˈmeɪʃ(ə)n ˌɡʌvənəns/ *noun* the practice of making sure that personal information held by a company is stored,
used and shared in a responsible
manner. Abbr **IG**

information handling /ˌɪnfə
ˈmeɪʃ(ə)n ˌhændlɪŋ/ *noun* same as
information management

information literacy /ˌɪnfə
ˈmeɪʃ(ə)n ˌlɪt(ə)rəsi/ *noun* the ability
to find relevant information for a particular situation or problem, and to interpret that information effectively

information management /ˌɪnfə
ˈmeɪʃ(ə)n ˌmænɪdʒmənt/ *noun* the
storage, searching, retrieval and
updating of information so that it is
easily accessible. Also called **information handling**

**information management
system** /ˌɪnfəmeɪʃ(ə)n
ˈmænɪdʒmənt ˌsɪstəm/ *noun* a
computer program that allows information to be easily stored, retrieved,
searched and updated. Abbr **IMS**

information manager /ˌɪnfə
ˈmeɪʃ(ə)n ˌmænɪdʒə/ *noun* a trained
person who controls the processing and
availability of information within a
company or organisation

information needs /ˌɪnfəˈmeɪʃ(ə)n
ˌniːdz/ *plural noun* the requirements of
a user or group for information on
specific subjects

information network /ˌɪnfə
ˈmeɪʃ(ə)n ˌnetwɜːk/ *noun* a group of
people or computers linked together so
that information can be passed around

information policy /ˌɪnfəˈmeɪʃ(ə)n
ˌpɒlɪsi/ *noun* a statement of policy
about the provision and accessibility of
information within an organisation

information presentation /ˌɪnfə
ˈmeɪʃ(ə)n ˌprezənteɪʃ(ə)n/ *noun* the
format of information, e.g. written,
spoken, or computer database form

information processing
/ˌɪnfəmeɪʃ(ə)n ˈprəʊsesɪŋ/ *noun* the
organisation, manipulation, analysis

and distribution of data, nowadays typically carried out by computers

information provider /ˌɪnfə
'meɪʃ(ə)n prə.vaɪdə/ *noun* a company or user who provides an information source for use in a videotext system, e.g. a company providing weather information or stock market reports

information qualifications /ˌɪnfə
'meɪʃ(ə)n ˌkwɒlɪfɪkeɪʃ(ə)nz/ *plural noun* degrees or diplomas indicating a level of training in information management

information quality assessment
/ˌɪnfə'meɪʃ(ə)n ˌkwɒlɪti ə.sesmənt/ *noun* a technique for assessing the level of satisfaction among users with the information provided

information relevance
/ˌɪnfəmeɪʃ(ə)n 'relɪvəns/ *noun* the value of the information to the enquirer

information retrieval /ˌɪnfə
'meɪʃ(ə)n rɪˌtriːv(ə)l/ *noun* the process of locating quantities of data stored in a database and producing useful information from the data

information retrieval centre
/ˌɪnfəmeɪʃ(ə)n rɪ'triːv(ə)l ˌsentə/ *noun* a research system providing specific information from a database for a user

information science /ˌɪnfə
'meɪʃ(ə)n ˌsaɪəns/ *noun* the study of the processes involved in storing and retrieving information

information services /ˌɪnfə
'meɪʃ(ə)n ˌsɜːvɪsɪz/ *plural noun* companies offering a service in the provision of information

information skills /ˌɪnfə'meɪʃ(ə)n
ˌskɪlz/ *plural noun* ability of users to access and retrieve the information they require

information source /ˌɪnfə
'meɪʃ(ə)n ˌsɔːs/ *noun* any book, document, database or person which provides information

information specialist /ˌɪnfə
'meɪʃ(ə)n ˌspeʃ(ə)lɪst/ *noun* a trained employee in information management

information storage
/ˌɪnfəmeɪʃ(ə)n 'stɔːrɪdʒ/ *noun* manual or electronic methods of storing information

information strategy /ˌɪnfə
'meɪʃ(ə)n ˌstrætədʒi/ *noun* a policy of a company or organisation about its use of information

information superhighway
/ˌɪnfəmeɪʃ(ə)n ˌsuːpə'haɪweɪ/ *noun* the worldwide computer network that includes the Internet, private networks and proprietary online services. It permits the rapid sending of many different forms of data, including voice, video and text.

information supplier /ˌɪnfə
'meɪʃ(ə)n sə.plaɪə/ *noun* a person or company that provides information on a specific subject

information system /ˌɪnfə
'meɪʃ(ə)n ˌsɪstəm/ *noun* a computer system used for the provision of information and designed according to user needs

information technology
/ˌɪnfəmeɪʃ(ə)n tek'nɒlədʒi/ *noun* the use of technologies from computing, electronics and telecommunications to process and distribute information in digital and other forms. Abbr **IT**

information term /ˌɪnfə'meɪʃ(ə)n
ˌtɜːm/ *noun* a word used for the organisation of information

information theory /ˌɪnfə
'meɪʃ(ə)n ˌθɪəri/ *noun* the mathematical study of the transmission, reception, storage and retrieval of information based on the statistical analysis of communication between humans and machines

'Shannon is most famous for his enormous paper, A Mathematical Theory of Communication, published in 1948 when he was in his early thirties. This paper spells out, among many other things, the fundamental limits of how fast we can transmit information. In fact, the whole field of information theory stems from Shannon's work.' [*VNU NET*]

information timing /ˌɪnfə'meɪʃ(ə)n
ˌtaɪmɪŋ/ *noun* a measure of whether information is provided in time to be of use

information tracking /ˌɪnfə'meɪʃ(ə)n ˌtrækɪŋ/ *noun* the facility to find records of related information from over a period of time

information universe /ˌɪnfə'meɪʃ(ə)n ˌjuːnɪvɜːs/ *noun* the idea of information being freely and equally available across the globe using new technology

information visualisation /ˌɪnfəmeɪʃ(ə)n ˌvɪʒuəlaɪ'zeɪʃ(ə)n/ *noun* the representation of data, e.g. in diagrammatic form, which helps users to understand and absorb it

infrared /ˌɪnfrə'red/ *noun* a form of invisible light, below the visible red level on the light scale. Abbr **IR**

infrastructure /'ɪnfrəˌstrʌktʃə/ *noun* basic structures which enable a country, society or organisation to function effectively

infringement of copyright /ɪnˌfrɪndʒmənt əv 'kɒpɪraɪt/ *noun* same as **copyright infringement**

inhibit /ɪn'hɪbɪt/ *verb* to prevent or slow down a process

in-house /ˌɪn 'haʊs/ *adjective* relating to staff who are employed to work directly for a company ○ *the in-house staff* ■ *adverb* done internally by a company ○ *We do all our data processing in-house.* ○ *The colour artwork cannot be done in-house and has to be sent outside.*

initial /ɪ'nɪʃ(ə)l/ *adjective* happening at the start of a process ■ *verb* to sign something using only the first letters of one's names

initialise /ɪ'nɪʃəlaɪz/, **initialize** *verb* to prepare a system or disk for use

initials /ɪ'nɪʃ(ə)lz/ *plural noun* the first letters of a person's names

Initial Teaching Alphabet /ɪˌnɪʃ(ə)l 'tiːtʃɪŋ ˌælfəbet/ *noun* an alphabet of 44 symbols, each representing a single sound in English, used to teach children to read

ink /ɪŋk/ *noun* a coloured liquid for writing or printing ■ *verb* to apply ink to

ink-jet printer /'ɪŋk dʒet ˌprɪntə/ *noun* a non-impact machine for printing the output of a computer using a system of electrically charged ink drops

ink pad /'ɪŋk pæd/ *noun* a pad of material soaked in ink for use with official stamps

ink rub /'ɪŋk rʌb/ *noun* dirty marks on printed paper, caused when it rubs against the ink on other pages during binding

innovation /ˌɪnə'veɪʃ(ə)n/ *noun* a new product or method of doing something

innumerate /ɪ'njuːmərət/ *adjective* lacking a basic knowledge of mathematics and unable to use numbers in calculation

in print /ˌɪn 'prɪnt/ *adjective* **1.** still being printed, still available in the bookshops or from the publisher ○ *a list of current books in print* ○ *The book was first published in 1902 and is still in print.* (NOTE: The opposite is **out of print** or **O/P**.) **2.** appearing in a book or journal

input /'ɪnpʊt/ *noun* information put into a computer memory ■ *verb* to enter data into a computer

input device /'ɪnpʊt dɪˌvaɪs/ *noun* a device such as a keyboard or barcode reader, which converts information into a form that a computer can understand and transfers the information to the processor. Compare **output device**

inscription /ɪn'skrɪpʃən/ *noun* words written on a monument, book or other object as a commemoration, dedication or greeting

insert /'ɪnsɜːt/ *noun* additional information printed on a separate sheet of paper and put inside a magazine or document

insert mode /'ɪnsɜːt məʊd/ *noun* an interactive computer mode used for editing and correcting documents

COMMENT: This is a standard feature on most word-processing packages where the cursor is placed at the required point in the document and any characters typed will be added, with the existing text moving on as necessary; when the insert mode is off, new text will erase the existing text.

in-service training /ˌɪn ˌsɜːvɪs 'treɪnɪŋ/ *noun* professional development training provided by an organisation for its employees

insight /'ɪnsaɪt/ *noun* understanding of a complex situation

INSPEC /'ɪnspek/ *noun* an abstracting and indexing service for electrical engineers

inspection copy /ɪn'spekʃən ˌkɒpi/ *noun* a copy of a publication sent or given with time allowed for a decision to purchase or return it

install /ɪn'stɔːl/ *verb* to set up equipment so that it is ready for use

installation costs /ˌɪnstə'leɪʃ(ə)n ˌkɒsts/ *plural noun* money required to put in the equipment required

instalment /ɪn'stɔːlmənt/ *noun* **1.** a small amount paid at regular intervals as part of a larger total ○ *They paid for the encyclopedia in six monthly instalments.* **2.** a part-section of a book or magazine published at regular intervals ○ *The novel has been serialised in ten instalments.*

instant replay /ˌɪnstənt 'riːpleɪ/ *noun* a feature of video recording systems which allows the viewer to see again the action that has just been recorded

institute /'ɪnstɪtjuːt/ *noun* an organisation set up for a particular group of people with a shared interest ■ *verb* to set up or establish something such as a policy or programme ○ *They instituted an information service in the branch library.*

Institute of Electrical and Electronics Engineers /ˌɪnstɪtjuːt əv ɪ ˌlektrɪk(ə)l ənd ˌelek'trɒnɪks ˌendʒɪnɪəz/ *noun* a professional membership body which promotes global technological advancement. Abbr **IEEE**

Institute of Information Scientists /ˌɪnstɪtjuːt əv ˌɪnfə'meɪʃ(ə)n ˌsaɪəntɪsts/ *noun* an organisation for the mutual support of employees in the field of information science. Abbr **IIS**

institutional repository /ˌɪnstɪtjuːʃ(ə)nəl rɪ'pɒzɪt(ə)ri/ *noun* a digital collection of all the information output by a single company or organisation, e.g. a hospital

instruct /ɪn'strʌkt/ *verb* to teach somebody how to do something

instruction /ɪn'strʌkʃən/ *noun* clear and detailed information about how to do something verbal, published in a manual or typed into a computer to cause the machine to work

instructional capital /ɪn ˌstrʌkʃ(ə)nəl 'kæpɪt(ə)l/ *noun* human capital which is a result of training employees, therefore treating them as an 'investment'

instruction note /ɪn'strʌkʃ(ə)n nəʊt/ *noun* a note directing the user of a catalogue to take an unusual search step

instrumentation /ˌɪnstrʊmen 'teɪʃ(ə)n/ *noun* dials which display information to indicate how a machine is working

insufficient /ˌɪnsə'fɪʃ(ə)nt/ *adjective* not enough

insulate /'ɪnsjʊleɪt/ *verb* to protect something from outside damage

insurance /ɪn'ʃʊərəns/ *noun* an agreement to pay a company fixed sums of money so that if damage or injury occurs, costs will be paid by the company

int *abbreviation* ONLINE international organisation

intake /'ɪnteɪk/ *noun* a quantity of people or things taken into something such as an organisation ○ *Their intake of new employees each year is increasing.*

integrated /'ɪntɪˌgreɪtɪd/ *adjective* combined or linked together

integrated book /'ɪntɪgreɪtɪd bʊk/ *noun* a book with text and illustrations on the same page

integrated database /ˌɪntɪgreɪtɪd 'deɪtəbeɪs/ *noun* a combined database which excludes repetition or redundant terms

integrated digital network /ˌɪntɪgreɪtɪd ˌdɪdʒɪt(ə)l 'netwɜːk/ *noun* a communications network that uses digital signals to transmit data

integrated library system /ˌɪntɪgreɪtɪd 'laɪbrəri ˌsɪstəm/ *noun* a library management system which deals with many library processes and works from a single bibliographic database

integrated package /ˌɪntɪgreɪtɪd 'pækɪdʒ/ *noun* combined applications on different topics stored on a central computer ○ *An integrated package can contain several programs including a database, spreadsheet, word processing and graphics.*

Integrated Services Digital Network /ˌɪntɪɡreɪtɪd ˌsɜːvɪsɪz ˌdɪdʒɪt(ə)l 'netwɜːk/ *noun* a service which provides high-quality telecommunications such as facsimile transmission and video conferencing. Abbr **ISDN**

integrity /ɪn'teɡrɪti/ *noun* reliability or honesty

intellect /'ɪntɪlekt/ *noun* a very intelligent and knowledgeable person

intellectual /ˌɪntɪ'lektʃuəl/ *adjective* having a highly developed ability to think, reason and understand, especially in combination with wide knowledge

intellectual assets /ˌɪntɪlektʃuəl 'æsets/ *plural noun* the knowledge, experience, and skills possessed by its employees that an organisation can use for its own benefit

intellectual capital /ˌɪntɪlektʃuəl 'kæpɪt(ə)l/ *noun* the idea of employees' skills and knowledge being a resource of their company, which can be directly linked to company turnover

intellectual property /ˌɪntɪlektʃuəl 'prɒpəti/ *noun* original writing, ideas, inventions, works of art or music which are the property of the creator, and protected by copyright law

intelligent /ɪn'telɪdʒənt/ *adjective* **1.** having a built-in electronic processing and data storage ability **2.** programmed to be able to adjust to changes in the environment and make deductions from information being processed

intelligent terminal /ɪnˌtelɪdʒ(ə)nt 'tɜːmɪn(ə)l/, **intelligent workstation** *noun* a computer terminal which can be programmed independently of the central processor and is capable of limited reasoning

intensity /ɪn'tensɪti/ *noun* a measure of strength of something such as a signal

inter- /ɪntə/ *prefix* combining with adjectives and nouns to describe the way they relate to each other ○ *inter-racial* ○ *inter-city*

interact /ˌɪntər'ækt/ *verb* to work with or relate to somebody or something

interactive /ˌɪntər'æktɪv/ *adjective* **1.** working together for the exchange of information **2.** relating to a computer program that responds to user activity, so that it can be changed while running ○ *The computer game was interactive, so the players could get answers to their questions.*

COMMENT: This system is often used in teaching to ask the student questions, which, if he answers correctly, will produce a sequence of film from the video disk.

interactive multimedia /ˌɪntəræktɪv ˌmʌlti'miːdiə/ *plural noun* systems of communication that use a variety of methods and can be controlled by the user in order to obtain information

interactive processing /ˌɪntəræktɪv 'prəʊsesɪŋ/ *noun* a computer mode that allows the user to enter commands, programs or data and receive immediate responses

interactive system /ˌɪntəræktɪv 'sɪstəm/ *noun* a computer system where the operator and the computer can communicate with each other

interactive video /ˌɪntəræktɪv 'vɪdiəʊ/ *noun* a system using a computer linked to a video disk player which allows the user to answer questions in order to move on to the next picture

interactive videotext /ˌɪntəræktɪv 'vɪdiəʊtekst/ *noun* a system which allows the user to select pages and display the information to gain information

interchange /ˌɪntə'tʃeɪndʒ/ *verb* to put data into a form that can be recognised by a differently-coded computer system

interchangeable /ˌɪntə'tʃeɪndʒəb(ə)l/ *adjective* able to be substituted for something else

intercom /'ɪntəkɒm/ *noun* a device with a microphone and loudspeaker which can be used to speak to somebody in another room

interdependent /ˌɪntədɪ'pendənt/ *adjective* dependent on each other

interdisciplinary studies /ˌɪntədɪsɪplɪnəri 'stʌdɪz/ *plural noun* academic studies that cross the conventional subject boundaries ○ *History, geography, religious studies and languages are sometimes taught together as interdisciplinary studies and called the humanities.*

interface /'ɪntəfeɪs/ *noun* **1.** the point at which two systems contact each other **2.** the point at which a system and a user make contact with each other

interference /ˌɪntə'fɪərəns/ *noun* unwanted signals causing difficulty in reception on a computer or broadcasting system

interim /'ɪntərɪm/ *noun* a short break in a process or series of events

interim report /ˌɪntərɪm rɪ'pɔːt/ *noun* a report written part-way through a process to show how much progress has been made

interleaf /'ɪntəliːf/ *noun* an extra sheet or page, usually a blank one, inserted into a book

interleave /ˌɪntə'liːv/ *verb* to add extra sheets or pages, usually blank ones, between the pages of a book, e.g. to allow for notes or to protect illustrations

interleaved /ˌɪntə'liːvd/ *adjective* denoting a book that has thin sheets of blank paper inserted between the pages of text

inter-library loan /ˌɪnə 'laɪbrəri ˌləʊn/ *noun* **1.** a system of lending books and documents between libraries **2.** a book, photocopy or material lent between libraries for their users ▸ abbr **ILL**

interlock /ˌɪntə'lɒk/ *verb* to fit things together so that they join firmly ■ *noun* a safety device that disables a process or piece of equipment if it might cause harm, e.g. a fusewire which prevents a circuit blowing

intermediary /ˌɪntə'miːdiəri/ *noun* a person who helps people or groups to come to an agreement

intermediate /ˌɪntə'miːdiət/ *adjective* halfway between two stages

intermediate storage /ˌɪntəmiːdiət 'stɔːrɪdʒ/ *noun* a tempo-rary place to store things until a more permanent place is found

intermittent /ˌɪntə'mɪt(ə)nt/ *adjective* happening occasionally rather than continually

intermittent error /ˌɪntəmɪt(ə)nt 'erə/ *noun* a mistake which occurs randomly and is difficult to trace

internal /ɪn't3ːn(ə)l/ *adjective* happening inside a place, person or object

internal consumption /ɪnˌt3ːn(ə)l kən'sʌmpʃ(ə)n/ *noun* the use of materials or information within a company or organisation

internalisation /ɪnˌt3ːnəlaɪ'zeɪʃ(ə)n/ *noun* a process by which individuals identify information which is relevant to them personally and so acquire values and norms which allow them to make decisions

internal phone /ɪnˌt3ːn(ə)l 'fəʊn/ *noun* a telephone on a network which enables communication with other offices within an organisation

internal politics /ɪnˌt3ːn(ə)l 'pɒlɪtɪks/ *noun* the relationships within an organisation which affect the way it works ○ *The internal politics of promotion within the library caused a lot of arguments.*

international /ˌɪntə'næʃ(ə)nəl/ *adjective* relating to different countries

International Aerospace Abstracts /ˌɪntənæʃ(ə)nəl 'eərəʊspeɪs ˌæbstrækts/ *plural noun* summaries of research done in the field of space exploration. Abbr **IAA**

International Copyright Information Centre /ˌɪntənæʃ(ə)nəl 'kɒpiraɪt ˌɪnfəmeɪʃ(ə)n ˌsentə/ *noun* an information service based at UNESCO headquarters in Paris. Abbr **ICIC**

international dialling code /ˌɪntənæʃ(ə)nəl 'daɪəlɪŋ ˌkəʊd/ *noun* a numerical code which allocates specific numbers to each country to make it possible to dial directly without using an operator

international direct dialling /ˌɪntənæʃ(ə)nəl ˌdaɪrekt 'daɪəlɪŋ/ *noun* a system of telephone communication which does not need an operator. Abbr **IDD**

International Federation of Library Associations and Institutions *noun* a not-for-profit international organisation based in The Hague, which promotes high standards in library and information provision. Abbr **IFLA**

International Information Centre for Standards in Information and Documentation *noun* an organisation established by UNESCO and ISO to promote the application of standards in information work. Abbr **ISODOC**

International Packet Switching Service /ˌɪntənæʃ(ə)nəl ˈpækɪt ˌswɪtʃɪŋ ˌsɜːvɪs/ *noun* an electronic link between terminals and computers in different countries. Abbr **IPSS**

International Serials Data System /ˌɪntənæʃ(ə)nəl ˈsɪərɪəlz ˌdeɪtə ˌsɪstəm/ *noun* an international network of serials libraries which promotes international standards of bibliographic description. Abbr **ISDS**

International Standard Bibliographic Description /ˌɪntənæʃ(ə)nəl ˌstændəd ˌbɪbliəʊɡræfɪk dɪˈskrɪps(ə)n/ *noun* a standardised way of formally describing catalogued pieces of information for later retrieval

International Standard Book Number /ˌɪntənæʃ(ə)nəl ˌstændəd ˈbʊk ˌnʌmbə/ *noun* a system of identifying publications by specific numbers relating to publishers and titles. Abbr **ISBN**

International Standard Music Number /ˌɪntənæʃ(ə)nəl ˌstændəd ˈmjuːzɪk ˌnʌmbə/ *noun* a system for identifying editions of published music. Abbr **ISMN**

International Standard Serial Number /ˌɪntənæʃ(ə)nəl ˌstændəd ˈsɪərɪəl ˌnʌmbə/ *noun* a system for identifying publications of journals and their publishers. Abbr **ISSN**

International Standards Organisation /ˌɪntənæʃ(ə)nəl ˈstændəz ˌɔːɡənaɪzeɪʃ(ə)n/ *noun* an organisation that controls the standards of production

for goods and services worldwide. Abbr **ISO**

Internet /ˈɪntənet/ *noun* a system of computer communication which allows international access to databases and electronic mail systems

Internet protocol /ˈɪntənet ˌprəʊtəkɒl/ *noun* a TCP/IP standard that defines how data is transferred across a network. Abbr **IP**

Internet protocol address /ˌɪntənet ˌprəʊtəkɒl əˈdres/ *noun* a unique, 32-bit number which identifies each computer connected to a TCP/IP network. Abbr **IP address**

Internet service provider /ˌɪntənet ˈsɜːvɪs prəˌvaɪdə/ *noun* a business that provides access to the Internet, usually for a monthly fee. Some large providers offer users a wide range of news, information and entertainment services. Abbr **ISP**

interoperability /ˌɪntərˌɒpərəˈbɪlɪti/ *noun* the ability of the component parts of a system to operate successfully together

interpret /ɪnˈtɜːprɪt/ *verb* **1.** to change what is spoken in one language to another ○ *My assistant speaks Italian, so he will interpret for us.* **2.** to decide on the meaning of a communication

interpretation /ɪnˌtɜːprɪˈteɪʃ(ə)n/ *noun* an explanation of the meaning of something

interpreter /ɪnˈtɜːprɪtə/ *noun* **1.** a person who is used to translate somebody's speech into another language **2.** software used to translate from one computer system to another

interrogate /ɪnˈterəɡeɪt/ *verb* **1.** to question somebody formally **2.** to work with an interactive computer program

'Until the early 1980s, when his [Ted Codd's] ideas were widely adopted, data was mostly stored in 'hierarchical' databases that were both inflexible and difficult to interrogate without a PhD in computer science.' [*Financial Times*]

interrogation /ɪnˌterəˈɡeɪʃ(ə)n/ *noun* the act of asking questions in order to obtain information

interrupt /ˌɪntəˈrʌpt/ *verb* to stop something happening temporarily

intervention /ˌɪntəˈvenʃən/ *noun* an action causing a change

interword spacing /ˌɪntəwɜːd ˈspeɪsɪŋ/ *noun* variable spaces between words used to justify line endings

intranet /ˈɪntrənet/ *noun* a private network of computers within a company which provide similar functions to the Internet

intrinsic /ɪnˈtrɪnsɪk/ *adjective* fundamental and important to a person or situation

introduction /ˌɪntrəˈdʌkʃ(ə)n/ *noun* **1.** the first part of written text or spoken information which tells what the rest of the document or talk is about **2.** a book that provides elementary information on a specific subject ○ *'An Introduction to Library Management'*

intuition /ˌɪntjuˈɪʃ(ə)n/ *noun* a feeling about something for which there is no proof

invalid /ɪnˈvælɪd/ *adjective* not legally acceptable

inventory /ˈɪnvənt(ə)ri/ *noun* a written list of the assets owned by an organisation ○ *The manager asked for an inventory of the library holdings.*

inversion /ɪnˈvɜːʃ(ə)n/ *noun* the act of changing something into its opposite

invert /ɪnˈvɜːt/ *verb* to turn something upside down

inverted commas /ɪnˌvɜːtɪd ˈkɒməz/ *noun* punctuation marks (' ') indicating speech or quotations

invest /ɪnˈvest/ *verb* to put money, time or energy into something or somebody in the hope that it will produce more money or better results

investigation /ɪnˌvestɪˈgeɪʃ(ə)n/ *noun* the process by which all the facts and aspects of a situation are examined

invisible Web /ɪnˈvɪzɪb(ə)l web/ *noun* same as **deep Web**

invitation to tender /ˌɪnvɪteɪʃ(ə)n tə ˈtendə/ *noun* a written or spoken request to a company or organisation to work out their charges for doing a job

invoice /ˈɪnvɔɪs/ *noun* an official document listing the goods or services supplied and stating the amount of money owed

io *abbreviation* in Internet addresses, the top-level domain for British Indian Ocean Territory

IP *abbreviation* Internet protocol

IP address /ˌaɪ ˈpiː əˌdres/ *abbreviation* Internet protocol address

IPSS *abbreviation* International Packet Switching Service

iq *abbreviation* in Internet addresses, the top-level domain for Iraq

IQ *noun* a measure of somebody's intelligence, obtained through a series of aptitude tests concentrating on different aspects of intellectual functioning. An IQ score of 100 represents 'average' intelligence. Full form **intelligence quotient**

ir *abbreviation* in Internet addresses, the top-level domain for Iran

IR *abbreviation* infrared

IRC /ˌaɪ ɑː ˈsiː/ *noun* a system that allows many users to participate in a chat session in which each user can send messages and see the text of any other user. Full form **internet relay chat**

irrelevant /ɪˈreləvənt/ *adjective* not important because it is not connected with the topic

irretrievable /ˌɪrɪˈtriːvəb(ə)l/ *adjective* unable to be found or obtained

is *abbreviation* in Internet addresses, the top-level domain for Iceland

ISBD *abbreviation* International Standard Bibliographic Description

ISBN *abbreviation* International Standard Book Number

COMMENT: An international system for books, in which each book is given its own particular number. Currently the ISBN is made up of ten digits; the first digit refers to the language (0 and 1 are the digits for English); the next group of digits (three, four or even six) refer to the publisher; the third group refer to the book; and the final digit is a check digit. From 2007, ISBNs will be made up of 13 digits, with the ISBN-10 number preceded by a 3-digit product code. ISBNs are used for cataloguing and ordering, and can be used for automatic stock movements if they are printed on the back of the book in the form of a barcode which can be read with a light pen.

ISBN-10 *noun* the original format for ISBNs, consisting of 10 numbers representing the group of origin, the publisher, the title and a final check digit

ISBN-13 *noun* the new format for ISBNs, adding a further 3 digits which represent the product code and allow a greater number of ISBNs to be generated in future

ISDN *abbreviation* Integrated Services Digital Network

ISDS *abbreviation* International Serials Data System

ISMN *abbreviation* International Standard Music Number

ISO *abbreviation* International Standards Organisation

ISODOC *abbreviation* International Information Centre for Standards in Information and Documentation

ISP *abbreviation* ONLINE Internet service provider

ISSN *abbreviation* International Standard Serial Number

COMMENT: An international system used on periodicals, magazines, learned journals, etc. The ISSN is formed of eight digits, which refer to the country in which the magazine is published and the title of the publication.

issue /ˈɪʃuː/ *noun* a particular edition of a journal or magazine ■ *verb* to give out or lend something ○ *The library books were issued to the students.*

issue card /ˈɪʃuː kɑːd/ *noun* a small card used in a manual library system of loan records

issue desk /ˈɪʃuː desk/ *noun* a counter in a library where items are recorded as on loan or returned

issue system /ˈɪʃuː ˌsɪstəm/ *noun* a system for controlling library loan records

it *abbreviation* in Internet addresses, the top-level domain for Italy

IT *abbreviation* COMPUT information technology

ITA *abbreviation* EDUC Initial Teaching Alphabet

ital. *abbreviation* PUBL **1.** italic **2.** italics

italic /ɪˈtælɪk/ *adjective* relating to a typeface in which the characters slope to the right

item /ˈaɪtəm/ *noun* one of a collection or list of objects

item number /ˈaɪtəm ˌnʌmbə/ *noun* a specific number which identifies an item in a collection

iterative searching /ˌɪtərətɪv ˈsɜːtʃɪŋ/ *noun* the process of searching for information by repeatedly asking questions until the solution is found

J

jacket /'dʒækɪt/ *noun* a paper or plastic cover for a book ■ *verb* to put a jacket on a book

jacket design /'dʒækɪt dɪˌzaɪn/ *noun* the design of a book jacket

jacket designer /'dʒækɪt dɪˌzaɪnə/ *noun* a person who designs book jackets

jam /dʒæm/ *verb* **1.** to stop working because something is blocked or stuck ○ *The printer's jammed.* **2.** to interfere with a radio or electronic signal so that it cannot be received clearly

JANET /'dʒænɪt/ *abbreviation* Joint Academic NETwork

jargon /'dʒɑːɡən/ *noun* a language that uses words and expressions in specific, often technical, ways that relate to a particular field of study

'According to a spokesperson for Barclays, the bank tested a much larger range of new words and phrases than the final set. 'The idea was to look at the language that banks use and eliminate the jargon that sometimes makes it difficult for customers to understand the bank and the bank to communicate with its customers', the spokesperson said.' [*Bank Marketing International*]

je *abbreviation* in Internet addresses, the top-level domain for Jersey

jiffy bag /'dʒɪfi bæg/ *noun* a padded envelope used to protect goods which are sent through the post

jigsaw puzzle library /'dʒɪɡsɔː ˌpʌz(ə)l ˌlaɪbrəri/ *noun* a UK library founded in 1933 and holding over 4000 wooden handcut jigsaws

JISC *abbreviation* Joint Information Systems Committee

jm *abbreviation* in Internet addresses, the top-level domain for Jamaica

jo *abbreviation* in Internet addresses, the top-level domain for Jordan

job /dʒɒb/ *noun* **1.** any task which needs to be done **2.** work that is done to earn money

job applicant /'dʒɒb ˌæplɪkənt/ *noun* somebody who applies to be considered for a job

jobbing printer /'dʒɒbɪŋ ˌprɪntə/ *noun* a person who undertakes small printing jobs

job description /'dʒɒb dɪˌskrɪpʃən/ *noun* an official statement of what a job involves

job scheduling /'dʒɒb ˌʃedjuːlɪŋ/ *noun* the process of allocating specific tasks to people and times

job specification /'dʒɒb ˌspesɪfɪkeɪʃ(ə)n/ *noun* detailed objectives for a job

join /dʒɔɪn/ *verb* **1.** to fasten two or more things together **2.** to become a member of an organisation

joint /dʒɔɪnt/ *noun* either of the creases between the spine and the front and back covers of a book, especially a hardback

Joint Academic NETwork /ˌdʒɔɪnt ˌækədemɪk 'netwɜːk/ *noun* a national communication system which uses electronic mail and other systems between universities. Abbr **JANET**

joint author /ˌdʒɔɪnt 'ɔːθə/ *noun* a person who writes a book in collaboration with others

joint authorship /ˌdʒɔɪnt 'ɔːθəʃɪp/ *noun* a situation in which several authors have written a book together and share the rights in it

joint imprint /ˌdʒɔɪnt ˈɪmprɪnt/ *noun* the imprints of two publishers which appear on a book that has been published by the two companies jointly

Joint Information Systems Committee /ˌdʒɔɪnt ˌɪnfəˈmeɪʃ(ə)n ˌsɪstəmz kəˌmɪti/ *noun* a professional body which works to promote the use of information systems to support education and administration needs. Abbr **JISC**

Joint Photographic Experts Group /ˌdʒɔɪnt fəʊtəˌɡræfɪks ˈekspɜːts ɡruːp/ *noun* full form of **JPEG**

journal /ˈdʒɜːn(ə)l/ *noun* a specialist magazine

journalese /ˌdʒɜːnəˈliːz/ *noun* a style of writing with clichés and hackneyed phrases often used by journalists

journalist /ˈdʒɜːn(ə)lɪst/ *noun* a person who writes for a newspaper or magazine

joystick /ˈdʒɔɪstɪk/ *noun* a hand-held control lever attached to a computer which can be used to play computer games

jp *abbreviation* in Internet addresses, the top-level domain for Japan

JPEG /ˈdʒeɪpeɡ/ *noun* a data file for pictures and photographs on the Internet. Full form **Joint Photographic Experts Group**

.jpeg /ˈdʒeɪpeɡ/, **.jpg** *suffix* a file extension for a JPEG file. Full form **Joint Photographic Experts Group**

jumpstation /ˈdʒʌmpˌsteɪʃ(ə)n/ *noun* a website whose primary function is to provide links to other websites, especially those relating to a particular subject

junior /ˈdʒuːniə/ *adjective* younger or lower in rank than another person

junk /dʒʌŋk/ *noun* information or hardware that is old and useless

junk mail /ˈdʒʌŋk meɪl/ *noun* unwanted publicity and advertisements sent through the post

justification /ˌdʒʌstɪfɪˈkeɪʃ(ə)n/ *noun* the process of adjusting the spacing in printed text so that the text starts and ends exactly at the margins

justify /ˈdʒʌstɪfaɪ/ *verb* **1.** to change the spacing between words or characters so that each line of the text ends exactly at the right-hand margin **2.** to give a good reason for something ○ *Can you justify the expenditure on children's books?*

juvenile /ˈdʒuːvənaɪl/ *noun* a young person

juxtapose /ˌdʒʌkstəˈpəʊz/ *verb* to put two things next to each other in order to emphasise the difference between them

K

K *abbreviation* thousand □ **£1k** £1000

Kb, Kbit *abbreviation* kilobit

KB, Kbyte *abbreviation* kilobyte ○ *The new disk drive has a 100GB capacity.*

ke *abbreviation* in Internet addresses, the top-level domain for Kenya

Keesings Contemporary Archives /ˌkiːsɪŋz kənˌtemp(ə)rəri ˈɑːkaɪvz/ *plural noun* a monthly publication listing world events reported in the press

Kelly's Directories /ˈkeliz daɪ ˌrekt(ə)riz/ *plural noun* a series of business directories listing products and services and the street names in Britain

Kermit /ˈkɜːmɪt/ *noun* a file transfer protocol which enables computer programs to be transferred from one system to another

key /kiː/ *noun* **1.** a button on a computer keyboard which is pressed to operate the machine **2.** something that is important ■ *verb* to type information using a computer or typesetting machine ○ *The entire text was keyed in Times italic.* ◊ **rekey**

keyboard /ˈkiːbɔːd/ *noun* a set of keys arranged in order and used to enter information into a computer or typewriter

keyboarder /ˈkiːbɔːdə/ *noun* a person who types information into a computer

keyboarding /ˈkiːbɔːdɪŋ/, **keying** /ˈkiːɪŋ/ *noun* the act of entering data on a keyboard

keyboard operator /ˈkiːbɔːd ˌɒpəreɪtə/ *noun* a person who works with a keyboard

key field /ˌkiː ˈfiːld/ *noun* a field which identifies important entries in a record, e.g. name and address

key function /ˈkiː ˌfʌŋkʃ(ə)n/ *noun* a stored command given to a specific key on a computer

key in /ˌkiː ˈɪn/ *verb* to enter text or commands on a computer by means of a keyboard

keynote /ˈkiːnəʊt/ *noun* the part of a policy or speech which is emphasised and given the most importance

keynote speech /ˈkiːnəʊt ˌspiːtʃ/ *noun* a speech at a conference which states the main topic for discussion

keypad /ˈkiːpæd/ *noun* **1.** a set of numerical keys often used for security devices to open doors by means of a known code **2.** numerical keys set separately on the right-hand side of a computer keyboard

keystroke /ˈkiːstrəʊk/ *noun* an act of pressing a key on a keyboard

key system /ˌkiː ˈsɪstəm/ *noun* a system which controls all other functions

keyword /ˈkiːwɜːd/ *noun* the most important word in a title or sentence

keyword and context /ˌkiːwɜːd ən ˈkɒntekst/ *noun* full form of **KWAC**

keyword in context /ˌkiːwɜːd ɪn ˈkɒntekst/ *noun* full form of **KWIC**

keyword out of context /ˌkiːwɜːd aʊt əv ˈkɒntekst/ *noun* full form of **KWOC**

keyword out of title /ˌkiːwɜːd əv ˈtaɪt(ə)l/ *noun* full form of **KWOT**

keyword search /ˌkiːwɜːd ˈsɜːtʃ/ *noun* a system of searching a database by using combinations of special words connected with the subject of the search

kg *abbreviation* kilogram □ **1kg** 1000 grams

kh *abbreviation* in Internet addresses, the top-level domain for Cambodia

ki *abbreviation* in Internet addresses, the top-level domain for Kiribati

kill /kɪl/ *verb* to erase or stop a computer program

kilobit /ˈkɪləbɪt/ *noun* a measure of 1,024 bits of data. Abbr **Kb**, **Kbit**

kilobyte /ˈkɪləʊbaɪt/ *noun* a unit of measurement for high capacity storage devices meaning 1,024 bytes of data. Abbr **KB**, **Kbyte**

King James Bible /ˌkɪŋ dʒeɪmz ˈbaɪb(ə)l/ *noun* same as **Authorised Version**

kiosk /ˈkiːɒsk/ *noun* a small, often wooden building, used for selling things

km *abbreviation* in Internet addresses, the top-level domain for Comoros

KM *abbreviation* knowledge management

kn *abbreviation* in Internet addresses, the top-level domain for St Kitts and Nevis

knockdown price /ˌnɒkdaʊn ˈpraɪs/ *noun* a price that is much lower than normal

know-how /ˈnəʊ haʊ/ *noun* knowledge about how to do specific tasks, especially technical or scientific ones

knowledge /ˈnɒlɪdʒ/ *noun* abstract information and understanding that somebody has about a subject

knowledgeable /ˈnɒlɪdʒəb(ə)l/ *adjective* possessing or showing a great deal of knowledge, awareness or intelligence

knowledge base /ˈnɒlɪdʒ beɪs/ *noun* the computerised data in an expert system required for solving problems in a specific area

knowledge-based system /ˈnɒlɪdʒ beɪst ˌsɪstəm/ *noun* a computer system that applies the stored reactions, instructions and knowledge of experts in a particular field to a problem

knowledge capital /ˈnɒlɪdʒ ˌkæpɪt(ə)l/ *noun* knowledge, especially specialist knowledge, that a company and its employees possess and that can be put to profitable use

knowledge harvesting /ˈnɒlɪdʒ ˌhɑːvəstɪŋ/ *noun* the activity of interviewing experts in a particular area and trying to capture their knowledge on the subject so it can be used by others

knowledge industry /ˈnɒlɪdʒ ˌɪndəstri/ *noun* businesses that specialise primarily in data processing or the development and use of information technology

knowledge management /ˈnɒlɪdʒ ˌmænɪdʒmənt/ *noun* the tast of coordinating the specialist knowledge possessed by employees so that it can be exploited to create benefits and competitive advantage for the organisation. Abbr **KM**

'Knowledge Management is important because many organisations are not truly 'hunting as a pack' and are thus not getting a decent return on their people's knowledge – or intellectual capital. Organisations that have grown by acquisition are in many cases nothing more than a federation of loosely coupled, and often antagonistic, units. Hence they are not punching their true weight.' [*Financial Times*]

knowledge mapping /ˈnɒlɪdʒ ˌmæpɪŋ/ *noun* the process of effectively documenting and representing knowledge harvested from experts

knowledge representation /ˈnɒlɪdʒ ˌreprɪzenteɪʃ(ə)n/ *noun* a way of writing down knowledge so that it can be understood by others, e.g. by putting it into diagram form

knowledge resources /ˈnɒlɪdʒ rɪˌzɔːsɪz/ *plural noun* documented knowledge on a subject such as effective management, which can be used to educate others

knowledge strategy /ˈnɒlɪdʒ ˌstrætədʒi/ *noun* a set of guidelines laying out the way that knowledge should be collated and shared within a company

knowledge transfer /'nɒlɪdʒ ˌtrænsfɜː/ *noun* the communication of specialised knowledge developed in part of an organisation to a wider group such as another part of the organisation or business customers

knowledge visualisation /'nɒlɪdʒ ˌvɪʒuəlaɪzeɪʃ(ə)n/ *noun* the process of mapping knowledge in the most effective way so that it can be shared with others

knowledge worker /'nɒlɪdʒ ˌwɜːkə/ *noun* **1.** somebody working in an industry that produces information rather than goods, e.g. management consultancy or computer programming **2.** an employee whose value to an organisation lies in the information, ideas and expertise that they possess

Kompass Directories /'kʌmpəs daɪˌrekt(ə)riz/ *plural noun* listings for different countries of most registered companies, e.g. of industrial companies with more than 10 employees who trade nationally in the UK

kp *abbreviation* in Internet addresses, the top-level domain for North Korea

kr *abbreviation* in Internet addresses, the top-level domain for South Korea

Kurzweil /'kʊrtsveɪl/ a trademark for an OCR reader which can recognise typefaces and reads printed text into a computer, converting the printed signs to code

kw *abbreviation* in Internet addresses, the top-level domain for Kuwait

KWAC /kwæk/ *noun* a library indexing system using keywords from the title and text as the index entries. Full form **keyword and context**

KWIC /kwɪk/ *noun* a library indexing system which uses the title or text to illustrate the meaning of the index entry. Full form **keyword in context**

KWOC /kwɒk/ *noun* a library indexing system using any relevant keywords not necessarily used in the text. Full form **keyword out of context**

KWOT /kwɒt/ *noun* an indexing system using words not in the title. Full form **keyword out of title**

ky *abbreviation* in Internet addresses, the top-level domain for Cayman Islands

kz *abbreviation* in Internet addresses, the top-level domain for Kazakhstan

L

la *abbreviation* in Internet addresses, the top-level domain for Laos

LA *abbreviation* Library Association

label /'leɪb(ə)l/ *noun* **1.** a piece of paper or card attached to something giving information about it such as its price or address **2.** a word or symbol used in computing to identify a piece of data ■ *verb* to attach a label to something with information on it such as its price or address

lag /læg/ *verb* **1.** to make slower progress than other people **2.** to slow down so that less is produced ○ *Production lagged and there had to be redundancies.*

laminate /'læmɪneɪt/ *verb* to cover a document with a thin film of glossy plastic for protection

lampoon /læm'puːn/ *noun* a written satirical attack, often with a humorous approach

LAN /læn/ *abbreviation* Local Area Network

landscape format /'lænskeɪp ˌfɔːmæt/ *noun* A4-size paper used sideways so that the longest side is at the top

COMMENT: Landscape format is not a normal book format, in that a portrait format book is easier to hold in the hand. Landscape formats are used for art books where many illustrations may be horizontal. Landscape books, especially large art books, are heavy and tend to pull apart at the spine, thus distorting the pages. They also have the disadvantage of not being easy to put on bookshelves, and are especially awkward for bookshop shelves, where the need to show the spine and title makes the book stick out from the shelf much further than others.

land use map /'lænd juːs ˌmæp/ *noun* a map used by planners which shows the way land is used in any given district

language /'læŋgwɪdʒ/ *noun* a system of sounds, signs or symbols used for communication

language dictionary /'læŋgwɪdʒ ˌdɪkʃ(ə)nəri/ *noun* a book that translates words from one language into another, as opposed to a monolingual dictionary which gives definitions within the same language

language laboratory /'læŋgwɪdʒ ləˌbɒrət(ə)ri/ *noun* a room equipped with tape recorders and computers which can be used for learning or teaching foreign languages

lapel microphone /lə'pel ˌmaɪkrəfəʊn/ *noun* a small microphone which can be pinned to clothing

lapsed /læpst/ *adjective* allowed to end or become invalid

lapsed user /ˌlæpst 'juːzə/ *noun* somebody who used to make use of a service but no longer does

laptop computer /ˌlæptɒp kəm'pjuːtə/ *noun* a computer that is small enough to be held on one's lap but not small enough for a pocket, usually having a screen, keyboard and disk drive

large crown octavo /ˌlɑːdʒ kraʊn ɒk'tɑːvəʊ/ *noun* a book format (198 x 129mm). Abbr **8vo**

large crown quarto /ˌlɑːdʒ kraʊn 'kwɔːtəʊ/ *noun* a book format (258 x 201mm). Abbr **4o**

large print book /ˌlɑːdʒ prɪnt 'bʊk/, **large type book** /ˌlɑːdʒ taɪp 'bʊk/

noun a book printed in a very large print size intended for people who have difficulty in seeing, usually found in public libraries and not available in bookshops

large print edition /ˌlɑːdʒ 'prɪnt ɪˌdɪʃ(ə)n/ *noun* a book printed with a large typeface to help people with poor eyesight to be able to read it

large scale /'lɑːdʒ skeɪl/ *adjective* **1.** large in number, amount or size **2.** referring to a company, activity or object which is larger than the norm

laser beam recording /'leɪzə biːm rɪˌkɔːdɪŋ/ *noun* the production of characters on a light-sensitive film by a laser beam controlled directly from a computer

laser disk /'leɪzə dɪsk/ *noun* a plastic disk containing information in the form of small etched dots that can be read by a laser, used to record images or sound in digital form

laser printer /'leɪzə ˌprɪntə/ *noun* a high quality computer printer

launch /lɔːntʃ/ *verb* to start a new activity or make a new product available to the public ■ *noun* the act of putting a new product on the market ○ *The launch of the new fiction series has been put back three months.* ○ *The company is geared up for the launch of the new series of school textbooks.* ○ *The management has decided on a September launch date.*

laureate /'lɔːriət/ ♦ **Poet Laureate**

law /lɔː/ *noun* a system of rules and regulations used by a government or society to control business agreements, social relationships and crime

law books /'lɔː bʊks/ *plural noun* books referring to the law, e.g. statutes, official publications and commentaries

law directory /'lɔː ˌdaɪrekt(ə)ri/ *noun* a book listing the registered law firms in a country

LAWLIB /'lɔːlɪb/ *noun* a subscription bulletin board on the Internet for the use of lawyers

law library /'lɔː ˌlaɪbrəri/ *noun* a library that specialises in the provision of books about the law, often to support university and college departments training lawyers

layout /'leɪaʊt/ *noun* the design of a page of printed matter including position on the page of illustrations, text and type sizes

lb /paʊndz/ *abbreviation* in Internet addresses, the top-level domain for Lebanon

LBF *abbreviation* London Book Fair

lc *abbreviation* **1.** lowercase **2.** in Internet addresses, the top-level domain for St Lucia

LC *abbreviation* LIBRARIES Library of Congress

LEA *abbreviation* Local Education Authority

lead /liːd/ *verb* to be in charge of or guiding an organisation or group

leader /'liːdə/ *noun* **1.** a person who manages or directs others ○ *the leader of the print workers' union* or *the print workers' leader* ○ *she is the leader of the trade mission to Nigeria* **2.** the product which sells best **3.** in information retrieval, the data at the beginning of a machine-readable record identifying and locating the information content **4.** a piece of blank tape at the beginning of a reel, which is fed into a machine **5.** same as **leading article**

leadership /'liːdəʃɪp/ *noun* the state of being in control of a group or organisation

leadership style /'liːdəʃɪp staɪl/ *noun* a method used to lead a company or organisation

leading article /ˌliːdɪŋ 'ɑːtɪk(ə)l/ *noun* the main article in a newspaper, written by the editor, expressing the newspaper's official point of view. Also called **leader**

lead-in page /'liːd ɪn ˌpeɪdʒ/ *noun* the first page in a videotext system which guides users to other pages

lead story /ˌliːd 'stɔːri/ *noun* the main news item on television or in a newspaper

lead term /ˌliːd 'tɜːm/ *noun* a term chosen by the indexer to head an entry

leaf /liːf/ *noun* a page of a book printed on both sides (NOTE: The plural is **leaves**.) ■ *verb* □ **to leaf through** to turn the pages of a document quickly without reading them carefully

leaflet /'liːflət/ *noun* a small folded piece of paper with printed information, often given away free as a form of advertising

leak /liːk/ *noun* a breach of security or loss of important information

leakage /'liːkɪdʒ/ *noun* the unofficial release of confidential information, usually to the media

leakproof /'liːkpruːf/ *adjective* not allowing breaches in secrecy or confidentiality

leaky /'liːki/ *adjective* allowing breaches in secrecy or confidentiality

learn /lɜːn/ *verb* to obtain knowledge or skill through study or training

learndirect /ˌlɜːndaɪ'rekt/ a trade name for a service which runs flexible courses in a number of workplace-friendly skills, which can be taken either at a drop-in centre or online

learned journal /ˌlɜːnɪd 'dʒɜːn(ə)l/ *noun* a specialised magazine on an academic subject

learning /'lɜːnɪŋ/ *noun* knowledge that has been obtained through study

learning curve /'lɜːnɪŋ kɜːv/ *noun* a graphical description of the speed of learning ○ *There's a lot to take in so it's a steep learning curve.*

learning disability /'lɜːnɪŋ dɪsəˌbɪlɪti/ *noun* a condition that either prevents or significantly hinders somebody from learning basic skills or information at the same rate as most people of the same age

learning-disabled /'lɜːnɪŋ dɪˌseɪb(ə)ld/ *adjective* prevented or hindered by a learning disability from learning basic skills or information at the same rate as most people of the same age

learning environment /'lɜːnɪŋ ɪn ˌvaɪrənmənt/ *noun* surroundings that are conducive to study and learning

learning management system /'lɜːnɪŋ ˌmænɪdʒmənt ˌsɪstəm/ *abbreviation* an online system that allows teachers and students to follow a course of study remotely, e.g. by placing course materials online. Abbr **LMS**

learning organisation /'lɜːnɪŋ ɔːɡənaɪˌzeɪʃ(ə)n/ *noun* an organisation whose employees are willing and eager to share information with each other, to learn from each other, and to work as a team to achieve their goals

lease /liːs/ *noun* a written contract for letting or renting a piece of equipment for a period in return for payment of a fee ■ *verb* to let or rent equipment for a period

leather /'leðə/ *noun* material made from the skins of animals, used for binding expensive books

leather binding /'leðə ˌbaɪndɪŋ/ *noun* the cover of a book, made from animal skin

leatherbound book /'leðəbaʊnd ˌbʊk/ *noun* a book that has been bound in leather

leave /liːv/ *noun* a period of time when somebody is absent from their job or study

lectern /'lektɜːn/ *noun* a stand with a sloping top on which a book or notes can rest in front of a standing speaker

lecture /'lektʃə/ *noun* a long talk on a specific subject given to a group of people, often used as a method of teaching in higher education

left-hand corner /ˌleft hænd 'kɔːnə/ *noun* the top or bottom corner at the left side of a page or envelope

left justification /ˌleft ˌdʒʌstɪfɪ 'keɪʃ(ə)n/ *noun* the process of aligning the left-hand margin on a piece of text so that the edge is even

left justify /ˌleft 'dʒʌstɪfaɪ/ *verb* to use computer commands which ensure that the text on the left side of a document is straight

legal /'liːɡ(ə)l/ *adjective* **1.** relating to the law ○ *a legal discussion* **2.** according to the law ○ *The contract was legal and binding.*

legal aid /ˌliːɡ(ə)l 'eɪd/ *noun* financial assistance with legal fees from the government, available to those who cannot afford a lawyer

legal deposit /'liːɡ(ə)l dɪˌpɒzɪt/ *noun* a system that entitles some libraries to receive by law one copy of every book or publication published in that country

legal tender /ˌliːg(ə)l 'tendə/ *noun* coins or notes that are officially part of a country's currency

legend /'ledʒənd/ *noun* **1.** a caption under a picture or diagram or on a coin or medal **2.** an explanation of the symbols on a map or diagram **3.** a story based on cultural traditions handed down

legible /'ledʒɪb(ə)l/ *adjective* clear enough to be read easily

COMMENT: Legibility is one of the requirements of text matter. Text is more easily read in roman serif typefaces than in italic or in sans faces, and should have line spacing of about 2pts between the lines (i.e. there should be more spacing between the lines than between words). Sans faces and italic are less legible, and closely spaced lines, or lines which are irregularly spaced, are more difficult to read than lines of closely spaced words with extra spacing between the lines.

legitimate /lɪ'dʒɪtɪmət/ *adjective* acceptable according to the law

lemma /'lemə/ *noun* a heading that indicates the topic of a work or passage (NOTE: The plural is **lemmata**.)

lending library /'lendɪŋ ˌlaɪbrəri/ *noun* a library which allows users to borrow items as opposed to a purely reference library

lengthen /'leŋθən/ *verb* to make something longer

lengthy /'leŋθi/ *adjective* lasting for a long time, especially excessively long ○ *lengthy delays*

lesson /'les(ə)n/ *noun* **1.** a period of time used to teach something to an individual or a group **2.** a short extract from sacred writings, read aloud during a religious service

let /let/ *verb* **1.** to allow somebody to do something **2.** to allow somebody to use something one owns in return for regular payments of rent

Letraset /'letrəset/ a trade name for a system of labelling or captioning documents and illustrations

letter /'letə/ *noun* **1.** a piece of writing sent from one person to another usually through the post **2.** a symbol used in writing which more or less represents one sound of a language

letterhead /'letəhed/ *noun* the name and address of a company or organisation printed at the top of their official notepaper

level /'lev(ə)l/ *noun* a point on a scale indicating amount, importance or difficulty ○ *sound level* ○ *level of inflation*

lexicographer /ˌleksɪ'kɒgrəfə/ *noun* a person who writes or edits dictionaries

lexicography /ˌleksɪ'kɒgrəfi/ *noun* the activity of writing and editing dictionaries

lexicon /'leksɪkɒn/ *noun* **1.** an alphabetical list of words specifically related to a language or a particular subject **2.** a dictionary, especially one of an ancient language such as Latin or Hebrew

liaise /li'eɪz/ *verb* to work together and keep each other informed

liaison /li'eɪz(ə)n/ *noun* co-operation and communication between different organisations or sections of an organisation

lib. *abbreviation* LIBRARIES **1.** librarian **2.** library

LIBNET /'lɪbnet/ *noun* the electronic mail service of the Australian Library and Information Association

librarian /laɪ'breəriən/ *noun* **1.** a person who is in charge of a library **2.** a person who has usually been trained in librarianship and who works in a library

librarianship /laɪ'breəriənʃɪp/ *noun* the study of organising and retrieving information so that it is accessible to other people

'Librarianship is a bipolar profession. On the one hand, librarians are custodians of treasure houses, whose responsibility for preserving collections of potentially rare, fragile and sometimes unique material can most easily be achieved by keeping people away from it. On the other hand, they are gatekeepers, charged with facilitating the most direct and fruitful access to the information and knowledge contained in their collections to all who may wish to use them.' [*The Times*]

library /'laɪbrəri/ *noun* a collection of books, documents, newspapers and audiovisual materials kept and organised for people to read or borrow

library and information science /ˌlaɪbrəri ənd ˌɪnfəˈmeɪʃ(ə)n ˌsaɪəns/ *noun* a course of study that covers all aspects of information and library management, e.g. resources, user services, organisation, evaluation, systems used, policy and representation. Abbr **LIS**

Library and Information Science Abstracts /ˌlaɪbrəri ənd ˌɪnfəˈmeɪʃ(ə)n ˌsaɪəns ˌæbstrækts/ *noun* an index of articles and current research in library science. Abbr **LISA**

library assistant /ˈlaɪbrəri əˈsɪstənt/ *noun* a person who works in a library as a helper but is not qualified as a librarian

Library Association /ˈlaɪbrəri əˌsəʊsieɪʃ(ə)n/ *noun* a UK professional body working to support librarians and information workers. Abbr **LA**

library binding /ˈlaɪbrəri ˌbaɪndɪŋ/ *noun* a strong, durable binding for books which will withstand heavy use

library card /ˈlaɪbrəri kɑːd/, **library ticket** /ˈlaɪbrəri ˌtɪkɪt/ *noun* a ticket which allows the holder to borrow library books

library edition /ˈlaɪbrəri ɪˌdɪʃ(ə)n/ *noun* a set of books, published in a series, either by a single author or on the same subject and with the same size and format

library equipment /ˈlaɪbrəri ɪˈkɪpmənt/ *noun* furniture and machinery needed to run a library

Library Information Service /ˌlaɪbrəri ˌɪnfəˈmeɪʃ(ə)n ˌsɜːvɪs/ *noun* a service provided by a library to users to answer their questions on any subject. Abbr **LIS**

library instruction /ˈlaɪbrəri ɪnˈstrʌkʃ(ə)n/ *noun* training in library management techniques

library licence /ˈlaɪbrəri ˌlaɪs(ə)ns/ *noun* a licence granted to a bookshop or to a local authority, allowing books to be bought at a discount for public libraries

library management system /ˈlaɪbrəri ˌmænɪdʒmənt ˌsɪstəm/ *noun* a computer system which deals with one or more library processes such as acquisitions, circulation and cataloguing

Library of Congress /ˌlaɪbrəri əv ˈkɒŋgres/ *noun* the national library of the United States, located in Washington DC and founded by an Act of Congress in 1800. It contains more than 28 million books and pamphlets as well as presidential papers, music, photographs and recordings. Abbr **LR**

Library of Congress Catalog /ˌlaɪbrəri əv ˈkɒŋgres ˌkætəlɒg/ *noun* a catalogue of the holdings of the Library of Congress in the USA, also available online. Abbr **LOCIS**

Library of Congress Catalog number /ˌlaɪbrəri əv ˌkɒŋgres ˈkætəlɒg ˌnʌmbə/ *noun* the number of the reference in the Library of Congress Catalog, printed inside a book published in the USA. Abbr **LOC**

Library of Congress Classification system /ˌlaɪbrəri əv ˌkɒŋgres ˌklæsɪfɪˈkeɪʃ(ə)n ˌsɪstəm/ *noun* an American system of organising documents for information retrieval. Abbr **LC**

library purchase /ˈlaɪbrəri ˌpɜːtʃɪs/ *noun* the purchase of books by a library from a library supplier

library school /ˈlaɪbrəri skuːl/ *noun* a department or college which runs courses to train library and information workers

library science /ˈlaɪbrəri ˌsaɪəns/ *noun* the study of librarianship

library supplier /ˈlaɪbrəri səˌplaɪə/ *noun* a company that supplies stationery, books, equipment and furniture needed for use in libraries

library supply /ˈlaɪbrəri səˌplaɪ/ *noun* a supply of books to libraries at a discount

library user /ˈlaɪbrəri ˌjuːzə/ *noun* a person who uses a library

library user education /ˌlaɪbrəri ˌjuːzər ˌedjʊˈkeɪʃ(ə)n/ *noun* training courses which help library users to use the library more effectively

libretto /lɪˈbretəʊ/ *noun* the words of an opera or other vocal musical production

licence /ˈlaɪs(ə)ns/ *noun* an official document giving permission to use or do something

license /ˈlaɪs(ə)ns/ *verb* to give official permission for something to happen

life cycle of records /ˌlaɪf ˌsaɪk(ə)l əv ˈrekɔːdz/ *noun* the creation, storage, retrieval for use, and disposal when no longer needed, of records

light-pen /ˈlaɪtpen/ *noun* a stylus with a light sensor used to scan barcodes

light-sensitive paper /ˌlaɪt ˌsensɪtɪv ˈpeɪpə/ *noun* paper that is sensitive to light, usually used for photographs

lightweight /ˈlaɪtweɪt/ *adjective* **1.** not heavy ○ *thin, lightweight paper* **2.** not thought to be of a high academic standard

Likert scale /ˈlaɪkɜːt skeɪl/ *noun* a system of measuring people's attitudes on a five-point scale, from positive to negative or vice versa

limit /ˈlɪmɪt/ *noun* a maximum predefined range used to restrict an action or thing ▪ *verb* to prevent something from becoming bigger

limited /ˈlɪmɪtɪd/ *adjective* small in amount or degree

limited company /ˌlɪmɪtɪd ˈkʌmp(ə)ni/ *noun* a company in which the shareholders are only legally responsible for debts to the amount of their shares if the company goes bankrupt

limited edition /ˌlɪmɪtɪd ɪˈdɪʃ(ə)n/ *noun* a work of art such as a book or painting which is only produced in very small numbers

limp /lɪmp/ *adjective* relating to a book cover that is not stiffened by boards but is made of more durable material than a paperback

limp binding /ˈlɪmp ˌbaɪndɪŋ/ *noun* a binding style using flexible material usually cheaper than hard boards

limp-bound edition /ˈlɪmp baʊnd ɪˌdɪʃ(ə)n/, **limp edition** /ˈlɪmp ɪˌdɪʃ(ə)n/ *noun* an edition of a book with a soft cover

Lindop Committee /ˈlɪndɒp kə ˌmɪti/ *noun* a British government committee which investigated and made recommendations about the security of information on computers in 1978

line /laɪn/ *noun* **1.** a row of words or figures in a text **2.** a type of product that a company makes or sells **3.** a long piece of wire used to connect communications ○ *a telephone line*

linear /ˈlɪniə/ *adjective* process in which things always happen one at a time following each other in a set order

line by line index /ˌlaɪn baɪ ˈlaɪn ˌɪndeks/ *noun* an index with entries consisting of one line only

line drawings /ˈlaɪn ˌdrɔːɪŋz/, **line illustrations** /ˈlaɪn ɪləˌstreɪʃ(ə)nz/ *plural noun* illustrations for a book which are drawn with a pen, or have tints, but which do not need to be reproduced as halftones

line editor /ˈlaɪn ˌedɪtə/ *noun* a piece of software that allows the operator to modify one line of text from a file at a time

line management /ˈlaɪn ˌmænɪdʒmənt/ *noun* a system of management using a hierarchical structure of jobs, so that everyone is responsible to the person immediately above them

line manager /ˈlaɪn ˌmænɪdʒə/ *noun* a person in a hierarchical structure of management who is responsible for the person or people immediately below

linguistics /lɪŋˈgwɪstɪks/ *noun* the study of language, its history, grammar, structure and use

link /lɪŋk/ *noun* **1.** a relationship between two or more things either by a physical connection or by a common idea which enables them to work together **2.** a hypertext connection which allows users to move to another related part of the Internet

link up /ˌlɪŋk ˈʌp/ *verb* to connect things to each other ○ *This computer can be linked up with others in the network.*

link word /'lɪŋk wɜːd/ *noun* a word used in writing or speaking to join ideas or sentences together

Linson /'lɪns(ə)n/ a trademark for a strong binding paper which is patterned to resemble cloth

LINUX /'lɪnəks/ a trademark for a computer operating system that is a free implementation of the UNIX operating system

LIS *abbreviation* 1. Library Information Service 2. library and information science

LISA *abbreviation* Library and Information Science Abstracts

list /'meɪlɪŋ lɪst/ *noun* 1. a series of items written down usually one under the other 2. a catalogue ○ *There is a price list for cars of different ages and models.* ■ *verb* to print or display certain items of information

list of abbreviations /ˌlist əv ə ˌbriːviˈeɪʃ(ə)nz/ *noun* a note in a reference book which lists the abbreviations used and what they stand for, usually printed at the beginning of the text, after the prelims or, in some reference works such as dictionaries, on the endpapers

list owner /'lɪst ˌəʊnə/ *noun* a person who controls an electronic mailing list

list price /'lɪst praɪs/ *noun* the price of a commodity according to a printed list

LISTSERV /'lɪstsɜːv/ *noun* a very large electronic mailing list manager

literacy /'lɪt(ə)rəsi/ *noun* the ability to read and write

'In a withering dossier, chief inspector Graham Donaldson concluded pupils were being failed by poor teachers and weak leadership and that a fifth were leaving school without basic literacy and numeracy skills.' [*Sunday Express*]

literal /'lɪt(ə)rəl/ *adjective* following the exact meaning of a word or phrase, without any additional meanings ■ *noun* a mistake made when keyboarding so that characters are transposed

literary /'lɪt(ə)rəri/ *adjective* related to literature

literary agent /'lɪt(ə)rəri ˌeɪdʒənt/ *noun* somebody whose job is to negotiate business contracts on behalf of an author

literary forensics /ˌlɪt(ə)rəri fə 'renzɪks/ *noun* the scientific examination of documents of disputed authenticity

Literary Marketplace /ˌlɪt(ə)rəri 'mɑːkɪtpleɪs/ *noun* an American publication listing people such as publishers, agents and translators (NOTE: The British equivalent is the **Writers' and Artists' Yearbook**.)

literary prize /'lɪt(ə)rəri praɪz/ *noun* an award given for a piece of writing judged to have literary value

literate /'lɪt(ə)rət/ *adjective* able to read and write

literature /'lɪt(ə)rətʃə/ *noun* 1. written works such as novels, plays and poetry, especially those considered to have artistic quality 2. printed information on a specific subject

literature search /'lɪt(ə)rətʃə sɜːtʃ/ *noun* a preliminary investigation when studying a subject to find all other related writing

literature survey /'lɪt(ə)rətʃə ˌsɜːveɪ/ *noun* a bibliography listing material on a given subject or sometimes in a given location

lithography /lɪ'θɒɡrəfi/, **litho** *noun* a method of printing in which the ink sticks to greasy areas of treated metal, stone or film and is then transferred to paper

COMMENT: Lithography was invented in 1798, by a German artist, Alois Senefelder. It was originally the art of drawing a design on stone in greasy ink, then printing from it. The surface now used is a metal plate, but the principle is the same: this is that a greasy surface attracts ink, while a wet surface repels ink. The design is drawn on the surface with greasy ink, the surface is then rolled with a damp roller to wet it, and then the inking roller passes over it, leaving ink on the parts which are greasy and not leaving ink on those parts which are wet.

lk *abbreviation* in Internet addresses, the top-level domain for Sri Lanka

LMS *abbreviation* learning management system

load /ləʊd/ *verb* □ **to load a file** to call a computer file so that it can be seen on screen and worked with

load sharing /ˈləʊd ˌʃeərɪŋ/ *noun* the process of using more people to even out the workload

loan /ləʊn/ *noun* something that is lent and must be returned □ **on loan** being borrowed ○ *The book is on loan from the library.*

loan collection /ˈləʊn kəˌlekʃ(ə)n/ *noun* a collection of books and materials available for borrowing, as opposed to a reference collection which cannot be taken away from the library

loan fee /ˈləʊn fiː/ *noun* a sum of money paid to borrow an item

loan period /ˈləʊn ˌpɪəriəd/ *noun* a period of time before an item that has been borrowed must be returned

LOC *abbreviation* Library of Congress Catalog number

local /ˈləʊk(ə)l/ *adjective* belonging or relating to the specific area where you live or work

Local Area Network /ˌləʊk(ə)l ˌeəriə ˈnetwɜːk/ *noun* a system linking computers, terminals and printers, within a restricted geographical area, which share the same stored information in the network memory. Abbr **LAN**

local collection /ˈləʊk(ə)l kəˌlekʃ(ə)n/ *noun* books and documents about a specific area close to where the collection is held

local directory /ˈləʊk(ə)l ˌdaɪrekt(ə)ri/ *noun* a collection of information about businesses and residents in a specified area arranged in alphabetical order of street names and also with classified trade entries

Local Education Authority /ˌləʊk(ə)l ˌedjuˈkeɪʃ(ə)n ɔːˈθɒrɪti/ *noun* an administrative body which controls the supply of education through schools and colleges in a local area of the UK. Abbr **LEA**

local history /ˌləʊk(ə)l ˈhɪst(ə)ri/ *noun* the history of a small area of a country

local interest title /ˌləʊk(ə)l ˈɪnt(ə)rəst ˌtaɪt(ə)l/ *noun* a book which is interesting to people living in a certain area, but less so to anyone else

local map /ˌləʊk(ə)l ˈmæp/ *noun* a map showing the area near to where you live or work

local newspaper /ˌləʊk(ə)l ˈnjuːzpeɪpə/ *noun* a newspaper that reports on local events and people

local press /ˌləʊk(ə)l ˈpres/ *noun* newspapers which cover news relevant to a local area and which are printed and sold in one small area of the country

local radio /ˌləʊk(ə)l ˈreɪdiəʊ/, **local TV** /ˌləʊk(ə)l tiː ˈviː/ *noun* broadcasting stations which concentrate on the news and issues relevant to a small local area

local record office /ˌləʊk(ə)l ˈrekɔːd ˌɒfɪs/ *noun* an archive store that keeps information about the particular area in which it is situated

locate /ləʊˈkeɪt/ *verb* **1.** to place or position something **2.** to find something

locator /ləʊˈkeɪtə/ *noun US* a device that helps somebody locate something such as a table or index

LOCIS /ˈləʊkɪs/ *abbreviation* Library of Congress Catalog

lock /lɒk/ *verb* to fasten something to prevent access □ **to lock a file** to prevent anyone from making changes to a computer file

lockdown /ˈlɒkdaʊn/ *noun* a procedure that prevents users of a computer network or intruders from the Internet from gaining access to files that are essential to the proper functioning of a computer system

log /lɒg/ *verb* to record something officially

log book /ˈlɒg bʊk/ *noun* **1.** a book in which entry and departure times to a particular place are recorded **2.** a book in which someone writes records of their activities especially related to travelling

logic /ˈlɒdʒɪk/ *noun* a way of thinking and reasoning which takes account of previous steps

log in /ˌlɒg ˈɪn/, **log on** /ˌlɒg ˈɒn/ *verb* to enter a password or code in order to gain entry to a computer system

logistics /ləˈdʒɪstɪks/ *plural noun* the organisation of something very complicated, especially of moving people and things from one place to another

logo /'ləʊgəʊ/ *noun* a special design which identifies the products and publicity material of a company or organisation

log off /ˌlɒg 'ɒf/, **log out** /ˌlɒg 'aʊt/ *verb* to enter data in order to close down and leave a computer system

long-distance /ˌlɒŋ 'dɪstəns/ *adjective* relating to journeys, communications or places that are far apart

long loan /'lɒŋ ləʊn/ *noun* an extended period for borrowing library items

long-term /ˌlɒŋ 'tɜːm/ *adjective* concerning a long period of time ○ *long-term planning* ○ *The long-term plans include the development of a music library.*

look up /ˌlʊk 'ʌp/ *verb* to search for information, e.g. by consulting a reference book

look-up /'lʊk ʌp/ *noun* a computer procedure in which a term or value is matched against a table of stored information

look-up table /'lʊk ʌp ˌteɪb(ə)l/ *noun* a collection of stored results that can be accessed very rapidly by a program without the need to calculate each result whenever needed. Abbr **LUT**

COMMENT: For computer graphics a look-up table may be a table of pixel intensity or colour information which increases the range of values that can be displayed. Since the values are stored in a look-up table they do not have to be computed each time they are called up, and execution time is reduced.

loop /luːp/ *noun* a series of actions that are performed repeatedly until the procedure has been completed

loose-leaf /'luːs liːf/ *adjective* having pages which can be removed or replaced

lossless compression /ˌlɒsləs kəm'preʃ(ə)n/ *noun* an image compression technique that can reduce the number of bits used for each pixel in an image without losing any information or sharpness

lossy compression /ˌlɒsi kəm'preʃ(ə)n/ *noun* an image compression technique that can reduce the number of bits used for each pixel in an image, but in doing so lose information

loudspeaker /ˌlaʊd'spiːkə/ *noun* a device that turns electrical signals into recognisable sound

low acid /ˌləʊ 'æsɪd/ *adjective* relating to paper that is mildly acidic in composition, but less prone to deterioration than standard acidic paper

lower case /ˌləʊə 'keɪs/ *adjective* relating to small letters such as a, b, c, as opposed to upper case A, B, C

low level language /ˌləʊ ˌlev(ə)l 'læŋgwɪdʒ/ *noun* a computer programming language that is similar to the machine language and difficult for non-expert users to understand

lr *abbreviation* in Internet addresses, the top-level domain for Liberia

LR *abbreviation* Library of Congress

ls *abbreviation* in Internet addresses, the top-level domain for Lesotho

lt *abbreviation* in Internet addresses, the top-level domain for Lithuania

lu *abbreviation* in Internet addresses, the top-level domain for Luxembourg

lunar month /ˌluːnə 'mʌnθ/ *noun* the period of time between one new moon and the next, usually about 28 days

LUT *abbreviation* look-up table

luxury edition /'lʌkʃəri ɪˌdɪʃ(ə)n/ *noun* an edition printed on fine paper with a superior binding

lv *abbreviation* in Internet addresses, the top-level domain for Latvia

ly *abbreviation* in Internet addresses, the top-level domain for Libya

lyric /'lɪrɪk/ *noun* a short poem expressing strong feelings in a songlike form

M

machine code /məˈʃiːn kəʊd/, **machine language** /məˈʃiːn ˌlæŋgwɪdʒ/ *noun* instructions and information shown as a series of binary figures which can be read by a computer

machine-readable /məˌʃiːn ˈriːdəb(ə)l/ *adjective* stored on a disk or tape in machine language, so that it can be read directly by a computer

Machine Readable Catalogue /məˌʃiːn ˌriːdəb(ə)l ˈkætəlɒg/ *noun* an automated system of cataloguing books and documents in a library. Abbr **MARC**

machine-readable code /məˌʃiːn ˌriːdəb(ə)l ˈkəʊd/ *noun* a set of signs or letters which a computer can read

machine translation /məˌʃiːn trænsˈleɪʃ(ə)n/ *noun* translation from one language into another carried out automatically by a computer

machinist /məˈʃiːnɪst/ *noun* a person whose job is to work a machine

magazine /ˌmægəˈziːn/ *noun* **1.** a regular weekly, monthly or quarterly publication containing articles, stories, photographs and advertisements **2.** a radio or television programme made up of several different items **3.** a container for slides to be used in an automatic projector

magnetic /mægˈnetɪk/ *adjective* relating to something that uses electrical magnetism to record and store information to be read by a computer

magnetic head /mægˌnetɪk ˈhed/ *noun* an electromagnetic device that reads, writes or erases data on a magnetic medium

magnetic strip /mægˌnetɪk ˈstrɪp/ *noun* a plastic strip with electronic data fixed to a plastic card, which can be read by a machine ○ *A library card often has a magnetic strip with details of its owner to prevent it being used by anyone else.*

magnetic tape /mægˌnetɪk ˈteɪp/ *noun* tape coated with a magnetic material so that electrical signals can be recorded on to it for speech, film or computer information

magnetic tape encoder /mæg ˌnetɪk teɪp enˈkəʊdə/ *noun* a device that directly writes data entered from a keyboard on to magnetic tape

magnetised /ˈmægnətaɪzd/, **magnetized** *adjective* converted into a magnet ○ *The library uses magnetised strips inside books to prevent theft.*

magnify /ˈmægnɪfaɪ/ *verb* to make something appear bigger or more important than it really is

magnitude /ˈmægnɪtjuːd/ *noun* the level, degree or importance of a signal or situation ○ *They did not appreciate the magnitude of the task.*

mail /meɪl/ *noun* letters and parcels delivered by the Post Office

mailbase /ˈmeɪlbeɪs/ *noun* a UK electronic mailing list service used by discussion groups. ◊ **bulletin board**

mail box /ˈmeɪl bɒks/ *noun* **1.** one of several boxes where incoming mail is put in a large building **2.** a box for putting letters, etc. which you want to post **3.** storage in an electronic mail system, where messages are kept for subscribers to access through their computers

mailing list /ˈmeɪlɪŋ lɪst/ *noun* **1.** a list of names and addresses kept by an organisation so that it can send people information or regular publications **2.** an electronic list of e-mail addressees or subscribers who usually have an interest in the same topic

mail merge /ˈmeɪl mɜːdʒ/ *noun* a word-processing program which allows a standard letter to be sent out to a series of different names and addresses

mailserver /ˈmeɪlsɜːvə/ *noun* a computer on the Internet which stores incoming mail and sends it to the correct user, and stores outgoing mail and transfers it to the correct destination server

mail shot /ˈmeɪl ʃɒt/ *noun* a large number of information or publicity leaflets sent out to a selected group of prospective customers

main /meɪn/ *adjective* most important

main catalogue /ˌmeɪn ˈkætəlɒg/ *noun* a full list of all the holdings in a library

main class /ˌmeɪn ˈklɑːs/ *noun* a major division of a general classification scheme

main entry /ˌmeɪn ˈentri/ *noun* the fullest entry in a catalogue, often with a tracing of related references

mainframe /ˈmeɪnfreɪm/, **mainframe computer** /ˌmeɪnfreɪm kəmˈpjuːtə/ *noun* a large-scale high-power computer system that can handle high-capacity memory and backing storage devices as well as servicing a number of operators simultaneously

main index /ˌmeɪn ˈɪndeks/ *noun* a general index which guides users to more specific entries

mainstream /ˈmeɪnstriːm/ *adjective* normal or conventional

mainstream research /ˌmeɪnstriːm rɪˈsɜːtʃ/ *noun* research that follows on from previous work done in the field

maintain /meɪnˈteɪn/ *verb* to keep something in good condition and up to date

maintenance /ˈmeɪntənəns/ *noun* the process of keeping something in good condition by giving it regular care and attention

maintenance contract /ˈmeɪntənəns ˌkɒntrækt/ *noun* an arrangement with a repair company to make regular checks and repairs at special prices

maintenance costs /ˈmeɪntənəns kɒsts/ *plural noun* money put into a budget for carrying out regular maintenance

maintenance of records /ˌmeɪntənəns əv ˈrekɔːdz/ *noun* the process of updating information or keeping records up to date

major /ˈmeɪdʒə/ *adjective* very important

major contributor /ˌmeɪdʒə kənˈtrɪbjətə/ *noun* a person who has supplied the most information or written text for a publication or meeting

majority /məˈdʒɒrɪti/ *noun* the larger part or greater number

malfunction /mælˈfʌŋkʃən/ *noun* failure to work properly ■ *verb* to fail to work properly

malware /ˈmælweə/ *noun* software such as viruses designed to cause damage or disruption to a computer system

man /mæn/ *verb* to provide the workforce for something ○ *They manned the exhibition stand all day.*

manage /ˈmænɪdʒ/ *verb* to direct or take responsibility for controlling somebody or something

manageable /ˈmænɪdʒəb(ə)l/ *adjective* able to be controlled easily because it is not too big or complicated

management /ˈmænɪdʒmənt/ *noun* the process of controlling an organisation, company or group

Management By Objectives /ˌmænɪdʒmənt baɪ əbˈdʒektɪvz/ *noun* a system of managing a company by stating the aims of the organisation as the basis of policy. Abbr **MBO**

management information service /ˌmænɪdʒmənt ˌɪnfə ˈmeɪʃ(ə)n ˌsɪstəm/ *noun* a department within a company that is responsible for information and data processing

management information system /ˌmænɪdʒmənt ˌɪnfə ˈmeɪʃ(ə)n ˌsɪstəm/ *noun* a system designed to collate all the information collected by an organisation and supplied to support anyone involved in decision making. Abbr **MIS**

'...of equal benefit has been the improvement in management information systems. In the past, banks and insurers were basing their risk decisions on inaccurate or out of date information; new technology has allowed companies to trade on real-time information with obvious implications for risk control and accuracy of pricing.' [*Investment Advisor*]

management of records /ˌmænɪdʒmənt əv ˈrekɔːdz/ *noun* the process of creating, storing, retrieving and disposing of records

management style /ˈmænɪdʒmənt staɪl/ *noun* any of several different ways of controlling, organising and motivating groups of people

management training /ˌmænɪdʒmənt ˈtreɪnɪŋ/ *noun* the training of managers by making them study the principles and practices of management

manager /ˈmænɪdʒə/ *noun* a person who is responsible for running a company, organisation or group

managerial /ˌmænəˈdʒɪəriəl/ *adjective* relating to the work of a manager

mandatory /ˈmændət(ə)ri/ *adjective* compulsory ○ *It is mandatory to pay taxes.*

manifesto /ˌmænɪˈfestəʊ/ *noun* a written statement of the intentions of a person or group of people who are standing for election

manipulate /məˈnɪpjuleɪt/ *verb* to control people, data or situations to produce a specific result

manipulation /mə,nɪpjʊˈleɪʃ(ə)n/ *noun* the act of moving, editing or changing text or data ○ *The high-speed database management program allows the manipulation of very large amounts of data.*

man-made /ˌmæn ˈmeɪd/ *adjective* made by people rather than formed naturally

manpower /ˈmænpaʊə/ *noun* a workforce or labour force which produces goods

manpower resources /ˈmænpaʊə rɪ,zɔːsɪz/ *plural noun* the number of people available for work

manual /ˈmænjuəl/ *noun* a document or book containing instructions about the operation of a system or machine ■ *adjective* done by hand rather than by machine

manual data processing /ˌmænjuəl ˈdeɪtə ,prəʊsesɪŋ/ *noun* the sorting and processing of information without the help of a computer

manual entry /ˌmænjuəl ˈentri/, **manual input** /ˌmænjuəl ˈɪnpʊt/ *noun* the act of entering data into a computer by an operator via a keyboard

manual system /ˈmænjuəl ,sɪstəm/ *noun* an information control system that uses handwritten rather than computerised records

manufacture /ˌmænjʊˈfæktʃə/ *verb* to make something in a factory

manufacturer /ˌmænjʊˈfæktʃərə/ *noun* a company which makes a product

manuscript /ˈmænjʊskrɪpt/ *noun* a typed or handwritten text of something before it is printed ○ *The advance on royalties will be paid on acceptance of the completed manuscript for publication.* Abbr **ms**

manuscript music book /ˌmænjʊskrɪpt ˈmjuːzɪk ,bʊk/ *noun* a book of paper ruled with five line staves for the writing of music

map /mæp/ *noun* a diagrammatic representation of an area of land

COMMENT: Maps are now mainly computerised and are output on plotters. This allows the information on a map to be stored as a database, which can be used to produce maps on different scales, with different colour designs, etc.

map pin /ˈmæp pɪn/ *noun* a sharp metal object with a small round coloured head used to indicate places on a map

marbled paper /ˌmɑːb(ə)ld ˈpeɪpə/ *noun* multi-coloured paper used by bookbinders usually for the endpapers of books

MARC /mɑːk/ *abbreviation* Machine Readable Catalogue

margin /'mɑːdʒɪn/ *noun* a blank space around a section of printed text between the printed text and the edge of the paper

margin of error /ˌmɑːdʒɪn əv 'erə/ *noun* the number of mistakes that are considered to be acceptable in a document or calculation

mark /mɑːk/ *noun* **1.** a sign or symbol written on a page **2.** the score or grade achieved for an assignment or examination ■ *verb* to assess work and award it a grade or score

marker /'mɑːkə/ *noun* an object that is used to show the position of something

marker pen /'mɑːkə pen/ *noun* a coloured pen used to indicate or highlight sections of text

market /'mɑːkɪt/ *noun* the number of people wishing to buy a product or the area of the world where it is sold ■ *verb* to organise the sale of a product by deciding the price, the areas where it will be sold and how it will be advertised

marketing plan /'mɑːkɪtɪŋ plæn/ *noun* a strategy for selling a product or service by planning the advertising and distribution within a selected market

market penetration /ˌmɑːkɪt ˌpenɪ 'treɪʃ(ə)n/ *noun* an expression of how much of the chosen market is reached by a product ○ *They estimated a 50% market penetration for the information service.*

marketplace /'mɑːkɪtpleɪs/ *noun* **1.** the potential number of people who will buy a product or use a service **2.** a place where goods or services can be sold or offered

market research /ˌmɑːkɪt rɪ'sɜːtʃ/, **market analysis** /ˌmɑːkɪt ə'næləsɪs/ *noun* the process of examining the possible sales of a product and the possible customers for it before it is put on the market

mark up /ˌmɑːk 'ʌp/ *verb* to prepare copy for printing by indicating such things as font size, typeface and layout

mass deacidification /ˌmæs ˌdiːæsɪdɪfɪ'keɪʃ(ə)n/ *noun* the process

of adding chemicals to acidic paper to neutralise the acid and prevent further deterioration, especially in old collections

mass market /ˌmæs 'mɑːkɪt/ *noun* a very large market, covering a large proportion of a population

mass market paperback /ˌmæs ˌmɑːkɪt 'peɪpəbæk/ *noun* a paperback book aimed at the mass market

mass media /ˌmæs 'miːdiə/ *noun* means of communication which reach large numbers of people, e.g. radio, television and newspapers

mass production /ˌmæs prə 'dʌkʃən/ *noun* the manufacture of large quantities of the same product

mass storage /ˌmæs 'stɔːrɪdʒ/ *noun* the storage and retrieval of large amounts of data

'"It's not unusual for universities or government bodies to have rooms that are floor to ceiling with magnetic tapes", says Kevin Murrell, a curator at Bletchley Park Computer Museum. "Ten or fifteen years ago this was the most common mass-storage medium, but today it's increasing difficult to read them".' [*New Scientist*]

mass storage device /ˌmæs 'stɔːrɪdʒ dɪˌvaɪs/ *noun* a computer backing store device such as a disk drive which is able to store large amounts of data

master /'mɑːstə/ *noun* **1.** the original document from which copies are made **2.** the most important person or device within a system ■ *verb* to learn something so that you can do it well

master catalogue *noun* a file in which every entry contains full bibliographical information. Also called **master file**

master copy /'mɑːstə ˌkɒpi/ *noun* the original document from which photocopies are made

master file /'mɑːstə faɪl/ *noun* **1.** same as **master catalogue 2.** the main copy of a computer file, kept for security purposes

mastermind /'mɑːstəmaɪnd/ *verb* to plan a complicated activity in detail and make sure it happens successfully

masterpiece /'mɑːstəpiːs/ *noun* an original creation in the arts which is of exceptional quality

master plan /'mɑːstə plæn/ *noun* a detailed plan to organise several difficult tasks

Master's degree /'mɑːstəz dɪˌɡriː/ *noun* an academic degree, usually awarded after one or two years of postgraduate study

match /mætʃ/ *noun* something that is equal to another in physical or mental characteristics ○ *The players were a perfect match for each other and the game ended in a draw.* ■ *verb* to find an item that has equal characteristics ○ *He had to match them for size and colour.* □ **to match a record** to search a database or record for a similar piece of information to the record you have

material /mə'tɪəriəl/ *noun* equipment or items needed for a particular activity

material requirements planning /məˌtɪəriəl rɪˈkwaɪəmənts ˌplænɪŋ/ *noun* a detailed statement of the equipment required for a specific task and its cost

matt /mæt/ *adjective* relating to paper that is not shiny, especially paper for photographs

matter /'mætə/ *noun* a situation that you have to deal with ○ *This is a matter which the library committee must decide.*

mature student /məˌtʃʊə 'stjuːd(ə)nt/ *noun* a student aged 25 or over who has gone into higher or further education later than is usual, especially after working or raising a family

maximise /'mæksɪmaɪz/, **maximize** *verb* 1. to make the most possible use of something 2. to make something as large or important as possible ○ *They aimed to maximise their profits.*

maximum /'mæksɪməm/ *noun* 1. the largest amount possible 2. the highest achievement possible

Mb, MB *abbreviation* megabyte

MBO *abbreviation* Management By Objectives

MBS *abbreviation* mind body and spirit

mc *abbreviation* in Internet addresses, the top-level domain for Monaco

md *abbreviation* in Internet addresses, the top-level domain for Moldova

means /miːnz/ *plural noun* 1. a method of doing something ○ *We have the means to store a large number of documents.* 2. the money that someone has to spend ○ *She has the means to buy a large house.*

measure /'meʒə/ *verb* to discover the size or quantity of something by using a calibrated instrument ■ *noun* 1. a set of scales or strip for measuring 2. an action taken to bring about a specific result ○ *Measures have been taken to reduce the loss of books.*

measurement /'meʒəmənt/ *noun* size in units such as centimetres or inches

COMMENT: In Britain, the measurements of paper sheets are normally given with the short side first (768 x 1008mm), while the physical measurements of a book are normally given with the height first and then the width. The format of this book is 198 x 129. Note that in many countries, the measurements are given with the width first and height second, leading to much confusion. The measurement of type is based on the point system (one point is 0.3515mm in Britain and the USA; 0.376mm in Europe).

mechanical /mɪ'kænɪk(ə)l/ *adjective* relating to something that has moving parts and uses power to perform tasks

mechanics /mɪ'kænɪks/ *plural noun* the way that something works or is done ○ *The mechanics of reading are difficult for children to learn.*

mechanism /'mekənɪz(ə)m/ *noun* 1. a piece of machinery 2. a method of doing something

media /'miːdiə/ *noun* the main means of communication as in radio, television and newspapers

media converter /'miːdiə kənˌvɜːtə/ *noun* a multi-disk reader device which can read data from various sizes and formats of disk

media coverage /'miːdiə ˌkʌv(ə)rɪdʒ/ *noun* the number of reports about a situation or event in the newspapers, radio or television

media management system /'miːdiə ˌmænɪdʒmənt ˌsɪstəm/ *noun* an operating system which allows physical storage media such as tapes or disks to be catalogued and replayed. Abbr **MMS**

media resource officer /ˌmiːdiə rɪ'zɔːs ˌɒfɪsə/ *noun* a person who is in charge of the management of audio-visual resources

media storage systems /'miːdiə ˌstɔːrɪdʒ ˌsɪstəmz/ *plural noun* systems for storing and retrieving non-book materials such as audio tapes, video tapes or illustrations

medical /'medɪk(ə)l/ *adjective* relating to the treatment and prevention of illness and injuries

medical abstracts /'medɪk(ə)l ˌæbstrækts/ *plural noun* a collection of summaries of medical articles in journals

medical directory /'medɪk(ə)l daɪ ˌrekt(ə)ri/ *noun* a list of medical institutions, practitioners and specialists

medical index /'medɪk(ə)l ˌɪndeks/ *noun* a list of bibliographical references to articles on medical subjects

medical journal /'medɪk(ə)l ˌdʒɜːn(ə)l/ *noun* a specialist magazine for medical practitioners

medical library /'medɪk(ə)l ˌlaɪbrəri/ *noun* a special library to support medical work

Medical Literature Analysis and Retrieval Service /ˌmedɪk(ə)l ˌlɪt(ə)rətʃə əˌnælɪsɪs ən rɪ'triːv(ə)l ˌsɜːvɪs/ *noun* a collection of databases operated by the National Library of Medicine. Abbr **MEDLARS**

medical publishing /'medɪk(ə)l ˌpʌblɪʃɪŋ/ *noun* the publishing of books on medical subjects

medieval manuscript /'mediiːvəl 'mænjuːskrɪpt/ *noun* a written manuscript dating from between 1100 and 1500 A.D.

medium /'miːdiəm/ *adjective* neither large nor small, but middle-sized ■ *noun* the means used to communicate or express oneself ○ *They communicated through the medium of the written word.* (NOTE: The plural is **media** or **mediums**.)

medium octavo /ˌmiːdiəm ɒk 'tɑːvəʊ/ *noun* a traditional book format of 9 x 5 3/4 inches

MEDLARS /'medlɑːz/ *abbreviation* Medical Literature Analysis and Retrieval Service

MEDLIB /'medlɪb/ *noun* a subscription bulletin board mainly used by doctors

Medline /'medlaɪn/ *noun* an information database mainly used by employees in medical professions

meet /miːt/ *verb* **1.** to make contact with somebody face to face **2.** to deal with a situation, need or requirement

meeting /'miːtɪŋ/ *noun* an event when people come together to discuss things

megabyte /'megəbaɪt/ *noun* a storage unit in computers, equal to 1,048,576 bytes, or 10^{22} bytes. Abbr **MB**, **Mbyte**

membership /'membəʃɪp/ *noun* the state of belonging to an organisation or group

membership list /'membəʃɪp lɪst/ *noun* a list of names and addresses of members of an organisation or group

membership ticket /'membəʃɪp ˌtɪkɪt/, **membership card** /'membəʃɪp kɑːd/ *noun* a card or ticket stating somebody's name and the name of the organisation of which they are a member

memo /'meməʊ/ *abbreviation* memorandum

memoir /'memwɑː/ *noun* a written account of somebody's life, especially one who has been well known in public life

memo pad /'meməʊ pæd/ *noun* a pad of headed paper used for internal messages

memorandum /ˌmemə'rændəm/ *noun* a note sent internally within a company or organisation

memorial volume /mɪ'mɔːriəl ˌvɒljuːm/ *noun* **1.** a book containing the names of people to be remembered **2.** a book written in memory of someone

memorise /'meməraɪz/, **memorize** *verb* to learn something so that you can remember it exactly

memory /'mem(ə)ri/ *noun* **1.** a person's ability to remember things **2.** the capacity to store information

menu /'menjuː/ *noun* a list of options displayed on screen for the user of a computer program

menu-driven /'menjuː ˌdrɪv(ə)n/ *adjective* relating to a computer program where the user can choose options from a menu

merchandise /'mɜːtʃəndaɪz/ *noun* goods that are bought, sold or traded ■ *verb* to sell goods and services

merge /mɜːdʒ/ *verb* to combine two data files on a computer. ◊ **mail merge**

merge sort /ˌmɜːdʒ 'sɔːt/ *noun* a software application in which the sorted files are merged into a new file

MERIT /'merɪt/ *noun* a US regional gateway with access to commercial services

MESH /meʃ/ *abbreviation* Medical Subject Headings for Medline

message /'mesɪdʒ/ *noun* a piece of information that you send or leave for somebody

message heading /'mesɪdʒ ˌhedɪŋ/ *noun* a title given to information to indicate its contents

message numbering /'mesɪdʒ ˌnʌmbərɪŋ/ *noun* identification of messages using a numerical system

metadata /'metədeɪtə/ *noun* descriptive information about the elements of a set of data, e.g. information contained in a webpage which describes the topics covered by that webpage

'Contivo Vocabulary Management Solution (VMS) (TM) provides a central semantics-based metadata repository, development tools, infrastructure, and code generators that automate data transformation for application integration across multiple platforms.' [*BusinessWire*]

metaphor /'metəfə/ *noun* an expression used to describe one thing in terms of another, without using the words 'like' or 'as', as in 'the librarian was a fountain of knowledge'

meteorological office /ˌmiːtiərə 'lɒdʒɪk(ə)l ˌɒfɪs/ *noun* a government office which records the forecasting and

occurrence of weather conditions worldwide

meteorology /ˌmiːtiə'rɒlədʒi/ *noun* the study of weather formation and conditions

methodical /mɪ'θɒdɪk(ə)l/ *adjective* having a careful, planned and ordered way of working

methodology /ˌmeθə'dɒlədʒi/ *noun* a system of ways and principles for doing something, e.g. in teaching or research

metric /'metrɪk/ *adjective* relating to a system of book and paper measurement, calculated in millimetres

COMMENT: The main metric stock paper sizes used in the UK are: metric quad crown (768 x 1008), metric large crown (816 x 1056), metric quad demy (888 x 1128), and metric quad royal (960 x 1272).

metric crown octavo /ˌmetrɪk kraʊn ɒk'taːvəʊ/ *noun* a book format (186 x 123mm)

mg *abbreviation* **1.** in Internet addresses, the top-level domain for Madagascar **2.** milligram

mh *abbreviation* in Internet addresses, the top-level domain for Marshall Islands

micro- /maɪkrəʊ/ *prefix* used to indicate a very small version of anything

micro computer /'maɪkrəʊ kəm ˌpjuːtə/ *noun* a small computer usually used as a stand-alone machine, i.e. one not connected to a network

microcontent /'maɪkrəʊˌkɒntent/ *noun* a single piece of data on the Internet which has its own URL or link and can be accessed by a hand-held device if needed, e.g. a weblog posting or a weather forecast

microcopy /'maɪkrəʊkɒpi/ *noun* a copy of a document which has been reduced in size

microfiche /'maɪkrəʊfiːʃ/ *noun* a small sheet of photographic film on which information is stored in very small print

microfiche reader /'maɪkrəʊfiːʃ ˌriːdə/ *noun* a machine that magnifies the writing on microfiche film and displays it in readable form on a monitor

microfilm /'maɪkrəʊfɪlm/ *noun* material for making microfiches ■ *verb* to make microfiches

micro image /'maɪkrəʊ ˌɪmɪdʒ/ *noun* a stored graphical image which is too small to be seen with the naked eye

microphone /'maɪkrəfəʊn/ *noun* an electronic device used to record sounds or to make them louder

microprocessor /'maɪkrəʊˌprəʊsesə/ *noun* a microchip which can be programmed to do a large number of tasks or calculations

Microsoft Disk Operating System /ˌmaɪkrəsɒft dɪsk 'ɒpəreɪtɪŋ ˌsɪstəm/ *noun* full form of **MS/DOS**

Microsoft Network /ˌmaɪkrəsɒft 'netwɜːk/ *noun* a vast online service to provide information, database links to the Internet and electronic mail especially for Windows users. Abbr **MSN**

middle management /ˌmɪd(ə)l 'mænɪdʒmənt/ *noun* a level of management which has responsibility for a part within the structure of a whole organisation

mid-user /'mɪd ˌjuːzə/ *noun* an operator who retrieves relevant information from a database for a customer or end user

migrate /maɪ'greɪt/ *verb* to transfer a file from one computer system or database to another

migration /maɪ'greɪʃ(ə)n/ *noun* a transfer of computer data, programs or hardware from one system to another

mil *abbreviation* in Internet addresses, the generic top-level domain for military organisation

milking machine /'mɪlkɪŋ məˌʃiːn/ *noun* a portable machine which can accept data from other machines and then transfer it to a large computer

millboard /'mɪlbɔːd/ *noun* thick paperboard used in binding books

millennium /mɪ'lenɪəm/ *noun* a period of one thousand years (NOTE: The plural is **millennia**.)

Mills and Boon /ˌmɪlz ən 'buːn/ *noun* a romantic novel published by, or of the kind typically published by, the firm of Mills and Boon, publishers of popular romantic fiction

mind body and spirit /ˌmaɪnd ˌbɒdi ən ' spɪrɪt/ *noun* a category of books dealing with alternative topics such as natural medicine, new faiths and oriental mysticism. Abbr **MBS**

mind map /'maɪnd mæp/ *noun* a diagram with nodes representing the the main points of a topic, with the links between them and any other relevant information also shown

mine /maɪn/ *noun* a rich source of something, especially information ■ *verb* to search through a source and extract information

'In addition, once the business processes have been optimised/re-engineered, the information technology function should provide tools to empower staff to search for and mine the data stores around the organisation.' [*Financial Times*]

mini- /mɪni/ *prefix* combining with nouns to indicate a smaller version of something ○ *mini-computer*

miniature /'mɪnɪtʃə/ *noun* **1.** a coloured picture in an illuminated manuscript **2.** a much reduced copy of a document **3.** a small, very detailed drawing or painting especially on ivory or vellum

minimise /'mɪnɪmaɪz/, **minimize** *verb* **1.** to reduce something to the smallest possible amount **2.** to make something seem unimportant

minimum /'mɪnɪməm/ *noun* the smallest amount possible

ministry /'mɪnɪstri/ *noun* a government department

ministry publication /'mɪnɪstri ˌpʌblɪkeɪʃ(ə)n/ *noun* a published report of the proceedings of a government department

Minitel /'mɪnɪtel/ *noun* a national information database in France accessible by telephone and home computer

minority /maɪ'nɒrɪti/ *noun* a group of people who form less than half of the total population of an area, e.g. in terms of race, religion or political opinion

minority sampling /maɪˌnɒrɪti 'saːmplɪŋ/ *noun* a method of surveying the needs and opinions of a minority group

mint /mɪnt/ *adjective* new

mint condition /ˌmɪnt kən'dɪʃ(ə)n/ *noun* the same condition as when new

minuscule /'mɪnɪskjuːl/ *adjective* extremely small

MIS *abbreviation* Management Information System

mis- /mɪs/ *prefix* combining with verbs or nouns to indicate that something is done badly or wrong ○ *misuse* ○ *mismatch*

miscalculate /mɪs'kælkjʊleɪt/ *verb* **1.** to add something up incorrectly **2.** to make a mistake in judging a situation

miscellaneous /ˌmɪsə'leɪniəs/ *adjective* relating to a collection of items that are all very different from each other

miscellany /mɪ'seləni/ *noun* a collection of written texts on a variety of subjects in one book

miseducate /mɪs'edjʊkeɪt/ *verb* to educate somebody in a wrong or inadequate way

misfile /mɪs'faɪl/ *verb* to file something such as a document in the wrong place

misinform /ˌmɪsɪn'fɔːm/ *verb* to give incorrect information to somebody

misleading title /mɪsˌliːdɪŋ 'taɪt(ə)l/ *noun* a title that does not indicate the subject matter or the form of the work

mismatch /'mɪsmætʃ/ *noun* a situation where two things are not correctly linked

misprint /'mɪsprɪnt/ *noun* a mistake in printing

misquote /mɪs'kwəʊt/ *verb* to state incorrectly what somebody has said or written

misread /mɪs'riːd/ *verb* **1.** to read something incorrectly **2.** to judge somebody's intentions incorrectly

miss /mɪs/ *noun* a document not retrieved by a computer search

missing /'mɪsɪŋ/ *adjective* not in the expected place

missing data /ˌmɪsɪŋ 'deɪtə/ *noun* information which is not available, so that a task cannot be completed

missing link /ˌmɪsɪŋ 'lɪŋk/ *noun* the missing piece of information in a chain of data, which makes it difficult to use the information

mission statement /'mɪʃ(ə)n ˌsteɪtmənt/ *noun* a statement of the aims and objectives of an organisation

missive /'mɪsɪv/ *noun* a letter, especially a long and detailed one

misspelt /mɪs'spelt/ *adjective* spelt wrongly

mistake /mɪ'steɪk/ *noun* an error

mixed ability class /ˌmɪkst əˌbɪlɪti 'klɑːs/ *noun* a class in a school or college where pupils have different levels of learning ability

mk *abbreviation* in Internet addresses, the top-level domain for Macedonia

ml *abbreviation* in Internet addresses, the top-level domain for Mali

MLA *abbreviation* **1.** Modern Language Association **2.** Museums, Libraries and Archives Council

mm *abbreviation* in Internet addresses, the top-level domain for Myanmar

MMS *abbreviation* media management system

mn *abbreviation* in Internet addresses, the top-level domain for Mongolia

mnemonic /nɪ'mɒnɪk/ *noun* a word, rhyme or sentence which helps you to remember other things, e.g., 'Richard Of York Gave Battle In Vain' which has the same first letters as the colours of the rainbow – Red, Orange, Yellow, Green, Blue, Indigo, Violet

mobile /'məʊbaɪl/ *adjective* able to be moved easily or to move by itself

mobile library /ˌməʊbaɪl 'laɪbrəri/ *noun* a specially adapted van which takes library books to residential areas at the same time each week

mobile storage files /ˌməʊbaɪl 'stɔːrɪdʒ ˌfaɪlz/ *plural noun* files that can be moved physically or electronically

mobile unit /ˌməʊbaɪl 'juːnɪt/ *noun* a complete set of filming and editing equipment which can be transported in a van for outside broadcasts

mock-up /'mɒk ʌp/ *noun* a model of a new product or building which can be used to show to potential customers

model /'mɒd(ə)l/ *noun* a theoretical statement of how a system will work which people can copy to achieve the same results

modem /'məʊdem/ *noun* an electronic device which converts binary to analogue signals so that data can be transmitted over the telephone network. Also called **dataset**

moderated list /ˌmɒdəreɪtɪd 'lɪst/ *noun* a mailing list in which a moderator reads all the material that has been submitted before it is distributed to the users on the list

moderated   newsgroup /ˌmɒdəreɪtɪd 'njuːzgruːp/ *noun* a newsgroup in which a moderator reads all the material that has been submitted before it is published in the newsgroup

moderator /'mɒdəreɪtə/ *noun* a person responsible for reading messages sent to a mailing list or newsgroup and editing any messages that do not conform to the rules of the list, e.g. by deleting commercial messages

Modern Language Association /ˌmɒdən 'læŋgwɪdʒ əˌsəʊsieɪʃ(ə)n/ *noun* a professional body that provides standard guidelines on writing research papers, e.g. document formatting and citing other sources. Abbr **MLA**

modification /ˌmɒdɪfɪ'keɪʃ(ə)n/ *noun* a small change to something usually made to improve it

modify /'mɒdɪfaɪ/ *verb* to change something, often in only a small way, usually in order to improve it

modular /'mɒdjʊlə/ *adjective* relating to a method of organising and teaching courses as a series of independent modules

module /'mɒdjuːl/ *noun* a small section of a larger programme which can also function as a unit in its own right

modus operandi /ˌməʊdəs ˌɒpə 'rændiː/ *noun* a particular and often personal way of working

moisture content of paper /ˌmɔɪstʃə ˌkɒntent əv 'peɪpə/ *noun* the amount of moisture in paper, shown as a percentage of the paper weight

MOMI /'məʊmi/ *abbreviation* Museum of the Moving Image

monitor /'mɒnɪtə/ *noun* a visual display unit used to show the text and graphics generated by a computer ■ *verb* to make regular checks to see how something or somebody is working

mono- /mɒnəʊ/ *prefix* used with nouns that have 'one' or 'single' as part of their meaning

monograph /'mɒnəgrɑːf/ *noun* a book on one specific subject

monolingual /ˌmɒnəʊ'lɪŋgwəl/ *adjective* using only one language ○ *a monolingual dictionary*

montage /'mɒntɑːʒ/ *noun* a combination of photographs, drawings or parts of pictures used for display or advertising

monthly /'mʌnθli/ *adjective* coming out regularly once a month ■ *noun* a magazine published once a month

Moon type /'muːn taɪp/ *noun* a system of reading for the blind, more easily learned than Braille and therefore often used by people who go blind late in life

morgue /mɔːg/ *noun* in journalism, a collection of miscellaneous reference material

morocco /mə'rɒkəʊ/ *noun* a soft leather made from goatskin, or a leather made in imitation of it from sheepskin or calfskin, used for covering books

morocco binding /mə'rɒkəʊ ˌbaɪndɪŋ/ *noun* a fine leather book covering made from goatskin

Morse /mɔːs/, **Morse code** *noun* a system for representing letters and numbers by signs consisting of one or more short or long signals of sound or light which are printed out as dots and dashes

mosaic /məʊ'zeɪɪk/ *noun* a picture made up of small dots as in a videotext system

mother tongue /'mʌðə tʌŋ/ *noun* the first language learned as a child

'[Zeljko Perovic, Assistant Minister for Foreign Affairs of Serbia and Montenegro] said that… non-

Albanian communities were being denied any meaningful participation in political life, to the extent that "not even basic access to documentation in their mother tongues is ensured".' [*M2 Presswire*]

motif /məʊˈtiːf/ *noun* **1.** an often repeated pattern or design **2.** the main subject which acts as the base for a work of art or music

motion picture /ˌməʊʃ(ə)n ˈpɪktʃə/ *noun* a film made to be shown in the cinema

motivate /ˈməʊtɪveɪt/ *verb* to encourage somebody to do something, especially to behave in a positive way

motivation /ˌməʊtɪˈveɪʃ(ə)n/ *noun* the feeling that you want to work hard

motive /ˈməʊtɪv/ *noun* a strong reason for doing something

mount /maʊnt/ *verb* **1.** to organise an event and ensure that it happens **2.** to fix something in a particular place, especially a piece of artwork or film on a card backing or in a frame

mounted picture /ˌmaʊntɪd ˈpɪktʃə/ *noun* a picture that is fixed on to a background to improve its appearance

mouse /maʊs/ *noun* a small hand device used to control the cursor on a computer screen (NOTE: The plural is **mice**.)

.mov *suffix* a file extension for a film file. Full form **movie**

move /muːv/ *verb* **1.** to change position **2.** to propose a motion or amendment at a meeting

movement /ˈmuːvmənt/ *noun* **1.** a gradual change in attitude or opinion **2.** a group of people who share the same beliefs or ideas

Moving Picture Experts Group /ˌmuːvɪŋ ˌpɪktʃəs ˈekspɜːts ˌgruːp/ *noun* full form of **MPEG**

mp *abbreviation* in Internet addresses, the top-level domain for Northern Mariana Islands

MP3 /ˌem piː ˈθriː/ *noun* a computer file standard for downloading compressed music from the Internet, playable on a multimedia computer with appropriate software. Full form

Moving Picture Experts Group, Audio Layer 3

.mp3 *suffix* a file extension for an MP3 file. Full form **Moving Picture Experts Group, Audio Layer 3**

MPEG /ˈempeg/ *noun* a data file for moving pictures on the Internet. Full form **Moving Picture Experts Group**

.mpeg /ˈempeg/, **.mpg** *suffix* a file extension for an MPEG file. Full form **Moving Picture Experts Group**

mq *abbreviation* in Internet addresses, the top-level domain for Martinique

mr *abbreviation* in Internet addresses, the top-level domain for Mauritania

ms *abbreviation* manuscript (NOTE: The plural is **mss**.)

MS/DOS /ˌem es ˈdɒs/ *noun* an operating system on personal computers. Full form **Microsoft Disk Operating System**

MSN *abbreviation* Microsoft Network

mt *abbreviation* in Internet addresses, the top-level domain for Malta

mu *abbreviation* in Internet addresses, the top-level domain for Mauritius

multi- /mʌlti/ *prefix* used to form adjectives describing things which have many parts

multicasting /ˈmʌltikɑːstɪŋ/ *noun* the process of sending data across a network to several recipients simultaneously

multicultural /ˌmʌltiˈkʌltʃərəl/ *adjective* relating to a community or philosophy that draws from many different races and cultures

multidisciplinary /ˌmʌlti ˈdɪsɪplɪnəri/ *adjective* studying or using several specialised subjects or skills

multi-disk reader /ˌmʌlti dɪsk ˈriːdə/ *noun* a device that can take in data from different sizes and formats of disk

multi-level indexing /ˌmʌlti ˌlev(ə)l ˈɪndeksɪŋ/ *noun* the process of indexing a document by both broad and narrow terms

multilingual *adjective* using several languages ○ *a multilingual dictionary of technical terms*

multilingual   thesaurus
/ˌmʌltilɪŋwəl θəˈsɔːrəs/ *noun* a collection of words providing synonyms in a variety of languages

multimedia /ˌmʌltiˈmiːdiə/ *noun* **1.** programs, software and hardware capable of using a wide variety of media such as film, video and music as well as text and numbers **2.** the use of film, video and music in addition to more traditional teaching materials and methods ▪ *adjective* using several different communication channels

multiple /ˈmʌltɪp(ə)l/ *adjective* having many parts, users or uses

multiple index /ˈmʌltɪp(ə)l ˌɪndeks/ *noun* a listing of contents from several documents on a related theme

multiplexer /ˈmʌltiˌpleksə/ *noun* a device for sending several data streams down a communications line and for splitting a received multiple stream into components

multi-tasking /ˈmʌlti ˌtɑːskɪŋ/ *noun* doing many things at the same time

multi-user system /ˌmʌlti ˌjuːzə ˈsɪstəm/, **multi-access system** /ˌmʌlti ˌækses ˈsɪstəm/ *noun* a computer system that allows several users to access a program at the same time

'Multi-user systems allow several users to all work on the same transport plan at the same time, points out Paragon. Companies benefit from central planning efficiencies, but allow local users to review and modify the transport plan for their own depot.' [*Motor Transport*]

multi-value words /ˌmʌlti ˌvæljuː ˈwɜːdz/ *plural noun* words that have different meanings in different contexts

multiversity /ˌmʌltiˈvɜːsɪti/ *noun* a university that has many affiliated or associated institutions such as research centres and colleges

multivolume /ˈmʌltiˌvɒljuːm/ *adjective* published in several volumes

museum /mjuˈziəm/ *noun* a building where old, interesting and valuable objects are stored and displayed to the public

museum catalogue /mjuˈziəm ˌkætəlɒg/ *noun* an organised list of the contents of a museum

Museum of the Moving Image /mjuˌziəm əv ðə ˌmuːvɪŋ ˈɪmɪdʒ/ *noun* a museum in London concerned with the history of the film industry. Abbr **MOMI**

Museums, Libraries and Archives Council /mjuˌziəmz ˌlaɪbrəriz ənd ˈɑːkaɪvz ˌkaʊns(ə)l/ *noun* a public body that works with libraries, museums and archiving bodies to promote collaboration and resource sharing. Abbr **MLA** (NOTE: The MLA was formerly called **Resource**.)

museum yearbook /mjuˈziəm ˌjɪəbʊk/ *noun* a listing of the museums in a country and their special collections and interests

music /ˈmjuːzɪk/ *noun* a combination of sounds made by people singing or playing musical instruments

music department /ˈmjuːzɪk dɪ ˌpɑːtmənt/ *noun* **1.** a teaching department in a college or university for the study of music theory and performance **2.** a section of a library which holds music scores, cassettes and discs **3.** a department in a shop which sells products connected with music

music dictionary /ˈmjuːzɪk ˌdɪkʃ(ə)nəri/ *noun* a reference book which gives information about music and musicians

music index /ˈmjuːzɪk ˌɪndeks/ *noun* a reference list of articles and research about music

music paper /ˈmjuːzɪk ˌpeɪpə/ *noun* paper ruled with staves of five lines for writing out music

muted /ˈmjuːtɪd/ *adjective* used to describe a weak reaction to a situation

mutual /ˈmjuːtʃuəl/ *adjective* shared in common between two or more people

mv *abbreviation* in Internet addresses, the top-level domain for Maldives

mw *abbreviation* in Internet addresses, the top-level domain for Malawi

mx *abbreviation* in Internet addresses, the top-level domain for Mexico

my *abbreviation* in Internet addresses, the top-level domain for Malaysia

myth /mɪθ/ *noun* a story made up a long time ago to explain natural phenomena or to justify religious beliefs

mz *abbreviation* in Internet addresses, the top-level domain for Mozambique

N

na *abbreviation* in Internet addresses, the top-level domain for Namibia

name catalogue /ˈneɪm ˌkætəlɒg/ *noun* a catalogue arranged alphabetically by the names of people or places

name entry /ˈneɪm ˌentri/ *noun* an index entry under the name of a person, place or institution

name plate /ˈneɪm pleɪt/ *noun* a small sign on or next to a door showing the name of the person or company who works in that room or building

narrative /ˈnærətɪv/ *noun* a story or poem which gives an account of a series of events ■ *adjective* told as a story

narrow term /ˈnærəʊ tɜːm/ *noun* an indexing term to indicate a specific field which is a subsection of a broader field

NASA /ˈnæsə/ *noun* a US government organisation concerned with space exploration and development ○ *The NASA database contains space travel information, and can be accessed through the Internet.* Full form **National Aeronautics and Space Administration**

national /ˈnæʃ(ə)nəl/ *adjective* belonging to one's own country

national archive /ˌnæʃ(ə)nəl ˈɑːkaɪv/ *noun* a storage library for keeping records of national importance

National Book Council /ˌnæʃ(ə)nəl ˈbʊk ˌkaʊns(ə)l/ *noun* an Australian organisation founded to bring together and support all who have an interest in books whether personal, commercial or educational

National Certificate /ˌnæʃ(ə)nəl sə ˈtɪfɪkət/ *noun* EDUC full form of **NC**

National Curriculum /ˌnæʃ(ə)nəl ˌkrɪmɪn(ə)l kəˈrɪkjʊləm/ *noun* the curriculum for pupils aged 5 to 16 taught in state schools in England and Wales

COMMENT: The National Curriculum is made up of three 'core' subjects, English, maths and science, and seven 'foundation' subjects, art, design and technology, geography, history, music, physical education and a foreign language.

National Diploma /ˌnæʃ(ə)nəl dɪ ˈpləʊmə/ *noun* EDUC full form of **ND**

National Discography /ˌnæʃ(ə)nəl dɪskˈɒgrəfi/ *noun* a central online database of all commercially recorded audio materials

National Educational Resources Information Services /ˌnæʃ(ə)nəl ˌedjʊkeɪʃ(ə)nəl rɪ ˌzɔːsɪz ˌɪnfəˈmeɪʃ(ə)n ˌsɜːvɪsɪz/ *noun* a database of educational and curriculum information. Abbr **NERIS**

National Federation of Abstracting and Indexing Services *noun* an American-based confederation of all the major abstracting and indexing services. Abbr **NFAIS**

National Foundation for Educational Research /ˌnæʃ(ə)nəl ˌfaʊndeɪʃ(ə)n fər ˌedjʊkeɪʃ(ə)nəl rɪ ˈsɜːtʃ/ *noun* a government-funded body in the UK which undertakes research into school education. Abbr **NFER**

National Health Service /ˌnæʃ(ə)nəl ˈhelθ ˌsɜːvɪs/ *noun* a system of public healthcare which operates in the UK. Abbr **NHS**

National Information Standards Organisation /ˌnæʃ(ə)nəl

ˌɪnfəmeɪʃ(ə)n   'stændədz
ˌɔːgənaɪzeɪʃ(ə)n/ *noun* a US organisation which develops and publishes standards for information management. Abbr **NISA**

National Information Systems
/ˌnæʃ(ə)nəl ˌɪnfə'meɪʃ(ə)n ˌsɪstəmz/ *noun* an international body under the guidance of UNESCO which encourages the standardisation of information services for all categories of users. Abbr **NATIS**

national library /ˌnæʃ(ə)nəl 'laɪbrəri/ *noun* a government-funded library which holds copies of all books published in that country

National Library for the Blind /ˌnæʃ(ə)nəl ˌlaɪbrəri fə ðə 'blaɪnd/ *noun* the principal source in Britain of materials published in Braille and Moon

National Library of Australia /ˌnæʃ(ə)nəl ˌlaɪbrəri əv ɒs'treɪliə/ *noun* the national library of Australia, in Canberra, established as an independent institution by an Act of Parliament in 1960. It was founded in 1901 as part of the Commonwealth Parliamentary Library.

National Library of Canada /ˌnæʃ(ə)nəl ˌlaɪbrəri əv 'kænədə/ *noun* the national library of Canada, founded in Ottawa in 1953

National Library of New Zealand /ˌnæʃ(ə)nəl ˌlaɪbrəri əv njuː 'ziːlənd/ *noun* the national library of New Zealand, in Wellington, created in 1966 by combining the collections of the General Assembly Library, the Alexander Turnbull Library and the National Library Service

National Library of Scotland /ˌnæʃ(ə)nəl ˌlaɪbrəri əv 'skɒtlənd/ *noun* the national library of Scotland, situated in Edinburgh and founded in 1925, having as its core the much older Library of the Faculty of Advocates. It is Scotland's only copyright deposit library.

National Library of Wales /ˌnæʃ(ə)nəl ˌlaɪbrəri əv 'weɪlz/ *noun* the national library of Wales, situated in Aberystwyth in Ceredigion and founded by royal charter in 1907. It is Wales's only copyright deposit library.

national media /ˈnæʃ(ə)nəl ˌmiːdiə/ *noun* the nationally distributed or marketed broadcast and print products of a country, e.g. major newspapers and television programming

national press /ˌnæʃ(ə)nəl 'pres/ *noun* newspapers which cover more general news and are sold in all parts of the country

National Record Office /ˌnæʃ(ə)nəl 'rekɔːd ˌɒfɪs/ *noun* a store in the UK of non-current and semi-current government records which have restricted access for 30 years

National Register of Archives /ˌnæʃ(ə)nəl ˌredʒɪstə əv 'aːkaɪvz/ *noun* a collection of lists of holdings of historical documents in private collections, libraries and record offices

National Sound Archive (UK) /ˌnæʃ(ə)nəl 'saʊnd ˌaːkaɪv/ *noun* a collection formed by a merger in 1983 of the British Institute of Recorded Sound and the British Library sound archive

national statistics /ˌnæʃ(ə)nəl stə'tɪstɪks/ *plural noun* government-produced facts and figures about various aspects of national life ○ *There is a quarterly government publication of national statistics called Social Trends.*

National Union Catalogue /ˌnæʃ(ə)nəl 'juːniən ˌkætəlɒg/ *noun* a cumulative author list of holdings in the USA, catalogued using Library of Congress printed cards

National Vocational Qualification /ˌnæʃ(ə)nəl vəʊˌkeɪʃ(ə)n(ə)l ˌkwɒlɪfɪ'keɪʃ(ə)n/ *noun* a certificate which can be gained in the UK after following a work-based course of post-school training in a specific skill. Abbr **NVQ**

NATIS /'nætɪs/ *abbreviation* National Information Systems

native speaker /ˌneɪtɪv 'spiːkə/ *noun* a person who speaks a language as a mother tongue. Abbr **NS**

NATLL *abbreviation* National Association of Toy and Leisure Libraries

natural language /ˌnætʃ(ə)rəl ˈlæŋgwɪdʒ/ *noun* a language that is used and understood by humans

natural language processing /ˌnætʃ(ə)rəl ˈlæŋgwɪdʒ ˌprəʊsesɪŋ/ *noun* the branch of computational linguistics concerned with the use of artificial intelligence to process natural languages, as in machine translation. Abbr **NLP**

navigable /ˈnævɪgəb(ə)l/ *adjective* relating to a website that is designed to enable the user to move between or through sections by clicking on usually highlighted computer links

navigate /ˈnævɪgeɪt/ *verb* to move between the different areas of a website by using the links provided in it

NBA *abbreviation* Net Book Agreement

nc *abbreviation* in Internet addresses, the top-level domain for New Caledonia

NC *noun* a UK qualification in a vocational subject that is roughly equivalent to a GCSE. Full form **National Certificate**

ND *noun* **1.** used in publishers' reports to indicate that it is not known when a book will be in stock. Full form **no date** **2.** a UK vocational qualification that is roughly equivalent to two A levels. Full form **National Diploma**

n.d. *abbreviation* an abbreviation used to indicate that the date of publication is not known. Full form **no date**

ne *abbreviation* in Internet addresses, the top-level domain for Niger

needs /niːdz/ *plural noun* what people require in order to do what they want to do ○ *A library must cater for all its users' needs.*

need to know /ˌniːd tə ˈnəʊ/ *phrase* relating to a basic security principle which restricts access to classified materials to essential users

negative /ˈnegətɪv/ *noun* a developed film in which the colour tones are reversed and used to produce a positive print

negative feedback /ˌnegətɪv ˈfiːdbæk/ *noun* comments which indicate that what has been proposed, done or made is not liked by the customers

negotiated environment /nɪˌgəʊʃieɪtɪd ɪnˈvaɪrənmənt/ *noun* working conditions agreed between employer and employee

negotiation /nɪˌgəʊʃiˈeɪʃ(ə)n/ *noun* discussions between people who have different viewpoints in which they try to reach an agreement

NERIS /ˈnerɪs/ *abbreviation* National Educational Resources Information Services

net /net/ *adjective* relating to a final amount when everything has been deducted ○ *a net profit*

Net /net/ *noun* ♦ Internet

Net Book Agreement /ˌnet ˈbʊk ə ˌgriːmənt/ *noun* formerly, the agreement between publishers and booksellers that books would be sold at an agreed price with no discounting allowed – abandoned in 1995/6. Abbr **NBA**

netlag /ˈnetlæg/ *noun* a temporary loss of contact between an Internet user and a server, usually caused by network delays

netsearch /ˈnetsɜːtʃ/ *noun* a program that allows the user to search for information on the Internet

net weight /ˌnet ˈweɪt/ *noun* the weight of something after the packaging has been deducted

network /ˈnetwɜːk/ *noun* a large number of people, organisations or machines that work together as a system ■ *verb* to join computers together so that they work as a system

networked system /ˌnetwɜːkt ˈsɪstəm/ *noun* a system in which several computers are linked together so that they all draw on the same database

Network Information System /ˌnetwɜːk ˌɪnfəˈmeɪʃ(ə)n ˌsɪstəm/ *noun* an electronic 'Yellow Pages' on the Internet. Abbr **NIS**

networking /ˈnetwɜːkɪŋ/ *noun* the act of linking computers so that users can exchange information or share access to a central store of information

neurocomputer /ˈnjʊərəʊkəm ˌpjuːtə/ *noun* a computer designed to imitate the human brain's ability to identify patterns, learn by trial and error, and find relationships in information

new acquisitions /ˌnjuː ˌækwɪ ˈzɪʃ(ə)nz/ *plural noun* new books which have been acquired by a library

new book number /ˌnjuː ˈbʊk ˌnʌmbə/ *noun* a temporary number assigned to a book which is required for borrowing before it is processed fully

new edition /ˌnjuː ɪˈdɪʃ(ə)n/ *noun* a book that has recently been reprinted with some updating and changes

new media /ˌnjuː ˈmiːdiə/ *noun* same as **e-media**

New Opportunities Fund /ˌnjuː ˌɒpəˈtjuːnɪtiz ˌfʌnd/ *noun* a fund of money raised by the National Lottery which is distributed to good causes, such as the training of librarians and information managers and the digitisation of information resources. Abbr **NOF**

news /njuːz/ *noun* information about things that have happened ○ *The business news is in the central pages of the paper.* ○ *Financial markets were shocked by the news of the devaluation.*

newsgroup /ˈnjuːzˌgruːp/ *noun* a feature of the Internet that provides free-for-all discussion forums

newsletter /ˈnjuːzletə/ *noun* a brief publication issued by an organisation to its members with internal news and information

newspaper /ˈnjuːzpeɪpə/ *noun* a daily or weekly publication consisting of a number of large sheets of folded cheap paper containing printed news articles and pictures

newspaper cutting /ˈnjuːzpeɪpə ˌkʌtɪŋ/ *noun* an article on a specific subject cut out of a newspaper page

newspaper index /ˈnjuːzpeɪpə ˌɪndeks/ *noun* an index to articles in past copies of newspapers, now usually held on a database, which can be accessed by keyword searching

NEWSPLAN /ˈnjuːzplæn/ *noun* a programme by the British Library to preserve British local newspapers in microfilm format

newsprint /ˈnjuːzprɪnt/ *noun* cheap paper on which newspapers and magazines are printed

newsreader /ˈnjuːzriːdə/ *noun* a computer program that allows somebody to read and post messages to Internet newsgroups

news-sheet /ˈnjuːz ʃiːt/ *noun* a small newspaper, with only a few pages, giving information and news to a limited number of people

newswire /ˈnjuːzwaɪə/ *noun* an Internet service providing the latest information on current events

newsworthy /ˈnjuːzwɜːði/ *adjective* considered to be important enough to be reported as news by the media

new technology /ˌnjuː tekˈnɒlədʒi/ *noun* electronic communication machines that have been recently invented

next /nekst/ *adjective* coming immediately after the present one

nf *abbreviation* in Internet addresses, the top-level domain for Norfolk Island

NFAIS *abbreviation* National Federation of Abstracting and Indexing Services

NFER *abbreviation* National Foundation for Educational Research

ng *abbreviation* in Internet addresses, the top-level domain for Nigeria

NHS *abbreviation* National Health Service

ni *abbreviation* in Internet addresses, the top-level domain for Nicaragua

niche /niːʃ/ *noun* an area in business which exactly fits the needs of a specialised group ○ *They found a niche in the market for their product so it sold well.*

nickname /ˈnɪkneɪm/ *noun* an alphabetical list of frequently used names on e-mail, giving the corresponding full and official names and easy access to addresses

niger morocco /ˈnaɪdʒə məˌrɒkəʊ/ *noun* good quality African leather, used for bindings

nil response /ˈnɪl rɪˌspɒns/ *noun* a reply to a survey question which indicates that there is nothing to record. Compare **non response**

NIS *abbreviation* Network Information System

NISA *abbreviation* National Information Standards Organisation

nl *abbreviation* in Internet addresses, the top-level domain for Netherlands

NLP *abbreviation* natural language programming

NNS *abbreviation* non-native speaker

no *abbreviation* in Internet addresses, the top-level domain for Norway

Nobel prize /nəʊˌbel ˈpraɪz/ *noun* an annual international prize for excellence awarded in various different fields, e.g. literature, science and peace work

node /nəʊd/ *noun* a piece of data in a database which has more than one link from it to other pieces of data

NOF *abbreviation* New Opportunities Fund

noise /nɔɪz/ *noun* **1.** electronic interference in an online search resulting in responses that are not useful **2.** an electronic signal present in addition to the wanted signal, resulting in noisy interference

nom de plume /ˌnɒm də ˈpluːm/ *noun* an assumed name used by a writer for professional purposes

non- /nɒn/ *prefix* not

non-book /ˈnɒn bʊk/ *adjective* not in the form of a book, or consisting of things other than books, e.g. as video tapes ○ *non-book media*

non-bookshop outlets *plural noun* places which are not bookshops but which sell books, such as supermarkets

non-current record /ˌnɒn ˌkʌrənt ˈrekɔːd/ *noun* a record which is no longer required for current business and so is assessed for storage or destruction

nondigital /nɒnˈdɪdʒɪt(ə)l/ *adjective* not processing, operating on, storing, transmitting, representing, or displaying data in the form of numerical digits, as a digital computer does

non-essential record /ˌnɒn ɪˌsenʃ(ə)l ˈrekɔːd/ *noun* information that is additional to the essential facts

nonfiction /nɒnˈfɪkʃ(ə)n/ *noun* writings that convey factual information rather than an imaginary story

non-native speaker /ˌnɒn ˌneɪtɪv ˈspiːkə/ *noun* a person who speaks a language after having learned it as a second or subsequent language later in life. Abbr **NNS**

non-numeric /ˌnɒn njuːˈmerɪk/ *adjective* expressed in letters or words

non-paper record /ˌnɒn ˈpeɪpə ˌrekɔːd/ *noun* a record kept in electronic format

'Since the advent of non-paper records, there has been a continuing controversy as to the merits of retaining a paper original after it has been reduced to some non-paper format. Originally, this controversy revolved around the relative merits of paper versus microfilm, but lately, the context has changed to paper versus images.'
[*Records Management Quarterly*]

non-preferred terms /ˌnɒn prɪˌfɜːd ˈtɜːmz/ *plural noun* an indexing term for sub-headings

nonreader /nɒnˈriːdə/ *noun* somebody who does not or cannot read, especially a child who has difficulty in learning to read

non response /ˈnɒn rɪˌspɒns/ *noun* a reply to a survey question which indicates that the question was not answered. Compare **nil response**

nonspecialist /nɒnˈspeʃ(ə)lɪst/ *noun* a person who is not qualified or expert in a specific occupation or field of study, though perhaps having a wide range of knowledge

non-verbal communication /ˌnɒn ˌvɜːb(ə)l kəˌmjuːnɪˈkeɪʃ(ə)n/ *noun* messages that are given by the use of body language rather than words

norm /nɔːm/ *noun* an average standard by which other behaviour can be judged

normal distribution /ˌnɔːm(ə)l ˌdɪstrɪˈbjuːʃ(ə)n/ *noun* a statistical term indicating that the majority of results will appear towards the centre of a graph with smaller amounts towards the top and bottom

notation /nəʊˈteɪʃ(ə)n/ *noun* a system of symbols used to express concepts like music or mathematics

note /nəʊt/ *noun* additional information in a catalogue or bibliography

notice /'nəʊtɪs/ *noun* a written announcement displayed so that everyone can read it ∎ *verb* to become aware of something

noticeboard /'nəʊtɪsbɔːd/ *noun* a board fixed to a wall so that information can be displayed for people to read

novel /'nɒv(ə)l/ *noun* a long fiction narrative story

novella /nə'velə/, **novelette** /ˌnɒvə 'let/ *noun* a short novel

novice user /ˌnɒvɪs 'juːzə/ *noun* a person who has little or no previous experience of using a system

np *abbreviation* in Internet addresses, the top-level domain for Nepal

n.p. *abbreviation* **1.** new paragraph **2.** no place of publication **3.** no price **4.** no printer's name

nr *abbreviation* in Internet addresses, the top-level domain for Nauru

NS *abbreviation* native speaker

NTBL *abbreviation* Nuffield Talking Book Library for the Blind

nu *abbreviation* in Internet addresses, the top-level domain for Niue

Nuffield Talking Book Library for the Blind /ˌnʌfiːld ˌtɔːkɪŋ bʊk ˌlaɪbrəri fə ðə 'blaɪnd/ *noun* the headquarters library of the British Talking Book Service for the Blind, based in Middlesex. Abbr **NTBL**

number /'nʌmbə/ *verb* to place the call number or the charging symbol on or in a book ∎ *noun* a symbol representing quantity, e.g. 1, 20, 64, 103 (NOTE: It is also written **no.**: *no. 15*. The plural is **nos.**: *nos. 2–20*.)

numbered edition /'nʌmbəd ɪ ˌdɪʃ(ə)n/ *noun* a limited edition where each copy has a number written in it

numeracy /'njuːm(ə)rəsi/ *noun* a competence in the mathematical skills needed to cope with everyday life and an understanding of information presented mathematically, e.g. in graphs or tables

numerate /'njuːm(ə)rət/ *adjective* able to calculate using numbers

'Half of all new recruits come straight from university; 30 per cent from business schools; and 20 per cent from existing jobs, where blue-chip experience is essential. Successful candidates must be numerate, able to tackle problems logically, have great communication skills and possess a spirit of entrepreneurship.' [*The Times*]

numeric /njuː'merɪk/, **numerical** /njuː'merɪk(ə)l/ *adjective* using numbers

numeric classification system /njuːˌmerɪk ˌklæsɪfɪ'keɪʃ(ə)n ˌsɪstəm/ *noun* a system of organising information for retrieval by using numbers in sequence

numeric data /njuːˌmerɪk 'deɪtə/ *noun* data in the form of figures

numeric keypad /njuːˌmerɪk 'kiːpæd/ *noun* part of a computer keyboard which is a programmable set of numbered keys

NVQ *abbreviation* National Vocational Qualification

NYP *abbreviation* a publisher's report to a bookseller who has tried to order a book that has not been published. Full form **not yet published**

nz *abbreviation* in Internet addresses, the top-level domain for New Zealand

O

OAI *abbreviation* Open Archives Initiative

obelus /ˈɒbələs/ *noun* a printed mark (†) used in modern editions of ancient manuscripts to indicate that the passage marked is thought not to be genuine

obiit /ˈəʊbɪɪt/ *verb* from the Latin word meaning 'died'; usually abbreviated to 'ob' ○ *ob. 1791*

obituary /əˈbɪtʃuəri/ *noun* a piece of writing about the character and achievements of somebody who has just died

objective /əbˈdʒektɪv/ *noun* what somebody is trying to achieve by a particular course of action ■ *adjective* not concerned with thoughts or feelings

oblique /əˈbliːk/ *adjective* **1.** indirect and difficult to understand **2.** sloping at an angle to the right

obscene /əbˈsiːn/ *adjective* shocking or offensive, usually because of pictures or references to naked people, sexual acts or bodily functions

obscene publication /əbˌsiːn ˌpʌblɪˈkeɪʃ(ə)n/ *noun* a book, film or any publication which offends against an accepted standard of decency

observation /ˌɒbzəˈveɪʃ(ə)n/ *noun* the act of watching somebody or something very carefully, especially for the purpose of research or study

obsolescent /ˌɒbsəˈles(ə)nt/ *adjective* becoming obsolete

obsolete /ˈɒbsəliːt/ *adjective* no longer needed because something newer or more efficient has been invented or designed

obtainable /əbˈteɪnəb(ə)l/ *adjective* easily available

obverse /ˈɒbvɜːs/ *noun* the opposite opinion in an argument or situation looked at from the opposite point of view

occasional publication /əˌkeɪʒ(ə)n(ə)l ˌpʌblɪˈkeɪʃ(ə)n/ *noun* a document that does not appear on a regular basis

occasional user /əˈkeɪʒ(ə)n(ə)l ˌjuːzə/ *noun* a person who does not use a service or system very often

occidental /ˌɒksɪˈdent(ə)l/ *adjective* relating to the countries of Europe and America, commonly known as the Western world

occupation /ˌɒkjʊˈpeɪʃ(ə)n/ *noun* a job or profession

occupational hazard /ˌɒkjʊpeɪʃ(ə)n(ə)l ˈhæzəd/ *noun* something unpleasant or even dangerous that somebody may encounter as a result of doing their job

OCLC *abbreviation* Online Computer Library Center

OCR *abbreviation* **1.** optical character reader **2.** optical character recognition

octavo /ɒkˈtɑːvəʊ/ *noun* a page made when a sheet of paper is folded three times, giving a 16-page section. Also called **eightvo**. Abbr **8vo**

octodecimo /ˌɒktəʊˈdesɪməʊ/ *noun* a book size of about 10 x 16 cm/4 x 4 ¼ in, or a book of this size. Abbr **18mo**

odd number /ˌɒd ˈnʌmbə/ *noun* a number which cannot be divided by 2 to give a whole number ○ *5 and 7 are odd numbers.*

OED *abbreviation* Oxford English Dictionary

offcut /'ɒfkʌt/ *noun* scrap paper left over when a sheet is trimmed to size

off-duty /ˌɒf 'djuːti/ *adjective* not at work for a period of time. Compare **on-duty**

office automation /ˌɒfɪs ˌɔːtə'meɪʃ(ə)n/ *noun* the use of machines and computers to carry out office tasks

officialese /əˌfɪʃə'liːz/ *noun* unclear, pedantic and verbose language considered characteristic of official documents

official name /əˌfɪʃ(ə)l 'neɪm/ *noun* the legal name for something

official publication /əˌfɪʃ(ə)l ˌpʌblɪ'keɪʃ(ə)n/ *noun* a document produced and published by official bodies, often kept by libraries as reference material

official title /əˌfɪʃ(ə)l 'taɪt(ə)l/ *noun* a title used by the cataloguer and appearing on the title page

offline /ɒf'laɪn/ *adjective* relating to a processor, printer or terminal that is disconnected from the network or central computer, usually temporarily ○ *Before changing the paper in the printer, switch it offline.*

offline newsreader /ˌɒflaɪn 'njuːzriːdə/ *noun* a piece of software that allows a user to read newsgroup articles when the computer is not connected to the Internet

offline printing /ˌɒflaɪn 'prɪntɪŋ/ *noun* a printout operation that is not supervised by a computer

offline processing /ˌɒflaɪn 'prəʊsesɪŋ/ *noun* processing by devices not under the control of a central computer (NOTE: The opposite is **on-line processing**.)

offset litho /ˌɒfset 'laɪθəʊ/ *noun* a printing process where the ink sticking to the image areas on film is transferred to rubber rollers for printing on to paper

off the record /ˌɒf ðə 'rekɔːd/ *phrase* used to indicate that something that is said should not be recorded or made public

OHP *abbreviation* overhead projector

OK /əʊ'keɪ/, **okay** *interjection* an informal word meaning 'correct' or 'yes', sometimes used as a computer prompt to ask if you want to continue

old stock /ˌəʊld 'stɒk/ *noun* books or documents that have been withdrawn from public use and either disposed of or kept in reserve

Olympic Games /əˌlɪmpɪk 'geɪmz/ *plural noun* international sports competitions at a very high level held every four years in a different country

om *abbreviation* in Internet addresses, the top-level domain for Oman

omission factor /əʊ'mɪʃ(ə)n ˌfæktə/ *noun* the number of relevant documents missed in a search

omission marks /əʊ'mɪʃ(ə)n mɑːks/ *plural noun* three dots (…) used in a quotation to show that something in the original has been left out

omit /əʊ'mɪt/ *verb* **1.** to leave something out or not put something in **2.** to fail to do something ○ *He omitted to transfer the new books to the acquisitions register, so no-one knew they had arrived.*

omnibus /'ɒmnɪbəs/ *noun* a collection of stories or articles by one or more authors bound into one book

omnibus edition /'ɒmnɪbəs ɪˌdɪʃ(ə)n/ *noun* an edition of a series of books or short stories in one volume

OMR *abbreviation* **1.** optical mark reader **2.** optical mark recognition

on /ɒn/ *preposition* **1.** placed on top of something **2.** done by a machine or instrument ○ *work on a computer* **3.** serving as a member of a council or committee ○ *She was on three committees.* **4.** □ **on approval** relating to goods that are kept for a short time by a customer without payment, so that they can decide to buy or return them □ **on demand** providing something only when it is asked for □ **on disk** held on a computer floppy disk which can be transferred to other machines □ **on hand** readily and immediately available □ **on screen** displayed on a computer screen rather than printed out □ **on site** in the building where the user is working

on-duty /ˌɒn 'djuːti/ *adjective* at work, usually for a set period of time. Compare **off-duty**

one-off /ˌwʌn 'ɒf/ *noun* something that happens or is made only once

onerous /'əʊnərəs/ *adjective* involving difficult or unpleasant work

one to one /ˌwʌn tə 'wʌn/ *adverb* working or talking with one person only

online /'ɒnlaɪn/ *adjective* **1.** connected to a mainframe computer often by a remote terminal ○ *The sales office is online to the warehouse.* ○ *We get our data online from the stock control department.* **2.** relating to data or information that is available when a terminal is connected to a central computer via a modem

online catalogue /'ɒnlaɪn ˌkætəlɒg/ *noun* access to a library's catalogue online, usually including a search facility

'Minister for Communications, Information Technology and the Arts, Helen Coonan, launched the new online catalogue Libraries Australia at Parliament House yesterday, which allows people to search for information across national, state and university libraries as well as most public, research, government, health and other specialist libraries.' [*Canberra Times*]

Online Computer Library Center /ˌɒnlaɪn kəmˌpjuːtə 'laɪbrəri ˌsentə/ *noun* a computer library service which provides its members with library resources electronically. Abbr **OCLC**

online database /ˌɒnlaɪn 'deɪtəbeɪs/ *noun* an interactive search, retrieve and update of database records using an online terminal

online editing /ˌɒnlaɪn 'edɪtɪŋ/ *noun* text editing by an editor or sub-editor on a terminal linked directly to the main computer

online information retrieval /ˌɒnlaɪn ˌɪnfə'meɪʃ(ə)n rɪˌtriːvəl/ *noun* a system that allows an operator of an online terminal to access, search and display data held in a main computer

online processing /ˌɒnlaɪn 'prəʊsesɪŋ/ *noun* processing by devices connected to and under the control of the central computer, in which the user remains in contact with the central computer while the processing is being carried out

Online Public Access Catalogue /ˌɒnlaɪn ˌpʌblɪk ˌækses 'kætəlɒg/ *noun* an electronic system for cataloguing library stock which can be used at a computer terminal to search for specific items. Abbr **OPAC**

online search /ˌɒnlaɪn 'sɜːtʃ/ *noun* a search of catalogues and databases for bibliographic records by direct computer contact with national, international or inter-library databases

online storage /ˌɒnlaɪn 'stɔːrɪdʒ/ *noun* data stored on a computer

online system /ˌɒnlaɪn 'sɪstəm/ *noun* a computer system that allows users who are online to transmit and receive information

online transaction processing /ˌɒnlaɪn træn'zækʃən ˌprəʊsesɪŋ/ *noun* interactive processing in which a user enters commands and data on a terminal that is linked to a central computer, with results being displayed on-screen

ONS *abbreviation* Office of National Statistics

on-screen /ˌɒn 'skriːn/ *adjective* with information being displayed on a screen ○ *The text is edited on-screen.*

on-the-job /ˌɒn ðə 'dʒɒb/ *adjective* done while you are working ○ *on-the-job training*

onus /'əʊnəs/ *noun* a duty or responsibility to do something ○ *The onus was on me to finish the job.*

op *abbreviation* opus

OP *abbreviation* out of print

OPAC /'əʊpæk/ *abbreviation* Online Public Access Catalogue

opaque /ə'peɪk/ *adjective* difficult to see through or understand

op. cit. /ˌɒp 'sɪt/ *abbreviation* 'in the work cited', short for 'opere citato', used in references after an author's name to refer to a book by the same person which has already been cited

open access /ˌəʊpən 'ækses/ *noun* a system of organising a collection where users can find what they want for themselves ○ *People have open access to the books in a public library.*

Open Archives Initiative /ˌəʊpən 'ɑːkaɪvz ɪˌnɪʃətɪv/ *noun* a body that promotes standards in archiving which allow systems to operate successfully together and exchange information. Abbr **OAI**

open back file /ˌəʊpən 'bæk ˌfaɪl/ noun a box file in the shape of a book for holding pamphlets and papers, with a back which can be easily opened

open day /'əʊpən deɪ/ noun a special day when the public are allowed to visit an institution

open entry /ˌəʊpən 'entri/ noun a catalogue entry which leaves room for additions ○ *The library did not have all the items in the set, so it used an open entry to allow for additions later.*

opening hours /'əʊp(ə)nɪŋ ˌaʊəz/ plural noun the hours during which a company, organisation or service is open to the public

open question /ˌəʊpən 'kwestʃ(ə)n/ noun a question that can be answered by different opinions or views

open-source /ˌəʊpən 'sɔːs/ adjective relating to software or information that is free to be accessed, distributed, copied and used by any person without licensing or copyright restrictions

Open University /ˌəʊpən ˌjuːni 'vɜːsɪti/ noun an institution of higher education in the UK which does most of its teaching by distance learning materials and the use of the national broadcasting networks. Abbr **OU**

OpenURL /ˌəʊpən juː ɑːr 'el/ noun a computer language which identifies the person trying to access a document online and uses metadata to take them to the most appropriate format or version of that document

operate /'ɒpəreɪt/ verb to work or make something work

operating instruction /'ɒpəreɪtɪŋ ɪnˌstrʌkʃən/ noun a command which explains how to work a machine

operating system /'ɒpəreɪtɪŋ ˌsɪstəm/ noun basic software which controls the running of a computer

operating time /'ɒpəreɪtɪŋ taɪm/ noun the time required to carry out a task

operational /ˌɒpə'reɪʃ(ə)nəl/ adjective in working order

operational indicators /ˌɒpəreɪʃ(ə)nəl 'ɪndɪkeɪtəz/ plural noun statistics which indicate how a system or organisation is functioning

operator /'ɒpəreɪtə/ noun a mathematical symbol, term or other entity that performs or describes an operation, e.g. a multiplication or subtraction sign

opinion /ə'pɪnjən/ noun a belief, view or judgement

op. no. abbreviation opus number

oppose /ə'pəʊz/ verb **1.** to express strong disagreement **2.** to contrast one thing to another deliberately in order to emphasise a particular point of view □ **as opposed to** contrasting two things when you want to emphasise the first one

opposite number /ˌɒpəzɪt 'nʌmbə/ noun a person who does the same job as you in a different department or institution

optical bar reader /ˌɒptɪk(ə)l 'bɑː ˌriːdə/ noun an optical device that reads data from a barcode. Also called **optical wand**

optical character reader /ˌɒptɪk(ə)l 'kærɪktə ˌriːdə/ noun a device that scans printed or written characters, recognises them and converts them into machine-readable codes for processing in a computer. Abbr **OCR**

optical character recognition /ˌɒptɪk(ə)l 'kærɪktə ˌrekəgnɪʃ(ə)n/ noun a technique for machine reading which uses special forms of type. Abbr **OCR**

optical disk /'ɒptɪk(ə)l dɪsk/ noun a rigid computer storage disk with data stored as tiny pits in the plastic coating, readable by laser beam

optical information system /ˌɒptɪk(ə)l ˌɪnfə'meɪʃ(ə)n ˌsɪstəm/ noun an encoded format for information storage, e.g. CD-ROM

optical mark reader /ˌɒptɪk(ə)l 'mɑːk ˌriːdə/ noun a device that can recognise marks or lines on a special form such as an order form or a questionnaire, and inputs them into a computer. Abbr **OMR**

optical mark recognition /ˌɒptɪk(ə)l mɑːk ˌrekəgˈnɪʃ(ə)n/ *noun* a process that allows certain marks or lines on special forms to be recognised by an optical mark reader, and input into a computer. Abbr **OMR**

optical scanner /ˌɒptɪk(ə)l ˈskænə/ *noun* a piece of equipment that converts an image into electrical signals which can be stored in and displayed on a computer

optical storage /ˌɒptɪk(ə)l ˈstɔːrɪdʒ/ *noun* data storage using visual mediums such as microfiche or optical disk

optical wand /ˈɒptɪk(ə)l wɒnd/ *noun* same as **optical bar reader**

optimisation /ˌɒptɪmaɪˈzeɪʃ(ə)n/, **optimization** *noun* making the best possible use of a situation or asset

optimism /ˈɒptɪmɪz(ə)m/ *noun* a feeling or belief that the future will be successful

option /ˈɒpʃən/ *noun* **1.** something that can be chosen **2.** freedom to choose something

opus /ˈəʊpəs/ *noun* a work of music or art, often abbreviated and used with an opus number to indicate the chronology of the work within a composer's total work ○ *Beethoven Op 23* Abbr **op**

opus number /ˈəʊpəs ˌnʌmbə/ *noun* a number which identifies when a work was written or, sometimes, published. Abbr **op. no.**

ORACLE /ˈɒrək(ə)l/ *noun* a teletext system used by the UK Independent Broadcasting Authority

oracy /ˈɔːrəsi/ *noun* the ability both to convey thoughts and ideas orally in a way that others understand and to understand what others say

ORBIT Infoline /ˈɔːbɪt ˌɪnfəʊlaɪn/ *noun* a database host specialising in patents, science, engineering, health and safety

order /ˈɔːdə/ *verb* **1.** to arrange things according to a system **2.** to ask for something to be brought or sent to you which you will then pay for ◇ **in order 1.** in sequence **2.** working properly

Ordnance Survey map /ˌɔːdnəns ˈsɜːveɪ ˌmæp/ *noun* a detailed map of Britain or Ireland known as the Ordnance Survey, originally used for military purposes. Abbr **O.S.**

org *abbreviation* in Internet addresses, the generic top-level domain for noncommercial organisations

organisation /ˌɔːgənaɪˈzeɪʃ(ə)n/, **organization** *noun* **1.** a company or group of people doing things together **2.** the structure of something, especially the way in which different parts are related to each other

organisational culture /ˌɔːgənaɪ ˌzeɪʃ(ə)n(ə)l ˈkʌltʃə/ *noun* the expectations and conventions in the management of an organisation

organisational learning /ˌɔːgənaɪ ˌzeɪʃ(ə)n(ə)l ˈlɜːnɪŋ/ *noun* learning which is structured so that it is highly efficient

oriental /ˌɔːriˈent(ə)l/ *adjective* of the East, especially China, Japan and nearby countries

orientation /ˌɔːriənˈteɪʃ(ə)n/ *noun* **1.** the direction of a page, either landscape (long edge horizontal) or portrait (long edge vertical) **2.** information or training that is necessary in order to understand a new subject, job, activity or situation

oriented /ˈɔːrientɪd/ *adjective* relating to the direction of the interests of a person or organisation

origin /ˈɒrɪdʒɪn/ *noun* **1.** the place or time of the beginning of something **2.** a country, place or social class of a person's parents or ancestors

original /əˈrɪdʒən(ə)l/ *noun* **1.** the first document from which copies have been made **2.** a piece of writing or music that is genuine and not a copy

orphan /ˈɔːf(ə)n/ *noun* the first line of a paragraph when it is printed by itself at the bottom of a column or page

orthodox /ˈɔːθədɒks/ *adjective* believed or accepted by most people

-ory /əri/ *suffix* forming adjectives with the sense of 'the nature of' ○ *advisory*

OS *abbreviation* out of stock

O.S. *abbreviation* Ordnance Survey

-ose /əʊz/ *suffix* forming adjectives with the sense of 'characterised by' ○ *grandiose*

OU *abbreviation* Open University

out- /aʊt/ *prefix* used with verbs to show that you can do the action better than another person ○ *They were outbid at the auction by someone with more money.*

outcome /'aʊtkʌm/ *noun* the result of an action or process

outlay /'aʊtleɪ/ *noun* an amount of money spent, especially at the beginning of a project

outlet /'aʊtlət/ *noun* the market for a product, shop or organisation which sells commodities

outline /'aʊtlaɪn/ *noun* **1.** the edge round an image **2.** a rough draft or summary ■ *verb* to describe the main features of something

outnumber /aʊt'nʌmbə/ *verb* to have more people or things than another group

out of date /ˌaʊt əv 'deɪt/ *adjective, adverb* no longer in general use or past the date for legal use ○ *Their computer system is years out of date.* ○ *They are still using out-of-date equipment.*

out of print /ˌaʊt əv 'prɪnt/ *adjective* relating to a book of which the publisher has no copies left and which is not going to be reprinted. Abbr **OP**

out of stock /ˌaʊt əv 'stɒk/ *adjective* relating to a publication of which the supplier or retailer has no copies at present. Abbr **OS**

output /'aʊtpʊt/ *noun* the amount that a person, organisation or machine produces ■ *verb* to print work done on a computer

output device /'aʊtpʊt dɪˌvaɪs/ *noun* a device such as a monitor or printer, which allows information in a computer to be displayed to the user. Compare **input device**

outside broadcast /ˌaʊtsaɪd 'brɔːdkɑːst/ *noun* a programme made for radio or television outside the studio

outside supplier /ˌaʊtsaɪd sə 'plaɪə/ *noun* a person who provides information from outside a company or organisation

outsource /'aʊtsɔːs/ *verb* to send work out to be done by freelance workers outside the company or organisation

outstanding /aʊt'stændɪŋ/ *adjective* **1.** excellent **2.** still to be done or completed ○ *Outstanding invoices must be paid by the end of the year.*

outweigh /aʊt'weɪ/ *verb* to be more important or significant than something else

overall /ˌəʊvər'ɔːl/ *adjective* including everything in general but not considering the details ○ *an overall view*

overcharge /ˌəʊvə'tʃɑːdʒ/ *verb* to ask for more money than is reasonable for a product or service

overdue /ˌəʊvə'djuː/ *adjective* past the due date ○ *overdue library books*

overdue notice /ˌəʊvə'djuː ˌnəʊtɪs/ *noun* a written request to a reader to return books or materials that are overdue

overhead projector /ˌəʊvəhed prə 'dʒektə/ *noun* a machine for displaying an image of transparent artwork on a screen, usually for the purposes of teaching or presentations. Abbr **OHP**

overink /ˌəʊvər'ɪŋk/ *verb* to cover in too much ink so that the printing image is unclear

overlap /'əʊvəlæp/ *noun* the point at which things start to be duplicated ○ *There was an overlap of ten minutes between the two periods of library duty.*

overlapping cover /ˌəʊvəlæpɪŋ 'kʌvə/ *noun* a paper cover which is not cut flush, but projects beyond the text pages

overlay /'əʊvəleɪ/ *noun* a transparent sheet used with overhead transparencies to add information at a specific time and place

overleaf /ˌəʊvə'liːf/ *adverb* on the other side of the page

overseas /ˌəʊvə'siːz/ *adjective* used in the UK to describe people from other countries ○ *They are not called overseas students now but international students.*

oversee /ˌəʊvə'siː/ *verb* to supervise a person or task

oversight /'əʊvəsaɪt/ *noun* an omission or a careless mistake because of failure to notice something

oversize /ˌəʊvə'saɪz/ *adjective* books and other printed materials that are larger than the standard book sizes and are often stored in a special area

overstock /ˌəʊvə'stɒk/ *verb* to keep more books, documents or information than is necessary for the users being served

overtime /'əʊvətaɪm/ *noun* time that is worked in addition to contracted hours and for which you are usually paid extra

overworked /ˌəʊvə'wɜːkt/ *adjective* working too hard or for too long

overwrite /ˌəʊvə'raɪt/ *verb* to replace an electronic file containing data or a computer program in memory or on a disk with a new file of the same name

own brand /ˌəʊn 'brænd/ *adjective* relating to goods packaged and marketed under a name belonging to the company selling them

ownership /'əʊnəʃɪp/ *noun* the position of owning something ○ *The ownership of information is a difficult matter to determine.*

Oxford English Dictionary /ˌɒksfəd ˌɪŋglɪʃ 'dɪkʃ(ə)nəri/ *noun* a complete collection of words and definitions for the English language, also available on CD-ROM. Abbr **OED**

P

p *abbreviation* page ○ *Table 6 is on p23 and tables 7–9 are on pp24 & 25.* (NOTE: The plural is **pp.**)

pa *abbreviation* in Internet addresses, the top-level domain for Panama

pack /pæk/ *noun* a packet of information containing items such as leaflets or maps relevant to a particular topic ■ *verb* to put things into containers or parcels so that they can be sent to another address

packet /ˈpækɪt/ *noun* a small parcel

packet switched data service /ˈpækɪt swɪtʃd ˈdeɪtə/, **packet switched network** /ˌpækɪt ˌswɪtʃɪd ˈnetwɜːk/ *noun* a service which transmits data in packets of set length. Abbr **PSN**

packet switching /ˈpækɪt ˌswɪtʃɪŋ/ *noun* a method of dividing data into small packets for transmission between terminals and networks

packing list /ˈpækɪŋ lɪst/, **packing slip** /ˈpækɪŋ slɪp/ *noun* a note sent with goods to say that the goods have been checked against the order

pad /pæd/ *noun* several pieces of paper joined together at one edge so that each piece can be torn off after use

PAD /pæd/ *noun* a device for making up the packets in a packet switching system. Full form **Packet Assembler/Disassembler**

padded envelope /ˌpædɪd ˈenvələʊp/ *noun* an envelope that has a soft lining to protect goods sent through the post

padding /ˈpædɪŋ/ *noun* unnecessary information put into a speech or written document to increase the length

page /peɪdʒ/ *noun* **1.** one side of a sheet of paper in a book, newspaper or magazine **2.** a computer text which will fill one sheet of paper when printed out **3.** a document or item of information on the Internet available through the World Wide Web ■ *verb* to call for somebody over the public address system in a large building such as a hotel or airport

page break /ˈpeɪdʒ breɪk/ *noun* a line on a screen of word-processed text which shows where the end of the printed page will occur

page layout /ˈpeɪdʒ ˌleɪaʊt/ *noun* a word-processing facility which allows the text to be formatted in different ways

page preview /ˈpeɪdʒ ˌpriːvjuː/ *noun* a word-processing facility which allows the shape of the text to be seen before printing

pager /ˈpeɪdʒə/ *noun* a small device carried in the pocket which allows someone to be called from a telephone in a central office by using a radio signal

paginal /ˈpædʒɪn(ə)l/ *adjective* exactly duplicating a previous edition or version, so that the same text appears on the same page in both

paginate /ˈpædʒɪneɪt/ *verb* to number the pages of a book or document

pagination /ˌpædʒɪˈneɪʃ(ə)n/ *noun* a system of numbering the pages in a document

COMMENT: Page numbers usually start with a series of roman numerals (i, ii, iii, etc.) for the prelims, and then change to Arabic numerals for the main text pages. The main text is paginated from page 1 again, with the result that the last folio in a book is rarely the same number as the actual extent.

paleography /ˌpæliˈɒɡrəfi/ *noun* the study of ancient writing and documents

palimpsest /ˈpælɪmsest/ *noun* a manuscript in which the first text has been partly erased and replaced by the second text

pamphlet /ˈpæmflət/ *noun* a small thin book, with at least 6 but not more than 48 pages and a paper cover, used to convey information

pamphlet box /ˈpæmflət bɒks/ *noun* a box specially designed to hold pamphlets within a storage system

p&p *abbreviation* postage and packing

panel /ˈpæn(ə)l/ *noun* **1.** a rectangular piece of paper on the spine of a book, giving the title and author **2.** a list of works by the same author printed on the page facing the title page

panellist /ˈpænəlɪst/ *noun* a person who sits with a group of other people to perform a group task ○ *The librarian was one of the interview panellists.*

paper /ˈpeɪpə/ *noun* **1.** a material made of cellulose fibres derived mainly from wood pulp, which is processed into thin sheets and used for writing, printing and drawing **2.** same as **newspaper 3.** part of a written examination **4.** a long essay on an academic subject

COMMENT: The first paper was made from old cloth, torn up, and mixed with water. Good quality paper is still made in this way, though most papers are now made from wood. The base material is wood which has been debarked, then shredded. If it is ground fine to make pulp it is called mechanical pulp; if it is mixed with various chemical substances to remove impurities and soften the tissues to form pulp, it is called chemical pulp. The pulp is laid on a wire mesh which retains the solid fibres and lets the water drain away. After most of the water has been removed, the paper is put through rollers which dry and calender it. Paper is made in many different qualities, each of which is suitable for a certain printing process, or for writing and drawing. Note that the paper usually constitutes the highest cost in book manufacture, especially where long printruns are concerned.

paperback /ˈpeɪpəbæk/ *noun* a book with a paper or light card cover ■ *adjec-*

tive with a thin flexible cover, instead of a hard cover

paperback original /ˌpeɪpəbæk ə ˈrɪdʒɪn(ə)l/ *noun* a book which is published first as a paperback and which later may be issued in a hard-cover edition

paperbased record /ˌpeɪpəbeɪst ˈrekɔːd/ *noun* a record kept on paper or card rather than on a computer

paper-bound /ˈpeɪpə baʊnd/, **paper-covered** /ˈpeɪpə ˌkʌvəd/ *adjective* denoting a book bound with a paper cover

paper deterioration /ˈpeɪpə dɪ ˌtɪəriəreɪʃ(ə)n/ *noun* the effect of age or damage on paper which causes it to discolour, tear or become brittle

paperless office /ˌpeɪpələs ˈɒfɪs/ *noun* an office that uses only electronic means of working, without any hard copy of materials

'The number of digital documents printed is increasing despite predictions of the paperless office, according to a new survey. Research firm Ovum revealed that 74% of firms said they were required to keep documents in hard copy format.' [*Printing World*]

papers /ˈpeɪpəz/ *plural noun* official documents, e.g. passport, identity card and visa

paper trail /ˈpeɪpə treɪl/ *noun* a sequence of documents that can be used by an investigator as a record of somebody's actions or decisions

paperweight /ˈpeɪpəweɪt/ *noun* **1.** a small heavy object, often decoratively designed, which can be placed on piles of paper to stop them blowing away **2.** the weight of a quantity of paper, used to describe its quality

COMMENT: In Britain, the weight of paper is calculated in grams per square metre (gsm). In the USA, it is expressed as the weight of 500 sheets of paper (i.e. a ream) of a standard 25 x 38 inch size, measured in pounds.

paperwork /ˈpeɪpəwɜːk/ *noun* the routine part of a job which involves tasks such as dealing with letters and writing reports

paradigm /'pærədaɪm/ *noun* a model or typical example of something

paragraph /'pærəgrɑːf/ *noun* a section of writing which contains one main idea, always starts on a new line, and is often indented

parallel edition /ˌpærəlel ɪ'dɪʃ(ə)n/ *noun* a publication in which different editions of the same work are published side by side, especially the same text in different languages

parallel processing /ˌpærəlel 'prəʊsesɪŋ/ *noun* computer operations that occur simultaneously

parallel publishing /'pærəlel ˌpʌblɪʃɪŋ/ *noun* the simultaneous production of a text in printed and electronic format

parameter /pə'ræmɪtə/ *noun* a limit which affects how something is done or made

paraphrase /'pærəfreɪz/ *verb* to summarise a person's ideas in one's own words

parchment /'pɑːtʃmənt/ *noun* writing material made from the thinly stretched skin of sheep or goats

parentheses /pə'renθəsiːz/ *plural noun* punctuation signs ( ) used to show that part of the text is an incidental comment or providing an explanation (often incorrectly called 'brackets')

parents' association /'peərənts əˌsəʊsieɪʃ(ə)n/ *noun* a group of parents who meet to discuss issues of importance to their children's schools

parliament /'pɑːləmənt/ *noun* a group of people who are elected to represent the citizens, and can make or change the laws of a country

parliamentary directory /ˌpɑːləment(ə)ri daɪ'rekt(ə)ri/ *noun* a list of the members of parliament with details about their careers

parliamentary paper /ˌpɑːləment(ə)ri 'peɪpə/ *noun* a policy statement issued by parliament either as a proposal for law or for consultation

parliamentary publication /ˌpɑːləment(ə)ri ˌpʌblɪ'keɪʃ(ə)n/ *noun* information or a report published by the government, e.g. by HMSO in the UK

parliamentary record /ˌpɑːləment(ə)ri 'rekɔːd/ *noun* a record of what is said in the debates in parliament, published in the UK as Hansard

participant /pɑː'tɪsɪpənt/ *noun* somebody who takes part in an activity or event

participate /pɑː'tɪsɪpeɪt/ *verb* to take part or become involved in something

partition /pɑː'tɪʃ(ə)n/ *noun* a screen or temporary wall used to separate one part of a room from another

partnership /'pɑːtnəʃɪp/ *noun* a relationship in which people or organisations work together with equal status

'The Vital Link is run by The Reading Agency and have been working in partnership with the National Literacy Trust and the National Reading Campaign to produce and disseminate teaching and learning resources based on the Quick Reads books for World Book Day.' [*Government Contracting Opportunities*]

part order /ˌpɑːt 'ɔːdə/ *noun* one or some of the items in a group of things ordered together

part-time /ˌpɑːt 'taɪm/ *adjective* working for only a part of full working hours

partwork /'pɑːtwɜːk/ *noun* a long work published in smaller parts at regular intervals

party line /ˌpɑːti 'laɪn/ *noun* **1.** a telephone line shared with other subscribers **2.** a policy followed by political parties

pass /pɑːs/ *noun* a complete run of a computer, printing machine or typesetting machine ○ *The first pass from the computer will not include the typesetting codes.*

password /'pɑːswɜːd/ *noun* a secret word or phrase that allows somebody to use a computer system or get into a building

paste /peɪst/ *verb* to place text, data or an image into a document electronically

patch /pætʃ/ *noun* the process of making small additions to a PostScript file without altering the original code underneath

patent /'pæt ənt/ *noun* an official right given to the inventor or originator of a product to control its manufacture and sale for a period of time ■ *verb* to register an invention with the patent office

patentee /,peɪtən'tiː/ *noun* the person in whose name a patent is registered

patent file /'peɪt(ə)nt faɪl/ *noun* patent specifications and drawings indexed by subject, country and number or name of patentee

patent office /'peɪtənt ,ɒfɪs/ *noun* a government office in the UK which controls the issuing of patents

Patents Information Network Bulletin /,peɪt(ə)nts ,ɪnfə'meɪʃ(ə)n ,netwɜːk ,bʊlətɪn/ *noun* the electronic information service of the Science Reference and Information Service of the British Library. Abbr **PIN Bulletin**

path /pɑːθ/ *noun* a particular course of action ○ *Here are many paths to success.*

patron /'peɪtrən/ *noun* a person or group that encourages and supports an activity, sometimes with money

pattern /'pæt(ə)n/ *noun* a particular way something is done or organised ○ *The work patterns need to be changed.*

pay /peɪ/ *noun* money received in return for work ■ *verb* **1.** to give somebody money in exchange for goods or services **2.** to be profitable ○ *These days there is a move towards making some library services pay.*

pay factor /'peɪ ,fæktə/ *noun* the effect of wages on the demand for work

payment /'peɪmənt/ *noun* a sum of money given to somebody in return for goods or services

payment date /'peɪmənt deɪt/ *noun* the date by which a bill must be paid

payphone /'peɪfəʊn/ *noun* a public telephone in which the user can pay for calls by coins or cards

payroll /'peɪrəʊl/ *noun* a list of employees who are paid wages or salaries by a company

PC *abbreviation* **1.** personal computer **2.** politically correct

PDA *abbreviation* personal digital assistant

PDF /,piː diː 'ef/ *noun* a data file generated from PostScript that is platform independent, application independent and font independent ○ *Acrobat is Adobe's suite of software used to generate, edit and view PDF files.* Full form **Portable Document Format**

pe *abbreviation* in Internet addresses, the top-level domain for Peru

peak /piːk/ *adjective* relating to the highest point or maximum value of a variable

peak demand /,piːk dɪ'mɑːnd/ *noun* the highest level of demand from users for services

peak time /'piːk taɪm/, **peak period** /'piːk ,pɪəriəd/ *noun* the time of day when most people do something

pedagogy /'pedəgɒdʒi/ *noun* the science or profession of teaching

peer /pɪə/ *noun* a person of the same age or social status

peerage /'pɪərɪdʒ/ *noun* a book listing the members of the nobility and giving information about their families

peg /peg/ *verb* to fix the value or level of something and prevent it from changing

pending /'pendɪŋ/ *adjective* awaiting attention, about to be dealt with soon

'We believe that with the continued importance of controlling and managing global content in a multinational business, our GIM solution is instrumental… SDL PhraseFinder 2005 leverages patent-pending technology to quickly and effectively identify terminology being used by an organisation.' [*Company News Feed*]

pending file /'pendɪŋ faɪl/ *noun* a file for keeping papers about matters which cannot be dealt with immediately

PEN International /,pen ,ɪntə 'næʃ(ə)nəl/ *noun* an international fellowship of writers in any genre which aims to promote freedom of expression and international cultural understanding

pen name /'pen neɪm/ *noun* a name taken by an author which is not his or her real name

People's Network /'piːp(ə)lz ˌnetwɜːk/ *noun* an online public library service managed by the Museums, Libraries and Archives Council

per /pɜː, pə/ *preposition* used to express ratio ○ *The rent was £250 per month.* ○ *The speed limit is 50 km per hour.* □ **per annum** each year ○ *She earns £25,000 per annum.* □ **per capita, per head** for each person ○ *What is the average per capita income?* □ **per cent** relating to a number which represents a part of a hundred ○ *10 per cent (10%) means 10 in every 100.*

percentage point /pə'sentɪdʒ pɔɪnt/ *noun* 1 per cent

perception /pə'sepʃən/ *noun* **1.** ability to notice things that are not obvious **2.** an opinion about somebody or something

perfect /pə'fekt/ *verb* to improve something until is completely correct ■ *adjective* without any mistakes

perfect binding /ˌpɜːfɪkt 'baɪndɪŋ/ *noun* same as **adhesive binding**

perfector /pə'fektə/, **perfecting press** *noun* a printing machine which prints on both sides of a sheet of paper

perforate /'pɜːfəreɪt/ *verb* to make holes in something so that it can be torn easily ○ *Sheets of stamps are perforated.*

perforated edge /ˌpɜːfəreɪtɪd 'edʒ/ *noun* an irregular edge left after tearing perforated paper

perforating stamp /'pɜːfəreɪtɪŋ stæmp/ *noun* a device that punches a mark by making a pattern of holes through the pages of a book

perforations /ˌpɜːfə'reɪʃ(ə)nz/ *plural noun* a series of very small holes made in paper to help to tear it in a straight line

perform /pə'fɔːm/ *verb* to do a task or action

performance indicator /pə 'fɔːməns ˌɪndɪkeɪtə/ *noun* a record that shows how well or badly an organisation is functioning

performance measurement /pə 'fɔːməns ˌmeʒəmənt/ *noun* the idea that skills and knowledge can be measured in terms of the value that they represent to a company

period /'pɪəriəd/ *noun* **1.** a particular length of time **2.** *US* a full stop ■ *interjection* used to emphasise that there is no more to be said about a subject

periodic /ˌpɪəri'ɒdɪk/ *adjective* happening occasionally but fairly regularly. Also called **periodical**

periodical /ˌpɪəri'ɒdɪk(ə)l/ *noun* a magazine or journal, especially a serious academic one ■ *adjective* same as **periodic**

periodical control /ˌpɪəri'ɒdɪk(ə)l kən,trəʊl/ *noun* a system for organising journals in a library

periodical index /ˌpɪəri'ɒdɪk(ə)l ˌɪndeks/ *noun* **1.** an index to one or more volumes of a periodical **2.** a cumulative subject index issued at stated intervals

periodic transfer /ˌpɪəriɒdɪk 'trænsfɜː/ *noun* the regular movement of records or data at specific time intervals ○ *Periodic transfer of records was done monthly.*

period of notice /ˌpɪəriəd əv 'nəʊtɪs/ *noun* time which must be worked after giving notice of leaving a job

peripheral /pə'rɪf(ə)rəl/ *adjective* not essential, attached to the edge of something else

peripherals /pə'rɪf(ə)rəlz/ *plural noun* items of hardware such as terminals, printers, monitors, etc. which are attached to a main computer system

perk /pɜːk/ *noun* a privilege or advantage additional to what is usual or expected ○ *A perk of writing book reviews is that you can keep the review copy.* (NOTE: **Perk** is short for 'perquisite'.)

permanence /'pɜːmənəns/ *noun* the ability of paper not to yellow or become brittle with age

permanent /'pɜːmənənt/ *adjective* expected to last for ever or for a very long time

permanent paper /ˌpɜːmənənt 'peɪpə/ *noun* acid-free paper

permeate /'pɜːmieɪt/ *verb* to spread through and affect every part

permit *noun* /'pɜːmɪt/ an official document allowing somebody to do a particular thing ○ *You have to have a permit to study in this library.* ■ *verb* /pə'mɪt/ to allow something to be done

permitted term /pə,mɪtɪd 'tɜːm/ *noun* a term that is used according to indexing conventions and must follow specific order rules

permutation /,pɜːmjʊ'teɪʃ(ə)n/ *noun* one of a set of ways in which things can be arranged ○ *There were so many permutations to the combination for the lock that it was very secure.*

persist /pə'sɪst/ *verb* to continue doing something even though it is very difficult or time-consuming

persistent /pə'sɪstənt/ *adjective* continuing to exist for a very long time

persistent identifier /pə,sɪst(ə)nt aɪ'dentɪfaɪə/ *noun* an Internet link to a resource which will work even if the resource is moved to a different location

personal /'pɜːs(ə)n(ə)l/ *adjective* belonging to you

personal attention /,pɜːs(ə)nəl ə'tenʃ(ə)n/ *noun* the action of dealing with a matter by oneself

personal computer /,pɜːs(ə)n(ə)l kəm'pjuːtə/ *noun* a small computer designed mainly for home or light business use. Abbr **PC**

personal development /,pɜːs(ə)n(ə)l dɪ'veləpmənt/ *noun* the process of gaining additional knowledge, skills and experience in order to develop your own talents and fulfil your own potential

personal digital assistant /,pɜːs(ə)n(ə)l ,dɪdʒɪt(ə)l ə'sɪstənt/ *noun* a small hand-held computer with facilities for taking notes, storing information such as addresses, and keeping a diary, usually operated using a stylus rather than a keyboard. Abbr **PDA**

personal environment /,pɜːs(ə)nəl en'vaɪrənmənt/ *noun* everything around you that affects your daily life

Personal Identification Number /,pɜːs(ə)n(ə)l aɪ,dentɪfɪ'keɪʃ(ə)n ,nʌmbə/ *noun* a short code given to people for use with credit and debit cards. Abbr **PIN**

personalised /'pɜːs(ə)nəlaɪzd/, **personalized** *adjective* printed with a person's name and/or address

personalised stationery /,pɜːs(ə)nəlaɪzd 'steɪʃ(ə)nəri/ *noun* letters, paper or cards printed with your address and sometimes your name

personal knowledge management /,pɜːs(ə)nəl 'nɒlɪdʒ ,mænɪdʒmənt/ *noun* a conceptual framework to organise personal knowledge so that it can be systematically applied and built upon. Abbr **PKM**

personnel /,pɜːsə'nel/ *plural noun* the people who work for an organisation

pf *abbreviation* in Internet addresses, the top-level domain for French Polynesia

pg *abbreviation* in Internet addresses, the top-level domain for Papua New Guinea

ph *abbreviation* in Internet addresses, the top-level domain for Philippines

phase /feɪz/ *noun* a particular stage in the development of something ■ *verb* to do something in stages

phased changeover /,feɪzd 'tʃeɪndʒ,əʊvə/ *noun* a change which takes place in stages over a period of time

phase in /,feɪz 'ɪn/ *verb* to introduce something gradually

phase out /,feɪz 'aʊt/ *verb* to stop using something gradually

PhD *abbreviation* Doctor of Philosophy

phone /fəʊn/ *noun* an electronic device which enables two people who each have one to talk to each other over a distance ■ *verb* to use a phone to contact another person

phone back /,fəʊn 'bæk/ *verb* to make a telephone call to somebody who has just called you

phone book /'fəʊn bʊk/ *noun* a book which lists names of people or companies with their addresses and telephone numbers

phone card /'fəʊn kɑːd/ *noun* an electronically coded card which enables the user to pay for calls on a public phone without using coins

phone number /'fəʊn ˌnʌmbə/ *noun* a set of figures which identifies the phone line that is being used

phonetics /fə'netɪks/ *noun* the study of speech sounds

phonetic script /fəˌnetɪk 'skrɪpt/ *noun* a system of writing the sounds of language by using one symbol for each sound

photocopier /'fəʊtəʊkɒpiə/ *noun* a machine that copies documents by photographing them very quickly

photocopy /'fəʊtəʊkɒpi/ *noun* an exact copy of a document produced by a photocopier, in black and white or colour ■ *verb* to make a copy of a document by using a photocopier

photograph /'fəʊtəɡrɑːf/ *noun* a picture formed by exposing light-sensitive paper to light using a camera

photograph directory /'fəʊtəɡrɑːf daɪˌrekt(ə)ri/ *noun* a list of photographs held by a special photo library, often catalogued by subject

photographic /ˌfəʊtə'ɡræfɪk/ *adjective* used to describe anything to do with photography or photographs

photography /fə'tɒɡrəfi/ *noun* the art or skill of producing photographs including use of a camera and the processing of the films

photogravure /ˌfəʊtəʊɡrə'vjʊə/ *noun* a printing method in which the paper is pressed directly on to the printing plate

photoprint /'fəʊtəʊprɪnt/ *noun* the final proof of a typeset copy

photostat /'fəʊtəʊstæt/ *noun* same as **photocopy**

phototext /'fəʊtəʊtekst/ *noun* characters and text produced by a phototypesetter

phototypesetter /ˌfəʊtəʊ'taɪpsetə/ *noun* a person who works with a computer and light-sensitive film to produce text ready for printing

COMMENT: The phototypesetter, rather like a large laser printer, normally uses the PostScript page description language and can generate type at 2,540 dpi; if the device is capable of outputting text and half-tone images, it is normally called an image setter.

PHP *noun* a programming language used for creating websites

physical /'fɪzɪk(ə)l/ *adjective* something that can be seen or touched, as opposed to a theoretical idea

physical record /ˌfɪzɪk(ə)l 'rekɔːd/ *noun* a manual form of a record rather than electronic

pica /'paɪkə/ *noun* a measurement of typeface equal to 12 point

pick up /ˌpɪk 'ʌp/ *verb* **1.** to learn a skill or an idea easily **2.** to improve ○ *The working conditions for the library staff picked up last month.*

PICS /pɪks/ *noun* a file format used to import a sequence of PICT files on an Apple Macintosh

PICT /pɪkt/ *noun* on an Apple Macintosh, a graphics file format that stores images in the QuickDraw vector format. Full form **picture**

picture /'pɪktʃə/ *noun* a drawing, painting or photograph

picture file /'pɪktʃə faɪl/ *noun* a collection of small pictures and cuttings, usually arranged by subject

picture library /'pɪktʃə ˌlaɪbrəri/ *noun* a storage system for pictures, which can be borrowed

'The Google deal allows customers to buy and rent selected video clips from ITN Archive, which contains 680,000 hours of news footage. ITN wants to develop its archive business. The model would be picture libraries such as US group Getty Images, whose annual turnover is £415 million.' [*The Mail on Sunday*]

picture processing /ˌpɪktʃə ˌprəʊsesɪŋ/ *noun* analysis of the information contained in an image, usually by computer, providing recognition of objects in the image

picture researcher /'pɪktʃə rɪ ˌsɜːtʃə/ *noun* somebody who looks for pictures relevant to a particular topic, so that they can be used as illustrations in a book, newspaper or TV programme

pie chart /'paɪ tʃɑːt/ *noun* a statistical diagram where the ratios are shown as sections of a circle

pigeonhole /'pɪdʒənhəʊl/ *noun* a small open section in a wall-mounted rack used as a temporary storage space or for delivery of personal mail

pilot /ˈpaɪlət/ *verb* to use a small-scale test to investigate whether a larger-scale operation will work ■ *adjective* done as a small test of a potential larger project ○ *A pilot scheme in a temporary building was used to see if a library was needed in the area.*

pin /pɪn/ *noun* a sharp piece of metal used for holding material or paper together

PIN /pɪn/, **PIN number** *abbreviation* Personal Identification Number

PIN Bulletin /ˈpɪn ˌbʊlətɪn/ *abbreviation* Patents Information Network Bulletin

ping /pɪŋ/ *noun* the length of time, in milliseconds, that it takes to send a message to an intranet, Internet or web address and receive a reply ■ *verb* to send a packet of data to an intranet, Internet or web address to check whether it is accessible or is responding

pipeline /ˈpaɪplaɪn/ *noun* a system for the spreading of information □ **in the pipeline** something which has already been started but has not yet produced an answer or result

piracy /ˈpaɪrəsi/ *noun* the act of illegally copying a piece of work under copyright

pirate /ˈpaɪrət/ *verb* to copy a patented or copyright work and sell it

COMMENT: The items most frequently pirated are books which can easily be printed from photocopied originals, music from CDs, or computer programs on magnetic disks which are relatively simple to copy.

pirate copy /ˌpaɪrət ˈkɒpi/ *noun* an illegal copy of a patented or copyright work

pixel /ˈpɪksəl/ *noun* the smallest unit of display on a computer screen whose colour or brightness can be controlled ○ *The picture was made up of several hundred pixels of different colours.* Full form **picture element**

COMMENT: In high resolution display systems the colour or brightness of a single pixel can be controlled; in low resolution systems a group of pixels are controlled at the same time.

pk *abbreviation* in Internet addresses, the top-level domain for Pakistan

PKM *abbreviation* personal knowledge management

pl *abbreviation* in Internet addresses, the top-level domain for Poland

place name /ˈpleɪs ˈneɪm/ *noun* the name by which a location is identified □ **dictionary of place names** an alphabetical list of places often with historical notes about their names

plagiarise /ˈpleɪdʒəraɪz/, **plagiarize** *verb* to copy somebody else's work and publish it as one's own

plagiarism /ˈpleɪdʒərɪz(ə)m/ *noun* the practice of copying and publishing somebody else's work as one's own

plagiarist /ˈpleɪdʒərɪst/ *noun* a person who copies other people's work without admitting what they have done

plaintext /ˌpleɪnˈtekst/ *noun* a term used in word processing to mean text that is in the standard font for that document without different types such boldface and italics

plan /plæn/ *noun* 1. a carefully worked out method of achieving objectives 2. a map ■ *verb* □ **to plan for** to make plans for a future event

planning /ˈplænɪŋ/ *noun* the process of working out in detail how to do something before starting to do it

planning department /ˈplænɪŋ dɪ ˌpɑːtmənt/ *noun* a local government department which decides how land in a given area will be used and what buildings may be put on it

plasticise /ˈplæstɪsaɪzd/, **plasticize** *verb* to put a plastic cover over a book jacket for protection

plate /pleɪt/ *noun* an illustration in a book often on better quality paper than the text

plate camera /ˈpleɪt ˌkæm(ə)rə/ *noun* a camera that uses glass plates instead of film

platen /ˈpleɪt(ə)n/ *noun* a roller which supports the paper in a printer

playback /ˈpleɪbæk/ *noun* the operation of a machine to reproduce sound or video pictures previously recorded

Play Matters /ˌpleɪ ˈmætəz/ *noun* the working title of the UK National Association of Toy and Leisure Libraries

plenary /ˈpliːnəri/ *adjective* attended by everyone who should be there ○ *The conference ended with a plenary session for all the participants.*

plot /plɒt/ *noun* a secret plan ■ *verb* to mark co-ordinates and draw a graph using them

plotter /ˈplɒtə/ *noun* a computer device that draws straight lines between two co-ordinates

COMMENT: Plotters are used for graph and diagram plotting and can plot curved lines as a number of short straight lines.

PLR *abbreviation* LIBRARIES Public Lending Right

plug /plʌg/ *noun* a device with metal pins which can be inserted into an electrical socket to provide power for a machine ■ *verb* to publicise a product or event in order to encourage people to buy or watch it

plug board /ˈplʌg bɔːd/ *noun* a board with several electrical sockets so that they are all connected to the same power supply

plug compatible /ˌplʌg kəmˈpætɪb(ə)l/ *adjective* computer or peripheral which can be used with another system simply by plugging it in with a special plug

plural /ˈplʊərəl/ *adjective* a grammatical term to describe words which refer to two or more things

pm *abbreviation* in Internet addresses, the top-level domain for St-Pierre and Miquelon

p-mail /ˈpiː ˌmeɪl/ *noun* same as **snail mail**

pn *abbreviation* in Internet addresses, the top-level domain for Pitcairn Island

pocket edition /ˈpɒkɪt ɪˌdɪʃ(ə)n/ *noun* a book small enough to be carried in a pocket

podcast /ˈpɒdkɑːst/ *noun* a service that allows subscribers to download a feed such as a radio show from the Internet on to their personal handset, e.g. an iPod

poem /ˈpəʊɪm/ *noun* a piece of imaginative writing which is arranged in a particular pattern of lines and sounds

poet /ˈpəʊɪt/ *noun* a person who writes poems

Poet Laureate /ˌpəʊɪt ˈlɔːriət/ *noun* a poet appointed by the British Queen to write poems for official occasions

point /pɔɪnt/ *noun* **1.** a place or position in time ○ *starting point* □ **to be on the point of** to be just about to start doing something □ **up to a point** partly but not completely ○ *It is true up to a point.* **2.** an idea or opinion ○ *He made a good point in the discussion.* ■ *verb* □ **to point out, to point to** to use a finger or stick to draw attention to something

pointer /ˈpɔɪntə/ *noun* a stick used to indicate something

point of presence /ˌpɔɪnt əv ˈprezəns/ *noun* a location where a user can connect to a network, e.g. a place where subscribers can dial in to an Internet service provider

point of sale /ˌpɔɪnt əv ˈseɪl/ *noun* the place where things sold in a shop are paid for. Abbr **POS, p.o.s.**

point size /ˈpɔɪnt saɪz/ *noun* the size of printed letters

COMMENT: In the UK and the USA, point sizes are based on the pica system; one point equals 0.3515mm (or 0.01384 inch); 12 points being one sixth of an inch, or 4.21mm or one pica em. In Europe, point size is based on the Didot point: one point equals 0.3759mm (or 0.0148 inch), and 12 points are one cicero.

policy /ˈpɒlɪsi/ *noun* a set of plans used as a basis for decisions

political /pəˈlɪtɪk(ə)l/ *adjective* concerned with the government or state

political correctness /pəˌlɪtɪk(ə)l kəˈrektnəs/ *noun* the use of language and behaviour that is not offensive or demeaning to any person or group of people

politically correct /pəˌlɪtɪkli kəˈrekt/ *adjective* designed not to offend any category of person. Abbr **PC**

politics /ˈpɒlɪtɪks/ *noun* the art or science of government

poll /pəʊl/ *noun* **1.** a survey in which a selected sample of people are asked their opinions about something **2.** the voting at a political election

polling station /ˈpəʊlɪŋ ˌsteɪʃ(ə)n/ *noun* a place where people go to vote at an election

polysemy /pəˈlɪsəmi/ *noun* the quality of words having two or more overlapping meanings

polyurethane   binding /ˌpɒlijʊərɪθeɪn ˈbaɪndɪŋ/ *noun* a strong adhesive binding used for heavy reference books offering good open-flat qualities. Abbr **PUR**

popular edition /ˌpɒpjʊlə ɪˈdɪʃ(ə)n/ *noun* a book with poorer paper and a lighter cover than the norm, sold at a cheaper price

population   coverage /ˌpɒpjʊˈleɪʃ(ə)n ˌkʌvərɪdʒ/ *noun* a selection of a survey population which considers all the different aspects to be covered

pop-up /ˈpɒp ʌp/ *adjective* containing cut-out figures that rise up as a page is opened ■ *noun* a book or card that contains pop-up figures

pop-up book /ˈpɒp ʌp ˌbʊk/ *noun* a book, usually for children, in which the pictures are cut out from the page so that they stand up when the book is opened

COMMENT: Used mainly for children's books, but also for some adult or more serious educational material.

pornography /pɔːˈnɒgrəfi/ *noun* publications of an obscene nature, usually in a sexual sense

port /pɔːt/ *noun* a socket or other physical connection allowing data transfer between a computer's internal communications channel and another external device

portable /ˈpɔːtəb(ə)l/ *adjective* easily carried ■ *noun* an easily carried machine such as a small computer or television

portal /ˈpɔːt(ə)l/ *noun* a website that provides links to information and other websites

portfolio /pɔːtˈfəʊliəʊ/ *noun* **1.** a collection of original works **2.** an area of responsibility held by a government minister **3.** a thin, flat case for carrying drawings and papers

portrait /ˈpɔːtrɪt/ *noun* a painting, drawing or photograph of a person

POS, p.o.s. *abbreviation* point of sale

position /pəˈzɪʃ(ə)n/ *noun* a person's job or status within a company

positive discrimination /ˌpɒzɪtɪv dɪsˌkrɪmɪˈneɪʃ(ə)n/ *noun* a policy which deliberately treats one group of people better than others because they have previously been unfairly treated

positive   feedback /ˌpɒzɪtɪv ˈfiːdbæk/ *noun* comments which indicate that what has been proposed, done or made is liked by the customers

'The new system allows users to search the site for their own purposes, rather than browse through all the collections – we have already had positive feedback from users and are looking forward both to having the full range of items available online, and to further developments that the system will enable us to achieve.' [*M2 Presswire*]

post /pəʊst/ *verb* **1.** to send letters and parcels through the mailing system **2.** to add the accession number to an index entry

post- /pəʊst/ *prefix* combining with nouns, adjectives and dates to indicate that something has happened after the stated time ○ *post-war* ○ *post-audit*

postage and packing /ˌpəʊstɪdʒ ən ˈpækɪŋ/ *noun* the cost of wrapping goods and paying for them to be delivered. Abbr **p&p**

postage stamp /ˈpəʊstɪdʒ stæmp/ *noun* a small official piece of paper which is stuck on to a letter or parcel to show that the cost of the postage has been paid

postal survey /ˈpəʊst(ə)l ˌsɜːveɪ/ *noun* a survey that is conducted by sending questionnaires through the post

postcard /ˈpəʊstkɑːd/ *noun* a card, often with a picture on one side, which can be written on and sent to somebody without an envelope

postcode /ˈpəʊstkəʊd/ *noun* a system of letters and numbers used by the post office to identify towns and roads to aid the delivery of letters

post-coordinate indexing system /ˌpəʊstkəʊɔːdɪnət 'ɪndeksɪŋ ˌsɪstəm/ *noun* a system in which information is organised under simple main headings but with devices whereby the user can combine them to produce compound subjects

postdated /pəʊst'deɪtɪd/ *adjective* dated later than the day of issue ○ *The cheque was postdated to the end of the month.*

poster /'pəʊstə/ *noun* a large notice or advertisement stuck to a wall or board

COMMENT: The standard format for a single sheet poster is double crown (30 x 20 inches).

postgraduate /pəʊst'grædʒuət/ *noun* **1.** a student who already has a first degree and is studying or doing research at a higher level **2.** *US* a graduate

posthumous /'pɒstjʊməs/ *adjective* published or printed after the author's death

posting /'pəʊstɪŋ/ *noun* a message sent to and displayed on an online facility such as an Internet newsgroup or bulletin board

postings list /'pəʊstɪŋz lɪst/ *noun* an alphabetical list of descriptors with the identification numbers of documents using them

post office /'pəʊst ˌɒfɪs/ *noun* a national organisation which controls the postal services within a country

postpone /pəʊst'pəʊn/ *verb* to rearrange for something to be done at a later date or time

postscript /'pəʊstskrɪpt/ *noun* an addition to the end of something such as a book, story or document

PostScript /'pəʊstskrɪpt/ a trade name for a standard page description language developed by Adobe Systems. PostScript offers flexible font sizing and positioning and it is most often used in DTP systems, high-quality laser printers and phototypesetters. ○ *If you do a lot of DTP work, you will benefit from a PostScript printer.*

potboiler /'pɒtbɔɪlə/ *noun* a work written purely to earn money with no literary merit

potential /pə'tenʃəl/ *noun* having the possibility to develop into something better ○ *The library needed a lot of work but had the potential to become a very efficient service.* ■ *adjective* capable of becoming something better in the future ○ *There is a large potential market for electronic information.*

powered /'paʊəd/ *adjective* worked by electricity or another source of energy ○ *gas-powered central heating*

Powerpoint /'paʊəpɔɪnt/ a trade name for a piece of software developed by Microsoft that allows users to create multimedia presentations

power supply /'paʊə səˌplaɪ/ *noun* a supply of electricity to a building or work site

pp *abbreviation* pages

pr *abbreviation* in Internet addresses, the top-level domain for Puerto Rico

practical /'præktɪk(ə)l/ *noun* a lesson or examination in which you are asked to do tasks rather than just read or write about them

practice /'præktɪs/ *noun* **1.** a repeated performance of something in order to learn to do it well **2.** a regular or standard course of action ○ *It is standard practice to keep reference books in a separate area of the library.* ◊ **in practice**

pre- /priː/ *prefix* combining with adjectives to indicate something done before

precede /prɪ'siːd/ *verb* to happen before something else happens

preceding record /prɪˌsiːdɪŋ 'rekɔːd/ *noun* a record that comes before the current one

precise /prɪ'saɪs/ *adjective* exact and accurate

PRECIS indexing /'preɪsi ˌɪndeksɪŋ/ *noun* a technique for subject indexing originally developed for the British National Bibliography. Full form **PREserved Context Index System**

precision /prɪ'sɪʒ(ə)n/ *noun* **1.** accuracy, exactness **2.** the number of relevant records returned by a search, expressed as a percentage of the total number of records returned

precision equipment /prɪˌsɪʒ(ə)n ɪ 'kwɪpmənt/ *noun* machines that are made to very accurate specifications

Pre-coordinate Indexing System /ˌprikəʊɔːdɪnət 'ɪndeksɪŋ ˌsɪstəm/ *noun* a system whereby the terms are combined at the indexing stage, used by the British National Bibliography

pref. *abbreviation* preface

preface /'prefəs/ *noun* an author's note which comes before the introduction and after any dedication

COMMENT: A preface is usually written by the author, and explains briefly why the book has been written and who the readers are expected to be. A foreword, on the other hand, can be written by the author, but is more usually by another person, often a famous person whose name might be expected to increase the sales of the book.

prefatory note /'prefæt(ə)ri nəʊt/ *noun* a note addressed to the reader, printed at the beginning of a book

preferment /prɪ'fɜːmənt/ *noun* promotion to a better job

preferred order /prɪˌfɜːd 'ɔːdə/ *noun* a set order in which the items in a classification scheme are arranged

preferred term /prɪˌfɜːd 'tɜːm/ *noun* a term used in a catalogue to gather together all synonymous and otherwise scattered entries ○ *Publications is the preferred term for books, documents, monographs, etc.*

prefix /'priːfɪks/ *noun* a word or letters added to the front of another word, which can change its meaning, e.g. 'undone', 'misread'

prejudice /'predʒʊdɪs/ *noun* an unfair and often negative feeling based on incomplete knowledge and information

prelims /'priːlɪmz/ *plural noun* the initial pages of a book, including the title page and table of contents, which precede the main text. Also called **front matter**

premise /'premɪs/ *noun* something that is supposed to be true and is therefore used as the basis for an argument

premises /'premɪsɪz/ *plural noun* land and buildings occupied by a business

pre-paid /priː'peɪd/ *adjective* paid for in advance of delivery

preparation /ˌprepə'reɪʃ(ə)n/ *noun* work done beforehand in order to be ready for something ○ *They made careful preparation for the open day.*

preparation of text /ˌprepəreɪʃ(ə)n əv 'tekst/ *noun* the process of making text ready for printing by editing and checking it

prepare /prɪ'peə/ *verb* to make something ready for use or for consideration ○ *The librarians were asked to prepare a report for the management meeting.*

preposition /ˌprepə'zɪʃ(ə)n/ *noun* the grammatical term for words such as 'by', 'with', 'on', 'under', which indicate place or direction

pre-printed form /ˌpriː ˌprɪntɪd 'fɔːm/, **pre-printed stationery** /ˌpriː ˌprɪntɪd 'steɪʃ(ə)n(ə)ri/ *noun* a form or notepaper that has some information already printed on it

prepublication /ˌpriːˌpʌblɪ 'keɪʃ(ə)n/ *adjective* relating to or occurring in the period before a book or other work is published

pre-recorded /ˌpriːrɪ'kɔːdɪd/ *adjective* recorded at an earlier time ○ *A message on a telephone answering machine is pre-recorded.*

pre-requisite /priː'rekwɪzɪt/ *noun* something that must be done before something else ○ *A reasonable standard of English is a pre-requisite to studying in an English-speaking country.*

prescribed text /prɪˌskraɪbd 'tekst/ *noun* an educational book which has been listed as required for a course of study or for an exam

prescription /prɪ'skrɪpʃən/ *noun* an instruction or plan for what needs to be done in a particular situation

prescriptive /prɪ'skrɪptɪv/ *adjective* giving rules and regulations for what should or should not be done

presell /ˌpriː 'sel/ *verb* to sell a book before its official publication date

present /'prez(ə)nt/ *noun* something given to a person as a gift ■ *verb* to introduce a person, idea or piece of information ■ *adjective* existing or happening now ○ *the present situation*

presentation /ˌprez(ə)n'teɪʃ(ə)n/ *noun* a talk about a specific subject given to provide information

preservation /ˌprezə'veɪʃ(ə)n/ *noun* the provision of suitable environmental conditions to ensure the condition of library stock

PREserved Context Index System /prɪˌzɜːvd ˌkɒntent 'ɪndeks ˌsɪstəm/ *noun* ♦ **PRECIS indexing**

pre-set /priː'set/ *adjective* set to specific levels before using ○ *The temperature of the heating in the library was pre-set to a comfortable level.*

press /pres/ *noun* **1.** a double-sided bookcase of not fewer than four tiers **2.** newspapers and the people who write for them ■ *verb* **1.** to put pressure on something ○ *Press the button to make it work.* **2.** to try to persuade somebody to do or say something

press coverage /'pres ˌkʌv(ə)rɪdʒ/ *noun* the amount of space or time given in newspapers or TV and radio news bulletins to one topic

press cutting /'pres ˌkʌtɪŋ/ *noun* one item cut from a newspaper

press guide /'pres gaɪd/ *noun* a reference book which lists the main newspaper publications throughout the world

pressmark /'presmɑːk/ *noun* same as **shelf mark**

press release /'pres rɪˌliːs/ *noun* a statement given by an organisation to the media to explain a situation from their point of view

Prestel /'prestel/ a trade name for a teletext system used in the UK marketed by British Telecom

prevent /prɪ'vent/ *verb* to make sure something does not happen

prevention /prɪ'venʃən/ *noun* an action which stops something from happening

preventive maintenance /prɪ ˌventɪv 'meɪntənəns/ *noun* regular checks and repairs to small faults so that they do not develop into large problems

preview /'priːvjuː/ *noun* the opportunity to see something before it is released to the general public

previous /'priːviəs/ *adjective* existing or happening before or earlier

price /praɪs/ *noun* the amount of money needed to buy an item

price bracket /'praɪs ˌbrækɪt/ *noun* a limited range of prices ○ *The goods were in the cheaper price bracket.*

price label /'praɪs ˌleɪb(ə)l/ *noun* a piece of paper or card attached to something to show its price

price list /'praɪs lɪst/ *noun* a list of the prices of everything in stock

pricing strategy /'praɪsɪŋ ˌstrætədʒi/ *noun* company policy about how much to charge for goods or services in order to make a reasonable profit

prima /'priːmə/ *noun* the first word of the next page printed at the bottom of a page

primary /'praɪməri/ *adjective* first, original, basic or most important

primary colour /'praɪməri ˌkʌlə/ *noun* one of the three colours, red, yellow and blue, from which all other colours can be made

primary education /ˌpraɪməri ˌedjʊ'keɪʃ(ə)n/ *noun* the first period of schooling usually up to the age of 11 years

primary operator /ˌpraɪməri 'ɒpəreɪtə/ *noun* the first person to operate a machine

primary record /ˌpraɪməri 'rekɔːd/ *noun* one of the first records on a subject

primary sampling /ˌpraɪməri 'sɑːmplɪŋ/ *noun* the first selected population for a survey

primary school /'praɪməri skuːl/ *noun* a school for young children usually for about the first six years of schooling

primary school textbook /ˌpraɪməri skuːl 'tekstbʊk/ *noun* a textbook used in schools teaching children up to about 11 years old

primary source /ˌpraɪməri 'sɔːs/ *noun* the original document from which information is extracted

primary user /ˌpraɪməri ˈjuːzə/ noun the first person to use a service

prime /praɪm/ adjective relating to the most important or typical example of something ■ verb to give somebody information about something

primer /ˈpraɪmə/ noun **1.** a simple instruction book or manual **2.** a basic or simple school book for children

prime time /ˈpraɪm taɪm/ noun the time of day when most people are expected to be watching television or listening to the radio

print /prɪnt/ verb to produce a book, magazine, newspaper or leaflet by a mechanical process

printed catalogue card /ˌprɪntɪd ˈkætəlɒg ˌkɑːd/ noun a pre-printed card containing the bibliographical details of a book for inclusion in a library catalogue

printed ephemera /ˌprɪntɪd ɪˈfemərə/ plural noun items such as theatre programmes, leaflets and advertising fliers which would normally be read and thrown away

printed index /ˌprɪntɪd ˈɪndeks/ noun an alphabetical list of words used in a text

printed matter /ˈprɪntɪd ˌmætə/ noun anything that is printed and can be read

printer /ˈprɪntə/ noun **1.** a machine that converts electronic data into readable form on paper **2.** a person or company that prints books, newspapers or other printed matter

printer buffer /ˈprɪntə ˌbʌfə/ noun a temporary store for character data waiting to be printed, used to free the computer before the printing is completed so making the operation faster

printer's imprint /ˌprɪntəz ˈɪmprɪnt/ noun a special mention of the name and address of the printer on the inside of a book or periodical

printing history /ˈprɪntɪŋ ˌhɪst(ə)ri/ noun details of the printing of a book such as the date of the original printing and dates of reprints, usually listed on the bibliographic page after the title page

printing press /ˈprɪntɪŋ pres/ noun a machine which presses paper on to type and prints text

print out /ˌprɪnt ˈaʊt/ verb to print information from a computer through a printer

printout /ˈprɪntaʊt/ noun a hard copy of a computer file

print run /ˈprɪnt rʌn/ noun the number of copies of a book printed at one time

print spooling /ˈprɪnt ˌspuːlɪŋ/ noun the automatic printing of a number of different documents in a queue at the usual speed of the printer, while the computer is doing some other task

print style /ˈprɪnt staɪl/ noun the typeface and fonts used in any particular document

prior /ˈpraɪə/ adjective **1.** having happened previously ○ unable to go due to a prior engagement **2.** being given priority over something else

priority /praɪˈɒrɪti/ noun something that must be dealt with first

privacy /ˈprɪvəsi/ noun the state of being left alone to do things

privacy of information /ˌprɪvəsi əv ˌɪnfəˈmeɪʃ(ə)n/ noun the act of keeping documents secret so that only authorised people are allowed to read them

'New rules for a passenger data collection scheme operated by US authorities may carry a nasty sting for travellers. The scheme – Advance Passenger Information System (Apis) – threatens to cause big delays at check-in and raises ethical questions about a passenger's right to privacy of information.' [*Financial Times*]

private /ˈpraɪvət/ adjective for the use of one person or group only

private sector /ˈpraɪvət ˌsektə/ noun services or industries that are owned by individuals or groups rather than by the state

pro abbreviation professional practice

probability /ˌprɒbəˈbɪlɪti/ noun the likelihood of something happening, often expressed as a fraction or percentage

probe /prəʊb/ *verb* to investigate a situation by asking a lot of questions

problematic /ˌprɒbləˈmætɪk/ *adjective* relating to a situation that involves difficulties and needs a solution

problem solving learning /ˌprɒbləm ˌsɒlvɪŋ ˈlɜːnɪŋ/ *noun* a method of teaching which sets problems for students to solve so that they learn how to reason

procedural knowledge /prəˈsiːdʒərəl ˌnɒlɪdʒ/ *noun* informal knowledge of how to perform tasks based on experience. Compare **propositional knowledge**

procedural memory /prəˈsiːdʒərəl ˌmem(ə)ri/ *noun* human memory of learned skills and how to perform tasks. Compare **declarative memory**

procedure /prəˈsiːdʒə/ *noun* a method of doing something which is generally accepted as being efficient

proceedings /prəˈsiːdɪŋz/ *plural noun* a published record of a meeting of a society or institution

proceeds /ˈprəʊsiːdz/ *plural noun* money that is made by an activity or event

process /ˈprəʊses/ *verb* **1.** to manipulate something into the required format **2.** to perform the necessary routines to a book before it can be borrowed, e.g. classifying, cataloguing, stamping, labelling and numbering

process colours /ˈprəʊses ˌkʌləz/ *plural noun* in printing, cyan, magenta and yellow

processing /ˈprəʊsesɪŋ/ *noun* the sorting of information

processor /ˈprəʊsesə/ *noun* a computer that is able to manipulate data according to given instructions. ◊ **word processor**

produce /prəˈdjuːs/ *verb* to make, create or show something ○ *He produced evidence to support his argument.*

product /ˈprɒdʌkt/ *noun* **1.** something that is made to be sold often in large quantities **2.** the result of previous actions or discussions

product development /ˌprɒdʌkt dɪˈveləpmənt/ *noun* the process of improving a product to meet the needs of the market

production /prəˈdʌkʃən/ *noun* the creation of something □ **on production of** when something is shown ○ *Goods can only be exchanged on production of a receipt.*

productivity /ˌprɒdʌkˈtɪvɪti/ *noun* the rate at which goods are manufactured

product life /ˈprɒdʌkt laɪf/ *noun* the length of time that a product is likely to be saleable

profession /prəˈfeʃ(ə)n/ *noun* a job that requires advanced education or training

professional /prəˈfeʃ(ə)nəl/ *noun* a person who works in one of the professions ■ *adjective* **1.** relating to work requiring a high level of training and done to a very high standard **2.** done for money rather than as a hobby

professional and reference publishing /prəˌfeʃ(ə)nəl ən ˈref(ə)rəns ˌpʌblɪʃɪŋ/ *noun* the publishing of special books for the professions and also reference titles

professional ethics /prəˌfeʃ(ə)nəl ˈeθɪks/ *noun* the conduct and behaviour expected of members of a professional organisation

professional judgement /prəˌfeʃ(ə)nəl ˈdʒʌdʒmənt/ *noun* the ability of somebody who has special knowledge or skill to assess a situation and recommend a course of action

professional organisation /prəˌfeʃ(ə)nəl ˌɔːgənaɪˈzeɪʃ(ə)n/ *noun* a group of people in the same profession who act to support other employees and to set standards for the way they work ○ *The Library Association is a professional organisation for all information employees.*

professional publishing /prəˌfeʃ(ə)nəl ˈpʌblɪʃɪŋ/ *noun* the publishing of books on law, accountancy and other professions

profit /ˈprɒfɪt/ *noun* the amount of money that somebody gains when they sell something for more than they paid for it ■ *verb* □ **to profit by, from** to gain advantage or benefit from something

proforma /prəʊˈfɔːmə/ *noun* a standard layout of a form

proforma invoice /prəʊˌfɔːmə ˈɪnvɔɪs/ *noun* an invoice sent to the purchaser of mail order goods which must be paid before the goods can be despatched

program /ˈprəʊɡræm/ *noun* a set of instructions for a computer ■ *verb* to write a program for a computer

programmed learning /ˌprəʊɡræmd ˈlɜːnɪŋ/ *noun* a learning method based on self-instructional materials that are designed to allow pupils to progress at their own pace, step by step, through structured sequences

programmer /ˈprəʊɡræmə/ *noun* a person who designs and writes instructions for a computer

programming engineer /ˈprəʊɡræmɪŋ ˌendʒɪnɪə/ *noun* an engineer in charge of programming a computer system

programming language /ˈprəʊɡræmɪŋ ˌlæŋɡwɪdʒ/ *noun* software that allows somebody to write instructions for a computer which it can then translate into a workable program

COMMENT: Programming languages are grouped into different levels: the high-level languages such as BASIC and PASCAL are easy to understand and use, but offer slow execution time since each instruction is made up of a number of machine code instructions; low-level languages such as ASSEMBLER are more complex to read and program in but offer faster execution time.

progress /prəˈɡres/ *verb* to improve or become more advanced

prohibit /prəʊˈhɪbɪt/ *verb* to forbid something by law

project /ˈprɒdʒekt/ *noun* **1.** a detailed study of a subject written up by a student **2.** a planned course of action ○ *They were involved in a large building project.* ■ *verb* to plan ahead

projection /prəˈdʒekʃən/ *noun* a forecast of a future amount from a set of data

project leader /ˌprɒdʒekt ˈliːdə/, **project manager** /ˌprɒdʒekt ˈmænɪdʒə/ *noun* the person in charge of a project

projector /prəˈdʒektə/ *noun* a mechanical device that displays films or slides on a screen

project team /ˈprɒdʒekt tiːm/ *noun* a group of people working together on a project

PROLOG /ˈprəʊlɒɡ/ *noun* a computer language used in the development of expert systems

prologue /ˈprəʊlɒɡ/ *noun* **1.** the introduction to something such as a play, book, film or long poem **2.** events which lead up to more serious consequences

promote /prəˈməʊt/ *verb* **1.** to advance somebody to a higher position within an organisation **2.** to encourage something to develop or succeed

promotion /prəˈməʊʃ(ə)n/ *noun* **1.** the act of upgrading somebody to a higher position **2.** a marketing activity to persuade people to buy goods or use a service ○ *The library had a special children's book promotion during the school holidays.*

prompt /prɒmpt/ *adjective* done on time, without delay ■ *noun* a symbol on a computer screen to remind the user to do something

pronunciation /prəˌnʌnsiˈeɪʃ(ə)n/ *noun* the way in which the sounds of a language are spoken and stressed

proof /pruːf/ *noun* **1.** facts or evidence to show that something is true **2.** a sample printed page made from type, for approval before mass printing

-proof /pruːf/ *suffix* added to nouns to show that something cannot be damaged ○ *The table surface was heatproof so hot pans could be put on it.*

proof correction mark /ˌpruːf kə ˈrekʃ(ə)n ˌmɑːk/ *noun* a special mark written on a proof text to show where and how it should be corrected

proofread /ˈpruːfriːd/ *verb* to read a text and mark any errors for correction before it is printed

proofreader /ˈpruːfriːdə/ *noun* a person whose job is to proofread texts

propaganda /ˌprɒpəˈɡændə/ *noun* information that is often untrue and biased, published and disseminated to influence people

proper noun /ˌprɒpə 'naʊn/ *noun* the grammatical term for a word that is the name of a person, place or institution and should be written with a capital letter

proportional /prə'pɔːʃ(ə)nəl/ *adjective* in proportion to the other parts

proportional spacing /prə ˌpɔːʃ(ə)nəl 'speɪsɪŋ/ *noun* a printing system where each letter takes the space proportional to the character width, so 'm' takes more space than 'i'

proposal /prə'pəʊz(ə)l/ *noun* a suggestion or plan, often written down and put forward as a discussion document

proposed system /prəˌpəʊzd 'sɪstəm/ *noun* a system that has been designed and suggested for use but is not yet installed

propositional knowledge /ˌprɒpə 'zɪʃ(ə)nəl ˌnɒlɪdʒ/ *noun* formal knowledge of hard facts which can be described as true or false. Also called **declarative knowledge**. Compare **procedural knowledge**

'Propositional knowledge is the formulation of 'if … then' statements based on the assumption that given causes have given predictable effects; that events have predictable, single and identifiable outcomes. Our thinking today is, in general, based on propositional knowledge; education and teaching methods are dominated by this paradigm also.' [*Management Learning*]

prospectus /prə'spektəs/ *noun* a document produced by an academic institution giving details about it for the information of potential students

protect /prə'tekt/ *verb* to keep something safe and free from damage

protection /prə'tekʃən/ *noun* the act of keeping something free from harm or damage

protective /prə'tektɪv/ *adjective* designed to keep things free from harm ○ *The books were covered in protective plastic.*

protest literature /'prəʊtest ˌlɪt(ə)rətʃə/ *noun* literature written and published to protest against something, usually a political situation

protocol /'prəʊtəkɒl/ *noun* **1.** a set of rules allowing unrelated information systems to communicate with each other **2.** a system of rules about the correct way to behave in formal situations

protocol converter /'prəʊtəkɒl kənˌvɜːtə/ *noun* a device used for converting protocols from one computer system to another, e.g. for converting data from a microcomputer to a phototypesetter

protocol standards /'prəʊtəkɒl ˌstændədz/ *plural noun* standards laid down to allow data exchange between any computer system conforming to the standard

prototype /'prəʊtətaɪp/ *noun* the first model of something that is completely new

provenance /'prɒvənəns/ *noun* the place of origin of something

provenance order /'prɒvənəns ˌɔːdə/ *noun* a document which proves that the origin of an item is genuine ○ *When genuine antiques are sold they require a provenance order or certificate.*

provide /prə'vaɪd/ *verb* to make something available

provider company /prə'vaɪdə ˌkʌmp(ə)ni/ *noun* a company which provides public Internet access links via the telephone network see also

province /'prɒvɪns/ *noun* a sphere of knowledge or activity

provisional /prə'vɪʒ(ə)n(ə)l/ *adjective* **1.** only for a short time **2.** likely to be changed

proximity operator /prɒk'sɪmɪti ˌɒpəreɪtə/ *noun* a Boolean operator that directs the search engine making a text search to locate pages in which the words it is looking for are near one another in any direction

pseudo- /sjuːdəʊ/ *prefix* used with nouns and adjectives to describe things that are not really what they claim to be

pseudonym /'sjuːdənɪm/ *noun* a name used by a writer which is not his or her real name

pseudonymous /sjuː'dɒnɪməs/ *adjective* written by an author under a pseudonym

PSN *abbreviation* packet switched network

PSTN *abbreviation* Public Switched Telephone Network

pt *abbreviation* in Internet addresses, the top-level domain for Portugal

pub. *abbreviation* **1.** published **2.** publisher **3.** publishing

publ. *abbreviation* **1.** publication **2.** published **3.** publisher

public /'pʌblɪk/ *adjective* open for anyone to use

public address system /ˌpʌblɪk ə'dres ˌsɪstəm/ *noun* a loudspeaker and microphone which enables a speaker to be heard by a large group of people

public archives /ˌpʌblɪk 'ɑːkaɪvz/ *plural noun* historical records which are accessible by the general public from a records office

publication /ˌpʌblɪ'keɪʃ(ə)n/ *noun* **1.** a book, newspaper or magazine which can be sold **2.** a leaflet which is given out to provide information **3.** the act of printing and distributing a book, newspaper or magazine **4.** the act of releasing information to the general public in printed form

publication data /ˌpʌblɪ'keɪʃ(ə)n ˌdeɪtə/ *noun* information about a book such as the date, publisher and ISBN, printed on the back of the title page

publication date /ˌpʌblɪ'keɪʃ(ə)n ˌdeɪt/ *noun* the year when a book was published. Also called **date of publication**

public domain /ˌpʌblɪk dəʊ'meɪn/ *noun* information that is unrestricted and accessible by the general public

publicise /'pʌblɪsaɪz/, **publicize** *verb* to make something widely known to the general public

publicity /pʌ'blɪsɪti/ *noun* advertisements and information materials which make something generally known

publicity handout /pʌ'blɪsɪti ˌhændaʊt/ *noun* an information sheet which is given to members of the public

publicity matter /pʌ'blɪsɪti ˌmætə/ *noun* advertisements or printed publicity material

Public Lending Right /ˌpʌblɪk 'lendɪŋ ˌraɪt/ *noun* the right of authors to receive a small fee every time their books are borrowed from public libraries in the United Kingdom. Abbr **PLR**

public librarian /ˌpʌblɪk laɪ'breəriən/ *noun* a trained information employee in the public library service

public library /ˌpʌblɪk 'laɪbrəri/ *noun* a library that serves the general public in a city, town or village

public record office /ˌpʌblɪk 'rekɔːd ˌɒfɪs/ *noun* a collection of historical archives organised for retrieval and use by the public

public sector organisation /ˌpʌblɪk ˌsektə ˌɔːgənaɪ'zeɪʃ(ə)n/ *noun* a company or organisation that is owned by the government rather than a private body

public service announcement /ˌpʌblɪk 'sɜːvɪs əˌnaʊnsmənt/ *noun* a government information announcement usually broadcast nationally

public service broadcasting /ˌpʌblɪk ˌsɜːvɪs 'brɔːdkɑːstɪŋ/ *noun* radio and television programmes that are accessible by everyone, as opposed to satellite and cable channels which require a subscription to be paid

public service provider /ˌpʌblɪk ˌsɜːvɪs prə'vaɪdə/ *noun* an electronic host providing interactive access to Telnet, e-mail and Usenet news

public speaking skills /ˌpʌblɪk 'spiːkɪŋ ˌskɪlz/ *plural noun* the ability to speak well and retain the interest of large groups of people

Public Switched Telephone Network /ˌpʌblɪk ˌswɪtʃt 'telɪfəʊn ˌnetwɜːk/ *noun* a form of automatic telephone exchange interconnecting worldwide. Abbr **PSTN**

publish /'pʌblɪʃ/ *verb* to arrange to have a book or article printed and usually distributed for sale

publisher /'pʌblɪʃə/ *noun* a person or company that publishes books, magazines and newspapers

publisher's binding /'pʌblɪʃəz ˌbaɪndɪŋ/ *noun* a binding style where the book is cased, with a plain cloth binding

publishing /'pʌblɪʃɪŋ/ *noun* the trade, profession or activity of preparing and producing material in printed or electronic form for distribution to the public

publishing house /'pʌblɪʃɪŋ haʊs/ *noun* a company that publishes books, magazines and newspapers

pull-down menu /'pʊl daʊn ˌmenjuː/ *noun* a list of options in a computer program which can be displayed on screen over work that is already being done

pull-out /'pʊlaʊt/ *noun* **1.** inserted pages in a magazine which can be easily removed and retained for reference **2.** a folded insert in a book or magazine which when opened out makes a large sheet, used e.g. for maps

pulp /pʌlp/ *noun* material produced from rags or ground wood, mixed with water, used for making paper ■ *verb* **1.** to take torn rags or ground wood and mix this with water and chemicals to produce smooth pulp for making paper **2.** to take printed paper or waste paper and produce pulp from it for making paper again ○ *The unsold copies in the warehouse were sent away to be pulped.*

pulp board /'pʌlp bɔːd/, **pulp card** /'pʌlp kɑːd/ *noun* thin board made from paper pulp, used for the cover boards of a book

pulp fiction /ˌpʌlp 'fɪkʃən/ *noun* cheap fiction which is considered by critics to have no literary value

punch /pʌntʃ/ *verb* **1.** to hit something hard **2.** to make holes in something so that it can be inserted into a ring file

punched card /ˌpʌntʃt 'kɑːd/ *noun* a card with holes in them in patterns which contain instructions or data for computers

punched card reader /ˌpʌntʃt 'kɑːd ˌriːdə/ *noun* a device that trans-

forms data on a punched card to a form that can be recognised by a computer

punched tape /ˌpʌntʃt 'teɪp/ *noun* a strip of paper tape that contains holes to represent data, formerly used in photo-typesetting, but now replaced by magnetic tapes and disks

punctuation /ˌpʌŋktʃu'eɪʃ(ə)n/ *noun* a system of symbols which enable a reader to make sense of written texts, e.g. full stops, commas, question marks

punctuation mark /ˌpʌŋktʃu 'eɪʃ(ə)n mɑːk/ *noun* a printed or written symbol, which cannot be spoken, but which divides up the text and helps to make its meaning clearer

COMMENT: The main punctuation marks are the question mark and exclamation mark; inverted commas (which show the type of text being written); the comma, full stop, colon and semicolon (which show how the words are broken up into sequences); the apostrophe (which shows that a letter or word is missing); the dash and hyphen and brackets (which separate or link words).

PUR *abbreviation* polyurethane binding

purchase /'pɜːtʃɪs/ *verb* to buy something

purchaser /'pɜːtʃɪsə/ *noun* a buyer

purchaser of information services /ˌpɜːtʃɪsə əv ˌɪnfə'meɪʃ(ə)n ˌsɜːvɪsɪz/ *noun* a person who pays for information to be provided

purport /pə'pɔːt/ *verb* to claim to be or have something ○ *The service purports to have a full range of business information.*

push button /'pʊʃ ˌbʌt(ə)n/ *noun* a switch which is worked by pushing

PVC *noun* a plastic material often used for covers of reference books because it can stand a great deal of handling. Full form **polyvinyl chloride**

pw *abbreviation* in Internet addresses, the top-level domain for Palau

py *abbreviation* in Internet addresses, the top-level domain for Paraguay

Q

qa *abbreviation* in Internet addresses, the top-level domain for Qatar

quad /kwɒd/ *noun* a sheet of paper four times as large as a basic sheet

qualification /ˌkwɒlɪfɪˈkeɪʃ(ə)n/ *noun* proof that a person has passed examinations or reached a particular level of skill

qualifier /ˈkwɒlɪfaɪə/ *noun* a word or phrase added to an index heading to differentiate it from other headings with the same spelling but different meaning

qualitative research /ˈkwɒlɪtətɪv rɪˌsɜːtʃ/ *noun* research which examines the quality of something rather than its quantity

quality /ˈkwɒlɪti/ *noun* a measure of how good or bad something is

quality assessment /ˈkwɒlɪti əˌsesmənt/ *noun* a method of measuring how well a company is performing in achieving its stated aims

quality control /ˈkwɒlɪti kənˌtrəʊl/ *noun* the work of a department in a company that checks that its products are of satisfactory standard

'"We identified that, by standardising on a system across all sites, we could reduce the amount of time and people needed to complete updates. The end result was improved content on the sites for our customers", [a spokesperson] said. The TV company hopes the new level of quality control will also encourage more visitors to its online stores.' [*Computing*]

quality newspaper /ˌkwɒlɪti ˈnjuːzpeɪpə/ *noun* a newspaper that is considered to have well-written and thoughtful views about topics

quango /ˈkwæŋgəʊ/ *noun* an independent advisory body set up by the government, but having separate legal powers within a restricted area of activity

quantify /ˈkwɒntɪfaɪ/ *verb* to represent something in terms of figures so that it can be counted or measured

quantitative research /ˈkwɒntɪtətɪv rɪˌsɜːtʃ/ *noun* research that examines the effects of something by using numbers and statistics

quantity /ˈkwɒntɪti/ *noun* the amount or number of items □ **in quantity** in large amounts

quarter /ˈkwɔːtə/ *noun* a fourth part of a whole

quarter binding /ˈkwɔːtə ˌbaɪndɪŋ/ *noun* a binding on a cased book, where the spine is covered with one material such as leather or cloth, and the rest of the cover is covered with another material such as paper

quarter-bound /ˈkwɔːtə baʊnd/ *adjective* denoting a book that is bound in one material, usually leather, on the spine and in another on the covers

quarter day /ˈkwɔːtə deɪ/ *noun* the last day of a quarter, every three months, when payments are due: Lady Day 25th March, Midsummer Day 24th June, Michaelmas 29th September, Christmas Day 25th December

quarter leather binding /ˌkwɔːtə ˈleðə ˌbaɪndɪŋ/ *noun* a binding where the spine is covered with leather and the rest of the cover with paper

quarterly /ˈkwɔːtəli/ *noun* anything that is issued or paid every three months

quarto /'kwɔːtəʊ/ *noun* a size of book made by folding a standard sheet of paper twice, to make four leaves or an eight-page signature. Abbr **4o**

quasi- /kweɪzaɪ/ *prefix* used with adjectives or less frequently with nouns, to describe things which are very like other things but not actually the same

quasi-official /ˌkweɪzaɪ əˈfɪʃ(ə)l/ *adjective* appearing to be official, but not really so

quasi-synonym /ˌkweɪzaɪ 'sɪnənɪm/ *noun* a word which appears to be similar in meaning to another, but actually is not

query /'kwɪəri/ *noun* **1.** a question, especially a note asking the author or editor to check the text **2.** a question mark ■ *verb* to ask a question about something or to suggest that something may be wrong ○ *The sub-editor has queried the date given in the index.*

query facility /'kwɪəri fəˌsɪlɪti/ *noun* a program, usually a database or retrieval system, that allows the user to ask questions and receive answers or access certain information according to the query

query language /'kwɪəri ˌlæŋgwɪdʒ/ *noun* a computer programming language in a database management system which allows a search to be done quickly and easily

question /'kwestʃ(ə)n/ *verb* **1.** to ask somebody a lot of questions **2.** to imply doubt about the truth of something

question mark /'kwestʃ(ə)n mɑːk/ *noun* a punctuation mark (?) used to show that a question is being asked

questionnaire /ˌkwestʃəˈneə/ *noun* a written list of questions given to people to answer to provide the information for a survey

questionnaire design /ˌkwestʃə 'neə dɪˌzaɪn/ *noun* the technique of writing questionnaires in order to avoid bias in the answers

queue /kjuː/ *noun* a line of people or tasks waiting to be dealt with

quick reference /ˌkwɪk 'ref(ə)rəns/ *noun* a system of finding answers to queries which provides rapid but not very detailed answers

quicksort /'kwɪksɔːt/ *noun* a method of sorting and ordering information very quickly on a computer

quorate /'kwɔːreɪt/ *adjective* having the minimum required number of people at a meeting

quota sampling /'kwəʊtə ˌsɑːmplɪŋ/ *noun* a method of selecting the population for a survey by choosing a fixed proportion of people from each group

quotation /kwəʊ'teɪʃ(ə)n/ *noun* the exact words said or written by somebody and used by another person

quotation dictionary /kwəʊ 'teɪʃ(ə)n ˌdɪkʃ(ə)nəri/ *noun* a collection of famous sayings and writings arranged alphabetically according to the authors

quotation marks /kwəʊ'teɪʃ(ə)n mɑːks/ *plural noun* punctuation marks, either single quotes (' ') or double quotes (" "), which mark the beginning and end of a written quotation

quote /kwəʊt/ *verb* to repeat the exact words written or said by somebody else ■ *noun* □ **in quotes** written inside quotation marks

quotidian /kwəʊ'tɪdiən/ *adjective* daily

quotient /'kwəʊʃ(ə)nt/ *noun* the level or degree of a quality ○ *The stress quotient in that job is very high.*

qwerty keyboard /'kwɜːti ˌkiːbɔːd/ *noun* the layout of keys on a computer keyboard, the first six letters on the top row from the left being QWERTY which gives it its name

R

rack /ræk/ *noun* a frame for holding things, often used for display purposes

radio /'reɪdiəʊ/ *noun* **1.** equipment used to broadcast speech, sounds and data over long distances **2.** broadcasting to the public using this equipment ○ *Radio is a powerful medium for information.*

Radio Frequency Identification

/ˌreɪdiəʊ ˌfriːkwənsi aɪˌdentɪfɪ'keɪʃ(ə)n/ *noun* full form of **RFID**

radio phone /'reɪdiəʊ fəʊn/ *noun* a mobile two-way communications system that can access the public telephone network

radio station /'reɪdiəʊ ˌsteɪʃ(ə)n/ *noun* the place from where a particular broadcasting company transmits its programmes

ragged margin /ˌrægɪd 'mɑːdʒɪn/ *noun* an uneven or unjustified right margin to a block of writing

RAM /ræm/ *abbreviation* random access memory

RAM chip /'ræm tʃɪp/ *noun* a chip that stores information allowing random access

R&D *abbreviation* research and development

random /'rændəm/ *adjective* done without any definite plan

random-access /ˌrændəm 'ækses/ *adjective* relating to the capability of a computer to obtain information from any memory location without having to begin its search at the memory's starting point and work through it in sequence

random access memory /ˌrændəm 'ækses ˌmem(ə)ri/ *noun* the primary working memory in a computer, used for the temporary storage of programs and data and in which the data can be accessed directly and modified

random error /ˌrændəm 'erə/ *noun* a computer error which has no special reason

random number /ˌrændəm 'nʌmbə/ *noun* a number that cannot be predicted

random sampling /ˌrændəm 'sɑːmplɪŋ/ *noun* a system of compiling unbiased samples in a survey population

Ranfurly Library Service /ˌrænfɜːli 'laɪbrəri ˌsɜːvɪs/ *noun* ♦ **Book Aid International**

range /reɪndʒ/ *noun* a large freestanding bookcase in a library that is built to hold books on both sides

rank /ræŋk/ *verb* to put into order according to size or merit

rapid /'ræpɪd/ *adjective* very quick

rare books /ˌreə 'bʊks/ *plural noun* relatively modern books which are not in print and are not easy to find

ratings /'reɪtɪŋz/ *plural noun* a measurement of size of the audience for TV programmes

raw data /ˌrɔː 'deɪtə/ *noun* data that has not yet been processed and compiled by a computer

re /riː/ *preposition* used in business English to refer to something which is to be discussed ○ *Re your letter of 12th Sept, I can now tell you...*

re- /riː/ *prefix* used with verbs and nouns to indicate repetition ○ *They will re-order the book when it becomes available.*

react to /ri'ækt tʊ/ *verb* to act in response to an earlier event

read /riːd/ *verb* to look at and understand what is written down

readable /'riːdəb(ə)l/ *adjective* **1.** able to be read, also implies well written and interesting **2.** in a form which can be processed e.g. by a machine ○ *data in computer-readable form*

reader /'riːdə/ *noun* a person or device that reads written or printed texts

readership /'riːdəʃɪp/ *noun* the number of people who read a publication

reading age /'riːdɪŋ eɪdʒ/ *noun* a child's competence in reading, measured against the average competence of children of the same age

reading group /'riːdɪŋ gruːp/ *noun* a group of people who meet regularly in a social situation to discuss a book, usually a book that the group has all read especially for that occasion

reading list /'riːdɪŋ lɪst/ *noun* a list of recommended books on a specific subject

reading matter /'riːdɪŋ ˌmætə/ *noun* anything which can be read

reading room /'riːdɪŋ ruːm/ *noun* a room in a library where users can sit and read quietly

Readme file /'riːdmiː faɪl/ *noun* a computer information file containing instructions about how to use a program or information on latest developments

read only memory /ˌriːd ˌəʊnli 'mem(ə)ri/ *noun* full form of **ROM**

read/write head /ˌriːd 'raɪt ˌhed/ *noun* a device in a disk drive that can read data on a disk or add data to a disk

ready /'redi/ *adjective* prepared and able to be used or to do something

ready money /ˌredi 'mʌni/ *noun* cash in notes and coins rather than cheques, cards or other electronic transfer forms

ready reference /ˌredi 'ref(ə)rəns/ *noun* easily accessible information

realise /'rɪəlaɪz/, **realize** *verb* **1.** to understand what is happening **2.** to make a physical representation of an idea as in a design

Really Simple Syndication /ˌrɪəli ˌsɪmp(ə)l ˌsɪndɪ'keɪʃ(ə)n/ *noun* full form of **RSS**

real-time system /'rɪəl taɪm ˌsɪstəm/ *noun* a computer system where data is inputted directly into the computer which automatically processes it to produce information that can be used immediately

ream /riːm/ *noun* 500 sheets of paper in a pack

COMMENT: For ordinary writing paper and handmade paper, a ream is 480 sheets, or 20 quires of 24 sheets each. For office paper or printing paper a ream is 500 sheets, or 20 quires of 25 sheets.

reback /riː'bæk/ *verb* to take the leather back off the spine of an old book and replace it

rebind /riː'baɪnd/ *verb* to remove an old binding from a book and replace it with another one ○ *The stock of paperback copies have been rebound in PVC.*

COMMENT: Rebinding means that the old covers have to be stripped off, new covers attached and the pages trimmed again. At least one or two millimetres will be lost at each of the three trimmed edges.

recall /rɪ'kɔːl/ *noun* **1.** retrieval of a document from an information store **2.** the number of relevant records returned by a search, expressed as a percentage of the total number of relevant records in the database ■ *verb* **1.** to request the return of a library book **2.** to bring back data or text on to the screen of a computer

'Extensive print management facilities include the ability to recall and resize previous copy jobs without rescanning, and the practical function of being able to monitor and amend print queues according to priority.' [*M2 Presswire*]

receive /rɪ'siːv/ *verb* to accept things that are sent or given to you

received opinion /rɪˌsiːvd ə'pɪnjən/ *noun* an opinion or method that is generally accepted as correct

Received Pronunciation /rɪˌsiːvd prəˌnʌnsi'eɪʃ(ə)n/ *noun* the standard accent of spoken British English with no regional variations. Abbr **RP**

recent /ˈriːs(ə)nt/ *adjective* happening only a short time earlier

recently /ˈriːs(ə)ntli/ *adverb* not long ago ○ *her recently-published book*

reception /rɪˈsepʃən/ *noun* **1.** the quality of radio or TV signal received **2.** an area for receiving visitors to a building

receptionist /rɪˈsepʃənɪst/ *noun* a person who works in a reception area, greeting and advising people who arrive

reciprocal /rɪˈsɪprək(ə)l/ *adjective* agreed because it is mutually beneficial ○ *a reciprocal arrangement which meant they both made a profit*

recode /riːˈkəʊd/ *verb* to change the coding in a retrieval system so that it will work in another system

recognise /ˈrekəgnaɪz/, **recognize** *verb* to see something and remember that it has been seen before

recognised fact /ˌrekəgnaɪzd ˈfækt/ *noun* a fact which is generally accepted as true

recognition /ˌrekəgˈnɪʃ(ə)n/ *noun* a process that allows something to be recognised

recommend /ˌrekəˈmend/ *verb* to advise that something is good or useful because you have experience of using it

recondite /rɪˈkɒndaɪt/ *adjective* **1.** requiring a high degree of scholarship or specialist knowledge to be understood **2.** dealing with material that is too difficult to be understood by those without special knowledge

reconfigure /ˌriːkənˈfɪgə/ *verb* to alter the structure of data within a system

record /ˈrekɔːd/ *noun* **1.** a written account either on paper or in electronic format **2.** a measurement of some achievement which has not been surpassed ○ *We have broken all sales records with this title.* ■ *verb* to write down or preserve something on film or tape so that it can be used for later reference

record analysis /ˈrekɔːd əˌnælɪsɪs/ *noun* an analysis of the information contained in a set of records

record clerk /ˈrekɔːd klɜːk/ *noun* a person who has the job of filing records

record control /ˈrekɔːd kənˌtrəʊl/ *noun* a system for organising records so that they can be traced, referred to or disposed of as necessary

record disposal /ˈrekɔːd dɪsˌpəʊz(ə)l/ *noun* the process of destroying records when they are no longer needed

recorded information /rɪˌkɔːdɪd ˌɪnfəˈmeɪʃ(ə)n/ *noun* information which has been recorded on tape or disk

record inventory /ˈrekɔːd ˌɪnvent(ə)ri/ *noun* a list of all the records held in a system

record management audit /ˈrekɔːd ˌmænɪdʒmənt ˌɔːdɪt/ *noun* an official check on the efficiency and effectiveness of the record management within an organisation

record management manual /ˈrekɔːd ˌmænɪdʒmənt ˌmænjuəl/ *noun* a book of instructions for users of the record management system

record management programme /ˈrekɔːd ˌmænɪdʒmənt ˌprəʊgræm/ *noun* a company policy programme for the control of records

record management software /ˈrekɔːd ˌmænɪdʒmənt ˌsɒftweə/ *noun* computer software which enables records to be stored and retrieved

record office /ˈrekɔːd ˌɒfɪs/ *noun* a form of archive library

record retrieval /ˈrekɔːd rɪˌtriːv(ə)l/ *noun* the process of finding documents and making them available

'[Data management software] PiImageX(TM) was developed specifically to increase efficiencies associated with underwriting and claim processing by reducing record retrieval turnaround times by as much as 40%.' [*Market Wire*]

record retrieval management /ˈrekɔːd rɪˌtriːv(ə)l ˌmænɪdʒmənt/ *noun* the organisation and control of record retrieval

records /ˈrekɔːdz/ *plural noun* documents which give information ○ *The names and addresses of authors are kept in the company's records.* ○ *We find from our records that our invoice number 1234 has not been paid.*

records information officer
/'rekɔːdz ˌɪnfəmeɪʃ(ə)n ˌɒfɪsə/ *noun*
1. an archivist who works in a records
office **2.** a company information
specialist who manages the record
supply

record storage /'rekɔːd ˌstɔːrɪdʒ/
noun a system of storing records so that
they can be retrieved easily

record supply /'rekɔːd səˌplaɪ/
noun the provision of records as
required

record transfer /'rekɔːd ˌtrænsfɜː/
noun the process of transferring records
from one system to another

record transfer document
/'rekɔːd ˌtrænsfɜː ˌdɒkjʊmənt/ *noun*
a form which gives details of the record
to be transferred and is used for record
control

record update /'rekɔːd ˌʌpdeɪt/
noun a system of keeping records up to
date by changing data as necessary

record vault /'rekɔːd vɔːlt/ *noun* a
secure room where confidential records
can be kept safely

recover /rɪ'kʌvə/ *verb* **1.** to replace a
cover on a document or book which has
been damaged **2.** to get back something
that has been lost

'With a few mouse clicks, even non-
technical end users can selectively
restore a deleted file, recover a
previous version of a file, or
completely restore the hard drive to a
pre-crash working state.' [*M2
Presswire*]

recoverable /rɪ'kʌv(ə)rəb(ə)l/
adjective able to be retrieved after being
lost

recoverable error /rɪˌkʌv(ə)rəb(ə)l
'erə/ *noun* a program error that can be
corrected without causing a computer
program to fail or data to be erased irre-
trievably. For example, if a user enters
obviously wrong data, the program
might request a different entry.

recovery procedure /rɪ'kʌv(ə)ri
prəˌsiːdʒə/ *noun* methods of finding
what has been lost, especially when
using a computer

rectify /'rektɪfaɪ/ *verb* to correct a
mistake

recto /'rektəʊ/ *noun* the right-hand
page of a book, usually given an odd
number

recur /rɪ'kɜː/ *verb* to happen again
once or several times

recurring subject /rɪˌkɜːrɪŋ
'sʌbjekt/ *noun* an item in a record
system that appears many times

redefine /ˌriːdɪ'faɪn/ *verb* to change
the function or value assigned to a variable

redirect /ˌriːdaɪ'rekt/ *verb* **1.** (*in
computing*) to send a message to its
destination by an alternative route **2.** to
send mail to a new address after it has
been delivered to the old one

red tape /ˌred 'teɪp/ *noun* official
rules and regulations which seem to
have no obvious value

reduce /rɪ'djuːs/ *verb* to make something smaller in amount

reduction /rɪ'dʌkʃən/ *noun* the act of
reducing something such as size or cost
○ *They were able to make a 75% reduction of the document on the photocopier
so fewer copies were needed and the
cost was less.*

redundancy /rɪ'dʌndənsi/ *noun*
words or symbols that do not add to
meaning

redundant /rɪ'dʌndənt/ *adjective* **1.**
no longer needed because it has been
replaced by a more up-to-date version **2.**
able to be removed from data without
losing any information

reel /riːl/ *noun* a circular holder around
which tape can be wound

reel off /ˌriːl 'ɒf/ *verb* to repeat information quickly from memory

reel to reel /ˌriːl tə 'riːl/ *adjective*
playing data on one tape on to another
without enclosing it in a cassette

referee /ˌrefə'riː/ *noun* a person who
provides information about whether
somebody known to them is suitable for
a particular job

reference /'ref(ə)rəns/ *noun* **1.** a
letter written by a person to support
somebody's application for a job **2.**
coded information which tells you
where to find a document or stored item
○ *our reference: PC/MS 1234* ○ *Please
quote this reference in all correspond-*

ence. **3.** an acknowledgement of somebody else's work quoted in a written document **4.** a source of information, e.g. a dictionary or an encyclopedia ○ *a reference book* **5.** a note directing a reader's attention to another source of information

reference book /ˈref(ə)rəns bʊk/ *noun* an information book such as a dictionary, encyclopedia or directory in which you can look things up

reference collection /ˈref(ə)rəns kəˌlekʃ(ə)n/ *noun* books in a library which can only be used within the library and cannot be borrowed

reference database /ˈref(ə)rəns ˌdeɪtəbeɪs/ *noun* a large database which can be searched for information on a particular subject

reference interview /ˈref(ə)rəns ˌɪntəvjuː/ *noun* a discussion between a user and the reference librarian to establish exactly what information is required

reference librarian /ˈref(ə)rəns laɪ ˌbreəriən/ *noun* a qualified person who works in a reference library to control the retrieval systems and supply information

reference library /ˈref(ə)rəns ˌlaɪbrəri/ *noun* a library where the books and documents can only be used within the building and cannot be borrowed

'Although copies of the sought-after video are not for sale, a copy is available to borrow from Crownhill Library. Copies are also held by the central reference library, and by local schools in the area.' [*Evening Herald*]

reference manual /ˈref(ə)rəns ˌmænjuəl/ *noun* a book of instructions about how to use a machine which can be referred to when learning how to use the machine or when problems occur

reference mark /ˈref(ə)rəns mɑːk/ *noun* a typographical symbol used to draw the attention of a reader to a note or bibliographical entry, e.g. an asterisk or number

reference material /ˈref(ə)rəns mə ˌtɪəriəl/ *noun* books, documents and materials kept in a reference library or designated area

reference number /ˈref(ə)rəns ˌnʌmbə/ *noun* a number or letter that identifies a document and makes it easier to find when it has been filed

reference request form /ˌref(ə)rəns rɪˈkwest ˌfɔːm/ *noun* a form which users fill in to give details of exactly which reference books or documents they require to be fetched from stock

reference source /ˈref(ə)rəns sɔːs/ *noun* any source of information which can be searched

reference tool /ˈref(ə)rəns tuːl/ *noun* an index or retrieval system which helps the user to search for information

referral /rɪˈfɜːrəl/ *noun* the act of sending something or somebody to a person who is better able to deal with them

referral centre /rɪˈfɜːrəl ˌsentə/ *noun* an organisation which directs researchers to information and appropriate sources but does not supply documents

refer to /rɪˈfɜː tuː/ *verb* **1.** to mention, deal with or write about something ○ *She referred to an article which she had seen in the Times.* **2.** to pass a question on to someone else to decide

reformat /riːˈfɔːmæt/ *verb* to format a computer floppy disk and so erase any data on it

refresh /rɪˈfreʃ/ *verb* to update an electronic device, especially a visual display unit or active memory chip, with data

refusal /rɪˈfjuːz(ə)l/ *noun* a deliberate statement that you will not do, say or allow something

regenerate /rɪˈdʒenəreɪt/ *verb* to reactivate something after a period of decline, so that it is improved

register /ˈredʒɪstə/ *noun* **1.** an official list of things such as names or events **2.** a ribbon attached to the binding of a book to act as a bookmark **3.** the fact of being correctly aligned with something else on a page ○ *The text is in register with the image.* ○ *The running heads are out of register.* ■ *verb* to make a record of something on an official list □ **to**

register for to put one's name on an official list for something

registration /ˌredʒɪ'streɪʃ(ə)n/ *noun* the act of recording something on an official list

registration card /ˌredʒɪ'streɪʃ(ə)n ˌkɑːd/ *noun* a card that is filled in with personal details to register for membership of something

regress /rɪ'gres/ *verb* to return to an earlier bad position

regular /'regjʊlə/ *noun* a person who frequently uses the same services ▪ *adjective* happening at equal intervals

regular edition /'regjʊlə ɪˌdɪʃ(ə)n/ *noun* an ordinary edition, as opposed to a particular type such as a de luxe or book club edition

regulate /'regjʊleɪt/ *verb* to control the behaviour of a situation or a machine

reimburse /ˌriːɪm'bɜːs/ *verb* to pay back money spent by somebody else while they were doing something for you

reinforced binding /ˌriːɪnfɔːst 'baɪndɪŋ/ *noun* a binding which is strengthened at the joints for heavy wear as in a library, or for a particularly heavy book

reinstate /ˌriːɪn'steɪt/ *verb* to give somebody back a job that has previously been taken away

reissue /riː'ɪʃuː/ *noun* a book or document that is made available again after a period of time ▪ *verb* to produce or publish again something that has not been available for a long time

reject *noun* /'riːdʒekt/ a product that is not up to standard, so is sold cheaply or not at all ▪ *verb* /rɪ'dʒekt/ to refuse to accept something

rekey /riː'kiː/ *verb* to re-enter lost text or data into a computer, or input text or data in a different form, using a keyboard

relate /rɪ'leɪt/ *verb* to show the connection between two things

related work /rɪˌleɪtɪd 'wɜːk/ *noun* a document which has some connection with another, e.g. a supplement or sequel

relational /rɪ'leɪʃ(ə)nəl/ *adjective* relating to a way of organising and presenting information in a database so that the user perceives it as a set of tables

relational database /rɪˌleɪʃ(ə)n(ə)l 'deɪtəbeɪs/ *noun* a database in which all the items of data can be interconnected. Data is retrieved by using one item of data to search for a related field.

relational index /rɪˌleɪʃ(ə)n(ə)l 'ɪndeks/ *noun* an index which shows the relationship between works by the use of symbols

relationship /rɪ'leɪʃ(ə)nʃɪp/ *noun* the way in which two things are connected or linked together

relative /'relətɪv/ *adjective* relating to the qualities of something by comparing it with something else

relative clause /'relətɪv klɔːz/ *noun* a clause that refers to and provides additional information about a preceding noun or pronoun, often beginning with a relative pronoun such as 'who', 'which' or 'that'

relatively /'relətɪvli/ *adverb* in comparison to other things ○ *A relatively small number applied this year compared to last year.*

relay /'riːleɪ/ *verb* to transmit, broadcast or repeat what has been said or written

release /rɪ'liːs/ *verb* to make something available

relevance /'reləv(ə)ns/ *noun* the relationship to the subject

'To the best of my knowledge no one has yet conducted tests on the recall and relevance ratios of Web site searches conducted using search engines, but it certainly seems that though with diligence and luck recall may be high, relevance is likely to be extremely low.' [*Information Technology and Libraries*]

relevance ratio /'reləv(ə)ns ˌreɪʃiəʊ/ *noun* the number of documents wanted in relation to the number retrieved which are relevant to the subject searched

relevant /'reləv(ə)nt/ *adjective* connected with and appropriate for what is being discussed or written about

reliability /rɪˌlaɪə'bɪlɪti/ *noun* the quality of being reliable

reliable /rɪ'laɪəb(ə)l/ *adjective* able to be trusted or depended on to function or behave as expected

relocate /ˌriːləʊ'keɪt/ *verb* to move data, people or an organisation from one place to another

reluctant user /rɪˌlʌktənt 'juːzə/ *noun* somebody who is forced to use a service but does not want to ○ *Some children are reluctant users of the school library.*

remainder /rɪ'meɪndə/ *noun* **1.** something left when demand has fallen **2.** a book sold cheaply to clear stock ■ *verb* to deal with a book as a remainder

remaindered publication /rɪˌmeɪndəd ˌpʌblɪ'keɪʃ(ə)n/ *noun* a book that will not be reprinted because demand has almost ceased and so the stock is sold cheaply

remedial /rɪ'miːdiəl/ *adjective* designed to correct a damaged situation or previous learning failure

remedy /'remədi/ *noun* a successful way of dealing with a difficult situation

remote access /rɪˌməʊt 'ækses/ *noun* access that is gained to a computer by means of a separate terminal

remote control /rɪˌməʊt kən'trəʊl/ *noun* a system of controlling a device from a distance by means of radio or electronic signals ○ *Using remote control she could listen to her answer-phone messages when she was away from the office.*

removable /rɪ'muːvəb(ə)l/ *adjective* able to be taken away ○ *The records which were no longer needed were removable.*

rename /riː'neɪm/ *verb* to give a different name to somebody or something ○ *They renamed all the computer files when they reorganised the system.*

renew /rɪ'njuː/ *verb* to extend the period of time for which a contract or a loan is valid ○ *They were told that they could not renew their books because*

they had been reserved by another reader.

renumber /'sɒnɪk/ *verb* to change the numbers on items or within a system

repaginate /riː'pædʒɪneɪt/ *verb* to change the numbers on the pages in a document

repetitive /rɪ'petɪtɪv/ *adjective* repeated many times

repetitive letter /rɪˌpetɪtɪv 'letə/ *noun* a standard letter which is reprinted with a different name and address each time

replace /rɪ'pleɪs/ *verb* **1.** to put something back where it was before **2.** to put a new item in the place of one that is broken, worn out or unsuitable ○ *The third paragraph should be deleted and replaced by the new text as shown.*

replacement /rɪ'pleɪsmənt/ *noun* a person or thing that takes the place of another ○ *The new library book was a replacement for the one that was lost.*

replace mode /rɪ'pleɪs məʊd/ *noun* an interactive computer mode in which new text entered replaces any previous text

replicate /'replɪkeɪt/ *verb* to make an exact copy of something such as an action or research method

report /rɪ'pɔːt/ *noun* a formal document that discusses a particular subject or states exactly what happened

report generator /rɪ'pɔːt ˌdʒenəreɪtə/ *noun* a word-processing facility for producing business reports on personal computers

repository /rɪ'pɒzɪt(ə)ri/ *noun* a book or archive store

representations /ˌreprɪzen'teɪʃ(ə)nz/ *plural noun* a formal request, complaint or statement made to an official body

representative /ˌreprɪ'zentətɪv/ *noun* a person who acts on behalf of another or of a group

reprint *noun* /'riːprɪnt/ copies of a book made from the original, but with a note in the publication details of the date of reprinting and possibly a new title page and cover design ■ *verb* /riː'prɪnt/ to print more copies of a book after all the others have been sold

reprinting /riːˈprɪntɪŋ/ *adjective* relating to a note indicating that a book cannot be supplied because it is being reprinted

reproduce /ˌriːprəˈdjuːs/ *verb* to produce copies of an item

reprographic equipment /ˌriːprə ˈɡræfɪk ɪˌkwɪpmənt/ *noun* machines such as photocopiers used to produce copies of documents and materials

reprography /rɪˈprɒɡrəfi/ *noun* the technique of producing copies

request /rɪˈkwest/ *verb* to ask formally for something

request document /rɪˈkwest ˌdɒkjʊmənt/ *noun* **1.** a form which must be filled in asking for a restricted document **2.** a document that has been requested for use in a closed access system

request form /rɪˈkwest fɔːm/ *noun* a form that is filled in to ask for an item which is not immediately available

require /rɪˈkwaɪə/ *verb* **1.** to need something **2.** to demand something from somebody □ **to be required to do** to have to do something because of a rule or regulation

requirement /rɪˈkwaɪəmənt/ *noun* something that is essential in order to do what you want

requisite /ˈrekwɪzɪt/ *adjective* necessary for a particular purpose ○ *They needed time to collect the requisite number of references.*

re-run /ˈriːrʌn/ *noun* a film or programme that is shown again

research /rɪˈsɜːtʃ/ *noun* work that is done to investigate something ■ *verb* to investigate a field of study and discover new facts about it

research and development /rɪ ˌsɜːtʃ ən dɪˈveləpmənt/ *noun* work in an organisation which researches new products or services and makes recommendations. Abbr **R&D**

research assistant /rɪˈsɜːtʃ ə ˌsɪstənt/ *noun* a person who helps a writer by doing research for him or her

researcher /rɪˈsɜːtʃə/ *noun* a person who carries out research

research establishment /rɪˈsɜːtʃ esˌtæblɪʃmənt/ *noun* an institution devoted to the work of research in a particular subject area

research tool /rɪˈsɜːtʃ tuːl/ *noun* a system of discovering or measuring facts, e.g. a questionnaire

'England's 149 public library authorities are being encouraged to save money by using a new online reference tool from the Museums, Libraries and Archives Council, the first initiative of its kind in the country.' [*Datamonitor NewsWire*]

reserve /rɪˈzɜːv/ *noun* a supply of things kept for use if the regular supplies have been used before replacements can be obtained

reserve collection /rɪˈzɜːv kə ˌlekʃ(ə)n/ *noun* **1.** a set of books for which there is little demand and which are kept in a closed store **2.** a set of books for which there is heavy demand as in an academic library and which are put in a short loan collection for limited period loan

reserved book /rɪˈzɜːvd bʊk/ *noun* a book that has been specially requested to be obtained as it is not available at the time of the request

reset /riːˈset/ *verb* to return a system to its original state so that it can start again

resident font /ˌrezɪd(ə)nt ˈfɒnt/ *noun* font data which is always present in a printer or device and which does not have to be downloaded

residual /rɪˈzɪdjuəl/ *adjective* remaining after everything else has been used

resist /rɪˈzɪst/ *verb* to refuse to accept or do something and even try to prevent it happening

resistance to change /rɪˌzɪstəns tə ˈtʃeɪndʒ/ *noun* a refusal to accept changes often in working conditions or practices

resolution /ˌrezəˈluːʃ(ə)n/ *noun* **1.** a formal decision taken at a meeting by means of a vote **2.** the solving of a problem ○ *The resolution of her difficulties with the immigration authorities took a long time.*

resource /rɪ'zɔːs/ *noun* information in a variety of formats which is useful and available

Resource /rɪ'zɔːs/ *noun* ◆ **Museums, Libraries and Archives Council**

resource-based learning /rɪˌzɔːs beɪst 'lɜːnɪŋ/ *noun* a method of teaching in which the student is allowed free access to resources in order to solve problems or undertake research on set topics

resource centre /rɪ'zɔːs ˌsentə/ *noun* a collection of books and audio-visual materials which is organised for people to use in schools or universities

respond /rɪ'spɒnd/ *verb* to reply or react to something said or done

response /rɪ'spɒns/ *noun* a reaction or reply to an event, action or statement

response rates /rɪ'spɒns reɪts/ *plural noun* the percentage of people who reply to a questionnaire or survey

responsibility /rɪˌspɒnsɪ'bɪlɪti/ *noun* □ **have responsibility for** to have a duty to deal with a situation or person because of one's position

responsible /rɪ'spɒnsɪb(ə)l/ *adjective* involving important duties and the need to make decisions □ **be responsible to** to work under a controlling person or body and have to report to them

restart /riː'stɑːt/ *verb* to begin again, often used as an option in computer systems

restore /rɪ'stɔː/ *verb* to return things to their previous state, position or owner

restrict /rɪ'strɪkt/ *verb* to limit something so that only a specific person or group can have access to it

restricted /rɪ'strɪktɪd/ *adjective* limited to particular uses or people

restricted access /rɪ'strɪktɪd ˌækses/ *adjective* only allowed to be seen or used by named individuals or groups ○ *If the information is classified as restricted access, only members can use it.*

result /rɪ'zʌlt/ *noun* the outcome of an event or activity ○ *The results of her exams were so good that she was given a scholarship for further study.*

retailer /'riːteɪlə/ *noun* a person who sells goods to the public

retainer /rɪ'teɪnə/ *noun* a fee paid to somebody so that they will be available to work for you when required

retention schedule /rɪ'tenʃ(ə)n ˌʃedjuːl/ *noun* a list of documents held for reference

retouch /riː'tʌtʃ/ *verb* to improve a photograph, painting or surface by painting over parts of it

retrain /riː'treɪn/ *verb* to teach somebody new skills, or learn new skills

retrieval /rɪ'triːv(ə)l/ *noun* the process of finding items that have been stored

retrieval system /rɪ'triːv(ə)l ˌsɪstəm/ *noun* a system of organising items so that information can be found quickly and easily

'Uttlesford District Council required a back-up and retrieval system to meet legislative demands regarding information management and to more cost-effectively and efficiently manage data. Data growth was outstripping capacity and the council needed to comply with government guidelines to make information available online.' [*Computer Weekly*]

retrieve /rɪ'triːv/ *verb* to get something back from where it has been stored

retrospective /ˌretrəʊ'spektɪv/ *adjective* concerned with things that take effect from an earlier date than when the decision is made ○ *The changes in the salary structure will be retrospective to last April.*

return /rɪ'tɜːn/ *noun* the act of giving something back ○ *The date for the return of all the library books is next week.* ■ *verb* to give something back or to change it so that it is in its earlier state again ○ *to return the company to its former position by investing a large amount of capital*

return key /rɪ'tɜːn kiː/ *noun* a key on a computer keyboard which gives the instruction for the machine to process the data entered

return on investment /rɪˌtɜːn ɒn ɪn'vestmənt/ *noun* a profit made by investing money in something which is financially successful. Abbr **ROI**

retype /riːˈtaɪp/ *verb* to type a word, phrase or document again, usually in order to make changes or to correct errors

revealing /rɪˈviːlɪŋ/ *adjective* giving away new, surprising or valuable information

revert /rɪˈvɜːt/ *verb* to return to an earlier state or system ○ *Although they spoke slowly to the foreigner at first they soon reverted to their normal speed of talking.*

review /rɪˈvjuː/ *noun* an evaluation of a book or other publication or a performance ■ *verb* to look again at a situation to assess what can be done

review copy /rɪˈvjuː ˌkɒpi/ *noun* a copy of a book given to a reviewer

revise /rɪˈvaɪz/ *verb* **1.** to change something so that it is more accurate **2.** to go over work done earlier in order to learn it more thoroughly

revised edition /rɪˈvaɪsd ɪˌdɪʃ(ə)n/ *noun* a book that has been reprinted with some changes, usually to bring it up to date

revised plan /rɪˌvaɪsd ˈplæn/ *noun* a plan that has been changed after consideration in order to make it more suitable for the task to be done

revision /rɪˈvɪʒ(ə)n/ *noun* **1.** the improvement and correction of a text **2.** a change which is made to improve something **3.** the activity of re-learning work in order to do an examination

reward /rɪˈwɔːd/ *noun* something given in return for doing a thing well

rewrite /riːˈraɪt/ *verb* to write something again with improvements

RFID /ˈɑːfɪd/ *noun* an electronic tracking chip which can be attached to books so that they can be automatically checked in and out. Full form **Radio Frequency Identification**

rhetorical question /rɪˌtɒrɪk(ə)l ˈkwestʃən/ *noun* a question that is used as a statement and does not expect an answer

rhyming dictionary /ˈraɪmɪŋ ˌdɪkʃ(ə)nəri/ *noun* a dictionary which organises words in groups of rhymes so that they are useful for writers of poetry

right aligned /ˌraɪt əˈlaɪnd/ *adjective* with the right-hand margin straight

right-hand corner /ˌraɪt hænd ˈkɔːnə/ *noun* the top or bottom corner at the right side of a page or envelope

right justification /ˌraɪt ˌdʒʌstɪfɪˈkeɪʃ(ə)n/ *noun* the process of aligning the right-hand margin on a piece of text so that the edge is straight

right justify /ˌraɪt ˈdʒʌstɪfaɪ/ *verb* to use a computer program to ensure that the right-hand margins of text are straight

rights /raɪts/ *plural noun* the legal right to publish something such as a book, picture or extract from a text

rigmarole /ˈrɪgmərəʊl/ *noun* a long, complicated story or procedure ○ *She told me some rigmarole about having lost her ticket.*

ring back /ˌrɪŋ ˈbæk/ *verb* to telephone somebody after they have telephoned you first

ring binder /ˈrɪŋ ˌbaɪndə/ *noun* a binder made of two hard covers with a ring attachment into which papers can be put, with holes punched in each sheet of paper to slip over the metal rings

ring off /ˌrɪŋ ˈɒf/ *verb* to finish a telephone call and replace the receiver

ring up /ˌrɪŋ ˈʌp/ *verb* to telephone somebody

risk /rɪsk/ *noun* the danger or chance of loss or injury □ **at your own risk** doing something with understanding of the danger and accepting responsibility for the outcome ■ *verb* to do something even though you know it may have dangerous or unpleasant results

RLOGIN /ˈɑːˌlɒgɪn/ *noun* a gateway to Internet files. ◊ **Telnet**

ro *abbreviation* in Internet addresses, the top-level domain for Romania

road atlas /ˈrəʊd ˌætləs/, **road map** /ˈrəʊd mæp/ *noun* a map which shows the roads that are passable by motor traffic but does not include very small roads or paths

road plan /ˈrəʊd plæn/ *noun* a map showing all the roads in an area

rogue site /ˈrəʊg saɪt/ *noun* a website that acquires visitors by having a domain name similar to that of a popular site

ROI *abbreviation* return on investment

role /rəʊl/ *noun* a function or position within an organisation

role playing /ˈrəʊl ˌpleɪɪŋ/ *noun* the activity of acting out the behaviour of somebody different from oneself as part of a training exercise

roll call /ˈrəʊl kɔːl/ *noun* a way of checking the people present by calling out their names and waiting for them to answer

rolling header /ˈrəʊlɪŋ ˈhedə/, **rolling footer** /ˌrəʊlɪŋ ˈfʊtə/ *noun* a title that is repeated at the top or bottom of every page in a document

roll of film /ˌrəʊl əv ˈfɪlm/ *noun* a length of film wound round itself and ready for use in a camera

ROM /rɒm/ *noun* a computer system which allows data to be read but not edited. Full form **read only memory.** ◊ **CD-ROM** (NOTE: There is no plural for ROM, and it is often used without the article: **The file is stored in ROM.**)

Roman /ˈrəʊmən/ *adjective* referring to ancient Italy, and especially to the Latin script

Romance language /rəˈmæns ˌlæŋgwɪdʒ/ *noun* any of the European languages that are almost entirely based on Latin, including French, Italian, Spanish, Portuguese and Romanian

romanisation /ˌrəʊmənaɪˈzeɪʃ(ə)n/, **romanization** *noun* transliterating a non-Western script into Roman characters

romanise /ˈrəʊmənaɪz/, **romanize** *verb* to transliterate a non-Western script into Roman characters ○ *a Romanised version of Chinese*

Roman numerals /ˌrəʊmən ˈnjuːmərəlz/, **Roman figures** *noun* figures written I, II, III, IV, or i, ii, iii, iv, etc. (as opposed to Arabic numerals such as 1, 2, 3, 4)

ROM cartridge /ˈrɒm ˌkɑːtrɪdʒ/ *noun* software stored in a ROM mounted in a cartridge that can be easily plugged into a computer

roster /ˈrɒstə/ ♦ **rota**

rota /ˈrəʊtə/ *noun* a list of people who take turns to do a job ○ *According to the rota it will be my turn to work late at the library on Friday.*

rotate /rəʊˈteɪt/ *verb* **1.** to move in a circular way **2.** to take turns to do a job until everyone has had a turn before starting again with the first one

rough trimmed /ˌrʌf ˈtrɪmd/ *adjective* relating to an art book whose pages are not all trimmed to the same measure, e.g. where only the excessively long or wide pages are trimmed

round off /ˌraʊnd ˈɒf/, **round down** /ˌraʊnd ˈdaʊn/ *verb* to approximate a number to a slightly lower one, e.g. 1.2 becomes 1

round up /ˌraʊnd ˈʌp/ *verb* to approximate a number to a slightly higher one, e.g. 1.9 becomes 2

roundup /ˈraʊndʌp/ *noun* a summary of everything that has been said and shown before ○ *The newscaster gave a roundup of the evening's news.*

routeing /ˈruːtɪŋ/ *noun* distribution of written information among members of staff according to a routeing list

routeing list /ˈruːtɪŋ lɪst/ *noun* a list of names attached to the front cover of a document which is passed round several people to be read

routine /ruːˈtiːn/ *adjective* done every day as a regular part of one's job ■ *noun* a procedure which, if followed, helps to perform tasks in an efficient and organised way

'In practice, Knowledge Management encompasses both technological tools and organizational routines in overlapping parts. Knowledge Management is not just about creating a new department and implementing technology but rather about a change management process.' [*M2 Presswire*]

row /rəʊ/ *noun* a horizontal line in a table, as opposed to columns which are vertical

royal /ˈrɔɪəl/ *adjective* a traditional size of book and paper (25 x 20 inches)

COMMENT: The metric royal paper sizes are: royal octavo (234 x 156mm), royal quarto (312 x 237mm); the quad royal sheet is (1272 x 960mm).

RP *abbreviation* **1.** reprinting **2.** Received Pronunciation

RSS *noun* a format which allows pieces of microcontent to be sent as an automatic feed from their source to another website or a handset device. Full form **Really Simple Syndication**

RTF *noun* a text file format which includes text commands that describe the page, type, font and formatting ○ *The RTF format allows formatted pages to be exchanged between different word-processing software.* Full form **rich text format**

.rtf *suffix* a file extension for an RTF file

ru *abbreviation* in Internet addresses, the top-level domain for Russian Federation

rubber-stamp /ˌrʌbə ˈstæmp/ *verb* to agree to something without discussion or thought ■ *noun* a small block of rubber, metal or wood which is used in combination with ink to make a mark on something to show that it is official or to show ownership

rubric /ˈruːbrɪk/ *noun* a set of rules or instructions like those at the beginning of an examination paper

rule /ruːl/ *noun* a regulation telling what is and is not allowed

ruled paper /ˈruːld ˌpeɪpə/ *noun* paper that has lines printed on it for writing on

ruler /ˈruːlə/ *noun* a long, flat object calibrated in inches or centimetres which is used for measuring or drawing straight lines

ruling /ˈruːlɪŋ/ *noun* an official decision which must be obeyed

run /rʌn/ *verb* **1.** to take charge of and be responsible for an organisation or activity ○ *The head librarian will be running the next course.* **2.** to make a machine work ○ *They run the computer every day.* **3.** □ **to run risks** to do things even though you realise the result may be dangerous or not what you expect ■ *noun* □ **in the long run** over a long period of time □ **in the short run** in the near future

run down /ˌrʌn ˈdaʊn/ *verb* **1.** to reduce the amount of work done by a department or organisation **2.** to criticise somebody aggressively

run-down /ˌrʌn ˈdaʊn/ *adjective* in poor condition

running title /ˌrʌnɪŋ ˈtaɪt(ə)l/ *noun* a title that appears throughout a book or document at the top of each page

rw *abbreviation* in Internet addresses, the top-level domain for Rwanda

S

sa *abbreviation* in Internet addresses, the top-level domain for Saudi Arabia

sabbatical /sə'bætɪk(ə)l/ *noun* a period of time during which a teacher or lecturer is allowed to leave their duties for the purpose of study or travel

saddle stitch /'sæd(ə)l stɪtʃ/ *noun* in bookbinding, a method of binding the pages of a small book or magazine together by folding it in half and stitching along the line of the fold

safe deposit box /ˌseɪf dɪ'pɒzɪt ˌbɒks/ *noun* a box for the safe keeping of personal documents, usually stored in a bank

safety measure /'seɪfti ˌmeʒə/ *noun* a regulation to ensure that activities do not endanger anyone

saga /'sɑːɡə/ *noun* **1.** a long story about a particular time in history or group of people **2.** a story written between the 12th and 14th century about the Norwegian Vikings

salary /'sæləri/ *noun* money that is paid, usually monthly, to somebody for their job

sales /seɪlz/ *plural noun* the quantity of a product or service that is sold ○ *Sales of information are becoming more common nowadays.*

sales department /'seɪlz dɪˌpɑːtmənt/ *noun* a department in a company which organises the sales of its products

sales force /'seɪlz fɔːs/ *noun* a group of sales people working for one company

sales literature /'seɪlz ˌlɪt(ə)rətʃə/ *noun* printed information such as leaflets or prospectuses which helps sales

Salon du Livre /ˌsælɒn du 'liːvrə/ *noun* a book fair in a French-speaking country, e.g. the Paris Salon du Livre

sample /'sɑːmpəl/ *noun* a small quantity of a product used to show what it is like

sans serif /ˌsænz 'serɪf/ *noun* a style of printing letters with all lines of equal thickness and no serifs

satellite /'sætəlaɪt/ *noun* a device sent into space to collect information or to be part of a communications system

satire /'sætaɪə/ *noun* writing which aims to make readers or an audience recognise the foolishness of people, organisations or events in an amusing way

satirical /sə'tɪrɪk(ə)l/ *adjective* using satire

satisfaction /ˌsætɪs'fækʃən/ *noun* a feeling of contentment that comes from having what you want

satisfactory /ˌsætɪs'fækt(ə)ri/ *adjective* acceptable or good enough for a purpose

saving /'seɪvɪŋ/ *noun* a reduction in the amount of time or money needed to accomplish a purpose

sb *abbreviation* in Internet addresses, the top-level domain for Solomon Islands

SBN *abbreviation* Standard Book Number

sc *abbreviation* **1.** single column **2.** in Internet addresses, the top-level domain for Seychelles

scale /skeɪl/ *noun* **1.** a set of marks or standards for measuring things **2.** the size or level of something in relation to what is usual ○ *Scale of development was very difficult to estimate.*

scan /skæn/ *verb* **1.** to look at something very quickly in order to see what it is about **2.** to examine periodicals routinely in order to keep users informed of new material **3.** to use a machine to read coded data ■ *noun* examination of an image or object to obtain data

scanner /'skænə/ *noun* a machine that converts documents, drawings or photographs into machine-readable form

COMMENT: A scanner can be a device using photoelectric cells as in an image digitiser, or a device that samples data from a process. One type of scanner reads the barcode on the product label using a laser beam and photodiode; another can read text and by recognising characters, stores them as data on a computer; yet another type will scan colour originals and carry out colour separations.

scanning /'skænɪŋ/ *noun* the action of examining and producing data from the shape of an object or drawing

scatter /'skætə/ *verb* to distribute things widely and without any order

scatter graph /'skætə grɑːf/ *noun* a diagram of individual points or values plotted on a two-axis graph

scavenging /'skævɪndʒɪŋ/ *noun* the act of searching through and accessing database material without permission

scenario /sɪ'nɑːriəʊ/ *noun* the way in which a situation is likely to develop ○ *The planners took account of the worst possible scenario.*

schedule /'ʃedjuːl/ *noun* **1.** a written list of information, e.g. prices, conditions, dates and times **2.** a detailed written programme of events and times ■ *verb* to include an activity in a plan or list

schema /'skiːmə/ *noun* an outline of a process, plan or database structure

scholarly books /'skɒləli bʊks/ *plural noun* books published on university and academic subjects

scholarly press /'skɒləli pres/ *noun* a publishing company which publishes scholarly books

school /skuːl/ *noun* **1.** a faculty, department, or institution that offers specialised instruction in an academic subject **2.** all the staff and students of an educational institution **3.** a place or period of activity regarded as providing knowledge or experience ■ *verb* to train somebody in a particular skill or area of expertise in a thorough and detailed way

school book /'skuːl bʊk/ *noun* an educational book, a book published for use in schools

school edition /'skuːl ɪˌdɪʃ(ə)n/ *noun* an edition of a book specially made for sale to schools

school librarian /ˌskuːl laɪ'breəriən/ *noun* a specially-qualified librarian employed to run the resource centre or library in a school

school library /ˌskuːl 'laɪbrəri/ *noun* **1.** a small library specially designed and stocked to cater for the needs of the pupils and staff of a school **2.** a library which is part of a school

'Inspectors said lack of funds meant many school libraries were unable to deliver the wide range of up-to-date books needed to support children's learning across the curriculum. "Reading is the cornerstone of learning but children need books to read. The school library is often a primary source of reading material for youngsters, as well as a vital learning resource".' [*The Independent*]

School Library Association /ˌskuːl 'laɪbrəri əˌsəʊsieɪʃ(ə)n/ *noun* a sub-section of the Library Association specially for the support of school librarians. Abbr **SLA**

School Library Service /ˌskuːl 'laɪbrəri ˌsɜːvɪs/ *noun* part of the public library service which supports school libraries and teachers. Abbr **SLS**

school of librarianship /ˌskuːl əv laɪ'breəriənʃɪp/ *noun* a department in an institute of higher education which trains librarians and information specialists

science /'saɪəns/ *noun* knowledge which can be tested and proved usually according to natural laws

science fiction /ˌsaɪəns 'fɪkʃən/ *noun* fiction books based on imaginative ideas about the future on this and other planets

scissors and paste job /ˌsɪzəz ən ˈpeɪst dʒɒb/ *noun* a book or article made almost entirely of passages from other works

SCONUL *abbreviation* Standing Conference on National and University Libraries

SCOOP /skuːp/ *abbreviation* Standing Committee on Official Publications

scope /skəʊp/ *noun* the area covered by an activity or piece of work

SCOPE /skəʊp/ *abbreviation* Systematic Computerised Processing in Cataloguing

score /skɔː/ *noun* a printed version of a musical work

Scottish Vocational Qualification /ˌskɒtɪʃ vəʊˌkeɪʃ(ə)nəl ˌkwɒlɪfɪ ˈkeɪʃ(ə)n/ *noun* a work-related qualification gained in Scotland after a period of post-school training. Abbr **SVQ**

scrapbook /ˈskræpbʊk/ *noun* a book of large blank pages into which cuttings, pictures and photographs can be stuck

scratch pad /ˈskrætʃ pæd/ *noun* an area of computer memory used for temporary storage of data

screen /skriːn/ *noun* a flat surface capable of displaying pictures and words ■ *verb* to investigate or check people or things for a specific fault or danger ○ *The information was screened to check that it was completely accurate.*

screen editor /ˈskriːn ˌedɪtə/ *noun* software that allows the user to edit text on screen, with one complete page of information being displayed at a time

screenful /ˈskriːnfʊl/ *noun* one complete frame of information displayed on a computer monitor

script /skrɪpt/ *noun* **1.** the written text of a play or film **2.** handwriting which is made to look like printing

scroll /skrəʊl/ *noun* a roll of paper or parchment containing writing ■ *verb* to move text up or down a computer screen one line at a time □ **to scroll downwards** to move down the text on screen

towards the end of a document □ **to scroll upwards** to move up the text on screen towards the beginning of a document

scrub /skrʌb/ *verb* to wipe information off a disk, or remove data from a store ○ *Scrub all files referring to 1994 taxes.*

sd *abbreviation* in Internet addresses, the top-level domain for Sudan

SD disk *abbreviation* single density disk

se *abbreviation* in Internet addresses, the top-level domain for Sweden

seal /siːl/ *verb* to close something so that it is airtight and cannot be opened easily ○ *Once an envelope is sealed it should only be opened by the addressee.*

search /sɜːtʃ/ *verb* to look through a document in order to find a specific item or word ■ *noun* the process of identifying a character, word or section of data in a document or file

search and replace /ˌsɜːtʃ ən rɪ ˈpleɪs/ *noun* a facility on a word processor which allows the user to find words or strings of characters and change them

search directory /ˈsɜːtʃ daɪ ˌrekt(ə)ri/ *noun* a website in which links to information are organised into a categorical, alphabetical hierarchy to provide the broadest response to a query

search engine /ˈsɜːtʃ ˌendʒɪn/ *noun* software that carries out a search of a database when a user asks it to find information. On the Internet there are many search engines that list all the websites and allow a user to find a website by searching for particular information.

search routine /ˈsɜːtʃ ruːˌtiːn/ *noun* software which allows the user to search for an item in a database

search skills /ˈsɜːtʃ skɪlz/ *plural noun* the ability to search efficiently through a database, reference or library for specific information

search strategy /ˈsɜːtʃ ˌstrætədʒɪ/ *noun* a plan for searching a database for information using specific keywords in order to maximise the use of computer time

search term /'sɜːtʃ tɜːm/ *noun* a word or phrase input into a database to find the relevant records

'Hopkins said web sites can increase the number of hits they receive from a search term in several ways, including increasing site content relating to that term or product and spending more on being listed as a sponsored link to that term on other sites, as well as search engines such as Google.' [*Retail Week*]

seasonal analysis /ˌsiːz(ə)n(ə)l ə'næləsɪs/ *noun* a method of analysing data which takes into account the seasonal variations throughout the year

second /'sekənd/ *noun* **1.** something that is counted as number two in a series **2.** a sixtieth part of a minute ■ *verb* to support a person or proposal

secondary /'sekənd(ə)ri/ *adjective* second in importance

secondary education /ˌsekənd(ə)ri ˌedjʊ'keɪʃ(ə)n/ *noun* the period of schooling between primary school and further or higher education, usually from about 11 to 16 or 18 years of age

secondary entry /ˌsekənd(ə)ri 'entri/ *noun* a catalogue entry which is not the main entry

secondary school /'sekənd(ə)ri skuːl/ *noun* a school that provides education after primary school

secondary source /ˌsek(ə)ndəri 'sɔːs/ *noun* a reference that has already been quoted in another document

second best /ˌsekənd 'best/ *adjective* considered to be slightly inferior, not the best of its kind

second-class /ˌsekənd 'klɑːs/ *adjective* less expensive or less comfortable than the best category ○ *The price of a second-class ticket is half that of a first class.*

secondhand /ˌsekənd'hænd/ *adjective* relating to something that has been previously owned by somebody else

second language /ˌsekənd 'læŋgwɪdʒ/ *noun* a language that somebody speaks quite fluently and uses for work but which is not their mother tongue

secondment /sɪ'kɒndmənt/ *noun* a limited period of time working at something away from one's usual duties

secret /'siːkrət/ *noun* a piece of information that is known only to a few people and is intentionally withheld from general knowledge

section /'sekʃən/ *noun* **1.** part of a book which is made from one sheet of paper ○ *The book is printed in 32-page sections.* ◊ **signature 2.** a supplement to a newspaper or magazine ○ *The paper has a special travel section on Saturdays.*

sector /'sektə/ *noun* a division of a group or area which is also part of a larger one

secure server /sɪˌkjʊə 'sɜːvə/ *noun* an Internet server that allows for the encryption of data and thus is suitable for use in e-commerce

Secure Sockets Layer /sɪˌkjʊə 'sɒkɪts ˌleɪə/ *noun* a secure format for sending documents which are encrypted and decrypted using two special keys. Abbr **SSL**

secure system /sɪˌkjʊə 'sɪstəm/ *noun* a system that cannot be accessed without the permission of the owner

security /sɪ'kjʊərɪti/ *noun* measures taken to make a place or person safe from attack or danger

security barrier /sɪ'kjʊərɪti ˌbæriə/ *noun* a device which prevents users leaving a library with materials that have not been checked out

security device /sɪ'kjʊərɪti dɪ ˌvaɪs/ *noun* something that ensures the safety of a place or person ○ *A password is a security device which protects computer files.*

security system /sɪ'kjʊərɪti ˌsɪstəm/ *noun* a system of alarms and guards which protects a building or organisation from burglars

see /siː/ *verb* an indexing command referring the user to a different entry □ **see also** an indexing command referring the user to additional entries for comparison or added information

seek /siːk/ *verb* to look hard for something or somebody □ **seek to do something** to attempt to do something

segment /'segmənt/ *noun* one part of the total which can be treated separately

select /sɪ'lekt/ *verb* to find and choose specific information or data

select committee /sɪ,lekt kə'mɪti/ *noun* a government committee chosen to do a particular task in a limited time

selection /sɪ'lekʃən/ *noun* a range of products and services available and chosen

selective /sɪ'lektɪv/ *adjective* choosing what to do, say or buy with great care

self-cover /,self 'kʌvə/ *noun* a cover which is printed on the same paper as the text of the book, used for brochures and small books

self-financing /,self faɪ'nænsɪŋ/ *adjective* not dependent on any outside source of funds

self-help /,self 'help/ *noun* provision of support through informal groups of people with similar experiences

self-study /,self 'stʌdi/ *noun* a form of education in which people can study at their own pace and in their own homes, often using courses or information available on the Internet

self-wrapper /,self 'ræpə/ *noun* same as **self-cover**

selling rights /'selɪŋ raɪts/ *plural noun* the legal right to sell specific goods or services

semantics /sɪ'mæntɪks/ *noun* a branch of linguistics which deals with the meanings of words

Semantic Web /sɪ,mæntɪk 'web/ *noun* a diagrammatic representation of all pieces of data and links between them on the World Wide Web

semester /sɪ'mestə/ *noun* one division of the academic year in colleges and universities

semi- /semi/ *prefix* combining with nouns and adjectives to form words which describe something that is only in a part state

semicolon /,semi'kəʊlɒn/ *noun* a punctuation sign (;) used to join rather than separate two parts of a sentence, as in 'the safe that had been broken into was on one side of the room; the other safe appeared to be intact'

semiliterate /,semi'lɪt(ə)rət/ *adjective* **1.** unable to read or write properly **2.** *US* having only limited understanding of a particular subject, especially a technical one

seminar /'semɪnɑː/ *noun* a meeting of a group of people called together to discuss a particular topic

semiotics /,semi'ɒtɪks/ *noun* the science of signs

semi-structured /,semi 'strʌktʃəd/ *adjective* partly controlled by a structure and partly free

semi-structured interview /,semi ,strʌktʃəd 'ɪntəvjuː/ *noun* an interview which is conducted partly with pre-written questions and partly giving the opportunity to talk freely

semi-structured questionnaire /,semi ,strʌktʃəd ,kwestʃə'neə/ *noun* a set of questions some of which are closed and some of which require open answers

send /send/ *verb* to arrange or cause something to be transported from one place to another, either physically as by post or electronically as in e-mail

sense /sens/ *noun* the possible meaning of words or phrases ■ *verb* to become aware of something either personally or through a machine

senseless /'sensləs/ *adjective* having no apparent meaning

sensible /'sensɪb(ə)l/ *adjective* able to think and behave in a logical and common-sense manner

sensitive /'sensɪtɪv/ *adjective* strongly able to be aware of feelings

sensitive subject /,sensɪtɪv 'sʌbjekt/ *noun* a topic that is liable to cause strong feelings when discussed

sensitivities /,sensi'tɪvɪtiz/ *plural noun* subjects that are likely to cause argument so must be approached very carefully

sentence /'sentəns/ *noun* a group of words which is complete in itself, containing a subject and a verb

separate /'sepəreɪt/ *verb* to cause two things to be apart and unconnected

separator /'sepəreɪtə/ *noun* a piece of card or plastic that keeps things apart

○ *The file had different colour separators for each division.*

sequel /'siːkwəl/ *noun* a book or film which continues the storyline of a previous one with the same characters

sequence /'siːkwəns/ *noun* an arrangement which follows a consecutive order

sequential /sɪ'kwenʃ(ə)l/ *adjective* in which things follow each other in a pre-arranged order

sequential access /sɪˌkwenʃ(ə)l 'ækses/ *noun* the state of information only being able to be accessed in a given order

'…no one is seriously expecting a tape replacement, in large part because tape volumes continue to vastly outstrip any competitive technologies. For all its sequential-access inconvenience and sheer old-fashioned aura, tape has remained the reliable performer at the end of the enterprise data chain.' [*Computing*]

sequential access storage /sɪ ˌkwenʃ(ə)l 'ækses ˌstɔːrɪdʒ/ *noun* a storage medium whose data is accessed sequentially

serial /'sɪəriəl/ *noun* **1.** a journal or magazine that is published at regular intervals **2.** a story published in regular instalments ■ *adjective* referring to a series

Serial Line Internet Protocol /ˌsɪəriəl laɪn 'ɪntənet ˌprəʊtəkɒl/ *noun* a dial-up phone link to the Internet. Abbr **SLIP**

serial number /'sɪəriəl ˌnʌmbə/ *noun* a number given to an item which identifies it by its position in a sequence

serial processing /ˌsɪəriəl 'prəʊsesɪŋ/ *noun* the organisation of journals so that they can be retrieved easily

serials crisis /'sɪəriəlz ˌkraɪsɪs/ *noun* the problems facing a library when subscriptions to academic journals become too costly to maintain

serials department /'sɪəriəlz dɪ ˌpɑːtmənt/ *noun* a section of a library with responsibility for organising the journals and periodicals purchased by the organisation

series /'sɪəriːz/ *noun* a group of related items ordered in a sequence, e.g. the volumes in a set of books ○ '*At Lady Molly's*' *is the seventh title in the* '*Dance to the Music of Time*' *series.*

series authority file /ˌsɪəriːz ɔː 'θɒrɪti ˌfaɪl/ *noun* a list of series headings used in a catalogue with the references made to them from other forms

series title /'sɪəriːz ˌtaɪt(ə)l/ *noun* the title given to a series of books, each one of which has its own separate title

serif /'serɪf/ *noun* **1.** a small decorative line added to letters in some fonts. ○ **sans serif 2.** a font which uses serifs, such as Times New Roman

server /'sɜːvə/ *noun* a computer with a large storage capacity which provides a function to a network of terminals

server farm /'sɜːvə fɑːm/ *noun* a business consisting of a group of Internet servers, all of which are linked to one another and are engaged in web hosting

service /'sɜːvɪs/ *noun* work which supports another person's or organisation's activities ■ *verb* to clean, adjust and repair a machine so that it keeps running

service agreement /'sɜːvɪs ə ˌɡriːmənt/, **service contract** /'sɜːvɪs ˌkɒntrækt/ *noun* an arrangement with the suppliers of a machine that they will maintain it regularly and repair it if it goes wrong

service point /'sɜːvɪs pɔɪnt/ *noun* a place in a library or information centre at which the public is served

service provider /'sɜːvɪs prə ˌvaɪdə/ *noun* a company that provides people and businesses with access to the Internet, usually charging a monthly fee

set /set/ *noun* a group of related items

setting /'setɪŋ/ *noun* **1.** the time and place where the action of a book or film happens **2.** the position of the controls on a machine ○ *There are two settings: fast and slow.*

sextodecimo /ˌsekstəʊ'desɪməʊ/ *noun* a size of book page traditionally created by folding a single sheet of standard-sized printing paper four times, giving 16 leaves or 32 pages

sg *abbreviation* in Internet addresses, the top-level domain for Singapore

SGML /ˌes dʒiː emˈel/ *noun* a hardware-independent standard which defines how documents should be marked up to indicate bolds, italics, margins and so on. Full form **standard generalized markup language**. ◊ **HTML, XML**

sh *abbreviation* in Internet addresses, the top-level domain for St Helena

shade /ʃeɪd/ *noun* a variation in the colour or black and white texture of printing produced by adding black ■ *verb* to colour in a section of a drawing by adding a darker colour or a textured pattern

shadow /ˈʃædəʊ/ *verb* to follow somebody closely throughout their working day in order to study what they do

share /ʃeə/ *noun* one of the parts into which the capital of a company is divided, which can be bought by investors ■ *verb* to own or use something together with somebody else

shared resources /ˌʃeəd rɪˈzɔːsɪz/ *plural noun* working materials which are used by several groups, e.g. schools or companies

'For example, the secondary school can now share the skills of its ICT technicians and admin staff with hard-pressed primary colleagues in activities such as preparing lessons and materials, and creating pupil displays. Such shared resources will free up teachers to be more productive and give them greater control over their working week.' [*The Guardian*]

sheaf /ʃiːf/ *noun* a bundle of long or thin things ◊ *He was carrying a sheaf of papers.*

sheet /ʃiːt/ *noun* a large flat piece of material or paper

sheet feed /ˈʃiːt fiːd/ *noun* a device that feeds single sheets of paper into a printer one at a time

shelf /ʃelf/ *noun* a horizontal piece of wood or metal attached to a wall, or in a bookcase or cupboard (NOTE: The plural is **shelves**.)

shelfback /ˈʃelfbæk/ *noun* the spine of a book

shelf label /ˈʃelf ˌleɪb(ə)l/ *noun* a written notice attached to a library shelf which indicates the classification of the books stored there

shelf life /ˈʃelf laɪf/ *noun* the period of time that an item is likely to last before it needs replacing

shelf list card /ˈʃelf lɪst ˌkɑːd/ *noun* a card which lists the items held on a particular shelf

shelf mark /ˈʃelf mɑːk/ *noun* the classification or call number of a book

shelf number /ˈʃelf ˌnʌmbə/ *noun* a number allocated to a shelf to assist the retrieval of books

shift /ʃɪft/ *noun* a period of time spent at work at any time during a 24-hour period ◊ *Librarians often have to work an afternoon and evening shift.*

shift key /ˈʃɪft kiː/ *noun* a key on a keyboard which raises a letter to a capital or combines with other command keys for word-processing and computing functions

ship /ʃɪp/ *verb* to transport goods by sea

shipment /ˈʃɪpmənt/ *noun* a quantity of goods, usually of the same kind, sent together to a destination by any form of transport, not just by sea ◊ *The shipment of library equipment has just arrived at the airport.*

shoot /ʃuːt/ *verb* to use a camera to take photographs or make a film

short /ʃɔːt/ *adjective* having only a few words or pages

shorten /ˈʃɔːt(ə)n/ *verb* to reduce the length of something

shorthand /ˈʃɔːthænd/ *noun* a system of signs and symbols which enables spoken words to be written down very quickly

short-handed /ˌʃɔːt ˈhændɪd/, **short-staffed** /ˌʃɔːt ˈstɑːft/ *adjective* without enough people to do the work required

shorthand typist /ˌʃɔːthænd ˈtaɪpɪst/ *noun* a person who takes down dictation in shorthand and then transcribes it into typewritten form

shortlist /'ʃɔːtlɪst/ *noun* a small group chosen from a larger group, from which the final choice is made ○ *Five titles were on the shortlist for the Booker Prize.* ■ *verb* to choose a few names of people or titles of books from a longer list, as a first step towards deciding on a person for a job or the winner of a competition ○ *Shortlisted candidates will be asked for an interview.*

short loan /'ʃɔːt ləʊn/ *noun* a restricted period for borrowing library items

short loan collection /ˌʃɔːt 'ləʊn kəˌlekʃ(ə)n/ *noun* books and materials in a library which are in heavy demand so can only be borrowed for a very limited time

short run /'ʃɔːt rʌn/ *noun* a print run of only a small number of copies

short-term /ˌʃɔːt 'tɜːm/ *adjective* only relevant to the near future

short-term planning /ˌʃɔːt tɜːm 'plænɪŋ/ *noun* decisions about what will be done in the near future

shot /ʃɒt/ *noun* a photograph or still frame from a film

shoulder /'ʃəʊldə/ *noun* the edge of the spine of a book, which sticks out slightly

show /ʃəʊ/ *verb* to take something to somebody and enable them to see it

show of hands /ˌʃəʊ əv 'hændz/ *noun* a method of counting votes by counting the number of raised hands

shred /ʃred/ *verb* to cut something into long thin strips

shredder /'ʃredə/ *noun* a machine that cuts paper into very small pieces, usually long thin strips, used to destroy confidential documents

shut down /ˌʃʌt 'daʊn/ *verb* **1.** to close a factory, shop or organisation permanently or temporarily **2.** to close down a computer or engine temporarily

si *abbreviation* in Internet addresses, the top-level domain for Slovenia

side /saɪd/ *noun* one surface of something flat such as a tape or piece of paper ○ *It is possible to record on both sides of this tape.*

side by side /ˌsaɪd baɪ 'saɪd/ *adjective* next to each other

side with /'saɪd wɪθ/, **side against** /'saɪd əˌgenst/ *verb* to support or oppose somebody in an argument

sign /saɪn/ *noun* a piece of wood, plastic or metal with words or pictures on it giving information ■ *verb* to write one's signature on a document □ **to sign for** to put your signature on an official document to say that you have received something □ **to sign in** write your name on a list to say that you have arrived □ **to sign on** to agree to a contract

signal /'sɪgn(ə)l/ *noun* a way of sending a message over a distance by physical or electronic methods

signatory /'sɪgnət(ə)ri/ *noun* a person who has the legal right to sign an official document

signature /'sɪgnɪtʃə/ *noun* **1.** a way of writing your name which is special to you and can be recognised as yours by other people **2.** a special authentication code such as a password which a user gives to prove their identity before accessing a system or before the execution of a task **3.** a sentence or paragraph used to end e-mail messages and comments posted on the Internet. Normally a signature should be short – no more than four lines – and might include a short advertisement for your services and your e-mail address. **4.** a printed sheet, folded into 16, 32 or 64 pages (NOTE: The folded set of printed pages is technically speaking a 'section', while the 'signature' is the identifying number or letter on it. However, 'signature' is commonly used to mean the set of pages themselves.)

COMMENT: Note that the folded set of printed pages is technically speaking a 'section' while the 'signature' is the identifying number or letter on it; 'signature' is however commonly used to mean the set of pages themselves.

signed edition /'saɪnd ɪˌdɪʃ(ə)n/ *noun* a copy of a book autographed by the author

significance /sɪg'nɪfɪkəns/ *noun* the importance, special meaning or value of something

significant /sɪgˈnɪfɪkənt/ *adjective* of particular importance

sign language /ˈsaɪn ˌlæŋgwɪdʒ/ *noun* communication, or a system of communication, by gestures as opposed to written or spoken language, especially the highly developed system of hand signs used by or to people who are hearing-impaired

silverfish /ˈsɪlvəfɪʃ/ *noun* a small silvery wingless insect with three long tail bristles and two long antennae, which feeds on the starch of books

Silver Platter Information /ˌsɪlvə ˈplætə ˌɪnfəmeɪʃ(ə)n/ *noun* an organisation set up specifically to provide information by using CD-ROM technology with microcomputers

similar /ˈsɪmɪlə/ *adjective* having features that are almost the same as something else

Simple Mail Transfer Protocol /ˌsɪmp(ə)l ˈmeɪl ˌtrænsfɜː ˌprəʊtəkɒl/ *noun* a standard protocol which allows electronic mail messages to be transferred from one system to another, normally used as the method of transferring mail from one Internet server to another or to send mail from a computer to a server. Abbr **SMTP**

simplify /ˈsɪmplɪfaɪ/ *verb* to make something less complex

simulate /ˈsɪmjʊleɪt/ *verb* to copy actions, feelings or objects to produce something that looks similar or acts in the same way

simultaneous /ˌsɪm(ə)lˈteɪniəs/ *adjective* happening at the same time

sine loco /ˌsaɪni ˈlɒkəʊ/ *phrase* a Latin phrase used in catalogue entries to signify no place of publication. Abbr **s.l.**

sine nomine /ˌsaɪni ˈnɒmɪneɪ/ *phrase* a Latin phrase used in catalogue entries to signify no known publisher. Abbr **s.n.**

single density disk /ˌsɪŋg(ə)l ˌdensɪti ˈdɪsk/ *noun* a standard magnetic disk able to store data. Abbr **SD disk**

single out /ˌsɪŋg(ə)l ˈaʊt/ *verb* to select one person or thing from a group

single-sided disk /ˌsɪŋg(ə)l ˌsaɪdɪd ˈdɪsk/ *noun* a computer disk which can only be used to store data on one side

single user /ˌsɪŋg(ə)l ˈjuːzə/ *adjective* to be used by one person

singular /ˈsɪŋgjʊlə/ *adjective* **1.** a grammatical term to describe words which refer to just one thing **2.** unusual or eccentric

SIS *abbreviation* strategic information services

site engineer /ˈsaɪt endʒɪˌnɪə/ *noun* an engineer who is allocated to a particular site to maintain the equipment and machines

site licence /ˈsaɪt ˌlaɪs(ə)ns/ *noun* an official permit to an institution and its staff to use particular software

situations vacant column /ˌsɪtjʊeɪʃ(ə)nz ˈveɪk(ə)nt ˌkɒləm/ *noun* a list of job advertisements printed in a newspaper

sixteenmo /ˈsɪkstiːnməʊ/ *noun* **1.** a book that is printed in 32-page sections **2.** an American book size about 6 or 7 inches high ▸ abbr **16mo**

16mo *abbreviation* sixteenmo

64mo *abbreviation* sixty-fourmo

sixty-fourmo /ˌsɪksti ˈfɔːməʊ/ *noun* a size of book page traditionally created by folding a single sheet of standard-sized printing paper six times, giving 64 leaves or 128 pages. Abbr **64mo**

size /saɪz/ *noun* **1.** the physical dimensions of something, which tell how big or small it is, usually indicated by its height and width **2.** a mixture of gelatine, alum and formaldehyde used to coat paper surfaces ■ *verb* to calculate the size of something □ **to size up** to study a person or situation and assess the best way of dealing with it

sj *abbreviation* in Internet addresses, the top-level domain for Svalbard and Jan Mayen Islands

sk *abbreviation* in Internet addresses, the top-level domain for Slovakia

skeleton key /ˈskelɪt(ə)n kiː/ *noun* a key that will open many different locks

skeleton service /ˈskelɪt(ə)n ˌsɜːvɪs/ *noun* a service run by the minimum number of people possible

skeleton staff /ˈskelɪt(ə)n stɑːf/ *noun* the smallest number of staff able to do the work

skill /skɪl/ *noun* a special ability, knowledge or training that enables somebody to do something well

skilled staff /ˌskɪld ˈstɑːf/ *plural noun* people who work with special knowledge in a particular job

skip /skɪp/ *verb* **1.** to miss something out **2.** to decide deliberately not to do something or go somewhere

skiver /ˈskaɪvə/ *noun* leather made by splitting a sheepskin, used as a cover material for de luxe books

sl *abbreviation* in Internet addresses, the top-level domain for Sierra Leone

s.l. *abbreviation* sine loco

SLA *abbreviation* School Library Association

slang /slæŋ/ *noun* words and expressions which are very informal and likely to change in meaning every so often

slash /slæʃ/ *noun* an oblique stroke used in typing (/) (NOTE: In printing it is more often called a **solidus**.)

slashed zero /ˌslæʃd ˈzɪərəʊ/ *noun* a printed sign (Ø) which puts an oblique stroke through zero to distinguish it from the letter O

sleeve /sliːv/ *noun* **1.** an envelope-type cover for disks, often with information or pictures on it **2.** a book jacket

slew /sluː/ *noun* rapid uncontrolled movement of paper in a printer when it is not connected to the feeder

slide /slaɪd/ *noun* **1.** a picture on positive transparent photographic film mounted in a frame **2.** an individual computer screen which can be produced as output in different formats

slide carousel /ˈslaɪd ˌkærəsel/ *noun* a container that allows slides to be fed into a projector

slide mount /ˈslaɪd maʊnt/ *noun* a frame around a slide which makes it easier to handle and store

slide projector /ˈslaɪd prəˌdʒektə/ *noun* a device that shines light through photographic slides in order to project them on to a screen

slide storage /ˈslaɪd ˌstɔːrɪdʒ/ *noun* a system of storage slides which keeps them clean, safe and easily retrievable

slide tape package /ˈslaɪd teɪp ˌpækɪdʒ/ *noun* a synchronised programme of slides and audio tape

slide viewer /ˈslaɪd ˌvjuːə/ *noun* a small portable box which enables slides to be viewed against a light source

SLIP /slɪp/ *abbreviation* Serial Line Internet Protocol

slipcase /ˈslɪpkeɪs/ *noun* a card box for an expensive book, which is open at one side so that the spine of the book is visible

slip pages /ˈslɪp ˌpeɪdʒɪz/, **slip proofs** /ˈslɪp pruːfs/ *plural noun* draft copies of text for printing which are printed on separate sheets of paper

slip-up /ˈslɪp ʌp/ *noun* a small unintentional mistake

slow fires /ˌsləʊ ˈfaɪəz/ *plural noun* an informal term to describe the gradual self-destruction of books made with acidic paper

slow motion /ˌsləʊ ˈməʊʃ(ə)n/ *noun* the act of playing back a film or video at a slower speed than when it was recorded

SLS *abbreviation* School Library Service

sm *abbreviation* in Internet addresses, the top-level domain for San Marino

small ad /ˈsmɔːl æd/ *noun* a short advertisement in a newspaper or magazine, usually advertising personal sales or wants

small caps /ˌsmɔːl ˈkæps/ *noun* a printing style which uses capital letters that are the same size as lower case letters

small-scale /ˈsmɔːl skeɪl/ *adjective* limited in size and extent ○ *The library's evening activities were kept small-scale to reduce costs.*

smart card /ˈsmɑːt kɑːd/ *noun* a plastic card with an electronic strip which can be read to identify the user on such things as credit cards

SMS /ˌes em ˈes/ *noun* a service that allows short text messages to be sent, e.g. between mobile phones and pagers.

Full form **short message service, short messaging service**

SMTP *abbreviation* Simple Mail Transfer Protocol

sn *abbreviation* in Internet addresses, the top-level domain for Senegal

s.n. *abbreviation* sine nomine

snail mail /'sneɪl meɪl/ *noun* mail sent through the postal service, as distinct from faster electronic mail. Also called **p-mail**

snap decision /ˌsnæp dɪ'sɪʒ(ə)n/ *noun* a decision taken quickly without much thought

snapshot /'snæpʃɒt/ *noun* a personal photograph taken quickly

so *abbreviation* in Internet addresses, the top-level domain for Somalia

social bookmarking /ˌsəʊʃ(ə)l 'bʊkmɑːkɪŋ/ *noun* personalised metadata added to recommended web resources by users, as a 'bookmark' to help others in the field find it

'Yahoo! last year also acquired del.icio.us, a social-bookmarking website that lets users share their favourite sites, music and other findings – allowing others to effectively look over their shoulders to find interesting stuff. "We're applying the wisdom of the crowds to find information", says Bradley Horowitz, Yahoo!'s head of search technology. "It's collaborative".' [*Time Magazine*]

social capital /ˌsəʊʃ(ə)l 'kæpɪt(ə)l/ *noun* the idea of the social networks created by and available to a person or company being a form of exploitable resource

social skills /'səʊʃ(ə)l skɪlz/ *plural noun* ability to communicate with other people at all levels of society

social trend /ˌsəʊʃ(ə)l 'trend/ *noun* the general direction of change in social behaviour

socket /'sɒkɪt/ *noun* a device with holes for a plug which connects a machine to the electricity supply

softback /'sɒftbæk/ *noun* PUBL same as **paperback** ■ *adjective* same as **paperback**

soft copy /ˌsɒft 'kɒpi/ *noun* text on screen as opposed to hard copy printed on paper

softcover /'sɒftkʌvə/ *noun* PUBL same as **paperback** ■ *adjective* same as **paperback**

software /'sɒftweə/ *noun* computer programs which instruct the hardware what to do

software development /'sɒftweə dɪˌveləpmənt/ *noun* the process of writing programs to implement an original idea

software documentation /'sɒftweə ˌdɒkjʊmenteɪʃ(ə)n/ *noun* instruction manuals which explain how to install and use computer programs

software engineer /'sɒftweə endʒɪˌnɪə/ *noun* a person who can write computer programs to fit specific applications

software installation /'sɒftweə ˌɪnstəleɪʃ(ə)n/ *noun* the process of putting a program on to a computer so that it can be used

software licence /'sɒftweə ˌlaɪs(ə)ns/ *noun* a contract between the producer and the purchaser of software about the use and copying of the program

software maintenance /'sɒftweə ˌmeɪntənəns/ *noun* modifications made to a program to keep it up to date

software package /'sɒftweə ˌpækɪdʒ/ *noun* a complete set of instruction manuals and installation disks which enable a program to be used

software piracy /'sɒftweə ˌpaɪrəsi/ *noun* the illegal copying of software

'Software piracy is one of the copyright sins. With many computer users in the habit of downloading music and films from the internet for free, cyber criminals are increasingly pushing pirated programs at a hungry audience… we have twice as many applications on our PCs today than we did three years ago.' [*The Guardian*]

software producer /'sɒftweə prəˌdjuːsə/ *noun* a publisher of computer programs for sale

software specification /'sɒftweə ˌspesɪfɪkeɪʃ(ə)n/ *noun* detailed information about a piece of software's abilities, functions and methods

solidus /'sɒlɪdəs/ *noun* an oblique stroke used in printing (/)

solution /sə'luːʃ(ə)n/ *noun* the answer to a problem

solve /sɒlv/ *verb* to find the answer to a problem or difficulty

sophisticated /sə'fɪstɪkeɪtɪd/ *adjective* complex and technically advanced

sort /sɔːt/ *verb* to put things in order ○ *The data can be sorted by name or number.*

sort code /'sɔːt kəʊd/ *noun* a combination of numbers which identifies the user

sorting office /'sɔːtɪŋ ˌɒfɪs/ *noun* the part of a post office where items to be delivered are sorted according to their destinations

sound /saʊnd/ *noun* a noise that can be heard ■ *adjective* strong, reliable or in good condition

sound effects /'saʊnd ɪˌfekts/ *plural noun* sounds produced artificially to make a play or film seem more realistic

soundproof /'saʊndpruːf/ *adjective* preventing sound from passing in or out

sound track /'saʊnd træk/ *noun* a track on the edge of a film on which the speech and music is recorded and synchronised with the pictures

source /sɔːs/ *noun* the place where something originally comes from

source language /'sɔːs ˌlæŋɡwɪdʒ/ *noun* the original language of a text which is being translated into another language

source term /'sɔːs tɜːm/ *noun* the first word looked up in an index search from which the searcher is directed to other terms

space /speɪs/ *noun* a gap or empty place intended for the storage of data ■ *verb* to arrange things with regular gaps in between them □ **to space out** to organise a series of things or events so that there are gaps or periods of time in between them

space bar /'speɪs bɑː/, **space key** *noun* a long bar at the bottom of a keyboard on a typewriter or computer which makes a single space into the text when pressed

spacing /'speɪsɪŋ/ *noun* the way in which gaps are inserted ○ *The spacing of words on that line is rather uneven.*

span /spæn/ *noun* a period of time

span of concentration /ˌspæn əv ˌkɒnsən'treɪʃ(ə)n/ *noun* a period of time for which a person is able to concentrate on doing something ○ *The average span of concentration on one activity for children is said to be only 15 minutes.*

spare /speə/ *adjective* extra to requirements and available for use

spare part /ˌspeə 'pɑːt/ *noun* a component for a machine that can be bought separately to replace one that is broken or worn out

spatial /'speɪʃ(ə)l/ *adjective* relating to space and shapes

spatial ability /'speɪʃ(ə)l əˌbɪlɪti/ *noun* the ability of a person to visualise the relationships between shapes

speaker /'spiːkə/ *noun* somebody who makes a speech. ◊ **loudspeaker**

special interest group /ˌspeʃ(ə)l 'ɪntrəst ˌɡruːp/ *noun* a community of people who have an interest in one specific area of study and development, e.g. computer-human interaction

specialise /'speʃəlaɪz/, **specialize** *verb* to study something in great depth so that you become an expert in that field

specialist /'speʃəlɪst/ *noun* an expert in one particular area of knowledge or skill

special librarian /ˌspeʃ(ə)l laɪ'breəriən/ *noun* a qualified librarian employed in a special library

special library /ˌspeʃ(ə)l 'laɪbrəri/ *noun* a library that is stocked to provide information in a particular area of study ○ *Research & Development departments of large firms often have their own special libraries.*

special offer /ˌspeʃ(ə)l 'ɒfə/ *noun* goods or services being sold at a specially low price usually for a short period of time

specifications /ˌspesɪfɪ'keɪʃ(ə)nz/ *plural noun* detailed instructions about work to be done or products to be supplied

specific entry /spə,sɪfɪk 'entri/ *noun* a catalogue entry under the actual subject rather than a broader term

specify /'spesɪfaɪ/ *verb* to state in detail what is required

specimen /'spesɪmɪn/ *noun* **1.** a small example of something which gives an idea of what the whole thing will look like **2.** one example of a species which shows what they all look like

specimen pages /ˌspesɪmɪn 'peɪdʒɪz/ *plural noun* printed pages produced by the printer for the publisher to show the proposed type style

specimen storage /'spesɪmɪn ˌstɔːrɪdʒ/ *noun* a system of organising the storing of physical objects so that they can be studied

speculate /'spekjʊleɪt/ *verb* to form a conjecture on the basis of incomplete facts or information

speculation /ˌspekjʊ'leɪʃ(ə)n/ *noun* **1.** a conclusion, theory or opinion based on incomplete facts or information **2.** reasoning based on incomplete facts or information

speech recognition /'spiːtʃ ˌrekəgnɪʃ(ə)n/ *noun* the ability of a machine to recognise the patterns of individual human voices, sometimes used in security systems

speech synthesiser /'spiːtʃ ˌsɪnθəsaɪzə/ *noun* a machine which takes information from a computer in electronic form and makes it recognisable as spoken words ○ *The blind student needed a speech synthesiser attached to his computer so that he could hear the written words.*

speed-read /'spiːd riːd/ *verb* to read something very fast using a learned technique of skimming the text

spellcheck /'speltʃek/ *verb* to check the spelling in a text by comparing it with a dictionary held in the computer

spellchecker /'speltʃekə/, **spelling checker** /'spelɪŋ ˌtʃekə/ *noun* **1.** a program which looks at the words of a

text in a computer, checks them against a dictionary of correctly spelled words, and indicates the words that are incorrect **2.** a dictionary of correctly spelled words, held in a computer, and used to check the spelling of a text

spellcheck facility /'speltʃek fə ˌsɪləti/ *noun* a software facility on a word-processing program which enables the user to check spellings against an inbuilt dictionary

speller /'spelə/ *noun* a book for teaching or improving spelling

spelling error /'spelɪŋ ˌerə/ *noun* a mistake made in spelling a word

spend /spend/ *verb* to exchange money for goods or time on activities

spider /'spaɪdə/ *noun* a computer program that searches the Internet for newly accessible information to be added to the index examined by a standard search tool

spike /spaɪk/ *noun* a sharp piece of metal which when mounted on a base can be used for temporary storage of papers needing attention

spine /spaɪn/ *noun* the edge of a book which is all that can be seen when a book is upright on a shelf

spine label /'spaɪn ˌleɪb(ə)l/ *noun* a label put on the spine of a book to indicate its library location

spine lettering /'spaɪn ˌlet(ə)rɪŋ/ *noun* the printing of the title and other details on the spine of a book

spine number /'spaɪn ˌnʌmbə/ *noun* a call or class number put on the spine of a library book

spine title /'spaɪn ˌtaɪt(ə)l/ *noun* the name of a book written down its spine

spinner /'spɪnə/ *noun* a display rack for books, which turns round

spiral binding /'spaɪrəl ˌbaɪndɪŋ/ *noun* a type of binding for collections of papers which uses a coiled wire inserted into specially punched holes

spiral bound book /ˌspaɪrəl baʊnd 'bʊk/ *noun* a book in a spiral binding

splice /splaɪs/ *verb* to join two pieces of magnetic tape or film together

splicing tape /'splaɪsɪŋ teɪp/ *noun* non-magnetic, transparent tape used to join two pieces of tape together

split catalogue /ˌsplɪt ˈkætəlɒg/ *noun* a catalogue in which the entries are divided by category and give separate alphabetical lists for details such as title, author and subject

split screen /ˈsplɪt skriːn/ *noun* a system where more than one text can appear on a screen at the same time, such as the text being worked on and a second text which can be called up for reference

split site /ˌsplɪt ˈsaɪt/ *adjective* referring to a school, college or university with buildings separated on different sites

sponsor /ˈspɒnsə/ *noun* a person or organisation that pays all or part of the expenses for an event or period of study ■ *verb* to pay to support an activity or person

spool /spuːl/ *noun* a round object on to which tape or film can be wound ■ *verb* to transfer data from a disc to a tape

spreadsheet /ˈspredʃiːt/ *noun* a computer program that allows the calculation of numbers in both columns and rows

spring back /ˈsprɪŋ bæk/ *noun* a binding for account books and other bound stationery which allows the pages to lie flat when open

sprinkled edge /ˈsprɪŋk(ə)ld ˌedʒ/ *noun* the edge of a book which has been sprayed with splashes of ink for decoration

sprocket /ˈsprɒkɪt/ *noun* a tooth on the edge of a wheel to pick up what passes over it

sprocket holes /ˈsprɒkɪt həʊlz/ *plural noun* a series of holes at the edge of paper which control its feed through a printer

SQL /ˌes kjuː ˈel/ *noun* a standardised language that is close to the structure of natural English, used for obtaining information from databases. Full form **structured query language**

square bracket /ˌskweə ˈbrækɪt/ *noun* either of a pair of symbols, [ ], used in keying, printing and writing especially to indicate the insertion of special commentary, e.g. that made by an editor

sr *abbreviation* in Internet addresses, the top-level domain for Suriname

SSL *abbreviation* Secure Sockets Layer

SSN *abbreviation* Standard Serial Number

st *abbreviation* in Internet addresses, the top-level domain for São Tomé and Príncipe

stable /ˈsteɪb(ə)l/ *adjective* steady and unmoving

stack /stæk/ *noun* **1.** a pile of things one on top of another ○ *a stack of order forms* **2.** a large and ordered collection of books kept in another area for reference

staff /stɑːf/ *plural noun* people who work for a company or organisation ■ *verb* to provide the staff for a company or organisation

staff levels /ˈstɑːf ˌlev(ə)lz/ *plural noun* the number of people who are employed to work for a company or organisation ○ *They were criticised for having inadequate staff levels.*

staff profile /ˌstɑːf ˈprəʊfaɪl/ *noun* records which show details of staff qualifications and work experience

staffroom /ˈstɑːfruːm/ *noun* a common room where staff can meet informally

staffroom library /ˈstɑːfruːm ˌlaɪbrəri/ *noun* a collection of books on work-related subjects kept in the staffroom for use by members of staff

stage /steɪdʒ/ *noun* one step in a process

stakeholder /ˈsteɪkhəʊldə/ *noun* somebody who has a vested interest in a company's success, e.g. shareholders, directors, employers or suppliers

stamp /stæmp/ *noun* something which marks another object to show that it has been processed ■ *verb* to use a rubber stamp to mark something ○ *The books are stamped with the date for return.*

stamp of approval /ˌstæmp əv ə ˈpruːv(ə)l/ *noun* a mark of approval given either verbally or by a physical mark

stand-alone /ˈstænd əˌləʊn/ *noun* a computer that can be used by itself without the help of larger networks

'"Our topic maps solution is a stand-alone system that can be fully integrated with an organisation's existing applications, regardless of where on the network they are", explains Kal Ahmed, founder of NetworkedPlanet. "It… removes the laborious task of manually searching through systems and folders to locate a particular document".' [*M2 Presswire*]

standard /ˈstændəd/ *noun* a level by which people or the quality of work can be judged ■ *adjective* normal or usual ○ *They received the standard letter of reply just like everyone else.*

standard author /ˌstændəd ˈɔːθə/ *noun* an author of literary merit who is part of the literature of a country

Standard Book Number /ˌstændəd ˈbʊk ˌnʌmbə/ *noun* an older form of the International Standard Book Number. Abbr **SBN**

standard deviation /ˌstændəd ˌdiːviˈeɪʃ(ə)n/ *noun* a statistical term to show how far things are different from the normal

standard format /ˌstændəd ˈfɔːmæt/ *noun* the most commonly used format for such things as documents, used many times without any change to the text

standardisation /ˌstændədaɪˈzeɪʃ(ə)n/, **standardization** *noun* the process of making sure that everything fits a standard or is produced in the same way ○ *standardization of cover design in a series*

standardise /ˈstændədaɪz/, **standardize** *verb* to make sure that everything conforms to the same standard

standard letter /ˌstændəd ˈletə/ *noun* a letter which is sent to several different addresses without any change in the text

Standard Serial Number /ˌstændəd ˈsɪəriəl ˌnʌmbə/ *noun* an older form of the International Standard Serial Number. Abbr **SSN**

standby /ˈstændbaɪ/ *noun* something that is kept ready for use in case of need

standing committee /ˈstændɪŋ kəˌmɪti/ *noun* a permanently established administrative body which supports the work of a large organisation

Standing Committee on Official Publications /ˌstændɪŋ kəˌmɪti ɒn əˌfɪʃ(ə)l ˌpʌblɪˈkeɪʃ(ə)nz/ *noun* an organisation that was set up in order to improve access to official publications. Abbr **SCOOP**

Standing Conference on National and University Libraries *noun* an advisory committee on special areas of concern such as buildings, staffing or specific subjects. Abbr **SCONUL**

standing order /ˌstændɪŋ ˈɔːdə/ *noun* **1.** a regular order for each edition of a serial or annual publication **2.** an instruction to your bank to pay a fixed regular amount of money to a named person or organisation

staple /ˈsteɪp(ə)l/ *noun* a small bent piece of metal which is forced into papers to hold them together ■ *verb* to join papers together using a stapler

stapler /ˈsteɪplə/ *noun* a tool used to force staples through papers or other materials to hold them together

star /stɑː/ *noun* same as **asterisk** ■ *verb* same as **asterisk**

start /stɑːt/ *noun* the place or time at which something begins ■ *verb* to create something from the beginning

starting point /ˈstɑːtɪŋ pɔɪnt/ *noun* the place from where somebody or something begins

start page /ˈstɑːt peɪdʒ/ *noun* the webpage to which a visitor to a website is automatically taken first, or the page to which a user is automatically taken first whenever he or she goes online

state /steɪt/ *noun* **1.** a country or nation **2.** the government of a country **3.** a condition of something ■ *adjective* relating to government-run organisations ○ *state schools*

statement /ˈsteɪtmənt/ *noun* a formal or official account of events

state-of-the-art /ˌsteɪt əv ði ˈɑːt/ *adjective* as technically advanced as possible

static /'stætɪk/ *adjective* unmoving and unchanging

station /'steɪʃ(ə)n/ *noun* a point in a network at which work can be input to the main system

stationary /'steɪʃ(ə)n(ə)ri/ *adjective* not moving

stationery /'steɪʃ(ə)n(ə)ri/ *noun* paper equipment in an office, e.g. envelopes and writing paper

statistics /stə'tɪstɪks/ *plural noun* facts presented in the form of figures

status /'steɪtəs/ *noun* a position in society or in a work schedule

STATUS /'steɪtəs/ *noun* an information retrieval package which works on the free text principle

STATUS/IQ /ˌsteɪtəs aɪ 'kjuː/ *noun* a software system for use with STATUS which understands natural English and can rank its findings in the order of perceived usefulness to the user

status line /'steɪtəs laɪn/ *noun* a line at the top of a computer screen which gives details of the file currently being worked on

statute /'stætʃuːt/ *noun* a regulation or law

statutory deposit copy /ˌstætʃʊt(ə)ri dɪ'pɒzɪt ˌkɒpi/ *noun* a copy of a book or other publication which has to be deposited with a national library according to law

statutory instrument /ˌstætʃʊt(ə)ri 'ɪnstrʊmənt/ *noun* a law or legal requirement

stave /steɪv/ *noun* a set of five lines on which music is written

STD *abbreviation* Subscriber Trunk Dialling

steering committee /'stɪərɪŋ kəˌmɪti/ *noun* a group of people in charge of stages of a project which decides the priorities and order of work

stem /stem/ *verb* to search a database by inputting only the stem of a word with indicators before or afterwards to show that extra letters may be attached

stencil /'stensəl/ *noun* a template of shapes or letters which can be used to produce a design or written information

step /step/ *noun* one of a series of stages used to accomplish a task

stereo /'steriəʊ/ *noun* an audio system or device that reproduces stereophonic sound ■ *abbreviation* stereophonic

stereophonic /ˌsteriə'fɒnɪk/ *adjective* where sound signals are directed through two speakers at once to give depth to the sound

sticky /'stɪki/ *adjective* referring to a website that attracts visitors, especially one that keeps them interested for a long time

still /stɪl/ *noun* one single frame from a video or film

stitch /stɪtʃ/ *verb* to bind the pages of a book, pamphlet or other publication with thread or staples

stock /stɒk/ *noun* the total quantity of items available for use or sale

stock availability /'stɒk əˌveɪləbɪlɪti/ *noun* the fact of whether an item is on the premises and ready for use or sale

stock control /'stɒk kənˌtrəʊl/ *noun* the process of keeping records of how much stock is bought and sold

stockroom /'stɒkruːm/ *noun* a room where items that are not immediately needed are stored

stock selection /'stɒk sɪˌlekʃ(ə)n/ *noun* the process of choosing items to hold on the premises

stocktaking /'stɒkteɪkɪŋ/ *noun* the process of checking the amount of available stock against records

stop list /'stɒp lɪst/ *noun* a list of words that cannot be used in a system

stop word /'stɒp wɜːd/ *noun* a word that is not significant for an index or library file so is not included, e.g. the word 'the'

storage /'stɔːrɪdʒ/ *noun* **1.** the process of placing or keeping goods in a store **2.** a place for storing things **3.** money charged for keeping goods in a store

storage facilities /'stɔːrɪdʒ fəˌsɪlɪtiz/ *plural noun* room or space in which to store items

storage system /'stɔːrɪdʒ ˌsɪstəm/ *noun* a system for organising items in store so that they can be retrieved

storage unit /'stɔːrɪdʒ ˌjuːnɪt/ *noun* a device attached to a computer for storing information on disk or tape

store /stɔː/ *noun* a place where items can be kept until needed ■ *verb* to place items into safe keeping

story /'stɔːri/ *noun* a narrative tale

storyboard /'stɔːribɔːd/ *noun* a planning document used by producers of broadcast programmes

strategic information services /strəˌtiːdʒɪk ˌɪnfəˈmeɪʃ(ə)n ˌsɜːvɪsɪz/ *plural noun* the provision of information to a company so that they can achieve some aim, e.g. increase customer awareness or understand the competition. Abbr **SIS**

'Inacom's efforts to transform itself into a computer services company did not work. It remained a tactical 'break and fix' shop rather than a provider of strategic information services, said Michell Hudnall of the Meta Group, a market research firm.' [*Financial Times*]

strategic planning /strəˌtiːdʒɪk ˈplænɪŋ/ *noun* policy planning for future developments within a company or organisation

strategy /'strætədʒi/ *noun* a plan which sets out the methods of achieving one's goals

streaming /'striːmɪŋ/ *noun* the reading of data from a storage device in one continuous operation, without processor intervention

street plan /'striːt plæn/ *noun* a map of the streets in a particular town. Also called **town plan**

string /strɪŋ/ *noun* **1.** an indexing term for a series of characters **2.** an indexing term to describe the lists of terms compiled by an indexer with details of how they relate to each other

stripe /straɪp/ *noun* **1.** a line of different colour from the background **2.** a thin magnetic strip on the side of a film opposite to the sound track to control its speed on playback

structure /'strʌktʃə/ *noun* an underlying plan which gives form to a system or activity ■ *verb* to organise or construct something according to an efficient or logical system

structured indexing language /ˌstrʌktʃəd ˈɪndeksɪŋ ˌlæŋgwɪdʒ/ *noun* the use of words in a specific order to construct index headings, as in 'libraries, special' instead of 'special libraries'

studies /'stʌdiz/ *noun* a particular subject of study, especially an educational course or academic specialisation

study /'stʌdi/ *verb* to learn about something by spending time reading about it and listening to experts

study aid /'stʌdi eɪd/ *noun* educational material such as a book or CD for sale to students who want to learn by self-study at home

study leave /'stʌdi liːv/ *noun* leave of absence from a course of study, granted for the purposes of carrying out additional research

STUMPERS-L /'stʌmpəz el/ *noun* an Internet bulletin board which lists difficult questions asked of librarians to see if any other librarians can help with the answers

style /staɪl/ *noun* the way in which a particular writer or editor uses words, sentences and layout to produce a recognisable publication

stylus /'staɪləs/ *noun* a small pointed object which is used in computer graphics to direct the cursor

sub- /sʌb/ *prefix* combining with nouns to give the meaning of less important

sub-contract /ˌsʌbkənˈtrækt/ *verb* to pay somebody else to do part of a job for you

subdomain name /ˌsʌbdəˈmeɪn ˌneɪm/ *noun* **1.** a second level of Internet domain names created by the administrator of the domain **2.** a subdivision of the two-letter country domain names into two- or three-letter organisational subdomains, e.g. 'ac.uk' for United Kingdom academic sites and 'com.au' for Australian commercial sites.

sub-editor /'sʌbedɪtə/ *noun* a person who corrects and checks articles in a newspaper before they are printed

sub-heading, **sub-head** *noun* a subsidiary heading which divides text into shorter sections

subject /'sʌbdʒɪkt/ *noun* an idea for study, discussion or treatment

subject bibliography /'sʌbdʒɪkt bɪbli,ɒɡrəfi/ *noun* a list of documents, articles and books that are relevant to a certain subject, with details such as author, publisher and date of publication

subject catalogue /'sʌbdʒɪkt ,kætəlɒɡ/ *noun* a catalogue which lists books according to their subjects

subject directory /'sʌbdʒɪkt daɪ,rekt(ə)ri/ *noun* an index of resources arranged primarily by subject area

subject entry /'sʌbdʒɪkt ,entri/, **subject heading** /'sʌbdʒɪkt ,hedɪŋ/ *noun* an index or catalogue heading which indicates the main subject of a document

subject index /'sʌbdʒɪkt ,ɪndeks/ *noun* a list of subjects covered by a library with the class numbers to indicate where materials can be found

subject librarian /'sʌbdʒɪkt laɪ,breəriən/ *noun* a librarian who is a specialist in a particular subject

subject line /'sʌbdʒɪkt laɪn/ *noun* a line in an e-mail that indicates the subject of the message

subject matter /'sʌbdʒɪkt ,mætə/ *noun* the subject of a book, talk or work of art

submission date /sʌb'mɪʃ(ə)n ,deɪt/ *noun* the last date by which an assignment, proposal or application can be sent to somebody

subordinate clause /sə'bɔːdɪnət klɔːz/ *noun* a clause that cannot stand alone as a separate sentence since its meaning depends on the meaning of the main clause and simply gives additional information. In the sentence 'We had to run because we were late', the clause 'because we were late' is the subordinate clause and 'We had to run' is the main clause.

subscribe /səb'skraɪb/ *verb* **1.** to agree to pay for and receive or use something over a fixed period of time, e.g. a periodical, series of books, or set of tickets to musical or dramatic performances **2.** to add one's name and e-mail address to a mailing list in order to receive messages from a website automatically, with or without charge

Subscriber Trunk Dialling /sʌb ,skraɪbə 'trʌŋk ,daɪəlɪŋ/ *noun* a system of automatic telephone connection all over the world which is then charged to your personal telephone account. Abbr **STD**

subscribe to /sʌb'skraɪb tʊ/ *verb* to pay money in order to receive copies of a regular publication or to gain access to a service

subscription /səb'skrɪpʃən/ *noun* money paid to become a member of an organisation or in order to receive regular publications

subscription library /səb'skrɪpʃən ,laɪbrəri/ *noun* a private library which people can join by paying a subscription

subscript letter /'sʌbskrɪpt ,letə/, **subscript number** *noun* a very small letter or number which is printed slightly below the line level of normal print

subsection /'sʌb,sekʃ(ə)n/ *noun* a small part of a larger section

sub-series /'sʌb ,sɪəriːz/ *noun* a series of publications with titles dependent on a previous series

subset /'sʌbset/ *noun* a smaller part of a large division of data

substantiate /səb'stænʃieɪt/ *verb* to supply evidence to prove that something is true

substitute /'sʌbstɪtjuːt/ *verb* to put or use something in the place of something else

subtitle /'sʌbtaɪt(ə)l/ *noun* **1.** the secondary title of a book **2.** words written at the bottom of a television or cinema screen to enable the spoken words to be read

succeed /sək'siːd/ *verb* **1.** to follow a person and take over their job **2.** to gain the intended result

successive /sək'sesɪv/ *adjective* following one after the other

sufficient /sə'fɪʃ(ə)nt/ *adjective* as much as is needed

suffix /'sʌfɪks/ *noun* a word or group of letters added to the end of a word which changes the grammar and meaning

suggestions book /sə'dʒestʃənz bʊk/ *noun* a book in which the users of a service can write their ideas for how to improve the service

summarise /'sʌməraɪz/, **summarize** *verb* to give a brief description of the main points

summary /'sʌməri/ *noun* a short version of something giving only the main points

Sunday supplement /ˌsʌndeɪ 'sʌplɪmənt/ *noun* a magazine that comes with a Sunday newspaper

super- /suːpə/ *prefix* combining with adjectives to suggest that something is of very high quality

superimpose /ˌsuːpərɪm'pəʊz/ *verb* to place something on top of something else

superior number /sʊˌpɪəriə 'nʌmbə/ *noun* a superscript number often used to indicate a footnote

Super Janet /'suːpə ˌdʒænɪt/ *noun* an updated version of the Joint Academic NETwork system of information transfer within the UK

superscript /'suːpəskrɪpt/ *noun* a small character printed at a higher level than the rest of the line of writing

supersede /ˌsuːpə'siːd/ *verb* to replace something which is old and out of date

supervise /'suːpəvaɪz/ *verb* to make sure that a person is working efficiently or that a task is done properly

supervisor /'suːpəvaɪzə/ *noun* a person who has the responsibility for supervising other people or machinery

supplementary /ˌsʌplɪ'ment(ə)ri/ *adjective* added to something else to improve it, update it or make it satisfactory

supplier /sə'plaɪə/ *noun* a person or company that provides goods, services or equipment

supply /sə'plaɪ/ *verb* to provide, give or sell something to somebody

support /sə'pɔːt/ *verb* to provide help, advice or finance to ensure that somebody or something else can work

suppress /sə'pres/ *verb* to prevent something from being known or done

surf /sɜːf/ *verb* to browse through a database ○ *surfing the Internet*

surface Web /'sɜːfɪs web/ *noun* data on the World Wide Web which can be found using ordinary search engines. Compare **deep Web**

surge /sɜːdʒ/ *noun* a sudden increase in something such as sales or electrical power

survey /'sɜːveɪ/ *noun* a detailed investigation often involving people's opinions

survey population /'sɜːveɪ ˌpɒpjʊleɪʃ(ə)n/ *noun* a selected sample for an investigation

sustain /sə'steɪn/ *verb* to keep or maintain something for a length of time

sv *abbreviation* in Internet addresses, the top-level domain for El Salvador

SVQ *abbreviation* Scottish Vocational Qualification

swap /swɒp/ *verb* to exchange information, giving one item and receiving another in its place

switch /swɪtʃ/ *verb* □ **to switch on** to connect a machine or equipment to a source of electrical power □ **to switch over** to change to another machine ◇ **to switch off 1.** to isolate a machine or equipment from a source of electrical power **2.** to stop listening

switchboard /'swɪtʃbɔːd/ *noun* a central control unit for a telephone system within an organisation, from which calls can be redirected to extension lines

switchboard operator /'swɪtʃbɔːd ˌɒpəreɪtə/ *noun* a person who receives calls to an organisation and redirects them

sy *abbreviation* in Internet addresses, the top-level domain for Syria

symbol /'sɪmbəl/ *noun* a shape, icon or picture which represents something else

symbolic /sɪm'bɒlɪk/ *adjective* representing something else ○ *Symbolic* *language uses words to represent items rather than just describing them.*

symposium /sɪm'pəʊziəm/ *noun* a conference of experts to discuss particular topics (NOTE: The plural is **symposia**.)

syndetic /sɪn'detɪk/ *adjective* connected by cross-references

syndetic catalogue /sɪn,detɪk 'kætəlɒg/, **syndetic index** /sɪn,detɪk 'ɪndeks/ *noun* a dictionary catalogue or index using a system of cross-referencing

synecdoche /sɪ'nekdəkiː/ *noun* a figure of speech which uses one species for the whole genus, e.g. 'pennies' for money in general

synonym /'sɪnənɪm/ *noun* a word of phrase which has almost the same meaning as another word or phrase

synopsis /sɪ'nɒpsɪs/ *noun* a summary of a longer text (NOTE: The plural is **synopses**.)

syntax /'sɪntæks/ *noun* a term in linguistics to describe the grammatical structure of a language

synthesis /'sɪnθəsɪs/ *noun* the artificial combination of ideas and styles

synthesise /'sɪnθəsaɪz/, **synthesize** *verb* to make an artificial combination from a variety of small components ○ *The computer is now able to synthesise sounds and make them seem like a human voice.*

synthesiser /'sɪnθəsaɪzə/ *noun* a machine which combines electrical sounds to make them recognisable as speech or music

SyQuest /'saɪkwest/ *noun* a manufacturer of storage devices, including a range of removable hard disk drives and backup units

system /'sɪstəm/ *noun* a set of rules or plans which are used to accomplish a task

system analyst /'sɪstəm ,ænəlɪst/ *noun* a person who works at finding out the strong and weak points in a system

'"The advantage Excalibur has is the search engine", says Leona Carpenter, senior system analyst at the British Library, where Excalibur has been used to digitise ageing microfilm of 18th century newspapers, and to digitise some of the library's printed catalogues and indexes.' [*The Guardian*]

Systematic Computerised Processing in Cataloguing *noun* a system used in university libraries for the systematic control of periodicals. Abbr **SCOPE**

systematic sampling /,sɪstəmætɪk 'sɑːmplɪŋ/ *noun* the use of a regular order of choice for the selection of a sample ○ *They chose to use the method of systematic sampling and interview every tenth person from the list of names.*

system design /,sɪstəm dɪ'zaɪn/ *noun* the process of deciding on the most appropriate system to provide the solution to a problem

system diagnosis /'sɪstəm daɪəg ,nəʊsɪs/ *noun* the process of finding faults in a system

systems analysis /'sɪstəmz ə ,næləsɪs/ *noun* a process of using a computer to suggest how a company should work by analysing the way in which it works at present

system software /,sɪstəm 'sɒftweə/ *noun* programs which make applications work on the hardware

sz *abbreviation* in Internet addresses, the top-level domain for Swaziland

T

T1 /ˌtiː ˈwʌn/ *noun* a high-capacity telephone line suitable for high-speed digital access to the Internet, handling 24 voice or data channels simultaneously

tab key /ˈtæb kiː/ *noun* one of the keys on a computer keyboard which enables the user to move through or arrange text in columns

table /ˈteɪb(ə)l/ *noun* a list of data arranged in rows and columns

table of contents /ˌteɪb(ə)l əv ˈkɒntents/ *noun* a list of contents in a book or magazine, usually printed at the beginning

tabloid /ˈtæblɔɪd/ *noun* a small-size newspaper with a less serious approach to the news than the broadsheets

tabulate /ˈtæbjʊleɪt/ *verb* to arrange work on a word processor using the tab key to move from one column or row to the next

tabulator /ˈtæbjʊleɪtə/ *noun* part of a computer which sets words or figures automatically in columns

tacit knowledge /ˌtæsɪt ˈnɒlɪdʒ/ *noun* human knowledge that takes the form of intuitions, judgments and learned skills, and is hard to define or record. Compare **explicit knowledge**

tact /tækt/ *noun* an ability to deal with people or situations without upsetting anyone

tactic /ˈtæktɪk/ *noun* a method of achieving what you want

tactical planning /ˈtæktɪk(ə)l ˌplænɪŋ/ *noun* discussion and decisions about future tactics

tactile feedback /ˈtæktaɪl ˌfiːdbæk/ *noun* information discovered by the sense of touch

tag /tæg/ *noun* a character or symbol attached to a record to aid retrieval

'Indexing tools provided by document capture software companies such as Captiva enable users to index – or tag – scanned images and assign them to specific, searchable files within a document imaging system.' [*Computer Weekly*]

tail end /ˌteɪl ˈend/ *noun* the final entry or activity in a series

tail off /ˌteɪl ˈɒf/ *verb* to become less in amount or value until it finally stops or disappears completely

take /teɪk/ *verb* to move something physically from one place to another □ **to take a message** to listen to information in order to pass it on to somebody else □ **to take a photograph** to use a camera to create a picture of something □ **to take into account** to consider a fact or aspect before making a decision

take out /ˌteɪk ˈaʊt/ *verb* **1.** to arrange to have something ○ *They made arrangements to take out a mortgage to buy the house.* **2.** to borrow a book from a library

talking book /ˌtɔːkɪŋ ˈbʊk/ *noun* a book that has been recorded on to an audio cassette, originally intended for people who cannot see well enough to read

talking newspaper /ˌtɔːkɪŋ ˈnjuːzpeɪpə/ *noun* a tape or cassette recording of a newspaper, usually for the use of blind people

talks /tɔːks/ *plural noun* **1.** a formal discussion **2.** an informal lecture

tally /'tæli/ *noun* an informal cumulative record of amounts collected ∎ *verb* to agree or correspond with another conclusion or total ○ *The figures in the accounts did not tally with the office records.*

tape /teɪp/ *noun* a narrow strip of plastic, coated with magnetic material on which to record sound or pictures

tape measure /'teɪp ˌmeʒə/ *noun* a flexible strip of metal or cloth marked with divisions of length

tape merging /'teɪp ˌmɜːdʒɪŋ/ *noun* the act of taking two tapes with data and combining them, usually by combining master tape with corrections or additions on a second tape

tape recorder /'teɪp rɪˌkɔːdə/ *noun* a machine that is used to record and play back sounds on audio cassettes or reel to reel tape

target audience /'tɑːɡɪt ˌɔːdiəns/ *noun* a group of people at which specific products, services or written or spoken information is aimed

target date /'tɑːɡɪt deɪt/ *noun* the date by which a task must be done

target language /'tɑːɡɪt ˌlæŋɡwɪdʒ/ *noun* the language that a text is translated into

target market /'tɑːɡɪt ˌmɑːkɪt/ *noun* the type of customer who is thought likely to buy specific goods or services

tariff /'tærɪf/ *noun* a charge made for goods or services

task /tɑːsk/ *noun* a job that has to be done

task identity /'tɑːsk aɪˌdentɪti/ *noun* a code that indicates which is the job to be done

taxonomy /tæk'sɒnəmi/ *noun* the principle of classifying and ordering items such as books, e.g. in a hierarchical structure

tc *abbreviation* in Internet addresses, the top-level domain for Turks and Caicos Islands

TCP /ˌtiː siː 'piː/ *noun* a standard data transmission protocol that provides full duplex transmission, in which the protocol bundles data into packets and checks for errors. Full form **transmission control protocol**

TCP/IP /ˌtiː siː piː aɪ 'piː/ *noun* a data transfer protocol used in networks and communications systems, often used in Unix-based networks. Full form **transmission control protocol/interface program**

teach /tiːtʃ/ *verb* **1.** to impart knowledge or skill to somebody by instruction or example **2.** to give lessons in or provide information about a subject

teacher librarian /ˌtiːtʃə laɪ 'breəriən/ *noun* a person who is qualified both as a teacher and as a school librarian

teacher's book /'tiːtʃəz bʊk/, **teacher's manual** /'tiːtʃəz ˌmænjuəl/ *noun* a book published to go with a set of students' books, giving the teacher answers to questions and suggestions for teaching

teaching tool /'tiːtʃɪŋ tuːl/ *noun* any document or audiovisual material that can be used for teaching

team teaching /ˌtiːm 'tiːtʃɪŋ/ *noun* a system of two or more teachers working together to teach a group of students

teamwork /'tiːmwɜːk/ *noun* the combined action of a group of people working well together

technical author /'teknɪk(ə)l ˌɔːθə/ *noun* a person who writes specialised instructions and manuals on technical subjects

technical college /'teknɪk(ə)l ˌkɒlɪdʒ/ *noun* a further education college in which students study practical rather than academic subjects

technical information centre /ˌteknɪk(ə)l ˌɪnfə'meɪʃ(ə)n ˌsentə/ *noun* an organisation which acquires, processes and distributes technical information

technical manual /'teknɪk(ə)l ˌmænjuəl/ *noun* a book that gives instructions about how to work a machine

technical support /ˌteknɪk(ə)l sə 'pɔːt/ *noun* a system by which the users of machines are helped by people who understand how they work

'As far as straight Internet access goes, look at features such as cost per month for unlimited access, quality of software bundled, the technical support hours. Internet Magazine publishes a list of access provider performance tests every month.' [*The Independent*]

technician /tek'nɪʃ(ə)n/ *noun* a person who specialises in working with and maintaining machines or scientific equipment

technique /tek'niːk/ *noun* a particular skill or ability which can be learned

technofreak /'teknəʊfriːk/ *noun* a technical expert in, or obsessive enthusiast of, information systems

technology /tek'nɒlədʒi/ *noun* the application of scientific knowledge to practical purposes. ◊ **information technology**

teething troubles /'tiːθɪŋ ˌtrʌb(ə)lz/ *plural noun* small difficulties which occur at the start of a project

TEFL *abbreviation* teaching of English as a foreign language

tele- /teli/ *prefix* meaning across a distance

telecommunication /ˌtelikə ˌmjuːnɪ'keɪʃ(ə)n/ *noun* the transmission of encoded sound, pictures or data over significant distances, using radio signals or electrical or optical lines

telecommunications /ˌtelikə ˌmjuːnɪ'keɪʃ(ə)nz/ *noun* the science and technology of using electronic equipment to send messages over a distance

telecomputing /'telikəm,pjuːtɪŋ/ *noun* the act of sending information to or receiving information from another computer via a modem or local area network

teleconferencing /'teli ˌkɒnf(ə)rənsɪŋ/ *noun* the act of several people using a telephone network to speak to each other at the same time

telecottage /'telikɒtɪdʒ/ *noun* a house where a person both lives and works

telegram /'telɪɡræm/ *noun* a message sent by telegraphy and then printed on to paper and delivered

telegraphy /tə'leɡrəfi/ *noun* a way of sending telegrams using radio or electric signals

telematics /ˌtelɪ'mætɪks/ *noun* the study of the processes involved in the long-distance transmission of computer data

telemedicine /'telimed(ə)sɪn/ *noun* the use of video links, e-mail, telephone or some other telecommunications system to transmit medical information, e.g. in consultations between a doctor and patient or in supervision of medical staff

telemessage /'telimesɪdʒ/ *noun* a message sent by telephone but delivered as a card

teleordering /'teli,ɔːdərɪŋ/ *noun* the ordering of goods by telephone which are then delivered to your address

telephone /'telɪfəʊn/ *noun* an instrument which can be used to talk to somebody over a long distance by means of dialling a series of numbers ■ *verb* to make contact with somebody at a distance by using a telephone

telephone call /'telɪfəʊn kɔːl/ *noun* a conversation with somebody on the telephone

telephone directory /'telɪfəʊn daɪ ˌrekt(ə)ri/, **telephone book** /'telɪfəʊn bʊk/ *noun* a book containing an alphabetical list of names, addresses and telephone numbers of people in a given city, town or area

telephone exchange /'telɪfəʊn ɪks ˌtʃeɪndʒ/ *noun* a building where telephone lines can be connected when a call is made

telephone extension /'telɪfəʊn ek ˌstenʃ(ə)n/ *noun* an extra telephone linked to the main line into the building

telephone operator /'telɪfəʊn ˌɒpəreɪtə/ *noun* a person who works in a telephone exchange, connecting calls and answering problems

telephone subscriber /'telɪfəʊn səb,skraɪbə/ *noun* a person who pays money to a telephone company in order to be able to connect a telephone to the national network

telephone switchboard /ˌtelɪfəʊn 'swɪtʃbɔːd/ *noun* a central point in a private telephone network where all the lines meet and can be connected

teleprocessing /ˈteliˌprəʊsesɪŋ/ *noun* the use of computer terminals in different locations, connected to a main computer, to process data. Abbr **TP**

telesales /ˈteliseɪlz/ *noun* the process of telephoning people without warning to try to sell them things

teleshopping /ˈteliˌʃɒpɪŋ/ *noun* using the telephone to do shopping which is then delivered to you

teletext /ˈtelitekst/ *noun* a system of transmitting written text using a television signal

COMMENT: Teletext constantly transmits pages of information which are repeated one after the other; the user can stop one to read it. This is different from viewdata, where the user calls up a page of text using a telephone line.

television /ˌteliˈvɪʒ(ə)n/ *noun* **1.** a system of transmitting pictures and sound over a distance so that they can be received and seen on a television set **2.** a device for receiving and displaying broadcast television programmes ▸ abbr **TV**

teleworker /ˈteliwɜːkə/ *noun* somebody who works from home by means of computers, modem, phone and fax machines

telex /ˈteleks/ *noun* a system of sending international messages using telephone lines, where the text is typed on one machine and immediately printed out at the receiving end

Telnet /ˈtelnet/ *noun* a remote login program that allows a user on one computer to access another on the same network

template /ˈtemˌpleɪt/ *noun* a thin sheet of metal or plastic with cut-out shapes which enable exactly the same shape to be reproduced many times

temporarily /ˌtempəˈreərəli/ *adverb* only for a short time

temporary /ˈtemp(ə)rəri/ *adjective* lasting only a short time

tender /ˈtendə/ *noun* a formal offer to supply goods or services at a stated price ▪ *verb* to make a formal offer to do something ○ *He tendered his resignation.* □ **to put work out to tender** to ask

for companies to state their price for doing a particular job

term /tɜːm/ *noun* **1.** a set or limited period of time ○ *The term of office for the chairperson is one year.* **2.** one of the three divisions of the academic year ○ *The year starts in October with the autumn term.* **3.** a word used in the terminology of indexing

terminal /ˈtɜːmɪn(ə)l/ *noun* a processor with screen and keyboard used to access a central computer system

terminal user interface /ˈtɜːmɪn(ə)l ˌjuːzə ˌɪntəfeɪs/ *noun* hardware and software used by a person at a terminal to enable contact with the central computer

terminate /ˈtɜːmɪneɪt/ *verb* **1.** to stop completely **2.** to end something

terminology /ˌtɜːmɪˈnɒlədʒi/ *noun* a set of specialised words and phrases belonging to a specific subject

terms /tɜːmz/ *plural noun* **1.** the headings, words and phrases used in a classification scheme **2.** conditions agreed between people for a sale or job

tertiary /ˈtɜːʃəri/ *adjective* third in order or stage of development ○ *Universities are the tertiary stage of education after primary and secondary schools.*

tertiary education /ˌtɜːʃəri ˌedjʊ ˈkeɪʃ(ə)n/ *noun* same as **higher education**

TESL *abbreviation* teaching of English as a second language

TESOL *abbreviation* EDUC teaching of English to speakers of other languages

test pattern /ˈtest ˌpæt(ə)n/ *noun* a design which uses different textures and colours on a television screen to see if all the components are adjusted properly

text /tekst/ *noun* the main part of a written document

textbook /ˈtekstbʊk/ *noun* an academic book on a particular subject used for study

text box /ˈtekst bɒks/ *noun* a box within a computer dialogue box in which characters such as text, dates or numbers can be typed and edited

text editing /ˈtekst ˌedɪtɪŋ/ *noun* work done on a word processor to change, add, delete or move words, phrases or paragraphs

text file /'tekst faɪl/ *noun* a stored file on a computer that contains text rather than digits or data

text formatter /'tekst ˌfɔːmætə/ *noun* a program that arranges a text file according to pre-set rules such as line width and page size

text illustrations /'tekst ˌɪləstreɪʃ(ə)nz/ *plural noun* illustrations printed on the text pages, and not on separate paper

text index /'tekst ˌɪndeks/ *noun* an index of some or all of the words in something such as a computer file or database field, used to aid searching and retrieval

text management /'tekst ˌmænɪdʒmənt/ *noun* facilities that allow text to be written, stored, retrieved, edited and printed

text processing /'tekst ˌprəʊsesɪŋ/ *noun* same as **word processing**

text retrieval /'tekst rɪˌtriːv(ə)l/ *noun* a facility on a word processor which allows the user to find the text of documents to be edited or worked with

text to table /ˌtekst tʊ 'teɪb(ə)l/ *noun* a facility on a word processor which allows the user to convert text into table form

textual analysis /'tekstʃuəl əˌnælɪsɪs/ *noun* investigation into the techniques used in a particular style of writing

tg *abbreviation* in Internet addresses, the top-level domain for Togo

th *abbreviation* in Internet addresses, the top-level domain for Thailand

The Bookseller /'bʊkselə/ *noun* a journal providing information especially interesting to booksellers and publishers

thematic catalogue /θiːˌmætɪk 'kætəlɒg/ *noun* a musical catalogue containing the main themes of a composer's works, usually arranged in chronological order

thermal imaging /ˌθɜːm(ə)l 'ɪmɪdʒɪŋ/ *noun* a technique which uses a TV camera sensitive to heat rather than light to produce pictures

thermal paper /ˌθɜːm(ə)l 'peɪpə/ *noun* paper which is chemically coated so that it can be used with a thermal printer

thermal printer /ˌθɜːm(ə)l 'prɪntə/ *noun* a printing machine which uses heat-sensitive paper

thesaurus /θɪ'sɔːrəs/ *noun* a type of dictionary that lists groups of synonyms

thesaurus strategy /θɪ'sɔːrəs ˌstrætədʒi/ *noun* in database searching, the practice of running multiple searches using similar words to find as many documents on a subject as possible

thesis /'θiːsɪs/ *noun* a piece of extended writing explaining the objectives, methodology and findings of a research project

thesis statement /'θiːsɪs ˌsteɪtmənt/ *noun* a sentence or short paragraph at the beginning of a thesis which describes the main idea explored in the text

third party /ˌθɜːd 'pɑːti/ *noun* a person who becomes involved in a situation but is not one of the main parties

32mo *abbreviation* thirty-twomo

thirty-twomo /ˌθɜːti 'tuːməʊ/ *noun* **1.** a size of book page traditionally created by folding a single sheet of standard-sized printing paper five times, giving 32 leaves or 64 pages **2.** a book printed in this format. Abbr **32mo 3.** an American book format about 4 or 5 inches high. Abbr **32mo**

Thomson's Local Directory /ˌtɒmsənz ˌləʊk(ə)l daɪ'rekt(ə)ri/ *noun* a private publication in most areas of the UK giving local information such as business telephone numbers, postcodes and maps

thorough /'θʌrə/ *adjective* very careful and complete

thread /θred/ *noun* an idea or theme which connects the different parts of a story together

3D /ˌθriː 'diː/ *abbreviation* three-dimensional

three-dimensional /ˌθriː daɪ'menʃ(ə)nəl/ *adjective* having width, breadth and depth and so appearing solid. Abbr **3D**

3G /ˌθriː ˈdʒiː/ *noun* a wireless communications technology designed to provide high-speed Internet access and transmission of text, digitised voice, video and multimedia. Full form **third generation**

three-quarter binding /ˌθriː ˈkwɔːtə ˌbaɪndɪŋ/ *noun* bookbinding in which the spine and most of the sides of a book are covered in the same material

thriller /ˈθrɪlə/ *noun* a novel telling of crime and criminals in an adventurous way

throughput /ˈθruːpʊt/ *noun* the amount of information processed in a given period of time

thumb index /ˈθʌm ˌɪndeks/ *noun* a method of indexing used especially for dictionaries and diaries, where rounded holes are cut into the foredge of a book, allowing a thumb to be placed in the hole and the book to be opened at the correct page quickly

thumb-index /ˈθʌm ˌɪndeks/ *verb* to provide a book with a thumb index ○ *The dictionary is thumb-indexed.*

tie-in /ˈtaɪ ɪn/ *noun* a book that is derived from or published together with a TV or radio programme

tier /tɪə/ *noun* one of a number of levels ○ *There were five tiers of shelves.*

.tif /tɪf/ *suffix* a file extension for a TIFF file. Full form **tagged image file format**

TIFF /tɪf/ *abbreviation* a standard file format used to store graphic images. Full form **tagged image file format**

COMMENT: TIFF is probably the most common image interchange format used by DTP software. Developed by Aldus and Microsoft, TIFF can handle monochrome, grey-scale, 8-bit or 24-bit colour images. There have been many different versions of TIFF that include several different compression algorithms

tilde /ˈtɪldə/ *noun* a pronunciation symbol (~) written over some letters in Spanish and Portuguese

tilt /tɪlt/ *verb* to alter the angle of something so that it is not vertical □ **tilt & swivel** used to describe a computer screen mounted on a pivot so that the angle and direction can be changed

time lag /ˈtaɪm læg/ *noun* a period of waiting between two related events ○ *There is sometimes a time lag between speakers who are interviewed on television from another country.*

time out /ˌtaɪm ˈaʊt/ *noun* time taken away from one's usual activities

timer /ˈtaɪmə/ *noun* a device which can be set or pre-set to measure the time taken to do an activity

timescale /ˈtaɪmskeɪl/ *noun* the length of time taken up by a particular activity ○ *Their timescale for writing the book was six months.*

timesharing /ˈtaɪmʃeərɪŋ/ *noun* an arrangement by which several people can be online to a computer at the same time

time slot /ˈtaɪm ˈslɒt/ *noun* a period of time allocated to a specific activity

timetable /ˈtaɪmteɪb(ə)l/ *noun* a schedule of times and activities such as bus and train services

title /ˈtaɪt(ə)l/ *noun* **1.** the name given to a book, play or TV programme **2.** the word used to indicate the status of a person, e.g. Mr, Mrs, Dr or Rev

title-a-line catalogue /ˌtaɪt(ə)l ə ˈlaɪn ˌkætəlɒg/ *noun* a catalogue in which the entries occupy only one line of type each

title bar /ˈtaɪt(ə)l bɑː/ *noun* a horizontal bar at the top of a computer screen which usually shows the names of the program and file that is currently in use

title catalogue /ˈtaɪt(ə)l ˌkætəlɒg/ *noun* an alphabetical list of book titles

title index /ˈtaɪt(ə)l ˌɪndeks/ *noun* an index of books in a library or publisher's catalogue listed under their titles

title page /ˈtaɪt(ə)l peɪdʒ/ *noun* a page at the beginning of a book which states the title and publication information

COMMENT: The title page is always a right-hand page. From the designer's point of view, a title page is designed both to attract the reader and at the same time give some idea of the contents of the book: this must be done using typography alone, although some title pages have illustrations or vignettes. The jacket or cover is designed in order to attract the purchaser to the book in the shop; the title page is designed to make the reader want to read it when he or she opens it

tj *abbreviation* in Internet addresses, the top-level domain for Tajikistan

tm *abbreviation* in Internet addresses, the top-level domain for Turkmenistan

tn *abbreviation* in Internet addresses, the top-level domain for Tunisia

to *abbreviation* in Internet addresses, the top-level domain for Tonga

TOEFL /'təʊf(ə)l/ a trademark for a standardised English language test taken by speakers of other languages who are applying to universities in the United States. Full form **Test of English as a Foreign Language**

TOEIC /'təʊɪk/ a trademark for a standardised English language test which measures comprehension, speaking, writing and reading skills, focusing especially on the areas of business, commerce and industry. Full form **Test of English for International Communication**

token effort /ˌtəʊkən 'efət/ *noun* the minimum amount of effort required so as to be seen to be trying to do something

toner /'təʊnə/ *noun* dry ink powder put into a photocopier to develop the image on the copy

toolkit /'tuːlkɪt/ *noun* **1.** a collection of information, resources and advice for a specific subject area or activity **2.** a bundle of software which can be used to set up a particular utility or service

tools /tuːlz/ *plural noun* a set of utility programs such as backup and format in a computer system

top down structure /ˌtɒp 'daʊn ˌstrʌktʃə/ *noun* a system in which policies are decided by people in authority rather than the people who actually do the work

topic /'tɒpɪk/ *noun* the subject of a document or for discussion

topic map /'tɒpɪk mæp/ *noun* a model of the structure of knowledge which represents a topic, the associations between this topic and other topics and the information sources in which this topic is referred to

'According to the company, [processing tool] TMCore05 is based on open standards to enable full integration with an organisation's existing file and content management applications. The solution utilises topic maps and enables employees to quickly retrieve information they need.' [*Telecomworldwire*]

top-level /'tɒp ˌlev(ə)l/ *adjective* relating to things that are discussed or decided by the people with the most power in a country, company or organisation

top-level domain /ˌtɒp ˌlev(ə)l dəʊ 'meɪn/ *noun* the part of an Internet address that identifies an Internet domain, e.g. edu (education), .com (commercial) or a two-letter country code.

top management /ˌtɒp 'mænɪdʒmənt/ *noun* the most senior members of a management hierarchy

topographical information /ˌtɒpəgræfɪk(ə)l ˌɪnfə'meɪʃ(ə)n/ *noun* a description of the physical features of a country

topology /tɒ'pɒlədʒi/ *noun* the relationships between parts linked together in a system such as a computer network

top secret /ˌtɒp 'siːkrət/ *adjective* highly confidential so having a restricted circulation to the people at the top level

touch pad /'tʌtʃ pæd/ *noun* a flat surface which is sensitive to touch and can be used to control a cursor on screen or on/off switches

touch screen /'tʌtʃ skriːn/ *noun* a computer display screen which is sensitive to touch and will react when touched according to pre-programmed information

town plan /ˌtaʊn 'plæn/ *noun* same as **street plan**

toy library /'tɔɪ ˌlaɪbrəri/ *noun* a collection of toys which can be borrowed by young children for short periods

tp *abbreviation* in Internet addresses, the top-level domain for Timor Leste

TP *abbreviation* teleprocessing

tr *abbreviation* in Internet addresses, the top-level domain for Turkey

trace /treɪs/ *verb* to find somebody or something after a prolonged search

tracing /'treɪsɪŋ/ *noun* **1.** a list of the headings an entry appears under in a catalogue **2.** a list of the references made to an entry from other entries in a catalogue

track /træk/ *noun* a concentric ring on a computer disk or tape which is used to store data in separate sections

tracking /'trækɪŋ/ *noun* lines on magnetic tapes or disks along which information is carried

tract /trækt/ *noun* a short article dealing with a religious or moral subject

tractor feed /'træktə fiːd/ *noun* a method of controlling paper feed by the use of holes on the edge of the paper and sprockets on the printer

trade /treɪd/ *noun* the activity of buying, selling or exchanging goods or services

trade book /'treɪd bʊk/ *noun* a standard edition of a book, meant for sale to the general public, as opposed to a de luxe or book-club edition

trade catalogue /'treɪd ˌkætəlɒg/ *noun* **1.** a book containing details of the goods manufactured or sold by a firm **2.** publisher's catalogue listing books for sale through retail bookshops

trade directory /'treɪd daɪˌrekt(ə)ri/ *noun* a book containing alphabetical lists and information about companies and organisations involved in trade in a particular area

trademark /'treɪdmɑːk/ *noun* a name, sign or symbol printed on something to show who it is made by

trade name /'treɪd neɪm/ *noun* the name under which a product is sold ○ *Some drugs are marketed under several different trade names.*

trade-off /'treɪd ɒf/ *noun* a compromise between two opposite points of view

trade paperback /ˌtreɪd 'peɪpəbæk/ *noun* a paperback edition of a book that is superior in production quality to a mass-market paperback

edition and is similar to a hardback in size

trail /treɪl/ *noun* a path followed by somebody or something

train /'treɪn ɒn/ *verb* to teach somebody the skills for a specific job

trainee /treɪ'niː/ *noun* a person who is learning how to perform specific tasks

trainer /'treɪnə/ *noun* a person who instructs others

training /'treɪnɪŋ/ *noun* the act of teaching somebody specific skills

training costs /'treɪnɪŋ kɒsts/ *plural noun* money needed by a company to pay for training its employees

training manual /'treɪnɪŋ ˌmænjuəl/ *noun* an instruction book which explains how to train somebody in a specific skill

training materials /'treɪnɪŋ mə ˌtɪəriəlz/ *plural noun* teaching materials used for training

training package /'treɪnɪŋ ˌpækɪdʒ/ *noun* a pack of teaching materials to help trainers to run courses

training programme /'treɪnɪŋ ˌprəʊgræm/ *noun* a schedule designed to teach specific skills within a given time

trans- /træns/ *prefix* used to form words with the meaning of moving across time or space

transaction /træn'zækʃən/ *noun* an action which involves the exchange of goods or information

transaction data /trænz'ækʃən ˌdeɪtə/ *noun* information about the data being processed

transaction processing /træn 'zækʃən ˌprəʊsesɪŋ/ *noun* the way in which a computer deals with instructions given by the user

transceiver /træn'siːvə/ *noun* a device that can both transmit and receive signals, e.g. a terminal or modem

transcribe /træn'skraɪb/ *verb* **1.** to produce a written version of spoken words ○ *His speech was transcribed so that it could be printed.* **2.** to write a written text in the alphabet of another language

transcript /'trænskrıpt/ *noun* a written form of something that was spoken

transcription /træn'skrıpʃən/ *noun* the act of transcribing data or copying a text

transfer /træns'fɜː/ *verb* to move something to another location

transferable skill /træns,fɜːrəb(ə)l 'skıl/ *noun* a skill that is not limited to a specific academic discipline, area of knowledge, job or task and is useful in any work situation, e.g. communication or organisational skills

'The introduction of this specialist qualification broadens the scope of our existing IT education programme. The theoretical and practical elements of the programme will provide students with transferable skills which are of tangible benefit in the industry.' [*M2 Presswire*]

transfer of records /,trænsfɜː əv 'rekɔːdz/, **transfer of materials** /,trænsfɜː əv mə'tɪərɪəlz/ *noun* the act of moving records or materials to another system or physical storage location

transform /træns'fɔːm/ *verb* to change completely

transformation /,trænsfə'meıʃ(ə)n/ *noun* the act of putting data into a different format, e.g. for data encryption purposes

transgressive fiction /trænz,gresıv 'fıkʃ(ə)n/ *noun* a literary genre characterised by graphic exploration of taboo topics, to which the work of writers such as the Marquis de Sade and William Burroughs belongs. It is based on the belief that knowledge is to be found at the very edge of human experience.

transistor /træn'zıstə/ *noun* a small electrical device which controls amplification in a machine such as a radio or television

translate /træns'leıt/ *verb* **1.** to change information from one language or format to another **2.** to convert ideas into action

translation bureau /,træns'leıʃ(ə)n ,bjʊərəʊ/ *noun* an office which translates documents for companies

translator /træns'leıtə/ *noun* **1.** a person who converts text and spoken words from one language to another **2.** a laptop computer that translates words into other languages

transliteration /,trænzlıtə'reıʃ(ə)n/ *noun* the writing of words of one language using the characters of another, e.g. Arabic using the Roman alphabet. ◊ **romanisation**

transmission /trænz'mıʃ(ə)n/ *noun* a programme broadcast on television or radio

transmit /trænz'mıt/ *verb* to send out information from one device to another by radio waves, cable or wire links

transmitter /trænz'mıtə/ *noun* a set of equipment used for broadcasting radio or television signals

transparency /træns'pærənsi/ *noun* transparent positive film which can be projected on to a screen by using a light source

transparent /træns'pærənt/ *adjective* easily seen through, recognised or understood

transport /'trænspɔːt/ *noun* a way of moving goods and people from one place to another ■ *verb* to carry something or somebody from one place to another

travel book /'træv(ə)l bʊk/ *noun* a book which describes a journey undertaken by the author, or the author's impressions of a foreign country, but not giving factual details of hotels, museums and other tourist information

travel guide /'træv(ə)l gaıd/ *noun* a book which gives tourist information about a place such as how to get there, what is worth visiting and which hotels to stay at

trawl /trɔːl/ *noun* a search for something, especially information ■ *verb* to search for something through a large amount of information or many possibilities

treatment /'triːtmənt/ *noun* a way of writing about something or somebody

tree /triː/ *noun* **1.** a diagram of a hierarchical structure that shows the relationships between components as branches **2.** a hierarchical data structure in which each element contains data and may be linked by branches to two or more other elements

tree diagram /'triː ˌdaɪəgræm/ *noun* INFO SCI same as **tree 1**

tree structure /'triː ˌstrʌktʃə/ *noun* a way of writing down the connections between items in an indexing string, using a system of branches rather than linear format

trend /trend/ *noun* a general movement in the way something is developing

trend analysis /'trend əˌnæləsɪs/ *noun* investigation of the direction and strength of the movement in a development

trial /'traɪəl/ *noun* a test of somebody or something to see if they are suitable for a particular situation

trial and error /ˌtraɪəl ənd 'erə/ *noun* the process of trying out different ways of doing things until the best way is found

trial user /'traɪəl ˌjuːzə/ *noun* a person who is asked to use a service to see if it works well

trim /trɪm/ *verb* to cut off a small portion of something around its edge

trivia /'trɪviə/ *noun* a collection of insignificant or obscure items, details or information

troubleshooter /'trʌb(ə)lˌʃuːtə/ *noun* a person who works at solving problems which occur in companies, organisations, systems or computer programs

true /truː/ *adjective* based on provable facts

truncation /trʌŋ'keɪʃ(ə)n/ *noun* the shortening of a search term by adding a symbol such as % or * to match all the forms with the same stem, e.g. LIBRAR% will find library, librarian, librarianship

trunk call /'trʌŋk kɔːl/ *noun* a long-distance telephone call

trust /trʌst/ *noun* a financial arrangement where a company keeps and invests money for someone

trust directory /'trʌst daɪˌrekt(ə)ri/ *noun* a book with an alphabetical list of trust companies

TS *abbreviation* typescript

tt *abbreviation* in Internet addresses, the top-level domain for Trinidad and Tobago

tuition /tju'ɪʃ(ə)n/ *noun* teaching or instruction, especially when given individually or in a small group

tune in /ˌtjuːn 'ɪn/ *verb* to adjust a radio receiver until the signal is at its strongest and clearest

Turbogopher /'tɜːbəʊˌɡəʊfə/ *noun* a Macintosh version of the gopher system for accessing the Internet

turnaround document /'tɜːnəraʊnd ˌdɒkjʊmənt/ *noun* a document used to record the details of a job and the time taken to complete it

turnaround time /'tɜːnəraʊnd ˌtaɪm/ *noun* the time taken to complete a job from beginning to end ○ *The turnaround time for photocopying a document is three hours.*

turnkey system /'tɜːnki ˌsɪstəm/ *noun* a complete system which is ready for immediate use

turn off /ˌtɜːn 'ɒf/ *verb* to disconnect the power supply from a machine

turn on /ˌtɜːn 'ɒn/ *verb* to connect the power supply to a machine

turnover /'tɜːnəʊvə/ *noun* **1.** the rate at which people leave a company and are replaced **2.** the amount of money taken for goods or services sold during a given period of time

turtle /'tɜːt(ə)l/ *noun* a computer peripheral, like a large mouse, used to draw graphics on a VDU ○ *Floor turtles are used in primary schools as teaching aids.*

tutor /'tjuːtə/ *noun* a teacher who is responsible for individuals or small groups, used especially at higher levels of education

tutorial /tju'tɔːriəl/ *noun* a chapter of a book or manual, or a section of a computer program, designed to provide instruction or training using exercises and assignments ■ *adjective* relating to or belonging to a tutor, or to the role and responsibilities of a tutor

tv *abbreviation* in Internet addresses, the top-level domain for Tuvalu

TV *abbreviation* television

TV station /ˌtiː ˈviː ˌsteɪʃ(ə)n/ *noun* a building where television programmes are produced

tw *abbreviation* in Internet addresses, the top-level domain for Taiwan

twelvemo /ˈtwelvməʊ/ *noun* **1.** a book made from a sheet which is folded to give twelve leaves or twenty-four pages **2.** a book with this format **3.** an American book size, 7–8 inches high ▶ abbr **12mo**

12mo *abbreviation* twelvemo

24mo *abbreviation* twenty-fourmo

twenty-fourmo /ˌtwenti ˈfɔːməʊ/ *noun* **1.** a book format produced when the printed sheet is folded to give 24 leaves, or 48 pages **2.** a book with this format **3.** an American book size, 5–6 inches high ▶ abbr **24mo**

two-dimensional /ˌtuː daɪ ˈmenʃ(ə)nəl/ *adjective* having only length and breadth and so looking flat

two-way radio /ˌtuː weɪ ˈreɪdiəʊ/ *noun* a radio transmitter and receiver in a single handset which allows two-way communication with another user

.txt *suffix* a file extension for a text file. Full form **text**

type /taɪp/ *noun* metal characters used for printing ■ *verb* to write using a computer keyboard

typeface /ˈtaɪpfeɪs/ *noun* the size and style of printing used, measured in 'points' which refer to the height of the characters

typescript /ˈtaɪpskrɪpt/ *noun* a type-written copy of a manuscript. Abbr **TS**

typeset /ˈtaɪpset/ *verb* to set text in type ready to be printed

typesetter /ˈtaɪpsetə/ *noun* a person or company that typesets text

typist /ˈtaɪpɪst/ *noun* a person whose job is to type up documents using a computer

typo /ˈtaɪpəʊ/ *noun US* a typographic error which is made while typesetting (*informal*) (NOTE: GB English is also **literal**)

typographic error /ˌtaɪpəˈɡræfɪk ˌerə/ *noun* a mistake made when typing

'…all name searches can be truncated without a wildcard (learned inf, learn, lea). Authority files exist for each word in a business name, so it is possible to look up uncertain spellings first. Unfortunately, the authority files reveal the large number of misspellings and typographic errors in the database (such as 'informatio').' [*Information World Review*]

typography /taɪˈpɒɡrəfi/ *noun* the design and methods used when working with type

tz *abbreviation* in Internet addresses, the top-level domain for Tanzania

U

U3A /ˌjuː θriː ˈeɪ/ *noun* a system of distance learning for people over the age of retirement. Full form **University of the Third Age (UK)**

ua *abbreviation* in Internet addresses, the top-level domain for Ukraine

UCAS /ˈjuːkæs/ *abbreviation* Universities and Colleges Admissions Service

UCC *abbreviation* Universal Copyright Convention

UDC *abbreviation* universal decimal classification

UFC *abbreviation* Universities Funding Council

ug *abbreviation* in Internet addresses, the top-level domain for Uganda

uk *abbreviation* in Internet addresses, the top-level domain for United Kingdom

UK *abbreviation* United Kingdom

ultimatum /ˌʌltɪˈmeɪtəm/ *noun* a warning that unless somebody conforms to regulations and instructions they will be punished

ultra- /ʌltrə/ *prefix* used with adjectives to indicate an extreme level

ultra-fiche /ˈʌltrə fiːʃ/ *noun* microfiche pages with images reduced more than ninety times

ultra-sonic /ˌʌltrə ˈsɒnɪk/ *adjective* sounds that are above the range of human hearing

ultra-violet light /ˌʌltrə ˌvaɪələt ˈlaɪt/ *noun* light which is just beyond the spectrum visible by the human eye. Abbr **UV light**

umlaut /ˈʊmlaʊt/ *noun* a pronunciation indicator of two dots above a vowel (e.g. ü), used especially in German

UN *abbreviation* United Nations

unabridged /ˌʌnəˈbrɪdʒd/ *adjective* complete and not shortened

unadulterated /ˌʌnəˈdʌltəreɪtɪd/ *adjective* complete with nothing added

unattributed /ˌʌnəˈtrɪbjʊtɪd/ *adjective* not attributed to a particular source of information or a particular creator

unauthorised /ʌnˈɔːθəraɪzd/, **unauthorized** *adjective* not officially allowed

unauthorised edition /ʌn ˌɔːθəraɪzd ɪˈdɪʃ(ə)n/, **unauthorised reprint** /ʌnˌɔːθəraɪzd ˈriːprɪnt/ *noun* a pirate edition of a book which has not been authorised by the publisher

uncensored /ʌnˈsensəd/ *adjective* not having been viewed by the official government censor and approved for showing to the public

uncertainty avoidance /ʌn ˈsɜːt(ə)nti əˌvɔɪdəns/ *noun* a system in which decisions are only made by people in full possession of all the facts

uncharted /ʌnˈtʃɑːtɪd/ *adjective* relating to an area that has had no maps made of it

uncorrupted /ˌʌnkəˈrʌptɪd/ *adjective* relating to a computer file or database that is free of errors or viruses

undercover /ˌʌndəˈkʌvə/ *adjective* done secretly to obtain information

under discussion /ˌʌndə dɪsˈkʌʃ(ə)n/ *adjective* being talked about but still to be decided

under-funded /ˌʌndə ˈfʌndɪd/, **under-financed** *adjective* not having enough money allocated to it to do its work properly

undergraduate /ˌʌndəˈgrædʒʊət/ *noun* a student at university who is working for a first degree

underground **literature** /ˈʌndəgraʊnd ˌlɪt(ə)rətʃə/ *noun* literature published by the underground press

underground press /ˈʌndəgraʊnd ˌpres/ *noun* illegal newspapers published in a country where publications are censored

underline *verb* to emphasise something either by talking about it strongly or by drawing a line under a written word or phrase

undocumented /ʌnˈdɒkjʊmentɪd/ *adjective* having no official papers to prove existence

unenlightening /ˌʌnenˈlaɪt(ə)nɪŋ/ *adjective* providing no useful information or insight

UNESCO /juːˈneskəʊ/ *abbreviation* United Nations Educational Social and Cultural Organization

unethical /ʌnˈeθɪk(ə)l/ *adjective* considered to be unacceptable according to a particular code of conduct

uneven pages /ʌnˌiːv(ə)n ˈpeɪdʒɪz/ *plural noun* the right-hand pages of a publication which bear the odd numbers

unexpurgated /ʌnˈekspəgeɪtɪd/ *adjective* not edited to remove words or passages considered offensive or unsuitable

uniform edition /ˈjuːnɪfɔːm ɪˈdɪʃ(ə)n/ *noun* a series of different books all with the same design

Uniform Resource Locator /ˌjuːnɪfɔːm rɪˈsɔːs ləʊˌkeɪtə/ *noun* an electronic address used to give access to files on the Internet. Abbr **URL**

unillustrated /ʌnˈɪləstreɪtɪd/ *adjective* having no illustrations

UNIMARC /ˈjuːnɪmɑːk/ *abbreviation* Universal Machine Readable Catalogue

uninformative /ˌʌnɪnˈfɔːmətɪv/ *adjective* not providing adequate information

union catalogue /ˈjuːnɪən ˌkætəlɒg/, **union list** /ˈjuːnɪən lɪst/ *noun* a combined bibliographic list of holdings for either institutions or subjects

unique /juːˈniːk/ *adjective* used to describe something of which there is only one example in the world

UNISIST /ˈjuːnɪsɪst/ *abbreviation* United Nations Information System in Science and Technology

unit /ˈjuːnɪt/ *noun* a small part of a large organisation with a specialised purpose

United Kingdom /juːˌnaɪtɪd ˈkɪŋdəm/ *noun* England, Scotland, Wales and Northern Ireland. Abbr **UK**

United Nations /juːˌnaɪtɪd ˈneɪʃ(ə)nz/ *noun* an international organisation to which most countries in the world belong, which works towards peace in the world and solving international problems. Abbr **UN**

United Nations Educational Social and Cultural Organization *noun* an international organisation through which richer countries can help poorer countries to develop. Abbr **UNESCO**

United Nations Information System in Science and Technology *noun* an international database for information about different areas of science and technology. Abbr **UNISIST**

United States of America /juːˌnaɪtɪd steɪts əv əˈmerɪkə/ *noun* a country in North America consisting of 50 states. Abbr **USA**

unit of enquiry /ˌjuːnɪt əv ɪnˈkwaɪri/ *noun* one item in a complex series of questions

universal /ˌjuːnɪˈvɜːs(ə)l/ *adjective* widespread and relevant to very large numbers of people

universal bibliographic control /ˌjuːnɪvɜːs(ə)l ˌbɪbliəgræfɪk kənˈtrəʊl/ *noun* a system of listing all the publications in the world

Universal Copyright Convention /ˌjuːnɪvɜːs(ə)l ˈkɒpɪraɪt kənˌvenʃ(ə)n/ *noun* an international agreement on copyright set up by the United Nations in Geneva in 1952. Abbr **UCC**. ◊ **convention**

universal decimal classification /ˌjuːnɪvɜːs(ə)l ˌdesɪm(ə)l ˌklæsɪfɪˈkeɪʃ(ə)n/ *noun* a system of classifying information by means of decimal numbering which is used worldwide. Abbr **UDC**

Universal Machine Readable Catalogue /ˌjuːnɪvɜːs(ə)l məˌʃiːn ˌriːd(ə)bəl ˈkætəlɒg/ *noun* a computer-generated index according to a specific system, which can be used worldwide. Abbr **UNIMARC**

Universities and Colleges Admissions Service /ˌjuːnɪvɜːsɪtiz ən ˌkɒlɪdʒɪz əd ˈmɪʃ(ə)nz ˌsɜːvɪs/ *noun* a centrally administered system for admissions to courses in all the universities and colleges of higher education in the UK. Abbr **UCAS**

Universities Funding Council /ˌjuːnɪvɜːsɪtiz ˈfʌndɪŋ ˌkaʊns(ə)l/ *noun* a government body which controls the money allocated to universities in the UK. Abbr **UFC**

university /ˌjuːnɪˈvɜːsɪti/ *noun* an institution of higher education where students study for degrees and academic research is done

university facility /ˌjuːnɪvɜːsɪti fə ˈsɪlɪti/ *noun* a building or equipment provided by a university for the work and leisure of its staff and students

university library /ˌjuːnɪvɜːsɪti ˈlaɪbrəri/ *noun* a library that caters specifically for the staff and students of a particular university

UNIX /ˈjuːnɪks/, **Unix** a trademark for a widely used computer operating system, developed in 1969 at AT&T Bell Laboratories, which can support multi-tasking in a multi-user environment

unjustified /ʌnˈdʒʌstɪfaɪd/ *adjective* with ragged margins, i.e. with no justification

unknown quantity /ˌʌnnəʊn ˈkwɒntɪti/ *noun* somebody or something about which nothing is known

unpaged /ʌnˈpeɪdʒd/ *adjective* not marked with page numbers. Abbr **unp.**

unprotected /ˌʌnprəˈtektɪd/ *adjective* having no security barriers and so able to be modified

UN publications catalogue /ˌjuː en ˌpʌblɪˈkeɪʃ(ə)nz ˌkætəlɒg/ *noun* a book containing bibliographic lists of documents published by the United Nations

unsigned /ʌnˈsaɪnd/ *adjective* having no signature to make it official

unstructured interview /ˌʌn ˌstrʌktʃəd ˈɪntəvjuː/ *noun* an interview which is free-ranging and not limited by pre-set questions

untranslated /ˌʌntrænsˈleɪtɪd/ *adjective* in its original language as opposed to being translated

up /ʌp/ *adjective* possessing up-to-date or accurate information

UPC *noun* an American barcode system used on packaging and book covers. Full form **universal product code**

up cursor key /ˈʌp ˌkɜːsə ˌkiː/ *noun* one of the four direction keys on a computer keyboard

updatable /ʌpˈdeɪtəb(ə)l/ *adjective* able to be updated easily, as with a website

update *noun* /ˈʌpdeɪt/ a news item which has the latest information on a topic already covered ■ *verb* /ʌpˈdeɪt/ to change information so that it is up to date and accurate

upgrade /ʌpˈgreɪd/ *verb* **1.** to improve something by bringing it up to date or adding more modern equipment **2.** to regrade a job, giving it a higher salary scale

upkeep /ˈʌpkiːp/ *noun* the act and cost of keeping buildings, equipment and services in good condition

upload /ˈʌpləʊd/ *verb* to send a file from one's computer to the hard disk of another computer, particularly used to refer to sending files over the Internet to another server. Compare **download**

upper case /ˌʌpə ˈkeɪs/ *adjective* relating to large letters such as A, B, C, as opposed to lower case a, b, c

COMMENT: To instruct upper case, the editor underlines the text with three lines. The term 'upper case' comes from the case in which metal type was kept in front of the compositor. The case was divided into many little compartments, the top half being for capitals and the bottom part for small letters.

up to date /ˌʌp tə ˈdeɪt/ *adjective* containing the latest known data

URL *abbreviation* Uniform Resource Locator

us *abbreviation* in Internet addresses, the top-level domain for United States

USA *abbreviation* United States of America

usage /ˈjuːsɪdʒ/ *noun* the generally accepted way that words are used, which may not necessarily be grammatically correct

use *noun* /juːs/ **1.** the ability or permission to use something ○ *They had the use of the library while they were attending the conference.* **2.** □ **in use**, **out of use** being or not being used □ **to be of use** /juːz/ to be useful ○ *A directory can be of use in many different ways.* ■ *verb* /juːz/ **1.** to employ somebody or something for a particular purpose **2.** to consume ○ *Colour televisions use much more electricity than black and white ones.*

Usenet /ˈjuːzˌnet/ *noun* a very large online bulletin board concerned with the news

user /ˈjuːzə/ *noun* a person who uses something

user education /ˈjuːzə ˌedjʊkeɪʃ(ə)n/, **user training** /ˈjuːzə ˌtreɪnɪŋ/ *noun* the process of teaching the users of a service how to make the best use of it

user-friendly /ˌjuːzə ˈfrendli/ *adjective* relating to language or software that makes interaction with a computer easy

user group /ˈjuːzə gruːp/ *noun* a group of people who use a service or facility and come together to discuss how it can be improved

user interface /ˈjuːzə ˌɪntəfeɪs/ *noun* hardware or software designed to make it easier for a user to communicate with a machine

'The [mobile handset] industry continues to struggle with cumbersome user interface issues, and manufacturers may be years away from an intuitive music-focused device that captures music lovers the way the iPod line has.' [*RCR Wireless News*]

user representative /ˈjuːzə ˌreprɪzentətɪv/ *noun* a person who speaks for other users and who voices their opinions

user resistance /ˈjuːzə rɪˌzɪstəns/ *noun* a feeling that some people have against using a particular facility or service

user study /ˈjuːzə ˌstʌdi/ *noun* research which investigates how users function and what they need

user views /ˈjuːzə vjuːz/ *plural noun* the opinions of people who make use of a facility or service

utility /juːˈtɪlɪti/ *noun* a service that is provided for everyone, e.g. water, gas or electricity

utility program /juːˈtɪlɪti ˌprəʊgræm/ *noun* a computer program that is concerned with routine activities such as searching, copying and replacing files

UV light *abbreviation* ultra-violet light

uy *abbreviation* in Internet addresses, the top-level domain for Uruguay

uz *abbreviation* in Internet addresses, the top-level domain for Uzbekistan

V

va *abbreviation* in Internet addresses, the top-level domain for Vatican City

vacate /vəˈkeɪt/ *verb* to leave a place or a job empty and available for other people

Vacher's Parliamentary Companion /ˌvæʃəz ˌpɑːləment(ə)ri kəmˈpænjən/ *noun* a reference book which gives information about all aspects of the UK parliament including biographical details of Members of Parliament

vade mecum /ˌvɑːdi ˈmeɪkəm/ *noun* a portable reference book

valid /ˈvælɪd/ *adjective* based on logical reasoning and so acceptable

validate /ˈvælɪdeɪt/ *verb* to prove that something is true, accurate or correct

valuable /ˈvæljʊəb(ə)l/ *adjective* **1.** worth a lot of money **2.** having great importance

valuation /ˌvæljuˈeɪʃ(ə)n/ *noun* the process of calculating how much something is worth

value /ˈvæljuː/ *noun* the amount that something is worth either in money or quantity ■ *verb* to estimate how much money something is worth

value added network /ˌvæljuː ˈædɪd ˌnetwɜːk/ *noun* a network which leases telecommunications links, adds services and markets the improved network

value added tax /ˌvæljuː ˈædɪd ˌtæks/ *noun* a tax on goods and services purchased which the seller must then pay to the government. Abbr **VAT**

values /ˈvæljuːz/ *plural noun* moral principles and beliefs

vandal /ˈvænd(ə)l/ *noun* a person who deliberately damages property

vandalism /ˈvændəˌlɪz(ə)m/ *noun* the act of deliberately damaging property

vanity publisher /ˈvænɪti ˌpʌblɪʃə/ *noun* a publishing house that publishes an author's work in return for payment from the author. Vanity publishers do not typically market or distribute their publications.

variable /ˈveəriəb(ə)l/ *noun* a factor in a situation that can change, or that can be measured according to a set of values ■ *adjective* not always the same ○ *Text was typed with variable spacing between the words.*

variance /ˈveəriəns/ *noun* difference from the norm

variorum /ˌveəriˈɔːrəm/ *adjective* **1.** having commentary or notes written by various editors or scholars **2.** containing different versions or readings of a text ■ *noun* an edition of a text with commentary or notes written by various editors or scholars, or with various different versions or readings

various dates /ˈveəriəs deɪts/ *noun* a series of volumes containing several works of different dates. Abbr **v.d.**

varnish /ˈvɑːnɪʃ/ *noun* a shiny coating applied to book covers or jackets to make them more durable, similar in appearance to lamination, but cheaper ■ *verb* to coat a book cover with varnish

VAT /ˌviː eɪ ˈtiː, væt/ *abbreviation* value added tax

vc *abbreviation* in Internet addresses, the top-level domain for St Vincent and the Grenadines

VCR *abbreviation* video cassette recorder

v.d. *abbreviation* various dates

VDC *abbreviation* virtual data centre

VDT *abbreviation* video display terminal

VDU *abbreviation* visual display unit

ve *abbreviation* in Internet addresses, the top-level domain for Venezuela

vellum /'veləm/ *noun* smooth, fine parchment or paper made from polished calf, sheep or goat skin

vending machine /'vendɪŋ mə ˌʃiːn/ *noun* an automatic machine which dispenses goods when money or a special key or card is put in the slot

vendor /'vendə/ *noun* somebody who sells things

Venn diagram /'ven ˌdaɪəgræm/ *noun* a graphical representation of the relationship between two or more sets of data

verbatim /vɜː'beɪtɪm/ *noun* an accurate word-for-word report of a speech or debate ■ *adverb* copying the spoken word exactly in writing ○ *She copied the speech down verbatim.*

verification /ˌverɪfɪ'keɪʃ(ə)n/ *noun* the act of checking that something is true and accurate

verify /'verɪfaɪ/ *verb* to check that something is true and accurate

vernacular /və'nækjʊlə/ *noun* a local dialect

verse /vɜːs/ *noun* **1.** a set of lines which forms one part of the pattern of a poem **2.** a group of sentences which forms a numbered division of a book of sacred writings

version /'vɜːʃ(ə)n/ *noun* a copy or form of something that is slightly different from the original

verso /'vɜːsəʊ/ *noun* the left-hand page of a book, usually given an even number

vertical /'vɜːtɪk(ə)l/ *adjective* upright, forming an angle of 90° to the ground

vertical filing /ˌvɜːtɪk(ə)l 'faɪlɪŋ/ *noun* a system of filing in which the organisation of records is from top to bottom rather than horizontal

vertical scrolling /ˌvɜːtɪk(ə)l 'skrəʊlɪŋ/ *noun* the act of moving text up or down a computer screen a line at a time

Very High Density /ˌveri haɪ 'densɪti/ *adjective* able to be encoded on both sides. Abbr **VHD**

Very High Frequency /ˌveri haɪ 'friːkwənsi/ *adjective* relating to a range of radio transmission frequencies which give clear reception. Abbr **VHF**

vg *abbreviation* in Internet addresses, the top-level domain for British Virgin Islands

VHD *abbreviation* Very High Density

VHF *abbreviation* Very High Frequency

via /'vaɪə/ *preposition* going through a person or place to reach a destination

VIATEL /'vaɪətel/ *noun* an Australian videotext service

video /'vɪdiəʊ/ *noun* a recording on video tape ■ *verb* to film something using a video camera

videobook /'vɪdiəʊbʊk/ *noun* an educational video that can be downloaded from a website as part of a training course

video camera /'vɪdiəʊ ˌkæm(ə)rə/ *noun* a portable camera for taking videos

video cassette /'vɪdiəʊ kəˌset/ *noun* a container for video recording tape which enables it to be played back by a VCR

video cassette recorder /ˌvɪdiəʊ kə'set rɪˌkɔːdə/ *noun* a machine which will record and play back television pictures

video conference /'vɪdiəʊ ˌkɒnf(ə)rəns/ *noun* a satellite TV link which enables several people to see and talk to each other at the same time

video conferencing /'vɪdiəʊ ˌkɒnf(ə)rənsɪŋ/ *noun* the holding of a meeting between people at a distance using video screens to enable the people taking part to see each other

videodisc /'vɪdiəʊdɪsk/ *noun* a read-only optical disk used to store large amounts of data and pictures

video display /ˈvɪdiəʊ dɪˌspleɪ/ *noun* a device that can display text or graphical information

video library /ˈvɪdiəʊ ˌlaɪbrəri/ *noun* a collection of video tapes available for hire

video nasty /ˌvɪdiəʊ ˈnɑːsti/ *noun* a film released on video which is extremely violent

video phone /ˈvɪdiəʊ fəʊn/ *noun* a telephone that has a video screen attached to it so that the callers can see the person they are talking to

video scanner /ˈvɪdiəʊ ˌskænə/ *noun* a device that enters pictures or diagrams to be input to a computer

video tape /ˈvɪdiəʊ teɪp/ *noun* magnetic tape which can be used to record pictures and play them back on a television set

Videotex /ˈvɪdiəʊteks/ *noun* a generic name for systems which display text on a television screen

videotext /ˈvɪdiəʊtekst/ *noun* a communications service linked to an adapted television receiver or video display terminal by telephone or cable television lines to allow access to pages of information. Systems can be one-way, allowing only for the display of selected information, or online or interactive, allowing for two-way communication.

view /vjuː/ *noun* an opinion about something ○ *I hold the view that every school should have a library.* ■ *verb* to look at or watch

Viewdata /ˈvjuːdeɪtə/ a trade name for a videotext system

COMMENT: The user calls up the page of information required, using the telephone and a modem, as opposed to teletext, where the pages of information are repeated one after the other automatically.

viewer /ˈvjuːə/ *noun* **1.** a person who looks at something **2.** an apparatus with a lightbox for looking at photographic slides

viewfinder /ˈvjuːfaɪndə/ *noun* an eyepiece in a camera which enables the photographer to see what is to be filmed

virement /ˈvaɪəmənt/ *noun* an authorised transfer of money from one budget to another for urgent purposes

virtual data centre /ˌvɜːtʃʊəl ˈdeɪtə ˌsentə/ *noun* a fully computerised data management system, including storage, access, publishing and archiving facilities. Abbr **VDC**

'The physical data centre may have disappeared entirely from many organisations by 2010. Outsourced virtual data centres could be the norm, rather than the exception, in small and medium-sized enterprises (SMEs). Thanks to the economies of scale that outsourcers can achieve, SMEs will have access to technology and applications far beyond their current reach.' [*Computing*]

virtual library /ˌvɜːtʃʊəl ˈlaɪbrəri/ *noun* an electronic stock of information which can be accessed via databases, but is not held in any one place

virtual reality /ˌvɜːtʃʊəl riˈæliti/ *noun* an electronic environment created by a computer which appears to be real to the viewer

virtual reference /ˌvɜːtʃʊəl ˈref(ə)rəns/ *noun* reference using computerised access to data, e.g. searching on the World Wide Web

virus /ˈvaɪrəs/ *noun* an infection in a computer system which can damage the software systems and the data

vis-à-vis /ˌviːz ə ˈviː/ *preposition* in comparison with

visit /ˈvɪzɪt/ *verb* □ **to visit a site** to read an electronic document on the World Wide Web

visitation /ˌvɪzɪˈteɪʃ(ə)n/ *noun* an official visit

Visnews /ˈvɪznjuːz/ *noun* a commercial library in the UK containing pictures and television news coverage

vistafoil /ˈvɪstəfɔɪl/ a trade name for a form of sticky, transparent plastic covering used to laminate books, pictures or work cards

visual aid /ˈvɪʒʊəl eɪd/ *noun* a teaching aid which enables the learner to see pictures or real examples of the subject being taught ○ *Slides, photographs, maps, charts, films are all visual aids.*

visual display unit /ˌvɪʒʊəl dɪ'spleɪ ˌjuːnɪt/, **visual display terminal** *noun* a device used with a computer and a keyboard to display words and graphics on a screen. Abbr **VDU**, **VDT**

visual education /ˌvɪʒʊəl ˌedjʊ'keɪʃ(ə)n/ *noun* the process of teaching how to read visual symbols

visual literacy /ˌvɪʒʊəl 'lɪt(ə)rəsi/ *noun* the ability to interpret visual signs and symbols

vital record /'vaɪtəl ˌrekɔːd/ *noun* a record which is currently in use and must be kept easily accessible

vn *abbreviation* in Internet addresses, the top-level domain for Vietnam

VOA *abbreviation* Voice of America

vocabulary /vəʊ'kæbjʊləri/ *noun* **1.** the number of words in a particular language or related to a specific subject ○ *The vocabulary of information handling is very specialised.* **2.** a set of words that are used for a specific purpose, e.g. for cataloguing

vocational qualification /vəʊ ˌkeɪʃ(ə)nəl ˌkwɒlɪfɪ'keɪʃ(ə)n/ *noun* a certificate which states that somebody has the training or skills needed to do a particular job

vocational training /vəʊ ˌkeɪʃ(ə)nəl 'treɪnɪŋ/ *noun* courses which teach people the skills for specific jobs or professions

Voice of America /ˌvɔɪs əv ə 'merɪkə/ *noun* a worldwide broadcasting network of American radio. Abbr **VOA**

voice-over /'vɔɪs ˌəʊvə/ *noun* a commentary or spoken text accompanying a television programme, advertisement or film by somebody who is heard but not seen

voice recognition /'vɔɪs ˌrekəgnɪʃ(ə)n/ *noun* the ability of a computer to recognise the characteristics of a human voice and respond appropriately

voice synthesiser /'vɔɪs ˌsɪnθəsaɪzə/ *noun* a computer reproduction of sounds similar to the human voice

volatile /'vɒlətaɪl/ *adjective* liable to change suddenly and unexpectedly

volatile memory /ˌvɒlətaɪl 'mem(ə)ri/, **volatile store** /'vɒlətaɪl stɔː/, **volatile storage** /ˌvɒlətaɪl 'stɔːrɪdʒ/ *noun* a memory or storage mechanism in a computer which loses data stored in it when the power supply is switched off

volume /'vɒljuːm/ *noun* **1.** a book, especially a large one **2.** one of a series in a set of books or journals **3.** the loudness of the noise produced by something

volume control /'vɒljuːm kən ˌtrəʊl/ *noun* a device that enables the user to control the loudness of the noise produced

volume signature /'vɒljuːm ˌsɪɡnətʃə/ *noun* the number of a volume, e.g. vol 1

volunteer /ˌvɒlən'tɪə/ *noun* somebody who works without being paid

VORTAL /'vɔːtəl/ *noun* a portal website that contains information for just one particular industry or interest group

vowel /'vaʊəl/ *noun* the five letters a, e, i, o, u in the Roman alphabet, at least one of which is required to make a word pronounceable in most western languages

vu *abbreviation* in Internet addresses, the top-level domain for Vanuatu

W

W3C /ˌdʌb(ə)l juː θriː ˈsiː/ *noun* a consortium of organisations, programmers, developers, industry executives and users which seeks to guide the future development of the World Wide Web and ensure that all web technologies are compatible with one another. Full form **World Wide Web Consortium**

w. a. f. *abbreviation* 'with all faults'

wage /weɪdʒ/ *noun* money paid to somebody, usually weekly, for their work

WAIS *abbreviation* Wide Area Information Server

waive /weɪv/ *verb* to decide not to enforce a regulation

waiver /ˈweɪvə/ *noun* permission to do something although it is not in accordance with the regulations

walled garden /ˌwɔːld ˈgɑːd(ə)n/ *noun* a browsing environment for viewing websites which provides a means of controlling the information and websites that a user is able to access. It may either protect users such as children from unsuitable information or direct users to specific, often paid content supported by an Internet service provider.

wall planner /ˈwɔːl ˌplænə/ *noun* a chart with empty spaces marked with the dates for each day of the year so that events can be written in

WAN /wæn/ *abbreviation* Wide Area Network

warning /ˈwɔːnɪŋ/ *noun* spoken or written advice about something bad that may happen

warranty /ˈwɒrənti/ *noun* a written guarantee given by a company against faulty goods or workmanship

waste /weɪst/ *verb* to spend money, time or effort on something that is not important

watermark /ˈwɔːtəmɑːk/ *noun* a distinctive mark impressed into the fabric of paper when it is made, which can be seen by holding the paper to the light

COMMENT: Watermarks are most often used in banknote paper, but they also appear in handmade paper and other fine papers. They are a useful way of dating old documents or antiquarian books.

waterproof /ˈwɔːtəpruːf/ *adjective* not allowing water to pass through ○ *Plastic book jackets are waterproof.*

.wav *suffix* a file extension for a sound file. Full form **waveform**

wavelength /ˈweɪvleŋθ/ *noun* **1.** the distance between corresponding points on consecutive cycles of light or sound **2.** the size of the radio wave used to broadcast programmes

weather satellite /ˈweðə ˌsætəlaɪt/ *noun* a satellite which collects meteorological information enabling changes in the weather to be forecast

web /web/ *noun* ♦ World Wide Web

web-based /ˈweb beɪst/ *adjective* found on the World Wide Web and not on a personal computer, e.g. Internet e-mail accounts such as Yahoo! Mail

web browser /ˈweb ˌbraʊzə/ *noun* a single file stored on a web server which contains formatted text, graphics and hypertext links to other pages on the Internet. A webpage is created using

HTML codes and is viewed with a browser.

webcasting /'webkɑːstɪŋ/ *noun* the use of the World Wide Web as a medium for broadcasting information

web content management /'web ˌkɒntent ˌmænɪdʒmənt/ *noun* formal organisation of the content on a company's website, including updating, branding, editorial access, formatting and supporting software considerations

web crawler /'web ˌkrɔːlə/ *noun* a program used to search through pages on the World Wide Web for documents containing a specific word, phrase or topic

web-enable /'web ɪˌneɪb(ə)l/ *verb* to make an electronic device or a software application capable of accessing the Internet

'The Sharing Wycombe's Old Photographs scheme or SWOP has been awarded a heritage Lottery Grant of £50 000 to digitise and web-enable the prints.' [*UK NewsQuest*]

web folio /'web ˌfəʊliəʊ/ *noun* a collection of webpages with an underlying defining theme, e.g. the pages of an electronic book or the electronic images of an artist's portfolio

webinar /'webɪnɑː/ *noun* a seminar given over the Internet

webliography /ˌwebli'ɒgrəfi/ *noun* 1. a list of documents available on the World Wide Web 2. a list or catalogue of all the web-based material relating to a specific subject

weblish /'weblɪʃ/ *noun* the form of English used globally online, with characteristic features such as the omission of apostrophes and capital letters, the use of abbreviations and the rapid absorption of new words

weblog /'weblɒg/ *noun* a frequently updated personal journal chronicling links at a website, intended for public viewing

webmaster /'webmɑːstə/ *noun* somebody who creates, organises or updates information on a website

Webology /web'ɒlədʒi/ *noun* an academic journal dedicated to the fields of library and information science

webpage /'webpeɪdʒ/ *noun* a computer file, encoded in HTML and containing text, graphics files and sound files, that is accessible through the World Wide Web

web portal /'web ˌpɔːt(ə)l/ *noun* a website that provides a wide range of information and resources that include everything a particular user might want from the Internet, on one site

web server /'web ˌsɜːvə/ *noun* a program that serves up webpages when requested by a client, e.g. a web browser

website /'websaɪt/ *noun* a computer program that runs a web server providing access to a group of related webpages

weed /wiːd/ *verb* to remove old and outdated items ○ *They need to weed the library stock every few years.*

weeding /'wiːdɪŋ/ *noun* the discarding of materials that are out of date or of no further use

weekly /'wiːkli/ *noun* a publication that is produced every week ■ *adjective* happening regularly once a week

weight /weɪt/ *noun* **1.** a measurement of how heavy something is **2.** a measurement of the 'strength' of a character in a typeface, i.e. light, normal, or bold **3.** a heavy object, often decorative, used to stop papers from falling or being blown away

COMMENT: Paper weight is usually calculated in gsm, and varies from about 30gsm (Bible paper) to about 150gsm (heavy cartridge). Board for paper covers is also calculated in gsm: a common cover weight is 240gsm. In the USA, paper weight is calculated in pounds per 500 sheets. Note that a heavy paper is not necessarily bulkier (thicker) than a lightweight paper.

weighting /'weɪtɪŋ/ *noun* a tariff or bonus added to something as a result of sorting things according to their importance or position ○ *The salary carried a London weighting to compensate for having to live in London where the cost of living is more expensive.*

wf *abbreviation* **1.** in Internet addresses, the top-level domain for Wallis and Futuna Islands **2.** workflow

what if? simulation /ˌwɒt 'ɪf ˌsɪmjʊleɪʃ(ə)n/ *noun* a management technique which is used for forward planning, in which questions are asked to predict what would happen in particular situations

Whitaker's /'wɪtəkəz/ *noun* a publishing house which produces comprehensive lists of books in print on CD, microfiche and hard copy

Whitaker's Almanac /ˌwɪtəkəz 'ælmənæk/ *noun* a reference book which gives details of the establishment, procedures and personalities in the UK as well as general knowledge about the rest of the world

white noise /'waɪt nɔɪz/ *noun* random noise on a broadcast transmitter which distorts other signals

white pages /ˌwaɪt 'peɪdʒz/ *noun* a database of users and their email address stored on the Internet to help other users find an email address

whitewash /'waɪtwɒʃ/ *noun* an official attempt to hide unpleasant facts

WHO /ˌdʌbəljuːeɪtʃ 'əʊ/ *abbreviation* World Health Organization

whole binding /'həʊl ˌbaɪndɪŋ/ *noun* same as **full binding**

whole bound book /ˌhəʊl baʊnd 'bʊk/ *noun* a book that has been completely covered in a binding material such as leather

wholesale /'həʊlseɪl/ *adjective* buying and selling goods in bulk to people who then sell them on in smaller quantities as retail goods

Who's Who /ˌhuːz 'huː/ *noun* a publication giving biographical details of well-known or important people

Wide Area Information Server /ˌwaɪd ˌeəriə ˌɪnfə'meɪʃ(ə)n ˌsɜːvəz/ *noun* an alphabetical list of electronic sources of information. Abbr **WAIS**

Wide Area Network /ˌwaɪd ˌeəriə 'netwɜːk/ *noun* a network of terminals with links outside the local area by radio, satellite and cable. Abbr **WAN**

widespread /'waɪdspred/ *adjective* available to a large number of people or over a large area

widow /'wɪdəʊ/ *noun* the last line of a paragraph printed by itself at the top of a page

Wi-Fi /'waɪ faɪ/ a certification trademark assuring the interoperability of wireless local area network products

wiki /'wɪki/ *noun* a type of website which is designed to be edited or added to by its users

Wikipedia /ˌwɪki'piːdiə/ *noun* an online encyclopedia which is made up of articles created and edited by users

wild card /'waɪld kɑːd/ *noun* a symbol such as * or ?, which will represent and call up all files when searching data

WIMP /wɪmp/ *noun* a description of an integrated software system that is entirely operated using windows, icons and a mouse-controlled pointer. Full form **windows, icons, mouse, pointer**

window /'wɪndəʊ/ *noun* **1.** a reserved section of a computer screen, with specific information, which can overwrite other sections on screen and can be selected at any time for editing or reference **2.** an opening in an envelope to show the address printed on the enclosed document

windowing /'wɪndəʊɪŋ/ *noun* **1.** the action of setting up a window to show information on the screen **2.** the act of displaying or accessing information via a window

Windows /'wɪndəʊz/ a trade name for a computer system developed by Microsoft, using icons, mouse and windows devised for use with software to make it more user-friendly than the purely keyboard-based systems

wipe /waɪp/ *verb* to remove all information from a disk

WIPO /'waɪpəʊ/ *abbreviation* World Intellectual Property Organization

wireless markup language /ˌwaɪələs 'mɑːkʌp ˌlæŋgwɪdʒ/ *noun* a standardised system for tagging text files, based on XML, which specifies the interfaces of narrowband wireless devices. Abbr **WML**

Wisden /'wɪzdən/ *noun* a reference book with details of everything related to the game of cricket, e.g. players, grounds, test matches and records

withdraw /wɪð'drɔː/ *verb* to remove something ○ *They were told to withdraw some of the old books from the library.*

withstand /wɪð'stænd/ *verb* to remain unharmed by an event or action ○ *Library books must be able to withstand constant usage.*

WML *abbreviation* COMPUT wireless markup language

word /wɜːd/ *noun* a separate item of language, which is used with others to form speech or writing that can be understood

word-process /ˌwɜːd 'prəʊses/ *verb* to edit, store and manipulate text using a computer

word processing /ˌwɜːd 'prəʊsesɪŋ/ *noun* the creation, retrieval, modification, storage and printing of text using a computer or other electronic equipment. Also called **text processing**

word-processing package /'wɜːd ˌprəʊsesɪŋ ˌpækɪdʒ/ *noun* software on a program disk with an instruction manual, which enables word processing to be carried out

word processor /ˌwɜːd 'prəʊsesə/ *noun* a computer that will run a word-processing program, usually used to create text

words per minute /ˌwɜːdz pɜː 'mɪnɪt/ *noun* a method of measuring the speed of a printer or a keyboarder. Abbr **WPM**

work /wɜːk/ *noun* **1.** a published document **2.** the tasks involved in a job

workaholic /ˌwɜːkə'hɒlɪk/ *noun* a person who cannot stop working to do other things

workbook /'wɜːkbʊk/ *noun* a textbook with exercises and spaces for the answers to be written in

work experience /'wɜːk ɪkˌspɪəriəns/ *noun* a situation in which a student spends some time doing a job to see whether he or she likes it

'Proposals include setting up a national World of Work programme to improve vocational training, provide work taster days for primary school pupils and use work experience to encourage girls to think about non-traditional jobs, as well as promote apprenticeships for women especially in sectors with skill shortages.' [*M2 Presswire*]

workflow /'wɜːkfləʊ/ *noun* **1.** the way that work is passed from one part of a production system to another **2.** an automatic system for passing on documents to users at each stage of the production process. Abbr **wf**

workforce /'wɜːkfɔːs/ *noun* all the people who work for a particular company or organisation

working capital /'wɜːkɪŋ ˌkæpɪt(ə)l/ *noun* money that is available immediately and not tied up in investments, property or equipment

working conditions /'wɜːkɪŋ kənˌdɪʃ(ə)nz/ *plural noun* the environment in which a job is done

working day /'wɜːkɪŋ deɪ/ *noun* a period of time spent working for money ○ *The standard working day is eight hours long.*

working hours /'wɜːkɪŋ ˌaʊəz/ *plural noun* **1.** the period when most people are at work, usually between around 9.00 am and 5.00 pm **2.** time spent at work rather than at home

working party /'wɜːkɪŋ ˌpɑːti/ *noun* a temporary group formed to investigate a particular situation

working population /'wɜːkɪŋ ˌpɒpjʊˌleɪʃ(ə)n/ *noun* people who have jobs

work of reference /ˌwɜːk əv 'ref(ə)rəns/ *noun* an important and well-known reference book ○ *It is the standard work of reference on tropical diseases.*

workplace /'wɜːkpleɪs/ *noun* a place at which work is done

worksheet /'wɜːkʃiːt/ *noun* a teaching aid prepared to give information and reinforce learning with exercises

workspace /'wɜːkspeɪs/ *noun* memory space available on a computer for temporary work

work standards /'wɜːk ˌstændədz/ *plural noun* the quality of work required by the management

work station /'wɜːk ˌsteɪʃ(ə)n/ *noun* a desk with a computer, keyboard and sometimes a printer

work study /'wɜːk ˌstʌdi/ *noun* a system of measuring the amount of work possible in the given conditions and during a particular time period

world atlas /ˌwɜːld 'ætləs/ *noun* a reference book containing maps of all the countries in the world and articles about them

world book /ˌwɜːld 'bʊk/ *noun* a reference book that contains information about all the countries in the world

WorldCat /'wɜːldkæt/ *noun* the online service provided by the OCLC, which covers online cataloguing, collection management, resource sharing, electronic content and data preservation

World Health Organization /ˌwɜːld 'helθ ˌɔːɡənaɪzeɪʃ(ə)n/ *noun* an international organisation that works to improve health, especially in poorer countries. Abbr **WHO**

world index /ˌwɜːld 'ɪndeks/ *noun* a reference book of abstracts of articles about all the countries of the world

World Intellectual Property Organization /ˌwɜːld ˌɪntɪlektʃʊəl 'prɒpəti ˌɔːɡənaɪzeɪʃ(ə)n/ *noun* an international organisation that provides guidelines and supports work for international copyright controls. Abbr **WIPO**

worldwide /'wɜːldwaɪd/ *adjective* happening throughout the world ○ *The recession appears to be worldwide.*

World Wide Web /ˌwɜːld ˌwaɪd 'web/ *noun* a hypertext representation of the Internet, a collection of the millions of websites and webpages which together form the part of the Internet that is most often seen by users. Abbr **www**

COMMENT: Each website on the World Wide Web is a collection of webpages, and each webpage contains text, graphics and links to other websites. Each page is created using the HTML language and is viewed by a user with a web browser. To navigate between webpages and websites is called surfing, which requires a computer with a link to the Internet and a web browser to view the webpages stored on the remote web servers.

World Wide Web Consortium /ˌwɜːld waɪd 'web kənˌsɔːtiəm/ *noun* ONLINE full form of **W3C**

WORM /wɜːm/ *noun* an optical disk storage system that allows the user to write data to the disc once, but the user can then read the data from the disc many times. Full form **write once read many times memory**

worthwhile /wɜːθ'waɪl/ *adjective* worth the time, money or effort spent on it

WPM *abbreviation* words per minute

wraparound /'ræpəˌraʊnd/ *noun* a system in word processing where the writer does not have to put in line endings, because the end of each line is automatically marked by the program

wrapper /'ræpə/ *noun* PUBL same as **dust jacket**

wrapround /'ræpraʊnd/ *noun* a cover which is wrapped round a book

write /raɪt/ *verb* to use a pen, pencil or computer to produce letters, numbers and symbols on paper so that other people can read them

write-off /'raɪt ɒf/ *noun* something that is so badly damaged that it cannot be repaired

write protect /ˌraɪt prə'tekt/ *verb* to make it impossible to write on or erase anything from a disk

write protect tab /ˌraɪt prə'tekt ˌtæb/ *noun* a tab on a disk which if moved prevents any writing to or erasing from the disk

writer /'raɪtə/ *noun* a person whose job is to write books or articles for money

written confirmation /ˌrɪtən ˌkɒnfə'meɪʃ(ə)n/ *noun* a written statement of something that has been said

wrong number /ˌrɒŋ 'nʌmbə/ *noun* a telephone connection to a number other than the one that was wanted

ws *abbreviation* in Internet addresses, the top-level domain for Samoa

Wuarchive /'wuːˌɑːkaɪv/ *noun* a large electronic archive with pictures

www *abbreviation* World Wide Web

WYSIWYG /'wɪziːwɪg/ *noun* a system in which the text and graphics on a computer screen are exactly the same as what will be printed out. Full form **what you see is what you get**

XYZ

x /eks/ *noun* a symbol used when the name of a person, place or amount is unspecified or to be kept secret ○ *He paid £x each to ten people.*

x-axis /'eks ˌæksɪs/ *noun* the horizontal axis of a graph

Xerox /'ziːrɒks/ a trade name for a type of photocopier ■ *verb* to photocopy a paper or document

XML /ˌeks em 'el/ *noun* a programming language designed for web documents which allows for the creation of customised tags for individual information fields. Full form **Extensible Markup Language**

x-rated /'eks ˌreɪtɪd/ *adjective* relating to a former category in the British film censorship system indicating a film with scenes of sex or violence only suitable for adult viewing

x-y co-ordinates /ˌeks 'waɪ kəʊ ˌɔːdɪnəts/ *plural noun* the horizontal and vertical axes of a graph

y /waɪ/ *noun* used to represent an unknown quantity ○ *Let y be the number of years since insurance was taken out.*

-y *suffix* added to nouns to form adjectives of quality, e.g. 'wordy'

yardstick /'jɑːdstɪk/ *noun* the standard by which other comparable things can be judged

y-axis /'waɪ ˌæksɪs/ *noun* the vertical axis of a graph

ye *abbreviation* in Internet addresses, the top-level domain for Yemen

yearbook /'jɪəbʊk/ *noun* a book published once a year with details and information about a particular organisa-tion or profession ○ *the education year-book*

yearly /'jɪəli/ *adjective* happening once a year or every year

-year-old *suffix* added to numbers to indicate the age of a person or thing ○ *a ten-year-old file*

yellow /'jeləʊ/ *verb* (*of paper*) to turn yellow when exposed to the light

'Only as I flicked through a childhood copy of The Wind in the Willows did horror strike. The book was disintegrating before my eyes. The once vivid, stiff cover was curling and fading… pages were yellowing and the paper so fragile you fear it would tear if you cast it a cross look. What on earth are these books made of? Are they the literary equivalent of the biodegradable coffin?' [*The Herald*]

yellowing /'jeləʊɪŋ/ *noun* the tendency of some paper to turn yellow when exposed to the light

Yellow Pages /ˌjeləʊ 'peɪdʒɪz/ *noun* a telephone directory printed on yellow paper, which is organised alphabetically according to the trade or business of the subscribers

yellow press /'jeləʊ pres/ *noun* a popular name for tabloid sensational newspapers

young adult book /ˌjʌŋ 'ædʌlt ˌbʊk/ *noun* a book written for adults but considered suitable for adolescents

yt *abbreviation* in Internet addresses, the top-level domain for Mayotte

yu *abbreviation* in Internet addresses, the top-level domain for Yugoslavia

za *abbreviation* in Internet addresses, the top-level domain for South Africa

zap /zæp/ *verb* to wipe off all data currently in the workspace ○ *He pressed CONTROL Z and zapped all the text.*

zero /ˈzɪərəʊ/ *verb* □ **to zero in on** to give full attention to a problem

zero-based budgeting /ˌzɪərəʊ beɪst ˈbʌdʒɪtɪŋ/ *noun* a financial policy taking zero as the starting point, without any prior assumptions ○ *They were working to zero-based budgeting so were not able to take out any loans to get started.*

zine /ziːn/ *noun* a self-published paper, Internet magazine or other periodical which is issued at irregular intervals and usually appeals to a specialist readership

ZING /zɪŋ/ *noun* a protocol for information retrieval maintained by the United States Library of Congress

.zip /zɪp/ *suffix* a file extension for a zip file

zip code /ˈzɪp kəʊd/ *noun* numbers in a USA address indicating the postal area. ◊ **postcode**

zip file /ˈzɪp faɪl/ *noun* a computer file with the extension '.zip' containing data that has been compressed for storage or transmission.

zm *abbreviation* in Internet addresses, the top-level domain for Zambia

zoo /zuː/ *noun* a compressing archive program for transferring electronic files

zoom /zuːm/ *verb* to enlarge an area of text on a computer screen so that it is easier to work on

zw *abbreviation* in Internet addresses, the top-level domain for Zimbabwe

SUPPLEMENTS

The Paris Principles
Three Types of Library Classification System
Major Classification Schemes
Five Laws of Library Science
Information Skills – The Big6™
Resources on the Web
Copyright and Data Protection Law in the UK
Book Prizes and Awards
Major Newspapers in the UK
Major Magazines in the UK

The Paris Principles

The eleven topics that should taken into account when developing cataloguing systems involving author/title entries. So named at the International Conference on Cataloguing Principles (ICCP) in Paris in 1961, which was organised by the IFLA. It was intended to serve as a basis for international standardisation in cataloguing. The principles apply to the choice and form of headings and entry words in catalogues of printed books (and other library materials having similar characteristics) in which entries under authors' names, or the titles of works, are combined in one alphabetical sequence.

The principles are:

> Functions of the catalogue
> Structure of the catalogue
> Kinds of entry
> Use of multiple entries
> Choice of uniform heading
> Single personal author
> Entry under corporate bodies
> Multiple authorship
> Works entered under title
> Entry word for personal names

Many other cataloguing codes now use these principle as their common basis: one of the most commonly used is AACR 2.

Three Types of Library Classification System

Enumerative:
> based on an alphabetic list of subject headings, which are then assigned numbers according to their subdivisions

Hierarchical:
> based on a 'tree structure', arranged from the most general to the most specific within a topic

Faceted:
> based on separate classifications of each text for each one of its different properties, which combine to give a unique reference number

Major Classification Schemes

Bliss Bibliographic Classification (BC)
A faceted classification system which uses only upper- and lower-case letters and typographical symbols to denote classes, and can be adapted to the specific need of a library's collection.

Brinkler Classification
A theoretical geographically-oriented system which files each text according to two main categories – one denoting subject and one denoting place. This is intended to serve the needs of every user equally, but would be a costly system to maintain.

Colon Classification
A system developed by S. R. Ranganathan and widely used in India. The call number is composed of the reference numbers attached to each facet of the text (publication date, author, setting, subject's covered, etc.) which are separated by colons.

Columbia-Dickinson System
A classification system for filing printed music, which arranges according to 5 main categories and then according to medium, form and composer.

Cutter Expansive Classification
A system which was never fully developed after the death of its inventor Charles Ammi Cutter. It divided subjects into a list given letters of the alphabet (a style later adopted for the Library of Congress system) and then by numbers denoting subject, geographical focus, author, form and edition date).

Dewey Decimal System (DDS)
A purely numerical classification system which divides all knowledge into 10 main categories (classes), then each of those into 10 subcategories (divisions), and finally each of those into a further 10 subcategories (sections) to give a 1,000-category system.

Library of Congress Classification (LC)
An enumerative system which bases its call numbers on a list of subject headings given a specific letter (e.g. J = Political Science), then into subcategories given a second letter (e.g. JZ = International Relations) and then by number (e.g. JZ4935-5160 = The United Nations).

Nippon Decimal Classification (NDC)
A system based on the Dewey Decimal 100-category system, used for mainly Chinese- and Japanese-language books (with the categories altered to reflect the cultural differences in subject coverage).

Universal Decimal Classification (UDC)
A powerful extension of the Dewey Decimal System which may be used to classify to any media stored in a library (e.g. CD-ROM, segments of film, maps, musical recordings etc.) It uses decimal numbers to categorise documents with symbols to represent additional information, e.g. relationship to other subjects, secondary subjects covered, language of text etc.

Five Laws of Library Science

The original 5 principles, as developed by S. R. Ranganathan, the 'father of library science in India':

1. Books are for use.
2. Every reader has his or her book.
3. Every book has its reader.
4. Save the time of the reader.
5. The library is a growing organism.

Proposed amendments by Michael Gorman, president of the American Library Association 2005–2006:

1. Libraries serve humanity.
2. Respect all forms by which knowledge is communicated.
3. Use technology intelligently to enhance service.
4. Protect free access to knowledge.
5. Honour the past and create the future.

Information Skills – The Big6™

A 6-step approach to information literacy developed by Mike Eisenberg and Bob Berkowitz. Each stage has two substages. The Big6™ provides a framework for approaching any information-based question. See www.big6.com for further details.

1. Task Definition
    –Define the information problem
    –Identify information needed

2. Information Seeking Strategies
    –Determine all possible sources
    –Select the best sources

3. Location and Access
    –Locate sources (intellectually and physically)
    –Find information within sources

4. Use of Information
    –Engage (e.g., read, hear, view, touch)
    –Extract relevant information

5. Synthesis
    –Organise from multiple sources
    –Present the information

6. Evaluation
    –Judge the product (effectiveness)
    –Judge the process (efficiency)

Resources on the Web

UK resources:

Association of Information Management
A body which undertakes recruitment, training, consultancy and lobbying services on behalf of those in information management.
www.aslib.co.uk

British Library
Online research services and collection information from the UK's national library.
www.bl.uk

Chartered Institute of Library and Information Professionals
The membership association which accredits university courses on librarianship in the UK.
www.cilip.org.uk

Consortium of Research Libraries in the UK
An organisation campaigning for the development of distributed libraries.
www.curl.ac.uk

Copac
Online access to the merged catalogues of the members of the Consortium of Research Libraries in the UK.
http://copac.ac.uk

International Association of Music Libraries – UK and Ireland branch
Represents and promotes the interests of music librarians and libraries.
www.iaml-uk-irl.org

National Archives
A record of registered archive repositories in the UK and abroad.
www.nationalarchives.gov.uk

School Library Association
Advisory and information services for those working in school libraries in the UK.
www.sla.org.uk

Society of Archivists
"Committed to working for high standards in the provision and care of archives and effective management of record systems."
www.archives.co.uk

Society of College, National and University Libraries
An organisation supporting libraries in institutes of higher education.
www.sconul.ac.uk

UK Patent Office
Information on copyrights, trademarks, patents and intellectual property.
www.patent.gov.uk

European resources:

Consortium of European Research Libraries
An association dedicated to preserving and sharing information on the cultural heritage of Europe.
www.cerl.org

European Bureau of Library, Information and Documentation Associations
Promoting the interests of the library and information science profession at European level, particularly on copyright and emerging technology issues.
www.eblida.org

European Commission Central Library
Online access to government publications from across Europe.
http://europa.eu.int/comm/libraries

European Library
"A portal which offers access to the combined resources (books, magazines, journals.... both digital and non-digital) of the 45 national libraries of Europe."
www.theeuropeanlibrary.org

European Patent Office
Information on copyright, trademarks, patents and intellectual property
www.european-patent-office.org

International resources:

American Library Association
The official website of the organisation.
www.ala.org

American Society for Information Science and Technology
A membership body for information professionals in the US.
www.asis.org

Arma International
A leading authority on records management, both paper and electronic.
www.arma.org

Association of Christian Librarians
An online community for librarians working in religious institutes of higher education worldwide
www.acl.org

Australian Library and Information Association
The official website of the organisation.
www.alia.org.au

Australian School Library Association
Online resources for school librarians in Australia.
www.asla.org.au

Canadian Association for School Libraries
Online resources for school librarians in Canada.
www.caslibraries.ca

Canadian Library Association
The official website of the organisation.
www.cla.ca

International Association of Law Libraries
A body for law librarians interesting in creating international distributed
libraries of resources.
www.iall.org

**International Association of Music Libraries, Archives and Documentation
Centres**
Encouraging and promoting the activities of music libraries, archives and
documentation centres worldwide.
www.iaml.info

International Association of School Librarianship
Support and guidance for those interested in school library development
worldwide.
www.iasl-slo.org

International Association of Technological University Libraries
A membership body concerned with libraries for those in technological
education.
www.iatul.org/

International Council on Archives
A membership body for information professionals worldwide.
www.ica.org

International Federation of Library Associations and Institutions
The leading international body representing the interests of library and
information services and their users.
http://ifla.org

Libraries on the Web
Links to the webpages of libraries across the world.
http://lists.webjunction.org/libweb/

Library and Information Science Wiki
An online encyclopedia on library and information management issues which
any user can edit and add to.
www.liswiki.com

Library and Information Society of New Zealand Aotearoa
The official website of the organisation.
www.lianza.org.nz

Library and Information Technology Association
A branch of the ALA concerned with emerging technologies in library
management.
www.lita.org

Knowledge Management Professional Society
A not-for-profit international organisation for knowledge workers.
http://kmpro.org

Music Library Association
Represents the interests of music librarians and libraries in the USA.
www.musiclibraryassoc.org

US National Commission on Library and Information Science
The official website of the government agency.
www.nclis.gov

World Intellectual Property Organisation
An international organisation dedicated to promoting the use and protection of
intellectual property.
www.wipo.int

Key Information Sources for Knowledge Workers:

Britannica Online
The famous encyclopedia's online database.
www.britannica.com

Global NewsBank
Archive news content from online and print publications and media broadcasts
worldwide, available by subscription.
www.newsbank.com/intllibr/global.htm

KnowUK
A digital reference library with access to more than 100 reference books.
www.knowuk.co.uk

Lexis Nexis
A searchable online database comprising the world's largest collection of public
records and research materials.
www.lexisnexis.com

ProQuest
Access to more than more than 5.5 billion pages of archived information
spanning 500 years for researchers.
www.proquest.co.uk

Xrefer
A digital reference library offering online access to over 200 reference books to
subscribers.
www.xrefer.com

Copyright and Data Protection Law in the UK

Copyright Act 1956

set up copyright protection for all original literary, dramatic, musical or artistic works made in the UK under the control of the Government

Data Protection Act 1984

introduced regulations on the storage, security and transferring of personal information of individuals held electronically by companies

Copyright, Designs And Patents Act 1988

introduced the rights for the author of a work to be identified as such, and to not suffer harm to their reputation through mistreatment of their works

EU Directive 92/100 1992

clarified intellectual property rights in relation to copying or distribution of a person's work

EU Directive 93/98 1993

made copyright periods uniform throughout the EU, extending post-mortem copyright protection of a work from 50 to 70 years in the UK

Trademarks Act 1994

made provision for registration of trademarks and sets out guidelines for what constitutes infringement

Data Protection Act 1998

expanded the 1984 Act to cover manual as well as electronic records; introduced the notions of 'sensitive' data and accountability of directors for company transgressions

Freedom of Information Act 2000

allowed access by members of the public to any and all information held by public bodies

Regulation of Investigatory Powers Act 2000

allowed those in authority to access and monitor all personal e-mail and telephone communications; forbade encryption which makes this difficult

Anti-Terrorism, Crime and Security Act 2001

allowed authorities greater access to personal information about suspected terrorists

Book Prizes and Awards

American Book Award
An annual award given in recognition of literary achievement by an American author, intended to be more open in terms of age, sex, race and genre of writing than other awards.

Australian/Vogel Literary Award
A prize given by Australian publishers Allen and Unwin for an outstanding unpublished manuscript by an author under the age of 35.

Author's Club Awards
Two awards made annually for outstanding works of literature, one for a first work of fiction and the other for a non-fiction work on architecture and the arts, each of £1,000.

BA/Book Data Author Of The Year Awards
A prize of £1,000 given to a British or Irish published author who has made the most impact over the course of the year according to a survey of bookshops.

BBC4 Samuel Johnson Prize
A prestigious prize for non-fiction writing, running since 1999. Each finalist receives £2,500 and the winner £30,000.

Betty Trask Awards
A total prize fund of £25,000, administered by the Society of Authors, for authors of an outstanding first novel 'of a romantic or traditional nature'.

Booktrust Early Years Awards
A prize given for outstanding illustrated books for pre-school children, running since 1999.

Bram Stoker Awards
A set of prizes honouring 'superior achievement' in horror writing, given for novels, short stories and anthologies by the Horror Writer's Association.

British Academy Book Prize
An award that honours academic books on the humanities and social sciences, which are written to appeal to a non-specialist audience.

Caldicott Medal
A prestigious award given by the American Library Association to the writer of an outstanding American illustrated book for children.

Carnegie Medal
An award made by CILIP to the writer of an outstanding book for children, written in English and published during the previous year in the UK.

Cholmondley Award
A prize of £2,000 given to each of four poets each year, running since 1966.

Commonwealth Writer's Prize
Awards up to £10,000 each for outstanding books and first novels from the Commonwealth areas, Africa, the Caribbean, Canada and South-East Asia.

Book Prizes and Awards *continued*

David Cohen British Literature Prize
An award given for lifetime achievement in the field of literature, administered by the Arts Council. The prize includes money to be used to fund further work.

Duff Cooper Award
A prize of £3, 000 given for the best work of history, biography or political science published in English or French.

Dundee Book Prize
An award of £6,000 and the chance of publication, awarded every two years for an unpublished manuscript.

Elizabeth Longford Prize for Historical Biography
Awards a prize of £3,000 for a work of historical biography published in the year preceding the awards.

Encore Award
A prize of £10,000 administered by the Society of Authors, given for an outstanding second novel published in the English language in the UK.

Eric Gregory Trust Fund Awards
A total prize fund of £24,000, to be shared between 4-6 authors of a published or unpublished collection of poetry.

George Orwell Memorial Prize
An award of £1,000 given for a political book, either fiction or non-fiction, which is accessible to a non-academic audience.

Guardian Award
A prestigious award for works of children's literature published in the UK during the preceding year, given by the Guardian Newspaper.

Guardian First Book Award
A prize for an outstanding piece of new writing published in the UK during the preceding year, given by the Guardian Newspaper.

Hans Christian Andersen Awards
An international prize presented every other year to authors and illustrators who have made a 'lasting contribution' to children's literature. Winners receive a gold medal.

Hawthornden Prize
An award given for 'a work of imaginative literature'. It is one of the oldest awards, running since 1919.

Hemingway Foundation/PEN Awards
A prize given to a first novel or book of short stories by an American author, founded by Ernest Hemingway's widow Mary in 1976.

Independent Foreign Fiction Prize
An award now administered by the Arts Council which honours works translated into English and published in the UK. The winning author and translator both receive £5,000.

Book Prizes and Awards *continued*

James Tait Black Memorial Prizes
Two awards given annually for works of fiction and biography, worth £3,000 each. It is one of the oldest literary awards still in operation, running since 1919.

John Llewellyn Rhys Prize
An award of £3,000 funded by the Mail on Sunday, given to an outstanding British or Commonwealth author under the age of 35.

John Newbery Medal
A prestigious award given by the American Library Association for an outstanding American work of children's literature.

J. R. Ackerley Prize for Autobiography
A prize of £1000 and a silver Dupont pen given for an outstanding work of autobiography by a British author, published in English.

Kate Greenaway Medal
An award made by CILIP to the writer of an outstanding illustrated book for children. The book must be written in English and have been published in the United Kingdom during the year preceding the presentation of the award.

Kerrie Group Irish Fiction Award
An annual prize of EUR10,000 for a published Irish author.

Kiriyama Prize
A double award given annually for the best fiction and non-fiction works which promote inter-cultural understanding between the West and the countries of South Asia.

Man Booker Prize for Fiction (also known as **The Booker Prize**)
A highly-prestigious award given to an author in the UK or Commonwealth, including a cash prize of £50,000 and also assuring some degree of literary success.

Man Booker International Prize
The international partner of the Man Booker Prize, given to an outstanding author whose work is generally available in English translation, with a cash prize of £60,000.

Manchester Book Award
A recently-established award for children's literature by a UK-resident author, which is judged by school library reading groups.

McKitterick Prize
A prize of £4,000 given for an exceptional first novel by an author over the age of 40.

Miles Franklin Literary Award
A prize of AU$28,000 given annually for an adult work of fiction depicting Australian life and culture.

Book Prizes and Awards *continued*

National Book Awards
An annual honour given in four categories of literary works, administered by the National Book Foundation in the US. The prize is $10,000 and a crystal sculpture.

Nestlé Smarties Books Prize
An award organised by Booktrust, given for children's books in 3 age categories.

Nobel Prize in Literature An immensely prestigious award given each year to an international author, with nominations made to the Swedish Academy. The prize, amounting to more than £720,000, is presented to the winner by the King of Sweden.

O. Henry Awards
Annual American awards given to exceptional short stories, especially those which have made a 'lasting contribution' to the art of short story writing.

Orange Prize for Fiction
An award given for an outstanding original novel by a female author of any nationality, published in the UK. The prize for the winner is £30,00 and a bronze sculpture.

Prix Décembre
A prize given for French literary works at the end of the year, generally for less conventional, 'mainstream' works than the Prix Goncourt.

Prix des Deux Magots
An annual French literary prize which is awarded for new fiction, running since 1933.

Prix Femina
An award given for an outstanding literary work in the French language, awarded by an exclusively female jury and sponsored by woman's magazine Femina.

Prix Goncourt
A highly-prestigious prize given annually by the Académie Goncourt for 'imaginative prose' in the French language.

Pulitzer Prizes
Annual awards given for works in fiction, non-fiction, history, poetry and biography by American authors, preferably written on an American theme.

Queen's Gold Medal for Poetry
An award given for an outstanding book of verse by a UK or Commonwealth citizen. The committee is chaired by the Poet Laureate.

Red House Children's Book Award
An annual prize for children's literature, judged by readers, which also generates a Pick of the Year list of recommended titles.

Book Prizes and Awards *continued*

Royal Society of Literature Ondaatje Award
An honour given to a published work by a UK or Commonwealth author, fiction or non-fiction, which best evokes the spirit of a place.

Saga Award for Wit
Awards a prize of £20,000 for a literary work by an author aged 50 or over which displays wit and humour.

Sagittarius Prize
A prize of £4,000 given for an exceptional first novel by an author over the age of 60.

Somerset Maugham Award
A prize of £6,000 to be spent on travel, awarded to an outstanding published British author under the age of 35.

Stonewall Book Award
An award given to literary works with a gay, lesbian, bisexual or transgendered (GLBT) theme, administered by the American Library Association.

Sunday Times Young Writer of the Year
Awards a purse of £5,000 to a published author in the UK under the age of 35.

Tir Na N-og Awards
An award in three categories celebrating Welsh-language literary works in fiction and non-fiction and for English language fiction by a Welsh author.

Wheatley Medal
A collaborative award administered by CILIP and sponsored by The Society of Indexers and Nielsen BookData, given for an outstanding printed index in a reference work.

Whitbread Book Awards
A set of literary awards given in 5 categories for best novel, first novel, children's book, poetry and biography, each winner receiving £5,000 and the overall winner receiving £25,000.

William Hill Sports Book of the Year Award
A prize given for a book with a sporting theme (excluding almanacs and listings), with a cash prize of £15,000 and other prizes worth £5,000.

WH Smith Literary Award
An annual honour given in the UK for literary works in English, including those in translation and by international authors, running since 1959.

National Newspapers in the UK

Daily Newspapers

Daily Express   *Circulation: 810,827*
Northern & Shell Building, 10 Lower Thames Street,
London EC4R 6EN.
Tel. 0871-434 1010
www.express.co.uk

Daily Mail   *Circulation: 2,350,694*
Northcliffe House, 2 Derry Street,
London W8 5TT.
Tel. 020-7938 6000
www.dailymail.co.uk

Daily Mirror   *Circulation: 1,684,660*
1 Canada Square, Canary Wharf, London E14 5AP.
Tel. 020-7293 3000
www.mirror.co.uk

Daily Record   *Circulation: 454,247*
1 Central Quay, Glasgow G3 8DA.
Tel. 0141-309 3000
www.dailyrecord.co.uk

Daily Sport   *Circulation: no figures available*
19 Great Ancoats Street, Manchester M60 4BT.
Tel. 0161-236 4466
www.dailysport.co.uk

Daily Star   *Circulation: 820,028*
Ludgate House, 245 Blackfriars Road,
London SE1 9UX.
Tel. 020-7928 8000
www.dailystar.co.uk

The Daily Telegraph   *Circulation: 901,667*
1 Canada Square, Canary Wharf, London E14 5DT.
Tel. 020 7538 5000
www.telegraph.co.uk

Financial Times   *Circulation: 419,249*
1 Southwark Bridge, London SE1 9HL.
Tel. 020-7873 3000
www.ft.com

The Guardian   *Circulation: 403,297*
119 Farringdon Road, London EC1R 3ER.
Tel. 020-7278 2332
www.guardian.co.uk

The Herald   *Circulation: 75,541*
Newsquest Ltd, 200 Renfield Street, Glasgow G2 3PR.
Tel. 0141-302 7000
www.theherald.co.uk

The Independent   *Circulation: 267,037*
Independent House, 191 Marsh Wall,
London E14 9RS.
Tel. 020-7005 2000
www.independent.co.uk

National Newspapers in the UK *continued*

Morning Star   *Circulation: no figures available*
People's Press Printing Society Ltd, William Rust House, 52 Beachy Road,
London E3 2NS.
Tel. 020-8510 0815
www.morningstaronline.co.uk

Racing Post   *Circulation: 74,552*
Trinity Mirror, Floor 23, One Canada Square, Canary Wharf,
London E14 5AP.
Tel. 020-7293 3291
www.racingpost.co.uk

The Scotsman   *Circulation: 65,194*
Barclay House, 108 Holyrood Road, Edinburgh EH8 8AS.
Tel. 0131-620 8620
www.scotsman.com

The Sun   *Circulation: 3,224,427*
News Group Newspapers Ltd, Virginia Street, London E1 9XP.
Tel. 020-7782 4000
www.the-sun.co.uk

The Times   *Circulation: 703,492*
1 Pennington Street, London E98 1TT.
Tel. 020-7782 5000
www.timesonline.co.uk

Weekly Newspapers

The Business   *Circulation: 178,528*
292 Vauxhall Bridge Road, London SW1V 1DE.
Tel. 020-7961 0000
www.thebusinessonline.com

Daily Star Sunday   *Circulation: 404,723*
Express Newspapers, Ludgate House, 245 Blackfriars Road, London SE1 9UX.
Tel. 020-7928 8000
www.megastar.co.uk

The Independent on Sunday   *Circulation: 230,053*
Independent House, 191 Marsh Wall, London E14 9RS.
Tel. 020-7005 2000
www.independent.co.uk

The Mail on Sunday   *Circulation: 2,292,258*
Northcliffe House, 2 Derry Street, London W8 5TS.
Tel. 020-7938 6000
www.mailonsunday.co.uk

News of the World   *Circulation: 3,773,705*
1 Virginia Street, London E98 1NW.
Tel. 020-7782 1000
www.newsoftheworld.co.uk

The Observer   *Circulation: 451,781*
3-7 Herbal Hill, London EC1R 5EJ.
Tel. 020-7278 2332
www.observer.co.uk

National Newspapers in the UK *continued*

The People   *Circulation: 905,494*
1 Canada Square, Canary Wharf, London E14 5AP. Tel. 020-7293 3000
www.people.co.uk

Scotland on Sunday   *Circulation: 84,192*
108 Holyrood Road, Edinburgh EH8 8AS. Tel. 0131-620 8620
www.scotlandonsunday.co.uk

Sunday Express   *Circulation: 829,064*
Northern & Shell Building, 10 Lower Thames Street, London EC4R 6EN.
Tel. 0871-434 1010
www.express.co.uk

Sunday Herald   *Circulation: 58,140*
200 Renfield Street, Glasgow G2 3QB.
Tel. 0141-302 7800
www.sundayherald.com

Sunday Mail   *Circulation: 549,129*
1 Central Quay, Glasgow G3 8DA.
Tel. 0141-309 3000
www.sundaymail.com

Sunday Mirror   *Circulation: 1,457,792*
1 Canada Square, Canary Wharf, London E14 5AP.
Tel. 020-7293 3000
www.sundaymirror.co.uk

The Sunday Post   *Circulation: no figures available*
D. C. Thomson & Co. Ltd, 144 Port Dundas Road, Glasgow G4 0HZ.
Tel. 0141-332 9933
www.sundaypost.com

Sunday Sport   *Circulation: 148,385*
840 Melton Road, Thurmaston, Leicester LE4 8BE.
Tel. 0116-269 4892
www.sundaysport.com

The Sunday Telegraph   *Circulation: 661,425*
1 Canada Square, Canary Wharf, London E14 5DT.
Tel. 020-7538 5000
www.telegraph.co.uk

The Sunday Times   *Circulation: 1,404,616*
1 Virginia Street, London E1 9BD.
Tel. 020-7782 4000
www.timesonline.co.uk

The Sunday Times Scotland   *Circulation: no figures available*
Times Newspapers Ltd, 124 Portman Street, Kinning Park, Glasgow G41 1EJ.
 Tel. 0141-420 5100
www.timesonline.co.uk

Wales on Sunday   *Circulation: no figures available*
Thomson House, Havelock Street, Cardiff CF10 1XR.
Tel. 029-2058 3583
www.icwales.co.uk

*(circulation figures net average October 2005, courtesy of the Audit Bureau of
Circulations – see www.abc.org.uk for further details)*

Major Magazines in the UK

	Circulation
Sky Magazine (TV Listings: Satellite/Cable)	6,783,581
Boots Health and Beauty (Women's Health & Beauty)	1,765,387
What's on TV (TV Listings: Radio & TV Guides)	1,673,790
The National Trust Magazine (Countryside & County: National)	1,655,088
U (magazine for Unison members) (General Interest: Miscellaneous)	1,465,833
Saga magazine (General Interest: Retirement)	1,245,006
Take a Break (Women's Weeklies)	1,200,397
TV Choice (TV Listings: Radio & TV Guides)	1,157,622
Radio Times (TV Listings: Radio & TV Guides)	1,080,199
Eyes Down (Leisure Interests: Games)	984,946
BBC Pre-Schools Magazines (Children's Magazines: Pre-School)	929,452
Reader's Digest (General Interest: Miscellaneous)	776,902
Debenhams Desire (Women's Lifestyle/Fashion)	745,126
Birds (the RSPB magazine) (Leisure Interests: Wildlife)	624,118
Glamour (Women's Lifestyle/Fashion)	609,626
Chat (Women's Weeklies)	609,163
Now (Women's Weeklies)	591,795
That's Life (Women's Weeklies)	569,631
Heat (Women's Weeklies)	560,438
FHM (Men's Lifestyle)	560,167
Time Magazine (News & Current Affairs: International)	551,114
Closer (Women's Weeklies)	540,044

Major Magazines in the UK *continued*

	Circulation
OK! (Women's Weeklies)	532,843
The Economist (News & Current Affairs: Business)	503,077
Exchange & Mart (Buying & Selling: General)	491,152
Woman (Women's Weeklies)	485,463
Good Housekeeping (Women's Lifestyle/Fashion)	475,838
Cosmopolitan (Women's Lifestyle/Fashion)	462,943
Yours (Women's Lifestyle/Fashion)	440,070
Woman's Weekly (Women's Weeklies)	425,568
Legion (General Interest: Miscellaneous)	425,462
Woman's Own (Women's Weeklies)	424,292
TV Times (TV Listings: Radio & TV Guides)	418,192
Emma's Diary Pregnancy Guide (Parenthood)	416,140
Best (Women's Weeklies)	398,289
The Vauxhall Magazine (Motoring & Motorcycling: Motoring)	394,846
Auto Exchange Group (Motoring & Motorcycling: Motoring)	392,598
Hello! (Women's Weeklies)	392,481
Marie Claire (Women's Lifestyle/Fashion)	381,281
New! (Women's Weeklies)	373,039
Motoring and Leisure (Motoring & Motorcycling: Motoring)	371,940
People's Friend (Women's Weeklies)	363,638
National Geographic (General Interest: Miscellaneous)	350,253

(circulation figures net average Jan-Jun 2005, courtesy of the Audit Bureau of Circulations – see www.abc.org.uk for further details)